MULTIPLE PERSPECTIVES
FOR DECISION MAKING
BRIDGING THE GAP
BETWEEN ANALYSIS AND ACTION

MULTIPLE PERSPECTIVES
FOR DECISION MAKING
BRIDGING THE GAP
BETWEEN ANALYSIS AND ACTION

HAROLD A. LINSTONE

with contributions by

ARNOLD J. MELTSNER • MARVIN ADELSON • BRUCE CLARY
PETER G. COOK • STEVE HAWKE • RUTH-ELLEN MILLER
ARNOLD MYSIOR • JOHN S. PEARSON, Jr. • JACK SHUMAN
LINDA UMBDENSTOCK • DONNA WAGNER • SUSAN J. WILL

Foreword by
IAN I. MITROFF

NORTH-HOLLAND
New York • Amsterdam • Oxford

Elsevier Science Publishing Co., Inc.
52 Vanderbilt Avenue, New York, New York 10017

Distributors outside the United States and Canada:

Elsevier Science Publishers B.V.
P.O. Box 211, 1000 AE, Amsterdam, The Netherlands

Cover illustration, "Holistico," by Guillermo Guzman

This book is based in part on research supported by the National Science Foundation, under Grant No. PRA 7910020.

Any opinions, findings, and conclusions or recommendations expressed in this book are those of the authors and do not necessarily reflect the views of the National Science Foundation.

Library of Congress Cataloging in Publication Data

Linstone, Harold A.
    Multiple perspectives for decision making.

    Includes index.
    1. Decision-making. I. Title.
HD30.23.L56   1984   658.4'03   84-7966
ISBN 0-444-00803-9

Manufactured in the United States of America

For Hedy and our sons, Fred and Clark

CONTENTS

XII LOOKING AHEAD: RISK, FORECASTING, AND PLANNING

XIII GUIDELINES FOR USERS OF MULTIPLE PERSPECTIVES

FOREWORD

The toys we play with tell us a lot about ourselves. Good toys, especially of the puzzle or game variety, are fun for several reasons. First, they are challenging. The correct solution is usually not readily apparent or easily attainable. A good puzzle or game demands some skill, knowledge, or dexterity. Second, unlike life, puzzles and games generally produce clearcut winners or losers, experts versus novices. Generally one and only one correct solution exists. Furthermore, it is generally very clear when one has either solved the puzzle or not. It is also rather easy to distinguish between expert and novice play. Thus there is little, if any, doubt regarding good versus bad performance. As a result, puzzles afford an immense degree of satisfaction to one who is able to work through them. In fact, such satisfaction is often in direct proportion to the degree of frustration inherent in getting to the correct solution. Third, and this aspect is generally least mentioned of all, a good game or puzzle is aesthetic. Either the pieces themselves or the puzzle as a whole has a nice shape. In other cases, the solution itself is elegant or aesthetically pleasing. Fourth, the means or process of arriving at the correct answer must itself be interesting or intrinsically rewarding. In other words, it must be fun or rewarding to "spend" one's time on playing the game. Fifth, one generally must be able to share one's skill or excellence with others. Even the most solitary of games has some social or sharing aspect, even if it is only to brag to others how good one is.

One of the reasons for the enormous popularity of Rubik's Cube is that it possesses all of these qualities to a high degree. Certainly, its aesthetic appeal is extremely high, not to mention its great portability. No one who has ever seen it could fail to be attracted to it; its sheer shape and colors alone exert a magnetic appeal.

And yet, for all the endearing and fascinating qualities of games and puzzles, problems involving human beings are infinitely more intriguing and, by the same token, infinitely more frustrating. It is absolutely vital to appreciate the differences between the two because all too many people assume that the way we solve puzzles should be *the* standard against which we measure success in solving society's problems. The plain fact of the matter is that such problems are radically different from puzzles of the Rubik's Cube variety in at least one very crucial respect. Unlike puzzles, society's problems do not have a single, correct solution that is recognized and accepted as such by all the contending parties, who are affected by the problem or who have a strong opinion on it. Problems like beauty and ugliness reside in the eye, and thereby ultimately, in the mind of the beholder. People have such different values and start from such totally different ideas as to what society should be that what is a problem and a good solution for one person is often an irrelevant, stupid, silly, or even evil idea for another. If these problems bear any resemblance to Rubik's Cube, it is only because each person has his or her own unique cube. No two cubes are exactly alike. If your cube has six sides, then mine has eight (a very strange "cube" indeed). If the colored sides of your cube are red, blue, green, white, orange, and black, then mine are light grey, dark grey, a mixture of black and blue, brown, etc. Even stranger, what is a nicely ordered shape, like a cube, to you may be a phantom object to me that changes its shape over time and in different parts of the country—a condition that is certainly true of social problems.

Why belabor all of this? For several reasons. Virtually all significant problems involve human beings, either singly or collectively. Business and military decisions, economic and health care planning, diffusion of technology and administration of justice, even Apollo lunar and space shuttle programs, cannot be adequately understood on a purely technical level. If sociotechnical and social systems are fundamentally not like Rubik's Cube, then we are seriously remiss in how we prepare people for working on a vast array of important problems and in the institutions we have designed for managing them in our society at large. Except for the humanities, education in the professions and sciences largely prepares people for tackling problems of the Rubik's Cube variety. Unless a problem is clearly stated and accepted by all parties as the "same," it is likely to be rejected as a "problem." Students from the humanities really fare no better. While they are certainly exposed to issues that have no single, widely agreed on solution, let alone formulation, only the most brilliant, to put it mildly, can translate this "exposure" from the great issues of the past to proposing novel solutions to the important issues of the present. Further, the present state of society renders the way we have designed education more suspect than ever. No single profession has a monopoly on defining or solving the great issues of the day. At every twist and turn, we are constantly reminded of the overwhelming complexity and interdependency of all issues. We live in a world wherein the so-called technical aspects of issues cannot be clearly separated from the social, legal, political, and moral aspects, if the language of "aspects" is even an acceptable way to think anymore. I defy anyone to try to separate the so-called technical aspects of Three Mile Island or the abortion controversy from the legal, political, moral, etc. aspects. Such a separation is, depending upon one's morality and politics, either immoral or politically irresponsible, if not just plain artificial and naive.

Alvin Toffler, in his book *The Third Wave,* may have put it best of all. Most of our institutions, including the modern University, were designed during the Second Wave, the age of the machine and the Industrial Revolution. One of the nice characteristics of a machine is that by definition it can be taken apart. It can be broken down into its separate parts, and the parts can be examined independently of one another. We cannot do this for social problems at all. Why? Because everything about them is subject to controversy. What's a "part" to one group is not to another, etc.

What then can we do? To start, we can recognize that at least four very different attitudes toward sociotechnical and social problems crop up repeatedly no matter what the issue. Second, our very survival, more than at any other time in our history, depends on our learning how to blend these four attitudes into a coordinated whole.

In their most extreme form, I have labeled these four attitudes or approaches: 1) the technological, quick-fix mentality, 2) the technological daydreaming mentality, 3) social daydreaming, and 4) social traditionalism.

Of all the four approaches, the technological, quick-fix mentality is the one most prone to view problems in Rubik's Cube-like terms. This attitude also tends to dominate corporate and government life in America. When it comes to treating problems, despite insistence about problems' differences, for all practical purposes they are essentially the same. If problems cannot be defined and solved quickly (i.e., in the very short run) and if complex problems do not have immediate, simple solutions, then this attitude leads to rejection: the problem is not worthy of even being considered a "problem."

A strong accompaniment of this attitude is a near exclusive focus on technical issues. Problems are discussed—even stronger, viewed—in highly complex technical terms, which are open only to "qualified experts." Some obvious examples are the economy, space research, almost all scientific research, and nuclear energy.

The near exclusive emphasis on technology means that those aspects of a problem that cannot be measured or are difficult to quantify are usually ignored. At its best, this position focuses on the doable, the feasible, and the sensible. Its insistence on measurement sets tough-minded standards of accountability; for something to be counted as worthy it must prove itself in the marketplace of goods, products, or ideas.

At its worst, this is short-term, myopic thinking. It sacrifices future businesses and ideas that by definition cannot be proven in the present for today's "bottom-line." Because problems are viewed as separate entities, each tends to be considered totally independent of the others. As a result, this attitude leads to a jump from issue to issue, problem to problem, without any overall scheme or plan.

Where the first attitude focuses on the here and now, the short term, what is known in terms of present, conventional, well-understood technology, the second attitude focuses on the technology of tomorrow. The best example of this approach is *Omni* magazine. The accent is on "the wonderful marvels of tomorrow's technology and how it is transforming our lives for the better." If we can only get through today's crises, then we are on "the verge of a revolution in thinking and technology that promises to transform us as 'never before'," or some such Sci-Fi public relations talk.

At its best, this attitude is marvelous for opening up new possibilities of what we might be, of suggesting sorely needed new ideas, and of reformulating old problems in such a way that entirely new solutions suggest themselves. At its worst, it is impractical daydreaming, of extending today's technologically fixated society indefinitely into the future and suggesting some marvelous technology wonder-world without suggesting any sensible way of how to get it from horrible here to terrific there.

The third attitude is similar to the second in that the emphasis in both is on tomorrow. The main difference is that where the second attitude is focused exclusively on technology, the third is focused on people—on interpersonal relations at the community and societal level. This attitude is concerned with the society of the future from a human standpoint. What new forms of human communities, living arrangements, and institutions will there be? What will it mean to be human in the future? Will our institutions be more effective from a human perspective? The best and the worst of this attitude parallels that of the third.

Finally, the last attitude parallels the first in that both are concerned with the here and now, the immediate short term, or the recent past. The difference is that the fourth attitude is concerned exclusively with people. The emphasis of this approach is on traditionally acceptable human behavior or time-tested standards of conduct. The Moral Majority is a good example. Anything that goes against the grain of traditional, sanctioned behavior is suspect, if not immoral.

Is it possible to get the best of each approach without the worst? Notice that we did not ask, "What is *the* answer?," for that would be to take us back into the exclusive clutches of the first approach.

Three considerations are critical. Unfortunately none of them is easy to realize, nor do we know how to do any of them truly well. The first, as I have pointed out, is to recognize that on all issues of any significance all four attitudes will either be present from the beginning or will surface in opposition to the others. By itself, this is healthy since it tends to counteract the one-sidedness of any approach. The second point is to appreciate that all four attitudes have a legitimate role to play in complex issues. This may be the hardest of all to do, for it demands distinguishing between legitimate and extreme forms of each attitude. By definition, an extreme position is one that recognizes only itself as legitimate. The difficulty with this is that nearly every position in our society thereby becomes extreme. Although difficult, unfortunately this may be the case. A pertinent example is, again, the Moral Majority. More Americans than we may suspect may indeed identify with the issues raised by the Moral Majority. As Yankelovich has pointed out in a recent article in *Psychology Today,* all of us, no matter what our social standing, feel victimized by something in our society at this time: the economy, crime, decreasing expectations, stress, anxiety, a general feeling of loss of control, or a growing inability to feel in charge of anything whatsoever. This does not mean, however, that Americans are ready to identify with the Moral Majority's "solution," their particular brand of social or moral traditionalism. The difficulty is to recognize *some* of the legitimacy of the *concerns* of the Moral Majority even if—particularly all the more that—we do not like the form in which they are expressed or their proposed "solutions."

The third point is no less difficult. This is the recognition that in reality all of the four approaches depend on one another, all the more that they oppose one another. No attitude can in actuality really go-it-alone. Take President Reagan's economic program. It's a mixture of all four attitudes. Despite all protestations to the contrary, it certainly has its technological quick-fix aspects. Given the intolerance of doubt and uncertainty, characteristic of life at the national level, one has no option but to overstate our magic cure-alls, particularly their potency. At the same time, we are instructed to "give the program a chance to work, give it enough time to prove itself *in the future*." Whoever said that religious belief was not a strong factor in *every* economic program?

All of which finally leads me to the present book. This volume is one of the very few I know of that is a serious and sustained effort to found a methodology for accomplishing the difficult task of blending the different attitudes toward problem solving that I have been discussing. This would be reason enough to applaud it. That it is also an excellent example of what it preaches is added cause for celebration. If my joy is tempered at all, it is only because the world is probably still unprepared to hear this book's message, let alone really take it seriously. As a culture we are still too hooked on puzzles to appreciate the vital differences between serious problem solving and toying with games.

If ever there was a time when we needed to understand the dynamics of complex problems—how to change, renew our institutions, propose new solutions to old problems, and create new problems that are capable of revitalizing our will and spirit—then surely that time is now. The problems we face at present are so complex that they defy simple statements, let alone simple solutions. The age of simple solutions, like that of cheap energy, is over. The problems we face make Rubik's Cube seem literally like child's play.

IAN I. MITROFF
Harold Quinton Distinguished Professor
 of Business Policy
Department of Management and Policy Sciences
Graduate School of Business
University of Southern California

PREFACE

The concept of multiple perspectives is presented in this work as a practical means to bridge the wide gap that exists between analysis and decision making in the realm of sociotechnical systems. It owes its development to Graham Allison's book, *Essence of Decision: Explaining the Cuban Missile Crisis* and to C. West Churchman's writings on inquiring systems. It has also benefited from a grant by the National Science Foundation's (NSF) Division of Policy Research and Analysis. These debts are gratefully acknowledged.

Following a brief introduction (Chapter I), we discuss the current dilemma (II) and describe earlier work on multiple perspectives (III). Our proposed approach is presented in Chapter IV. In consonance with the law that "an ounce of application is worth a ton of abstraction," Chapters V to X focus on a wide spectrum of illustrations and applications. Some readers may wish to sample one or more of these chapters before embarking on the full journey through the text.

We first consider past decisions made in the public and private sectors by means of these perspectives (Chapters V and VI, respectively). Then we proceed to an ongoing living system where the investigator is an actual participant (VII). In Chapters VIII to X, we deal with NSF technology assessments, which were at different stages of completion during our study. Robustness rather than theory building is the main concern. Chapter XI analyzes, and draws lessons from, these experiences. In Chapter XII we look ahead to the use of the perspectives in risk analysis, forecasting, and corporate planning. The final chapter (XIII) offers 16 guidelines for the user.

On the basis of the applications to date, we envision the user to be a decision maker or analyst in the private or public sector. Corporate managers and business strategists, policy and systems analysts, operations researchers and management scientists, government agency heads, and institutional administrators may find the concept of practical value. Finally, it can add new dimensions to the education of students in fields such as engineering, computer science, business, and economics—who will have to bridge the future gaps.

The contributors who made this volume possible are listed on pp. xxi and xxiii. Arnold J. Meltsner, the Deputy Principal Investigator on the NSF grant, was a constant source of ideas and encouragement. Marvin Adelson's unique insights at crucial points also deserve special acknowledgment. Consultants and support staff are listed on p. xxiii. I express my deep appreciation to them, as well as to my students, for their faith, perceptions, and unstinting efforts. My gratitude is extended to Guillermo Guzman of Saltillo, Mexico, for permission to use his beautiful engraving, "Holistico." Last but not least, I must mention Ethel Whitson, who was the ideal administrative assistant and crisis manager.

HAROLD A. LINSTONE

Lake Oswego, Oregon
June 15, 1983

BIOGRAPHIES

HAROLD A. LINSTONE   Chapters I, II, III, IV, V, VI, VIII, IX, XI, XII, XIII, Appendices B, C, and D

University Professor at Portland State University; first Director of its Systems Science Doctoral Program and Futures Research Institute; Editor-in-Chief of the journal, *Technological Forecasting and Social Change* (now in its 25th volume); Co-editor of the books, *Futures Research: New Directions, The Delphi Method,* and *Technological Substitution;* President of Systems Forecasting, Inc.; twenty years' industrial experience at Hughes Aircraft Company and Lockheed Aircraft Corporation (with the latter as Associate Director of Corporate Development Planning-Systems Analysis); Visiting Scientist at the International Institute for Applied Systems Analysis in Austria; and Visiting Professor at the Universities of Rome and Washington; doctorate in Mathematics, University of Southern California.

The Contributors

ARNOLD J. MELTSNER   Chapters IX, XI, XIII, Appendices A and B

Professor at the Graduate School of Public Policy, University of California, Berkeley; Deputy Principal Investigator on NSF Multiple Perspectives project; Editor of the book, *Politics and the Oval Office,* and Author of *Policy Analysts in the Bureaucracy.*

MARVIN ADELSON   Chapters IX and XI

Professor at the Graduate School of Architecture and Urban Planning, University of California, Los Angeles; formerly Principal Scientist, Systems Development Corporation.

BRUCE CLARY   Chapters V, X, and Appendix B

Associate Professor, Public and Environmental Administration Program, University of Wisconsin, Green Bay; formerly Assistant Professor of Public Administration, Portland State University.

PETER G. COOK   Chapter VI

Manager of Software Development, Four-Phase Systems, Inc., Cupertino, California.

STEVE HAWKE   Chapter VI

Chief Field Engineer, Portland General Electric Company, Oregon; currently pursuing doctorate in Systems Science Ph.D. Program, Portland State University, Oregon.

RUTH-ELLEN MILLER   Chapter IX

Consulting Policy Analyst and Project Facilitator; currently pursuing doctorate in Systems Science Ph.D. Program, Portland State University.

ARNOLD MYSIOR   Chapter VIII

Practicing Psychologist, member of Mysior-Runion and Associates, Washington, D.C.; formerly Director of the Psychological Center at Georgetown University; Author of *Society—A Very Large System.*

JOHN S. PEARSON, Jr.   Chapter V
Former Senior Vice President-Corporate Development, Surety Life Insurance Company; graduate
degrees in Actuarial Science and Economics; student in Systems Science Ph.D. Program,
Portland State University.

JACK SHUMAN   Chapter VIII
Senior Physical Scientist, National Oceanic and Atmospheric Administration, Department of
Commerce, Rockville, Maryland; Associate Director of Research, Austin Lindberg, Ltd.,
McLean, Virginia; doctorate in History of Social Systems, Georgetown University.

LINDA UMBDENSTOCK   Chapters VII and XI
Senior Research Associate, Center for Health and Social Services Research; doctorate in Systems
Science, Portland State University, 1981.

DONNA WAGNER   Chapter X
Assistant Professor, University of Bridgeport; doctorate in Urban Studies, Portland State
University, 1979.

SUSAN J. WILL   Chapter V
Program Administrator, Community Mental Health Services Department of Health and Social
Services, Division of Mental Health and Developing Disabilities, State of Alaska, Juneau.

CONSULTANTS AND SUPPORTING STAFF

The very valuable advice and assistance of the following individuals is gratefully acknowledged.

JACK BURBY
Senior Editorial Writer, *Los Angeles Times;* author of *The Great American Motion Sickness.*

JOSEPH F. COATES
President of Joseph Coates, Inc.; formerly with the Office of Technology Assessment of the U.S. Congress.

YEHEZKEL DROR
Professor of Political Science, The Hebrew University; author of *Crazy States, Ventures in Policy Sciences,* and *Design for Policy Sciences.*

MAGOROH MARUYAMA
Professor, Uppsala University, Sweden; visiting Professor, UCLA Graduate School of Management.

PAUL MOLNAR
Staff Associate, Nero & Associates, Inc., Portland, Oregon; co-author of *Technological and Social Change: A Transdisciplinary Model.*

FREDERICK ROSSINI
Professor, Department of Social Sciences, Georgia Institute of Technology; co-author of *A Guidebook to Technology Assessment and Impact Analysis.*

LAWRENCE BURT
Student in Systems Science Ph.D. Program, Portland State University.

HEATHER RODE
Student in Systems Science Ph.D. Program, Portland State University.

XU LI DA
Student in Systems Science Ph.D. Program, Portland State University.

The helpful comments of Dr. Kennith Foster of the Office of Arid Lands Studies, University of Arizona, Dr. Martin Ernst of Arthur D. Little, Inc., Wayne Boucher of the National Electronic Funds Transfer Commission, and Dr. Paul C. Nutt of Ohio State University are also appreciated.

FIGURES

TABLES

PERMISSIONS

Cover drawing "Holistico" by Guillermo Guzman

Rashomon by Fay and Michael Kanin, Random House, Inc.   p. 25

In a Grove by R. Akutagawa, Liveright Publishing Co.   p. 33–34

How Washington Really Works by C. Peters, Addison-Wesley
Publishing Co.   pp. 102–103

The Caine Mutiny by Herman Wouk, Doubleday & Co.
(BSW Literary Agency, Inc.)   p. 340

The Politics of Mistrust by A. Wildavsky and E. Tenenbaum,
Sage Publications   p. 341

I

INTRODUCTION

H. LINSTONE

Two things fill my heart with never-ending awe: the complexity of the total social system . . . and the self within.

Paraphrase of Immanuel Kant by C. West Churchman

It began as "scientific management" with Frederick Taylor in 1911 and gathered steam with World War II's operations research. The Battle of the Atlantic called for submarine search, and the Battle of Britain for vectoring of interceptor aircraft. Mathematical analysis could and did help. The War also was a turning point in the design of new systems, marking a level of complexity that required "systems analysis." Radar, fire control systems, and guided missiles, as well as nuclear weapon strategy, created a strong need for systems analysts. Researchers developed game theory and decision analysis as well as technological forecasting tools. The flowering of Camelot-on-the-Potomac brought systems analysis to Washington. Cost-effectiveness analysis and the Planning-Programming-Budgeting System became *de rigueur* among the cognoscenti in the bureaucracy. And the industrial part of the defense complex had to learn to play the game.

By 1967, the Dean of the School of Electrical Engineering of the Massachusetts Institute of Technology (MIT) proclaimed:

> I doubt if there is any such thing as an urban crisis, but if there were, MIT could lick it in the same way we handled the Second World War [Thompson, 1971:48].

The same year Congressman Emilio Q. Daddario introduced to Congress H.R. 6698, a bill designed to stimulate discussions to formalize the concept of technology assessment and strengthen the legislative process in the area of technology policy. The pinnacle of the expectations placed on systems analysis at the time is found in Max Ways' survey "The Road to 1977," in *Fortune:*

> The further advance of this new style (systems analysis) is the most significant prediction that can be made about the next ten years. By 1977 this new way of dealing with the future will be recognized at home and abroad as a salient American characteristic [Ways, 1967:94].

The optimism exuded by Ways and many others was based on solid evidence of the success of systems analysis[1] in dealing with purely technological systems and the anticipation of its wider application to the design and decisions of systems that are not purely technological.

A decade later, bleak reality had displaced euphoria; this skepticism is reflected in the words of Ida Hoos (1979:192)

> In our technological era, the dominant paradigm is so technically oriented that most of our problems are defined as technical in nature and assigned the same treatment—doctoring by systems analysts. The "experts" are methodological Mer-

---

[1]For convenience we shall usually subsume under this label various related subjects and spin-offs, such as cost–benefit analysis, risk analysis, decision analysis, operations analysis, technological forecasting, technology assessment, and impact analysis.

lins. . . . Technology assessments are conducted by latter-day intellectual *condottieri*, the brains-for-hire. . . .

Most of the technology assessments I have reviewed . . . must be taken with a large measure of skepticism lest they lead us to regrettable, if not disastrous, conclusions.

Nuclear war, as exemplified by a U.S.–Soviet nuclear weapons exchange, had earlier been cited as ideally suitable to systems analysis. It was seen as a "well-structured" system, and endless computer modeling and gaming have been conducted. But Fallows (1981:140) now observes:

The best minds of the defense community have been drawn toward nuclear analysis, but so were the best minds to be found in the monastery, arguing the Albigensian heresy in the fourteenth century.

The approach works as long as other nuclear powers do the same. But because no one has experience fighting a nuclear war, our theoretical scenarios have "no more foundation in fact than other theologians' fiery visions of hell" (Fallows, 1981:170). And in an era of nuclear proliferation, a heretic will arise sooner or later.[2]

In his book *Evil and World Order,* W.I. Thompson (1976) considers the systems analysis approach to societal systems as *the* evil. He notes that history provides one example after another of well-intentioned efforts culminating in evil. As the Declaration of the Rights of Man in 1789 ended in the Reign of Terror, the drive for quantifiable measures of effectiveness in Vietnam led *The Best and the Brightest* to the concept of the body count, which was then travestied in incidents such as My Lai. The routines of science and technology, development of information theory, and transformation of management and policy into sciences all made complex, living organisms into mechanistic feedback loops.

Systems theorists' efforts at *Redesigning the Future* (Ackoff), creating a *Liberty Machine* (Beer), developing a *World Dynamics* model (Forrester), and *A Strategy for the Future* (Laszlo) are seen as the ultimate hubris.[3] To Thompson (1976:109), "the tongue cannot taste itself, the mind cannot know itself, and the

---

[2] The whole deterrence concept depends on "rational" decision making. Yet history is hardly reassuring on this point when we look at other mass destruction decisions. One-quarter of Europe's population died in the Thirty Years' War over a religious question; one-third of Great Britain's population was killed in the War of Roses over an argument between two families. And in our time, six million Jews were killed by a culturally advanced nation to preserve its Aryan purity. Recent research has also exposed the illusory nature of the assumption that nuclear systems analysis can be treated as "well-structured." Carl Sagan, Freeman Dyson, and other scientists have pointed to the meteorological effects (e.g., dense smoke darkening much of the earth, winter weather in summer) as examples of our ignorance *in 1983* of nuclear war.

[3] In fairness, we must also recognize that general systems theorists, such as Gerald Weinberg (1975), and cyberneticists, such as Heinz von Foerster (1977), have well understood the limitations of the conventional systems approach and the need for complementary world views.

system cannot model itself." To Adams (1972:444), these models "can never be anything but cargo cult models, superficial caricatures of one minority's view of the world."

In the area of corporate management, a recent article in the *Harvard Business Review* on "Managing Our Way to Economic Decline" notes that principles of management fashionable in the 1960s and 1970s encouraged in American managers a preference for "analytic detachment rather than insight that comes from 'hands-on' experience" (Hayes and Abernathy, 1980:68). Disillusionment and reaction are now evident: in 1982 "corporate strategists {are} under fire" (Kiechel, 1982b:34).

Richard M. Cyert, coauthor of *A Behavioral Theory of the Firm* and now President of Carnegie-Mellon University, muses:

> As a professor of organization theory and management, I used to wonder about the practical value of these academic fields. For the last eight years, I've had some first-hand experience finding out. . . . And I've concluded that the study of management makes a useful, but only a limited, contribution to the practicing manager.
>
> Organization theory hasn't provided me any framework to judge possible appointees. The theory hasn't even been very useful in developing new organizational structures. . . . Finally, theory doesn't shed much light on how a manager should get information about how his organization operates [*Wall Street Journal* April 7, 1980].

My 20 years of systems analysis activity—in industry (corporate planning), institute (RAND), and academe (developing a systems science doctoral program)—mirrored this shift from confidence to concern. I experienced a deepening frustration with the chasm between systems analysis and decision making (Linstone, 1969). And my conviction grew that "better" systems analysis would not bridge this chasm. The 1976–1978 project on *The Use of Structural Modeling for Technology Assessment* made the dilemma very vivid. In the "Conclusion" section of the final report, I wrote:

> There is still only lip service paid to any but "rational" or traditional "systems analysis" approaches and models in addressing the technology assessment process [Linstone et al., 1978:132].

Decision making inherently involves organizations and individuals, whose perspectives are very different from those of "rational" systems analysts or technology assessors. The signpost that showed a way out of the dilemma was Allison's (1971) book *Essence of Decision: Explaining the Cuban Missile Crisis,* which used three models to "see" a single decision process. This work is the direct result of that encounter.

Perspectives which differ in their underlying paradigms unavoidably create a kind of "Catch 22" situation. In consonance with the modes of inquiry preferred by scientists and technologists, we could regard analyses such as technology assessment (TA) as scientific endeavors and deal with the formulation of theorems, design of models, and validation of hypotheses. But virtually all writers on TA agree that it is not a science—some call it an art. And our fundamental concept, the use of multiple perspectives, inexorably moves us beyond the paradigms associated with science and technology. Experimental design and validation of hypotheses are intraparadigmatic: they operate only *within* the framework of a perspective. They cannot prove that a model gives the most useful or "correct" representation of reality; they cannot give assurance that the variables chosen are sufficiently inclusive or appropriate. They tell us nothing about other perspectives.

Were we able to confine ourselves to the paradigms of science and technology, our work would be viewed with empathy by those who embrace that world view, including most practitioners of these analyses. Yet it is precisely the focus on a single perspective or world view—that of the rational actor—that is, in our opinion, the primary source of their inadequacy. Thus we may invoke the wrath of the purists; the use of multiple perspectives makes us *ipso facto* heretical to the adherents of any one perspective. Orthodox systems analysts and management scientists are likely to view us as iconoclasts. Our purpose, however, is not to debunk or to urge abandonment of their conventional modes of analysis, but to create or nourish an awareness of the need to step beyond the confines of their paradigms. Our proposed route is that of pluralism or multiplicity of perspectives.

It is not an easy path for most. Westerners find it difficult to grasp the Japanese acceptance of two religions simultaneously: Buddhism and Shintoism. Technologists may find it even more difficult to live with at least three perspectives simultaneously.

It should be emphasized that the concept of multiple perspectives has been demonstrated in several contexts, for example, understanding of the Cuban missile crisis and management of policy modeling in public sector bureaucracies. The illustrations in this book also cover a spectrum. They have in common the following factors:

- ill-structured nature of the problem (typically sociotechnical systems);[4]

- significant policy and/or decision analysis content;

- significant human aspects (societal or individual).

Thus strategic planning, venture analysis, risk analysis, the design or management of complex systems, social impact assessment, and environmental impact statements offer significant opportunities for the introduction of multiple perspectives.

---

[4]Rittel and Webber (1973) use the term *wicked* problems—in contrast to *tame* problems.

II

THE USUAL PERSPECTIVE
AND ITS LIMITATIONS

H. LINSTONE

Give a small boy a hammer, and he will find that everything he encounters needs pounding.

Kaplan's Law of the Instrument

Daran erkenn ich den gelehrten Herrn!
Was ihr nicht tastet, steht euch meilenfern,
Was ihr nicht rechnet, glaubt ihr, sei nicht wahr.

Goethe, *Faust,* Part II

Science and technology represent the most successful "religion" of modern times. From Galileo to the Apollo lunar landing, from Darwin to recombinant DNA, the paradigms[1] of science and technology have yielded dazzling triumphs. This world view includes the following characteristics:

1. the definition of "problems" abstracted from the world around us, and the implicit assumption that problems can be "solved";
2. optimization, or the search for a *best* solution;
3. reductionism, that is, the study of a system in terms of a very limited number of elements (or variables) and the interactions among them;
4. reliance on data and models, and combinations thereof, as modes of inquiry;
5. quantification of information;
6. objectivity, the assumption that the scientist is an unbiased observer outside of the system he or she is studying (that is, truth is observer-invariant);
7. ignoring or avoiding the individual, a consequence of reductionism and quantification (for example, the use of averages) as well as objectivity;
8. a view of time movement as linear (that is, at a universally accepted pace reckoned by precise physical measurement with no consideration of differential time perceptions, planning horizons, and discount rates).

Applied mathematics and modeling have been used as tools by scientists and engineers for a very long time, and their evolution continues in accordance with these characteristics. They serve system designers remarkably well in the analysis of today's complex hardware and software.

Frequently, cause-and-effect modeling is carried out to study the static and dynamic behavior of the variables that describe the system and its environment. Structural models and system dynamics are illustrative of such tools (Linstone, et al. 1978). Theoretical models are "validated" by empirical data. Rationality is assumed to determine decisions, for example, the alternative with the most efficient performance will be selected. Figure 1a schematically summarizes the general approach.[2]

The success of this mode of thought and its paradigms has led very naturally to increasing pressure to extend its use beyond science and technology, that is, to society and all its systems. This attitude is typified by the planning, programming, and budgeting drive in the 1960s and the popularity of econometric and cost–benefit models in the 1970s. Organizations become cybernetic systems, utility theory determines preferences, social indicators are synthesized, decision analysis provides the key to decision making, and policy analysis selects strat-

---

[1] We could alternatively use the term *operating principles*.
[2] A typical well-structured systems problem treated very successfully by such analysis is the optimization of the Long Island (N.Y.) blood distribution system (from regional blood centers to hospitals). Because blood can be administered only within 21 days of collection, wastage is of serious concern. The analysts were able to model the system and revise the distribution pattern to cut wastage from 20 to 4% (Brodheim and Prastacos, 1979)!

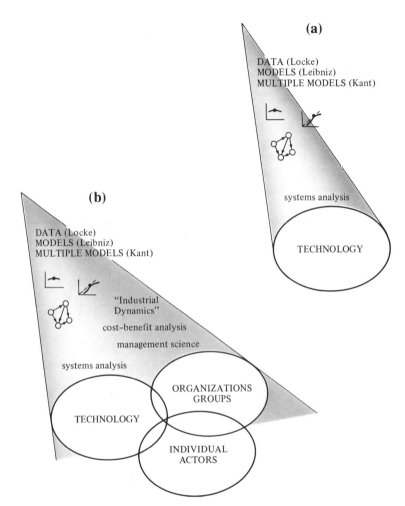

FIGURE 1. The technical perspective: (**a**) originally applied to purely technological systems; (**b**) later extended to complex sociotechnical systems, which invariably involve social entities and individuals.
Note: The set of circles represents the system being viewed (the "what"), and the beams show the perspective (the "how").

egies. There is a mathematical theory of war and, of course, "management science." Systems analysis is now described more broadly as the application of "the logical, quantitative, and structural tools of modern science and technology" to complex sociotechnical problems (Quade and Miser, in press:2). James Miller (1978) breaks down all living systems, from cells to nations and supranational organizations, into subsystems that can be categorized in terms of 19 types.[3] This elaborate tour de force tries to do for systems what Mendeleyev's periodic table achieved for chemical elements. Hugh Miser (1980:146) in his state-of-the-art review of systems analysis and operations research for the centennial issue of *Science*, recalls Nobel Laureate Herbert Simon's description of systems analysis as a "celebration of human rationality" and concludes:

> The challenge is to enlarge this celebration to include the rational management of all of society's systems and their problems.

Figure 1b portrays this vision. Ida Hoos (1972:87) refers to this as the "man on the moon" magic: ie., the oft-repeated rhetorical question, "If we can put a man on the moon, why can't we_____?," where the blank can be filled in by 1) "reduce crime in our cities," 2) "develop an adequate public transportation system," 3) "rid America of poverty," 4) "offer the Japanese stronger competition in cars and steel," 5) "provide work for all," and so on.

Without question, the technical perspective is ideal for well-structured systems problems, such as those encountered in the manned space program. Why, then, does deep trouble result when relying on it in ill-structured problem areas? To answer this question, we will examine the eight characteristics listed above in more detail.

A. THE PROBLEM–SOLUTION VIEW

When we talk about a "problem" we assume a solution exists. We have been brainwashed in school: a textbook presents a problem only if there is a solution (often in the back of the book). Such books do not point out that in the living world every new solution provided by a technology creates new problems. Public health measures cut the death rate but this result in turn led to a global population explosion. Introduction of European agricultural techniques in Africa produces food in the short term and desertification in the long term. It would be more nearly correct to state that we shift problems rather than solve them.[4]

---

[3]There are eight subsystems that process matter-energy (for example, ingestion), nine that process information (for example, encoder), and two that process both (for example, reproduction). Thus the encoder in a cell is a component-producing hormone, and in a national government it is a press secretary. All 19 subsystems are seen as critical to the continuation of life at any given level of living-system complexity and hence for the evolutionary process.

[4]A complex problem usually has several solution concepts (S) each of which leads to several new problems (P), etc. In other words we have a tree/branch structure with levels of P and S succeeding each other indefinitely into the future. Some Ps are of the diminishing ripple type, and some have an amplifying effect ("the cure is worse than the illness").

B. OPTIMIZATION OR THE "BEST" SOLUTION SEARCH

Cost–benefit analysis and linear programming are typical of the search for the optimal solution. It usually comes as a shock to those nurtured on this paradigm that complex living systems have not organized themselves in accordance with such an optimization principle. As Holling (1977:129) notes, ecological systems sacrifice efficiency for resilience or trade avoidance of failure (the *fail-safe* strategy familiar to engineers) for survival of failure (*safe-fail* strategy). They seek to minimize the cost of failure rather than the likelihood of failure. They strive to maximize their options, rather than confine them by selecting the "best" one. They do not "manage" themselves by manacling themselves.[5] Evolution shows that their safe-fail strategy is eminently suited to a world that is inherently unpredictable at certain times.

C. REDUCTIONISM

Von Foerster's (1972:1) First Law expresses the reductionist process rather well:

> The more complex the problem which is being ignored, the greater are the chances for fame and success.

If a system is complex, we simplify it by dividing it into subsystems. If we still cannot handle the subsystems, we reduce the system further. Finally we arrive at problems we can solve; fame and success come with publishing. The process leads inexorably to a plethora of papers that deal profoundly with unimportant, even trivial, problems.

Modeling is undoubtedly the most basic and pervasive means of simplifying complex systems for the purposes of analysis. We shall postpone a discussion of this subject to the next section.

The use of averages (for example, statistical mechanics in physics, per capita gross national product in economics) and probabilities (for example, structural failure, health risk) has permitted treatment of systems with very large numbers of elements, each behaving in a unique way. None will dispute the resulting success in effecting reduction of complexity. Not surprisingly, probabilities have been extended to areas such as planning. We hear talk of a "most probable" scenario. Unfortunately, it either comprises so few elements (events and trends) that it is meaningless or so many that, even if each had a 90% chance of occurrence, the product would have a very low likelihood. For example, for 20

---

[5]The dictionary tells us that "to manage" means "to control or direct the use of." As Von Foerster (1977:107–108) notes, this implies that management reduces the degrees of freedom of the technological system being managed. In probing more deeply, it is ominous to find that *manage* is related to the word *manacle*, "a device for confining the hands, usually consisting of two metal rings that are fastened about the wrist and joined by a metal chain." Much of American industry looks at technology assessment and environmental impact statements in precisely these terms, that is, as efforts to shackle technology.

elements each with an independent 90% probability, the scenario has only 12% likelihood. If all alternative scenarios have a lower probability, does this make the 12% scenario a "most probable" one? History is strewn with events that had a powerful impact but were calculated to have a very low probability (for example, Three Mile Island accident). The clients of the forecast are usually less interested in probabilities than in circumventing catastrophe and moderating the effects of failure. The analyst's familiar "expected value" calculation may miss the mark completely in providing a meaningful measure of risk for the decision maker.

As Berlinski (1976:131–132) so aptly put it:

> Complexity begets nonlinearity. But linear theory is where the theorems are. Buridan's ass perished between two such choices.

There are few straight lines in our world. But the jump in difficulty of solution when we move from linear to nonlinear systems is enormous. Hence the predilection for linearization is as understandable in the case of economists today as it was for physicists a century earlier.[6]

Another example of the reductionism common in analysis is the representation of a system as a set of elements with pairwise relationships denoting the interactions. If there are three elements (A, B, and C), there exist six possible relations (for example, $A–B$, $C–B$). If the pairwise qualification is removed, there are at least 49 interactions (for example, $AB–ABC$, $B–B$, $BC–A$). Anyone with a family or corporation knows that there are numerous nonpair relationships (for example, father–children). For a system of ten elements, this number rises to over one million. (The formula is $(2^n - 1)^2$.) Such a calculation bares the vast simplification underlying conventional systems analysis.

A recent fashion in reductionism is the transfer of entire theories from one field to another (often falsely presented as an example of interdisciplinarity). One such case is the adoption of thermodynamics by some economists, for example, the "entropy state" of Georgescu-Roegen (1972). In the context of the science-technology world view it is tempting to reduce complexity by taking an existing law, albeit derived for closed physical systems, and apply it to open social systems. But the Second Law of Thermodynamics really does not address the evolution of living systems from single cells to *Homo sapiens*. Such systems are becoming increasingly organized, oblivious to the running-down postulated by the Law. In human beings, each fertilized egg recreates potential (that is,

---

[6]A personal note: I am reminded that, as a budding mathematician, I was duly impressed by the powerful theorems that can be derived for "regular" or "analytic" functions (that is, those that are differentiable in a region). Only much later was I made aware that, among all functions, those that are regular constitute "a set of measure zero." This translates into the statement that *almost no* functions are regular.

negentropy), and the transfer of information about technology among different cultures may have a similar effect.[7]

A concrete illustration of the fruits of reductionism is provided by the Pentagon. Several years ago, a computerized war game resulted in such a command and control breakdown that the entire computer-dominated Worldwide Military Command and Control System was reexamined.

> The question is whether the traditional reductionist approach to understanding can make workable such a "holistic" challenge as a worldwide U.S. military command and control system [*Science*, 1980:410].

D. RELIANCE ON DATA AND MODELS

A reflection of the reductionism just noted is the self-imposed constraint of the science-technology perspective to certain modes of inquiry (Churchman, 1971):

1. Lockean—empirical, agreement on observations or data, truth is experiential and does not rest on any theoretical considerations;
2. Leibnizian—formal model, theoretical explanation, truth is analytic and does not rest on raw data of an external world;
3. Kantian—theoretical model and empirical data complement each other and are inseparable, truth is a synthesis, multiple models provide synergism (for example, particle and wave theories in physics).

Not only the hard sciences, but the soft ones as well, see their legitimation almost exclusively in terms of these modes of inquiry. A recent *Fortune* Series on new management strategies mirrors the same tendency in advising corporate planners (Kiechel, 1981). The McKinsey S curves,[8] Porter U curve, growth and market share matrix, Lewis strategy grid, and Mitchell price/equity return slope are the 1981 vintage "in" models. They have replaced the experience curve and the old dog/cow/star grid. Such are the magic tonics peddled by the modern patent medicine salesmen to the corporate world (Cicco, 1982). They are essential elements in a process sometimes termed "the sea gull model of consulting": "you flew out from Boston, made a couple of circles around the client's head, dropped a strategy on him, and flew back" (Kiechel, 1982b:36).

The widespread use of simple curves in economics reflects the dominance of models as a source of insight into economic processes. From supply and demand curves we moved to isoquants. The learning curve explained the benefits of increased production, namely, reduced cost; the Phillips curve suggested that unemployment and inflation were inversely related. Most recently, the Laffer

---

[7]Berlinski (1976:14) quotes Paul Samuelson in his Nobel lecture: "There is really nothing more pathetic than to have an economist or a retired engineer trying to force analogies between the concepts of physics and the concepts of economics" [*Science*, 1971:994].

[8]Simply a series of logistic growth curves familiar to every forecaster.

curve demonstrated that there is an optimal tax rate (that is, one that maximizes government revenue).

Each curve represents an engagingly simple model and provides valuable, albeit limited, insights. The trouble begins when we overreach ourselves by claiming that the model *approximates the real world system*. As we realize that, contrary to the Phillips curve, unemployment and inflation actually can rise simultaneously, as in the 1970s, we search for a more complex model and expect it to represent the system. In this way, an avalanche of increasingly detailed models is easily triggered. Their popularity is evident. As Daniel Bell put it, the Phillips curve "provided more employment for economists . . . than any public works program since the construction of the Erie Canal" (Gardner, 1981:23).

Emphasis on certain types of models easily leads to a kind of "group think." As system dynamics or input–output modeling proliferates and the number of modelers multiplies, conferences, papers, and books create a community. Shared interest and mutual reinforcement increasingly turn attention to baroque model improvements and compulsive extensions. In the process, the core assumptions are left behind untended.

Another facet of the problem is the unwarranted jump from simulation to duplication, that is, the assumption that a computer can duplicate human behavior because it can simulate it. We understand the computer's operation; we do not understand that of the brain. The latter produces mental states; the former does not. A computer program can simulate a learning process but cannot create a thinking machine, regardless of its sophistication. The computer's formal operations, using symbols, do not imply that the symbols have meaning to the computer (Searle, 1982). Thus the reality created by the computer model in the mind of the programmer or user can never be a duplication of a human or societal reality. Unfortunately, this distinction is often overlooked—an understandable lapse for those whose computer modeling experience was built on the simulation of purely technological systems.

In its most extreme form, modeling becomes an end rather than a means. The dedicated modeler reminds one of Pygmalion, the sculptor king of Greek mythology. He fashioned a beautiful statue of a girl and fell in love with it. Responding to his plea, the goddess Aphrodite brought the statue to life, and Pygmalion married his model. Today's modelers, mesmerized by the vast computer capacity, may also become wedded to their creations: *the models become the reality*. The computer's ability to handle large-scale models is confused with an ability to represent sociotechnical system complexity. Clearly, modeling seems to be fun for modelers,[9] but it also can be a nightmare for the real-world problem solver.

---

[9]In a recent survey of structural modeling techniques, Linstone et al. (1978) found over 100 types in this very limited area.

This discussion of the role of models suggests a subtle distinction between two approaches:

1. striving to *represent* a complex sociotechnical system by replicating it in a mathematical format (for example, simulation using a large-scale, computerized, albeit severely constrained, model),
2. seeking abstract models to serve as *thinking aids,* revealing possible clues or illuminating some aspect of system behavior in a different way (usually such models are simple enough to abandon without regret, occasionally elegant enough to cherish).

In the latter case, we harbor no illusion that the model *represents* the system; we use the model merely as a key to unlock a new insight or point to a hidden link. Role 2 makes modeling an exceedingly valuable learning tool, but it is role 1 that so frequently leads us astray. Hence the maxim suggested by Berlinski (1976:83) for the mathematical modeler: "start simply and use to the fullest the resources of [mathematical] theory." As he observes, it is this prescription taken neatly in reverse that characterizes the world dynamics modeling of Forrester (1971) and Meadows et al. (1972), that is, an imposingly complex system of equations subjected to "an analysis of ineffable innocence." Role 1 is clearly reflected in Forrester's (1971:18) own words in his explanation of system dynamics:

> All systems that change through time can be represented by using only levels and rates. The two kinds of variables are necessary but at the same time sufficient for representing any system.

Role 1 was also implied in the urban planners' growing conviction during the 1960s that they could rely on large-scale computer models to analyze urban structure and policy. But as Lee (1973:163) concludes in his *Requiem for Large-Scale Models:*

> None of the goals held out for large-scale models have been achieved, and there is little reason to expect anything different in the future. For each objective offered as a reason for building a model, there is either a better way of achieving the objective (more information at less cost) or a better objective (a more socially useful question to ask).

The lesson has been learned at great expense. His advice for future modeling efforts is one of common sense: 1) balance theory and objectivity with intuition, 2) start with a problem that needs solving, not a methodology that needs applying, 3) build only very simple models.

Outstanding examples of role 2 are found in the work of Lotka (1956) and Volterra on predator–prey relations, of Glansdorff and Prigogine (1971), as well as Thom (1975), on complex system stability and divergence effects, also in the writings of Marchetti (1977:ff). On the other hand, much of the General Systems

Theory to date fails in role 2. It abstracts system models in general to such stratospheric levels that any potentially useful substance evaporates in the process, that is, it becomes an end in itself (Berlinski, 1976:2–11).

For analysts, it is difficult to appreciate that, as we move beyond the pure science-technology domain, other systems of inquiry may prove more fruitful. Here are several candidates:

4. Hegelian—dialectic confrontation between opposing models or plans leading to resolution, truth is conflictual as typified in a courtroom trial;
5. Merleau–Ponty—reality as currently shared assumptions about a specific situation, acceptance of a new reality is negotiated out of our experience, truth is agreement that permits action;
6. Singerian—pragmatic meta-inquiring system which includes application of other systems as needed; the designer's psychology and sociology are inseparable from the physical system representation; ethics is swept into the design.[10]

If we concentrate on the individual we should also mention Kant's noumena:

7. Noumena—reality beyond the perception of our senses, a world that we can only intuit, to which we are linked through our unconscious mind— in such a world there is no temporal distinction of past, present, and future.

Thus we see that there is much out there beyond data-based, model-based, and complementary multimodel systems of inquiry. Kellen (1968:24–25) urges us to:

> . . . realize the limitations of the knowledge you can obtain under the best of circumstances and with the most thorough use and study of the "data". . . . Some people are now fanatics in the realm of methodology. . . . But any extensive use of, or trust in, any methodology can only lead you astray, and you can get the help which new methods and machines offer only if your consumption remains sparing, your methodological diet balanced, and your attitude skeptical.

Plamenatz (1972:45) writes in his work on Machiavelli:

> The ideas about the great man and his role in history of a sometimes careless historian may be more perceptive and realistic than those of the most scrupulous recorder of facts.

The science–technology world view also places great stress on cause-and-effect relationships. But pause to consider a comment of Toynbee (1972:97):

---

[10]For an appreciation of philosopher Edgar A. Singer, Jr., particularly his importance for the study of socio-technical systems, see Churchman (1982, Chapt. 10).

Typical Questions Posed by Inquiring Systems

Suppose we are given a set of technology assessment statements. Our Inquiring Systems can be simply differentiated from one another in terms of the kind of characteristic questions each of them would address to the assessor or to his set of statements. Each question in effect embodies the major philosophical criterion that would have to be met before that inquirer would accept the statement.

- The Lockean analyst or Inquiring System would ask something like:
  Since data are always prior to the development of theory, how can one, independent of any formal technology assessment model, justify the assessment by means of some objective data or the consensus of some group of expert judges that bears on the assessment? What are the statistics? What is the probability you are wrong? Is that a good estimate?

- The Leibnizian analyst or Inquiring System might ask:
  How can one, independent of any empirical considerations, give a rational justification of the assessment? What is the model you are using? How was the result deduced and is it precise and certain?

- The Kantian analyst or Inquiring System would ask:
  Since data and theory always exist side by side, does there exist some combination of data or expert judgment plus underlying theoretical justification for the data that would justify the assessment? What alternative assessments exist? Which of these satisfies my objectives?

- The Hegelian analyst or Inquiring System might ask:
  Since every assessment is a reflection of a more general theory or plan about the nature of the world as a whole system, i.e., a world view, does there exist some alternative sharply differing world view that would permit the serious consideration of a completely opposite assessment? What if the reverse happens and why wouldn't that be more reasonable?

- The Merleau–Ponty analyst or Inquiring System might ask:
  What is the shared reality? How does it facilitate the generation of policy options? How does the assessment create an impetus for desirable action? What kind of reality is most effectively negotiated by the parties at interest?

- The Singerian analyst or Inquiring System would ask:
  Have we taken a broad enough perspective of the basic assessment? Would other perspectives help? Have we from the very beginning asked the right question? To what extent are the questions and models of each inquirer a reflection of the unique personality of each inquirer as much as they are felt to be a "natural" characteristic or property of the "real" world?

Source: Mitroff and and Turoff (1973) and Scheele (1975).

> In my search up to the present point, I have been experimenting with the play of soul-less forces . . . and I have been thinking in deterministic terms of cause and effect. . . . Have I not erred in applying to historical thought, which is a study of living creatures, a scientific method of thought which has been devised for thinking about inanimate nature? And have I not also erred further in treating the outcomes of encounters between persons as cases of the operation of cause and effect? The effect of a cause is inevitable, invariable, and predictable. But the initiative that is taken by one or the other of the live parties to an encounter is not a cause; it is a challenge. Its consequence is not an effect; it is a response. Challenge and response resembles cause and effect only in standing for a sequence of events. The character of the sequence is not the same. Unlike the effect of a cause, the response to a challenge is not predetermined . . . and is therefore intrinsically unpredictable.

Prigogine et al.'s (1977) concept of order through fluctuation posits another source of unpredictability: the phase when a system becomes unstable and experiences temporary "macroscopic indeterminacy" before reaching a new stability state. The new state may depend on one fluctuation that is itself of no significance.

E. QUANTIFICATION

In ancient Greece the Pythagoreans attempted to preserve the purity of their mathematical expressions by putting to death the man who discovered incommensurables. Today the computer has become the ideal instrument to fuel the drive for quantification. A new version of Gresham's Law states that "quantitative analyses tend to drive out qualitative analyses." Zadeh's fuzzy set theory (1965) has even been developed to quantify qualitative terms and, in the manner of a shoehorn, squeeze them into the computer input format. Churchman (1979:20) points up the paradox: "fuzzy set theory runs the danger of becoming precise about fuzziness."

The developed nations are, culturally speaking, measuring societies. We measure national military strength by comparing the number of our strategic weapons systems with those of the Soviet Union, ignoring the fact that accuracy is far more significant than quantity and that the ability to destroy the enemy's industrial capacity four times may not be better than destroying it twice. We measure individuals by their "worth" in dollars and societies by their gross national products in dollars. No wonder, therefore, that the candid admission by David Stockman, current Director of the U.S. Office of Management and Budget— "none of us really understands what's going on with all these numbers"—caused consternation in Washington (*New York Times,* Nov. 13, 1981:17). Yankelovich's comment on the subject reminds one of the circles of Hell in Dante's *Inferno:*

> The first step is to measure whatever can be easily measured. This is OK as far as it goes.
> The second step is to disregard that which can't be measured or give it an arbitrary quantitative value. This is artificial and misleading.

The third step is to presume that what can't be measured easily really isn't very important. This is blindness.

The fourth step is to say that what can't be easily measured really doesn't exist. This is suicide [Smith, 1972:271–272].

Compare this attitude with that of another culture, Papua New Guinea. Fuglesang (1977:96) writes:

In many villages they do not use measures, because people's life-style is such that they have no need for it. In other villages people may measure the size of houses, fields, or gardens in "paces," which are sometimes called "feet". . . [The technical expert] will be disenchanted by the fact that a "pace" is not a fixed standard measure. It will vary with the man who is doing the pacing. In villages I lived in, in Zambia, people were perfectly happy with that, because they knew the man.

Quantification engenders self-delusion. Tversky and Kahneman (1974:1129) have found that:

People tend to overestimate the probability of conjunctive events and to underestimate the probability of disjunctive events . . . [such biases] are particularly significant in the context of planning. The successful completion of an undertaking, such as the development of a new product, typically has a conjunctive character: for the undertaking to succeed, each of a series of events must occur. [This leads] to unwarranted optimism in the evaluation of the likelihood that a plan will succeed or that a project will be completed on time. Conversely, disjunctive structures are typically encountered in the evaluation of risks. A complex system, such as a nuclear reactor or a human body, will malfunction if any of its essential components fails. Even when the likelihood of failure is slight, the probability of an overall failure can be high if many components are involved . . . people will tend to underestimate the probabilities of failure in complex systems.

The fundamental claim of the think tank is that it deals with its materials objectively. But of course it cannot do so when the materials do not lend themselves to objective analysis. . . . This is its great weakness when it ventures into policy matters. . . . The non-scientific part has to be done in non-scientific ways, which is to say, non-think-tank ways. The characteristic error is to deal with the unquantifiable as if it were quantifiable.

I once spent the better part of a week in argument with a remorselessly humorless colleague who wanted to assign numerical values to the phrases "desirable," "probably desirable," [etc.]. I said that language was used because language conveys certain things to the intelligence that numbers cannot. He regarded this as primitive prejudice or as "theology."

Source: W. Pfaff (1981:79).

F. OBJECTIVITY

Editors of scientific and technological publications have traditionally frowned on the use of the first-person singular or plural. Authors have resorted to arduous circumlocutions to banish *I* or *we* from their texts, lest they be tainted with subjectivity. Yet the assumption of objectivity on the part of scientists and technologists is revealed more and more frequently as a myth. Churchman (1968:86) writes of the social sciences:

> One of the most absurd myths of the social sciences is the "objectivity" that is alleged to occur in the relation between the scientist-as-observer and the people he observes. He really thinks he can stand apart and objectively observe how people behave, what their attitudes are, how they think, how they decide . . . [it is a] silly and empty claim that an observation is objective if it resides in the brain of an unbiased observer.

Mitroff (1974:248) lays to rest objectivity in its traditional meaning in the physical sciences with his study of Apollo moon scientists:

> It is humanly impossible to eliminate all bias and commitment from science . . . [we cannot] pin our hopes for the existence of any objective science on the existence of passionless unbiased individuals.

Von Foerster (1977:107–108), a cyberneticist, insists that objectivity cannot occur in the relation between the scientist as observer and the people he observes. The claim that the properties of an observer must not enter into the description of his observation is nonsense, because without the observer there are no descriptions; the observer's faculty of describing enters, by necessity, into his descriptions.

If objectivity cannot be assumed for the scientist in his proverbial ivory tower, it would seem foolhardy indeed to carry this assumption over to technology management in a real world setting. The "real world" is a complex system in which virtually "everything interacts with everything"—and this includes the manager. That being the case, the choice of model and data, of problem definition and boundaries, is always partly subjective.

G. IGNORING OR AVOIDING THE INDIVIDUAL

From Adam Smith to West Churchman, concern has been expressed over the danger of ignoring the individual and losing him in the aggregate view. Smith said 200 years ago:

> The man of system . . . seems to imagine that he can arrange the different members of a great society with as much ease as the hand arranges the different pieces upon a chessboard; he does not consider that the pieces upon the chessboard have no other principle of motion besides that which the hand impresses upon them; but that, in the great chessboard of human society, every single piece has a principle

of motion of its own altogether different from that which the legislature might choose to impress upon it [Schneider, 1948:247].

Churchman (1977:88–90) makes the following observations:

> Economic models have to aggregate a number of things, and one of the things they aggregate is you! In great globs you are aggregated into statistical classes. . . .
>
> Jung says that, until you have gone through the process of individuation . . . you will not be able to face the social problems. You will not be able to build your models and tell the world what to do. . . .
>
> From the perspective of the unique individual, it is not counting up how many people on this side and how many on that side. All the global systems things go out: there are no trade-offs in this world, in this immense world of the inner self. . . . All our concepts that work so well in the global world do not work in the inner world. . . . We have great trouble describing it very well in scientific language, but it is there, and is important. . . .
>
> To be able to see the world globally, which you are going to have to be able to do, and to see it as a world of unique individuals . . . that is really complexity.

In retrospect we encounter instance after instance where individuals were crucial in the interaction of a technology with society: Wernher Von Braun's leadership in rocket and space vehicle development, Rachel Carson's book *The Silent Spring*. In these cases we have an impact of individuals on technology. Conversely, technology may have a tremendous impact on the individual. Television ended the career of Senator Joseph McCarthy, radio broadcasts of fireside chats worked powerfully for President Franklin Roosevelt, and television coverage of the space program made folk heroes of the astronauts.

H. PERCEPTIONS OF TIME

The science-technology world view is concerned with physical space-time, with time as a dimension or variable essential in grasping the dynamics of a complex system. Distortions intrude through the relativity theory, for example, perceptions of time vary with observer velocity in an Einsteinian universe. Similarly, economists apply a discount rate to future dollars to determine their present value; the basis traditionally is the cost of capital. Aside from such rather mechanistic alterations, this perspective sees time as moving linearly, to a universally accepted pace determined by precise physical measurement. Thus Forrester, Meadows, Mesarovic, and Pestel may exercise their system dynamics models over 50- to 130-year periods, but the computational time increment is independent of society and individuals, geographical locale, and era. We shall use the term *technological time* for this case.

By contrast, every individual has a *personal time* conception. A person's time horizon is dictated by the expected life span, position in Maslow's hierarchy of needs, and/or other individual considerations.

A person alone is a different entity from a person in groups of 3, 11, 40, 4,000, 60,000, and so on up. . . .

All the studies I know about dealing with mass psychology in its relation to individual psychology, and vice versa, grow out of that academic stuffiness that invariably falls upon the men who devote themselves to such things. . . . The thing demands a certain amount of that high courage known as humor, and it demands knowing personally people like the grocer's boy, hundreds of children around the age of 6 and 8, and very few, if any, professors.

James Thurber letter to E.B. White
January 20, 1938
Reprinted in the Los Angeles Times
December 30, 1980:115.

The individual applies a psychological discount rate to his perception of future problems and opportunities, which is totally distinct from the economist's dollar discount rate based on the cost of capital. The psychological discount rate means, in effect, that the individual looks at the future as if through the wrong end of a telescope (Linstone and Simmonds, 1977:5–6). Distant objects appear smaller than they really are. Similarly, problems far in the future are of less concern to us than equally serious problems in the near term (Figure 2). The highest discounting occurs where immediate personal survival is the prime concern; the lowest rate occurs in an affluent, well-educated family in a stable Western setting.

FIGURE 2. The discounting phenomenon: world population crisis. Zero discount rate case based on Meadows' *Limits to Growth* standard run (1972:124). *Note:* The application of a 5% discount rate to the population increase has the apparent effect of reducing a crisis 75 years from now to insignificance.

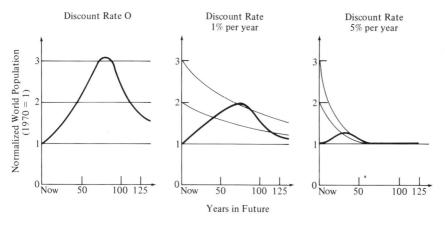

TABLE 1. Jung's Typology and Time Orientations

Jung type	Time focus		Discounting
Sensation	Present		Highest
Feeling	Past	⎫⎧	Selective bias
Intuition	Future	⎭⎩	High/moderate
Thinking	Past–present–future		Moderate

Source: Linstone and Simmonds (1977:10).

Time discounting varies with age and with psychological type [11] Table 1 suggests the Jung typology and related time orientations. As the Marschallin in *Der Rosenkavalier* observes, "Die Zeit, die ist ein sonderbar Ding" (time is a strange thing).

Even our daily newspaper raises the subject:

> The dimension of time has become a great paradox of the modern world. Words and images are transmitted instantly, people almost as fast. But the context and the meaning do not come through the blur of impression which seems to make adjustment slower and more difficult [*New York Times*, Dec. 28, 1979:A-6].

The experiments of Tversky and Kahneman (1974) demonstrate how human beings apply a discount rate to their own pasts and thus distort the integration of their personal experience. Recent events tend to be overstressed in comparison with more remote ones.

Let us now turn from the individual to organizations or social entities. Neither technological time nor personal time prevails. Organizations have a longer time horizon than individuals; they do not expect to die like human beings. This does not mean they use a zero discount rate, merely a lower one than individuals. *Social time* is multigenerational. Organizations have, in fact, a curious blend of long- and short-time horizons. There is the motivation of self-perpetuation and the pressure of meeting next month's payroll and protecting next year's budget. As in the case of individuals, organizations have a spectrum of time horizons. Small companies contrast with large ones, medieval Christian with modern Western societies, rich European with poor African states. Thus the discount rate depends both on the conception of time *and,* to a lesser degree, organizational and individual differences (Figure 3).

Consider once more the case of Papua New Guinea:

> There is something we could call "village time." It is not measured in hours, minutes or seconds, but in seasons or moons. . . . Women would tend to measure

---

[11]Leaders in government, religion, and industry are often distinguished by their atypical time orientations. Farsightedness means an unusually low personal discount rate—in the United States, Washington and Lincoln are examples (Loye, 1978). Today, Israel's Begin uses a biblical time scale and Iran's Khomeini sees the 16th century as close: both individuals seem past, rather than future, oriented.

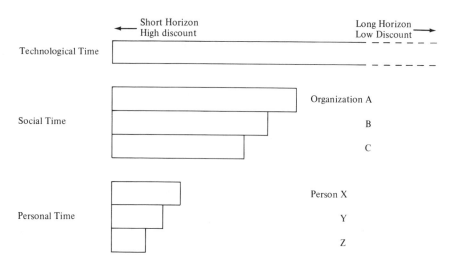

FIGURE 3. Relative time horizons: a schematic. *Note:* For qualification see text.

the time by the chores of the day, which are very regular in a village setting. There is the time for gathering firewood or making the fire. There is the time for weeding the garden and the time for preparing the big meal of the day [Fuglesang, 1977:96].

The importance of such discounting in the decision-making context can hardly be overestimated: decisions are drastically altered as the discount rate varies. Consider the choice between major national investments in two alternative energy forms: coal and large-scale solar energy. A proposed 20-year coal mining program absorbs relatively constant investment from year to year, whereas the solar program necessitates a much higher initial investment with much lower subsequent costs. If a zero discount rate is used, the solar alternative is likely to show a lower total cost over the 20-year period; if a modest discount rate is used, the coal alternative is preferred in terms of cost. The reason is simple: the discount factor shrinks the higher coal costs in the distant future, but hardly reduces the very high solar energy costs in the immediate future. Thus the decision maker's preference is strongly dependent on the assumed discount rate.

Recent history also points to the pervasive presence of discounting. Following the oil shock in 1973, a great interest developed in alternative energy sources (solar, synthetic fuels, etc.). Today, there is a temporary oil glut, and the support for these alternatives has been sharply curtailed. Discounting of the future focuses our attention on the immediate or near-term situation. Over the longer term, this myopia could mean that the optimistic energy forecasts will prove self-defeating (Kahn, 1982:140). (For another illustration, see Linstone, 1975.)

In contrast to the mainstream (or positive) discounting phenomenon, we should mention the environmentalist position, seen in ethical terms by Churchman (1977:87): the preference for a negative discount rate, which implies that the future is *more* important than the present! This means that we believe our grand-children are more important than we. Because they cannot vote or form a vested interest group, we should act as conservators for them.[12]

The discount rate is also at the heart of Julian Simon's discussion of the question, Does population growth reduce the standard of living? Using the family analogy, he argues that the answer is "yes" in the short run, but "no" in the long run. "Whether you wish to pay the present costs for the future benefits depends on how you weigh the future relative to the present" (1981:6).

Research is urgently needed to extend our limited grasp of differential dis-counting (see Section XII D1).

As a final note on discounting we observe that physical space as well as time is commonly discounted. Events occurring far from our physical location (e.g., home, city) are of less interest than those taking place close to us. Residents of Santa Monica Bay, California, are more troubled by oil drilling off their shore than in the Gulf of Mexico. This is known as the NIMBY syndrome: "*not in my backyard*."[13]

These, then, are eight important paradigms that govern our usual perspective of complex systems. They also suggest why so much of systems analysis is an "inside job," performed for other analysts who share the same paradigms—and not necessarily for the audience that needs it.

---

[12]See also Heilbroner (1974:115).
[13]For a schematic representation see Figure 24.

MULTIPLE PERSPECTIVES:
THE LITERATURE

H. LINSTONE

WOODCUTTER: All those different stories—I began to doubt my
senses. I couldn't understand—I still can't understand—why
they all lied.

WIGMAKER: Did they?

WOODCUTTER: They must have! I know what I saw with my own
eyes.

WIGMAKER: Why should I trust *your* eyes any more than those of
the other three? Like I told you—people see what they want to
see and say what they want to hear.

> *Rashomon*
> Fay and Michael Kanin

In Chapter II we reviewed a series of paradigms integral to the way we normally look at systems problems. We were concerned with the "how" rather than the "what," that is, *how* we usually look at the problem rather than *what* we are looking at. We will continue in this vein and focus on the question: Does recent literature suggest how we can look at problems differently?

In a narrow sense, the concept of multiple models is widely recognized. We emphasize that we refer to the use of multiple models *simultaneously* or in parallel, not sequentially. The latter is exemplified by the Copernican and Ptolemaic models, one replacing the other as the "correct" view of the world.

Accepting multiple models requires a considerable degree of intellectual sophistication or maturity. Im mathematics, the 19th century challenged us with Euclidean, Riemannian, and Lobachevskian geometries; anthropology used the triad of culture, society, and personality (Kluckhorn and Mowrer, 1944). In the social sciences, Etzioni (1967) bases his model of "mixed scanning" on political and systems approaches to decision making.

Religions, like early science, strongly depended on *one Weltanschauung* as a base for authority. The fear of unsettling alternative perspectives was, and is, reflected in inquisitions, witch hunts, ostracism by colleagues, and other techniques of persecution.[1]

We prefer the word *perspective* over *model* (which Allison uses) to emphasize that we are considering different sets of paradigms, not merely different mathematical formulations.

A. ALLISON'S MODELS

Graham Allison (1969, 1971) has used three models to examine the Cuban missile crisis: model I, the rational actor; model II, the organizational process; and model III, the bureaucratic politics. Table 2 suggests the origins of these models.

Both models I and II could be built on a solid base of 1950's and 1960's scholarship. The RAND "school" and its disciples produced a plethora of rational actor guidelines and case studies, for example, Dror (1968) and Quade and Boucher (1967). The organizational process model was drawn largely from the Simon–March school of organizational decision making (March and Simon, 1958; Simon, 1958). Many of Allison's model II propositions are taken from Cyert and March (1963). Their research is a response to the dominant assumption in economics that the activity of business firms is solely a function of market dynamics. They present an alternative "process-oriented" theory whereby the internal structure of the firm plays an equally significant role. Similar to Allison's questioning of the assumption of rational choice in foreign policy making, Cyert and March challenge the axiom that profit is the only motive behind business decisions. Instead, they argue that goals are reached through bargaining and

---

[1]However, the need to move beyond a framework of paradigms to interpret occurrences within that framework was already recognized in the Biblical Book of Job. The explanation of the phenomenon of great suffering and misfortunes afflicting virtuous human beings was basically this: The infallibly fair judgment of the Deity can only be understood in a context beyond the grasp of man, his bounded realm of action and life span.

TABLE 2. A Comparison of the Multiple Perspectives and Their Sources.[a]

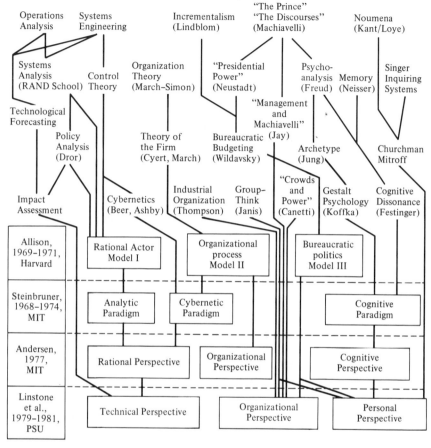

[a]Note: Only representative sources are shown.

compromise among the major subunits within the organization. Maximization of profit is only one consideration. In the prevailing economic theories of the firm (and Allison's model I), decision makers are assumed to have complete information about alternatives. Cyert and March, in contrast, posit a process of problem solving characterized by incomplete information and biased toward dominant perspectives within the organization.

The foundations of Allison's first two conceptual models (I and II) are stronger than those of the third. Organizations are easier to analyze than individuals and permit more ready generalization, hence propositions. (We recall the quotations from Adam Smith and Churchman in Chapter II.) In his afterword, Allison (1971:274) notes, "Model III tells a fascinating story, but is enormously complex. The information requirements are often overwhelming." The use of a "rational-actor" model and an "organizational-process" model for a case study of a 1962 presidential crisis was self-evident, considering the strong countercurrents of the time. Rationality was the hallmark of *The Best and the Brightest*, the whiz kids brought in by Secretary of Defense McNamara to the dismay of the apparatchik dominated by career civil servants, true "organization men." In the five years prior to the formation of the Harvard May Group (Allison, 1971:ix), models I and II were, so to speak, involved in public confrontation all over Washington. Model III subsequently signified the recognition that two models could not encompass all the crucial aspects of the decision-making process. The main descriptors of the Allison models are shown in Table 3. Allison himself stresses that his models II and III are not the only alternative conceptual models. He specifically mentions a model IV, based on Steinbruner's cognitive processes of individuals (Allison, 1971:255, 329).[2]

B. STEINBRUNER'S PERSPECTIVES

Steinbruner's *The Cybernetic Theory of Decision* (1974) is partly based on his study of the application of multiple perspectives to decisions concerning the proposed multilateral force for NATO (his 1968 MIT doctoral dissertation). Like Allison, he is concerned with dimensions of political analysis and, like Allison, defines three perspectives with separate paradigms (Table 2). They are termed rational or analytic, cybernetic, and cognitive; Table 4 summarizes the characteristics.

The *analytic* paradigm refers to the operations research/systems analysis process of evaluating alternatives and determining preferred decisions by suitable measures. Often a model is the means by which causal learning takes place.

In his *cybernetic* paradigm, Steinbruner sees the systems engineering concept of the servomechanism or automatic feedback as a fundamentally different basis for decision making. Instead of causal learning, we have learning through error control.[3] This means we are more concerned with the process than with the outcome state. The critical simplification in complex problems here lies in reducing variety and limiting uncertainty. Much input is filtered out because the established repertory of responses (that is, the set of standard operating procedures) is not programmed to accept it. The relevance of this paradigm to organizations is apparent. But the quasi-exclusive concern with the control mechanism also imposes limits: it cannot explain all significant aspects of the organizational view of a sociotechnical system.

It should be noted that cyberneticists themselves represent a considerable spectrum of views. Some recognize a different control concept, but in all other respects take a rational-actor view in their analysis of the system. Others, such as Heinz Von Foerster (1977), take a much broader perspective.

---

[2]Trotter (1971) also studied the Cuban missile crisis (using nine different models), concluding that a cognitive perspective provided the best explanation for American decision making in that situation.

[3]The Watt governor and the thermostat are examples of error-control systems; the electric toaster is a cause-control system (see Appendix B, Statement 8).

TABLE 3. Allison's Models

	Model I—rational actor	Model II—organizational process	Model III—bureaucratic politics
Basic unit of analysis	Action as choice of total system	Action as organizational output in framework of present capabilities and constraints	Action as political resultant (bargaining, compromise)
Organizing concepts	Unitary decision maker (for example, government)	Constellation of loosely allied units topped by leaders	Players ("where you stand depends on where you sit")
	One set of goals (for example, national)	Problems factored; power fractionated	Parochial priorities and perceptions
	Problem seen by unitary decision maker	Parochial priorities	Goals include personal interests
	Solution a steady-state choice among alternatives	Goals are constraints defining acceptable performance of organization	Players' impact based on relative power
	Action a rational choice based on goals/objectives, alternatives/ options, consequences, and value maximizing selection	Sequential attention to goals	Action channels structure the game
		Standard operating procedures (SOPs)	Rules sanction some tactics (bargaining, coalitions, bluff) but not others
		Programs and repertoires	
		Avoidance of uncertainty	
		Problem-directed search	
		Central coordination and control	
Dominant inference pattern	Actions are maximizing means to achieve ends	Behavior of organization at time t similar to $t-1$, at $t+1$ similar to t	Action resultant of bargaining game among individuals, groups
General propositions	Likelihood of any action results from a combination of relevant values and objectives, perceived alternative courses of action, estimates of various sets of consequences, and net valuation of each set of consequences	Standard routines: program is a cluster of SOPs satisfying rather than maximizing (first acceptable rather than best alternative)	Peculiar preferences and stands of individual players
		Long-range planning institutionalized, then disregarded	Styles of play vary
	Increase in costs of an alternative reduces likelihood of its selection	Incremental change	Face of issue differs from seat to seat
	Decrease in costs of an alternative increases likelihood of its selection	Trade-offs neglected	Fuzziness useful to get agreement
		Organizational health implies growth, imperialism	Focus on immediate decision rather than on doctrine
		Administrative feasibility a major dimension	Views:
		Directed change possible when organization is in crisis	Looking down—options
			Looking sideways—commitment
			Looking up—show of confidence
			Frequent misperception
			Misexpectations
			Miscommunications

Source: Allison (1971).

TABLE 4. Steinbruner's Perspectives

Analytic paradigm	Cybernetic paradigm	Cognitive paradigm
Analytic evaluation of alternative outcomes	Uncertainty reduction by routinization	Much information processing is done without conscious direction
Models used for causal learning	Servomechanism or feedback control	Inferential memory, consistency, reality, simplicity, and stability as basis for mental information processing
Decision based on optimal choice	Learning through automatic error control	Structure of cognitive operations has regularities bearing on decision process
Decision maker makes assessment of relative values	Problem fractionalization	Strong beliefs exist despite uncertainty
New information added as in Bayesian statistics	Decision making by recipe rather than blueprint	Strong reliance on negative logic
Collective decision making assumes equivalence with theoretical individual	Survival or perpetuation is a decision criterion (not optimization or satisficing)	Thought patterns: grooved thinking, uncommitted thinking, and theoretical thinking

Source: Steinbruner (1974).

The *cognitive* paradigm rests on cognitive psychology, specifically on three claims:

1. There are regularities in the decision process that have to do with the structure, as opposed to the content, of cognitive operations.
2. The full human mental apparatus is engaged in the simplest of operations, such as direct, immediate perception.
3. Most of what happens in the human mind is not accessible to direct, conscious experience. In other words, a great deal of information processing is conducted independently of conscious direction.

Inferential memory, consistency, reality, simplicity, and stability provide the basis of this paradigm:

- inferential memory—an overall structure in operationalizing the memory;
- consistency—a tendency to keep internal belief relationships consistent with one another (and filter out inconsistent ones)[4];

---

[4]Here is the basis for the difficulty in accepting multiple perspectives. As Churchman (1977:90) noted: "The mature individual is the individual who can hold conflicting world views together at the same time, and act, and live, and that his or her life is enriched by that capability—not weakened by it."

- reality—the human mind is in contact with its environment (Freud's reality principle);

- simplicity—cognitive inference mechanisms work to keep the structure of belief as simple as possible;

- stability—cognitive inference mechanisms resist change in the core structure of beliefs.

Cognitive thinking is taken to follow one of three patterns:

- grooved thinking—routinized by tradition and experience, akin to the cybernetic process;

- uncommitted thinking—adoption of generalized concepts embedded in larger, theoretical belief structures: these are associated with a sponsor; sequential adoption of different belief structures, that is, oscillation among them ("He was of the mind of the last person he talked to");

- theoretical thinking—adoption of very abstract and extensive belief structures that are internally consistent and stable over time; theological faith in one world view ("the Communist conspiracy").

This paradigm is quite distinct from Allison's model III, bureaucratic politics. To summarize, Steinbruner's first paradigm bases the decision on whatever information is available to build a model of critical relationships; the second paradigm controls uncertainty by mechanistic feedback and decision rules; and the third rests on a certain belief structure in the human mind.

C. ANDERSEN'S PERSPECTIVES

Allison's book appeared in 1971 and has been widely used at Harvard, MIT, and elsewhere. In 1974 Massachusetts began to implement a comprehensive policy reform of special education, "Chapter 766." A system dynamics simulation was constructed as an element of this effort. Andersen's work—an MIT doctoral dissertation as was Steinbruner's, examines the impact of that model on the decision-making process using a "rational," "organizational," and "cognitive" perspective (Andersen, 1977). The central features of the Andersen perspectives are summarized in Table 5 and are compared with those of Allison and Steinbruner in Table 2. Andersen appears to have taken his *rational* perspective directly from Allison's model I, his *organizational* perspective similarly from Allison's model II, and his *cognitive* perspective from Steinbruner's cognitive paradigm. As Andersen (1977:66) writes:

> There was some question concerning what the third perspective should be. The most active candidates for the third slot were a bureaucratic politics model as articulated by Allison, a purely political model, or a form of a cognitive model. The details of the case study helped to make this choice.

TABLE 5. Andersen's Three Perspectives

Rational perspective	Organizational perspective	Cognitive perspective
Alternatives specified	Multiple actors, parochial interest	Limited information process capability
Consequences assessed		
Goals or objectives	Goals as constraints ("don't go above or below")	Tendency to filter out inconsistent images
Choice (often by optimization)	Sequential attention to goals ("grease the squeaky wheels")	Store and recall information consistent with past experience
Decisions collective (single actor)		
Problem bounded	SOPs	Focus on simplistic hypotheses rather than scan options
	Decomposable environments	
	Problem directed search	Small-peer-group reinforcement (use of task force)
	Importance of information channeling	
		Reality socially constructed (Merleau–Ponty)
	Short-run actions and corrections based on feedback	
	No prediction of long-term consequences	
	Limited flexibility	

ROLE OF MATHEMATICAL MODELS (FOR EXAMPLE, SYSTEM DYNAMICS) IN PERSPECTIVE

Highlight problem definition	Focus attention on long-term goals	Expand information processing capabilities (ability to handle many variables and interactions)
Evaluate consequences of alternative policies	Ignore sequence of goal attention	
Explicitly present trade-offs		Aid formation of images and analogies
Forum for collective decisions (replaces diverse mental models)	Provide guidelines for problem-directed search	
	Aid organizing information processing	Counteract simple extrapolations
	Ignore short-run feedback	Force causal hypotheses and then clarify trade-off
	Aid development of interagency policies	Impact depends on the relative social positioning of the model and the user
	Tend to develop infeasible policies	

Source: Andersen (1977).

A comparison of Tables 3 and 5 shows the differences in emphasis in the third perspective. Allison is concerned with bargaining, Andersen with learning and mental decision processes. Allison focuses on governmental action as a resultant of compromise, perceptions, styles of play, personal goals, and rules of the game. Andersen deals with the individual's limited information processing capability, inferential memory, focusing rather than scanning as a basis for choice, and small-group interactions leading to a shared reality. It is thus apparent that Andersen's cognitive model deals not only with the individual but with small groups.

Andersen (1977:25) concluded:

> . . . when taken together, the three perspectives create a view of model use within bureaucracies that is richer, more complex, and generates deeper insights than any view taken one at a time. . . .

D. OTHER SOURCES

The commonality of Allison, Steinbruner, and Andersen is that *each places three perspectives on one subject of study.*[5] It a device also known to writers and historians and transcends decision analysis.[6] In literature, Akutagawa's *Rashomon and Other Stories* (1952:19–33) provides a classic example. His short piece "In a Grove" consists of a series of testimonies about a corpse:

WOODCUTTER: It was I who found the body. Apparently he must have made a battle of it before he was murdered.

TRAVELING BUDDHIST PRIEST: The unfortunate man was walking toward Sekiyama with a woman accompanying him on horseback.

POLICEMAN: The man that I arrested? He is a notorious brigand called Tajomaru. . . . Tajomaru must be the murderer.

OLD WOMAN: The corpse is the man who married my daughter. . . . He was of a gentle disposition.

TAJOMARU'S CONFESSION: I killed him. . . . I had made up my mind to capture her. . . . I didn't want to kill him. . . . She asked that either her husband or I die. She said it was more trying than death to have her shame known to two men . . . I untied him . . . we crossed swords. When he fell . . . she was gone.

CONFESSION OF A WOMAN WHO HAS COME TO THE SHIMIZU TEMPLE: The

---

[5]Two other names should be mentioned in the political science area. Lowenthal (1972) analyzed the Dominican intervention, and Art (1973) viewed several recent episodes in American foreign policy from several perspectives. Both concluded that beliefs and mind sets of leaders provided crucial perspectives.

[6]It is also present in Western religious traditions. In Judaism, for example, God is viewed in three perspectives: God as nature (Malhuyot), God as history (Zihronot), and God as revelation (Shoferot).

man in the blue silk kimono, after forcing me to yield to him, laughed mockingly as he looked at my bound husband. . . . I fell unconscious. I came to and found that the man in blue silk was gone. . . . I went up to my husband. "Takehiro," I said to him, "I cannot live with you. I'm determined to die . . . but you must die too. You saw my shame." . . . . Despising me, his look said only, "Kill me." I stabbed the small sword through the lilac-colored kimono into his breast.

STORY OF THE MURDERED MAN, AS TOLD THROUGH A MEDIUM: The robber made his brazen proposal. "Once your virtue is stained, you won't get along with your husband, so won't you be my wife instead? It's my love for you that made me violent toward you." . . . She said, "Then take me away with you wherever you go". . . . When she was going out of the grove, . . . she suddenly . . . pointed to me . . . and said, "Kill him! I cannot marry you as long as he lives". . . . At these words the robber himself turned pale. [He knocked her down]. He looked at me "What would you like done with her?" . . . She ran away. . . . He disappeared. I took it [the sword] up and stabbed it into my breast.

The fundamental difference between the single- and multiple-perspective modes of thinking is also discussed in an interesting way by Isaiah Berlin in his essay *The Hedgehog and the Fox*. The title is based on a fragment from the Greek poet, Archilochus: the fox knows many things, but the hedgehog knows one big thing.

There exists a great chasm between those, on one side, who relate everything to a single central vision, one system less or more coherent or articulate, in terms of which they understand, think and feel—a single universal, organizing principle in terms of which alone all that they are and say has significance—and, on the other side, those who pursue many ends, often unrelated and even contradictory, connected, if at all, only in some *de facto* way . . . related by no moral or aesthetic principle; these last lead lives, perform acts, and entertain ideas that are centrifugal rather than centripetal . . . moving on many levels. . . . The first . . . belongs to the hedgehogs, the second to the foxes. (Berlin, 1967:1–2)

Historian Fernand Braudel divides his distinguished work on *The Mediterranean* into three parts:

1. the almost timeless history of man and his interaction with the physical, inanimate environment;
2. the social history of groups and groupings that generate forces leading, for example, to wars;
3. history on the scale of individual men.

. . . a history of brief, rapid, nervous fluctuations, by definition ultra-sensitive; the least tremor sets all its antennae quivering . . . as such it is the most exciting of all, the richest in human interest, and also the most dangerous [Braudel, 1972:20–21].

He sees historical time as "geographical time, social time, and individual time," bringing to mind our view of future time in Figure 3.

Mitroff and Blankenship (1973:340) inform us that the mode of inquiry for whole systems differs so radically from that of traditional methodology that it raises severe challenges to some of the most basic tenets underlying science. Noting that such systems are conceptualized in radically different, even divergent, ways by different users, they develop guidelines for the analysis of holistic systems:

1. at least two radically distinct disciplines of knowledge must be brought to bear;
2. at least two radically distinct kinds of conceptualizers (personality types) must be brought to bear;
3. at least two radically distinct philosophical inquiry models must be brought to bear.

By "radically distinct" disciplines they do not mean, for example, operations research and engineering, but operations research and law. Different conceptualizers are convergers and divergers, problem formulators and problem solvers. Inquiry models are equivalent to the inquiring systems discussed in Chapter II.[7]

The general systems theory and cybernetics communities have produced a number of "heretics" who trespass beyond the rational actor perspective. Weinberg's General Law of Complementarity states that "any two points of view are complementary." He meant that two observers viewing the same situation find 1) neither can reduce his view to that of the other and 2) their views are not entirely independent, that is, certain things can be derived about each from the other. (Weinberg, 1975:119–120). Weinberg recognizes the limits to reductionism and the resistance of scientists to accept the possibility of "truth" in complementary perspectives. His quotation from Blackburn (1971:1007) clearly reflects this concern:

> If the practice of science continues its present one-sided and underdimensional course, new scientists will be recruited primarily from among those people to whom such a view of the world is most congenial. Yet such people are least fitted, by temperament and training, to hold in mind the complementary truths about nature that our looming task will require.

Von Foerster dismisses the superficial analogies frequently used by rational actor analysts in expanding their range of subject matter from physical to social systems (Figure 1a to 1b). Von Foerster (1977:105) considers them not merely misleading, but dangerous:

> The conceptual problem-solving apparatus that Western culture has developed [i.e., the rational actor perspective] is incapable not only of solving the societal problems, but even of perceiving these problems.

---

[7]Popper tells us that we cannot study "whole" systems scientifically (Mitroff and Blankenship, 1973:346). While we do not disagree, this does not answer our need to study whole systems.

Here we have a cyberneticist perceiving management no longer as control of observed systems—reducing the degrees of freedom of the system, but rather in terms of autonomy, self-management, and ethics—increasing the degrees of freedom of the system. A different paradigm emerges as the perspective changes.

In the area of social program evaluation, Crowell (1980) also converges on the need for multiple perspectives.[8] The dominant perspective for him is the "scientific" evaluation research as practiced by professional evaluators (for example, measuring programs by common criteria, observational procedures, and cause-and-effect relationships). This perspective is obviously very similar to Allison's and Andersen's rational perspectives.

Crowell's "new" paradigm balances quantitative and qualitative procedures, considers ambiguities and differences between observers as essential aspects in the evaluative task, and is unfazed by different perceptions of a given process. He recognizes that "validity," as usually understood, is inherently intraparadigmatic.

The new paradigm is denoted as multiple perspective evaluation (MPE) and represents, in a collective sense, the use of a mix of perspectives, in contrast to exclusive reliance on the dominant one (single-perspective evaluation or SPE). In the case of staff training in group homes for the mentally retarded, Crowell (1980:47–72) notes that SPE may easily proceed to solve a research problem whereas MPE would see the need to solve an evaluation problem. He then examines the implications of MPE on the evaluation of mainstreaming programs for the mentally retarded. A major requirement imposed by MPE is the very significant differences in training evaluators, and a potential benefit is

> a new image of ourselves and retarded persons as co-designers of a social system where the quality of life is directly proportional to our participation in the design process.

In the field of risk analysis, Fischhoff (1979:353) suggests that poor judgments could be improved by adopting

> . . . a variety of perspectives, hoping that the biases each produces will cancel one another out. For example, showing different ways to look at value issues might help people understand what their desires really are.

Indeed, much of the recent surge of activity in risk analysis (for example, at Decision Research, Inc, and the International Institute for Applied Systems Analysis) may be readily placed in the context of multiple perspectives. Its success in providing important insights is gratifying; we will return to this area in Section XII A.

---

[8]The term *multiple perspectives* was previously used in this context by House (1977). Crowell apparently developed his ideas independently of Allison, Steinbruner, and Andersen.

In his text on managerial decision making, Harrison (1975:306,312) expresses the need for a "multidimensional perspective" encompassing four aspects of arriving at, and implementing, the best choice among alternatives:

1. integrative—emphasizing the inseparability of the several stages in the total process;
2. interdisciplinary—emphasizing the fusion of the quantitative disciplines and the behavioral sciences, as well as the influence of the environment;
3. interlocking—emphasizing the limitations and constraints imposed on the rational decision maker both within and without the organization as he pursues a satisficing choice
4. interrelational—emphasizing the interrelatedness of decision making in all the functions of the manager, with particular emphasis on planning and control

Noel Tichy's "rope theory" of management sees corporate organizations in terms of three intertwined "strands": technical, political, and cultural.

Finally, Barbara Kellerman reviews Allison's decision models and suggests three additional models to supplement them (Hill et al., 1979:89–90).

1. *Model IV—Small-Group Process Model.* It recognizes that small groups have their own special dynamic and that much public policy is formulated in small-group situations. This model is reminiscent of some aspects of Andersen's cognitive perspective (Table 5), which also sees small groups developing a shared reality.
2. *Model V—Dominant Leader Model.* A policy decision is the resultant of the personality and behavior of the dominant leader, that is, "the buck stops here."
3. *Model VI—Cognitive Process Model.* This is similar to most of Steinbruner's and Andersen's cognitive perspectives (Tables 4 and 5) because it places the emphasis on our limited abilities in information processing, mental conceptualization, and consistency with past experiences.

These examples suffice to show that the idea of simultaneously applying multiple perspectives is hardly new. For other relevant literature, the reader is referred to Appendix B. We now propose to make the concept a conscious, quasi-routine procedure in studying sociotechnical systems in general.

IV

OUR PROPOSED PERSPECTIVES

H. LINSTONE

I have said it thrice: What I tell you three times is true.

Lewis Carroll, *The Hunting of the Snark*

Computo, ergo sum. Particeps sum, ergo sum. Cogito, ergo sum.

Adapted from René Descartes

We have already stressed the need to separate the two questions: *"what* are we looking at?" and *"how* are we looking at it?" Let us consider them now in more detail.

A. WHAT ARE WE VIEWING?

In its most general form, a system involves nature, man, society, and technology, singly or in the various possible combinations (Figure 4a). Here are some examples:

- man—a biological system,

- nature—the solar system,

- technology—a communications satellite,

- nature/technology—a waterwheel,

- man/society—a legal system,

- nature/man/society—a primitive village,

- man/society/technology—an information system.

Our primary concern will be *sociotechnical* systems, where the problems and issues must deal not only with the technological aspect but with the social and human facets surrounding and interacting with it. Technology is embedded in an environment of human beings—it helps, hurts, and changes them. They, in turn, can make decisions to develop, limit, alter, or stop technology. Human beings are considered here in two ways: as social entities (companies, vested interests, states) and as individuals (specific decision makers, personal impacts). We simplify the schematic of Figure 4a to highlight the relationships in sociotechnical systems and focus on three overlapping areas: technical, social/organizational, and individual/personal.[1] Figure 4b offers a convenient means to point out the various components or elements of interest. For purposes of explanation we shall assume that the starting point is a technology.

1. Technology

The starting element, shaded in Figure 4b, is taken to be a specific technology, for example, fluoridation of water, off-shore oil drilling, or nuclear power plants. It represents what the technical expert is looking at, for example, the concerns of a nuclear physicist or engineer in developing a breeder reactor or a practical fusion energy source. In the case of electronic funds transfer (EFT), the tech-

---

[1]Because we must also deal with the nonhuman, nontechnical aspects of the environment, that is, the natural physical setting in which people and technology operate, we use the convention of including these aspects in the technology domain of the schematic.

(a)

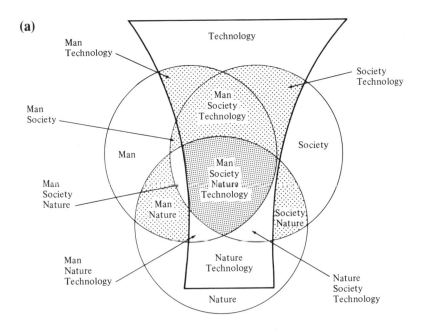

Organizational Aspects

(b)

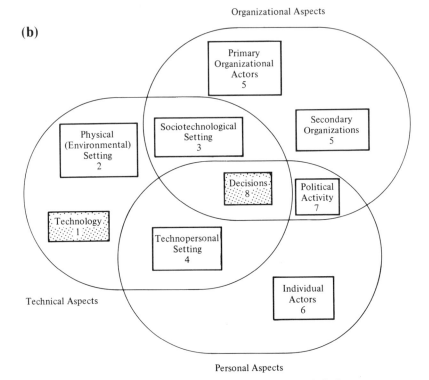

FIGURE 4. Viewing systems: **(a)** system types; **(b)** our sociotechnical system.

nology involves data input devices, linking of information loops, secure information storage systems, and so on.

2. Physical Environment Setting

The technical aspect of the "environment" of a technology recognizes clearly the land, sea, air, and space with all its inanimate and living components. Element 2 in Figure 4b refers to such systems, which physically impact on, or are impacted by, the technology. Examples include the altered ozone level of the atmosphere resulting from chemical exhaust products, and the level of the subsurface water table in areas of interest for guayule crops and for on-site solid-waste management.

3. Sociotechnical Setting

Here we have situations where the technical and organizational elements mingle. Technologies interact with organizations and groups in many ways. The Nuclear Regulatory Commission (NCR) was established to deal with a technology; computers alter group decision-making processes and office operations; telecommunications galvanize the formation of common interest groups. Cost–benefit analysis is a technical means to evaluate some of these interactions.

4. Technopersonal Setting

Technology affects, and is affected by, the individual. Such interactions cannot be understood by only looking at individuals collectively, that is, as groups. Telecommunications have an impact on the human psyche (Houston, 1976); computers constitute a prosthesis of certain parts of the brain and the impact may vary from one individual to another. Computer output may overrule common sense because of its aura of scientific quantification. Television creates a reality of its own; in Paddy Chayefsky's film *Network,* the desperate commentator, anchorman, Howard Beale, rants:

> You people sit there, night after night. You're beginning to believe this illusion we're spinning here. You're beginning to think the tube is reality, and your own lives are unreal. This is mass madness.

The other side of the coin is the effect of individuals on a technology. Ralph Nader's *Unsafe at Any Speed,* and Wernher von Braun's fascination with space vehicles affected technological developments. The relation of Edwin Land to camera technology, of Dutch Kindleberger, Robert Gross, and Donald Douglas to aircraft technology exemplify the crucial role of individuals in technology impact, policy, and implementation.

5. Organizational Actors

Because organizations are as old as human society and much older than science, organizational entities existed long before cybernetic or other theories of organization. The family, clan, village, state, church, club, union, party, and company are all examples of organizations that interact with technology. There are victims, beneficiaries, advocates, opponents, and regulators who become involved with the impact and control of technology. There are primary and secondary actors. For example, in the struggle for the Apollo program, The National Aeronautic and Space Administration (NASA) and the U.S. Air Force (USAF) were primary actors, but the Army and Navy were secondary actors. USAF was in competition for budgets with the other services, and this competition affected its interest in the Apollo program.

The most basic societal unit, the family, has been strongly affected by technology. Mobility has brought with it the nuclear family, isolation of the elderly, and rootlessness of the young.

Organizations may be described in formal terms (see Appendix B), such as the following:

- cohesion—formal or informal nature, leadership;
- organization boundaries—members, environment, task goals, techniques;
- allocation design—structure, power resources;
- control design—communication patterns, programmed responses, decision rules, nonroutine decision processes;
- incentive reward design—motivational assumptions.

Another very important social unit is the *crowd,* which gives man's lust for power its freest rein. The history of civilization may be seen as the history of combatting crowds, whereas bureaucracies (public and private) represent modern domesticated crowds. The crowd always wants to grow; it offers internal equality; it loves density; and it needs direction (Canetti, 1962).

6. Individual Actors

An individual in a crowd or an organization may be quite different from the same individual by himself. As a member of a group he surrenders responsibility—a heavy burden. But this relief is usually tempered by a loss of freedom and creativity.

An entrepreneur who propels a technology from concept to marketplace, a charismatic politician who finds an issue in a technology, or a terrorist who uses a new technology must be understood as an individual actor. There are visionaries and realists, promoters and obstructionists, operators and theoreticians, and their activities are as important as those of organizations. Identification by name may clearly not be possible in the case of an emerging technology where implementation agencies, regulators, and lead industries have not yet crystallized, as would be the case for an existing technology. Nevertheless, personality criteria, warning indicators, and other useful clues, as well as desiderata pertaining to key actors should be considered in dealing with new technology, particularly in connection with the policy and implementation aspects. The aim is analogous to that of an intelligence organization developing a profile of a political personality (for example, Hitler, Khomeini) to anticipate decision patterns (for example, the work of Walter C. Langer (1972)).

Key executives in a corporation impress their world view on the organization. When a leader is bold and dynamic, the corporation may take considerable technological risks.[2] When the leadership is conservative, the corporation shows it—investments are cautious, flexibility is minimal, innovation is uncomfortable. Of course, when the same characteristic applies to an entire industry (for example, auto, steel, tire and rubber), we revert back to the organizational actors (element 5 above).

Although the six elements mentioned thus far can be discussed very meaningfully in terms of *what* is being analyzed, out concern with the remaining elements (7 and 8) really lies much more in the *how* than the *what*. We are dealing with processes rather than objects or entities.

7. Political Action

This element represents the well-recognized interplay between organizations and individuals.

8. Decisions

This element represents the direct outcome of the political activity in element 7, for example, a decision to adopt and implement a policy. It also signifies the indirect consequence of all other elements (1 through 6) and is shaded in Figure 4b as the culmination of the cycle originating with element 1. This does not mean that the process ends here. A decision may itself impact the technology (element 1) and alter its evolution, leading to changed effects on elements 2 through 7, and consequently again to the decision element 8. A decision may alternatively affect elements 2 through 7 directly. In either case, there is continuing change. Almost never can we consider a sequence (for example, elements 1 through 8) as static or not subject to iteration or alteration over time. This fits the notion that any analysis of a complex, dynamic system should not be a one-time exercise but a continuing activity. The values may change and alter organizations (element 5), or new actors (element 6) may appear following an admin-

---

[2]Such a leader must, of course, surround himself with appropriate lieutenants. Placed in a senescent management setting the active, exuberant leader may well fail—and quit.

istration change. Finally, we emphasize that the starting point in the decision process need not be a technology, but may be an organization or other element in Figure 4b.

An interesting rational/analytic perspective technique, to identify potential mismatches in introducing a technology into a cultural setting, has been developed by Fried and Molnar (1978). To estimate matches and mismatches they use three "zones"; these can be related to our elements as follows:

- technological zone—elements 1 and 2,

- managerial zone—elements 3 and 5,

- political zone—elements 7 and 8.

Table 6 shows examples of our eight elements drawn from Lawless' (1977) 45 case studies of technology and social shock. Not surprisingly we have many examples in these case descriptions of elements 1, 2, 3, 5, 7, and 8, with few of elements 4 and 6. The focus on the individual tends to be hidden or submerged by the far more easily tracked organizationally related items.

B. HOW ARE WE VIEWING?

Building on the work of Allison, Steinbruner, and Andersen, we now adapt the concept of multiple perspectives to the study of sociotechnical systems.[3] Such "study" will not confine itself strictly to the decision process, as did Allison et al. For example, we will also be able to illuminate the weaknesses of the forecasting process using multiple perspectives.

We propose a *technical* perspective (T), an *organizational* perspective (O), and a *personal* perspective (P). The word *perspective* is used to distinguish *how* we are looking from *what* we are looking at (that is, an element).[4] For example, the element may be an organization. Using the technical perspective (T) we may see the organization as a hierarchical structure, model it using system dynamics, and apply decision analysis or other tools of management science. The organizational perspective (O) sees the same organization as a powerful or weak unit; a living system fighting competitors, cohesive or divided; a collection of baronies (divisions, departments) with a weak king (president, chief executive officer) or a strong chief with loyal lieutenants running the subunits; a powerful staff and weak line, or vice versa. The personal perspective (P) may see the same organization as job security, an opportunity to exert power, or a step to gain prestige. Thus each perspective sees the world through a different filter.

In relating the *how* and the *what,* we posit that the use of the T perspective to study the technical element, O perspective to study the organizational element, and P perspective to study the individual element are vital but by no means

---

[3]Earlier and less detailed versions of this work were published in Linstone (1980) and Linstone et al. (1981a,b)

[4]The three perspectives are symbolized in the Guzman engraving reproduced on the cover.

TABLE 6. The Eight Elements—Illustrated by Lawless' Case Studies

Our element	Lawless case	Illustration
1. Technology	DMSO (dimethyl sulfoxide)— Suppressed Wonder Drug?	Interest revived 75 years after initial synthesis as a possible means to recover useful chemicals from wood pulp wastes. Uses were found as industrial solvent and drug carrier.
2. Physical setting	The Donora, Pennsylvania Air Pollution Episode	In October 1948 20 deaths and nearly 6000 illnesses occurred due to a combination of a prolonged temperature inversion and industrial emissions.
3. Sociotechnical setting	The Nuclear Power Controversy	The Atomic Energy Commission takes initiative in facilitating nuclear power generation by cooperating with industry in research and development.
4. Technopersonal setting	The Fluoridation Controversy	Dentist Frederick McKay spends his off-hours for three decades on finding the cause of mottled teeth, notes lack of decay 20 years before serious studies were done.
5. Organizational actors	Abuse of Medical and Dental X-Rays	National Council on Radiation Protection and Measurement formed in 1929 collaborated with radiological societies and x-ray industries to set first standards for exposure.
6. Individual actors	The Thalidomide Tragedy	Dr. Frances Kelsey was new to the U.S. Food and Drug Administration bureaucracy and thalidomide was her first case. She resisted continued pressure from drug manufacturers due to her own considerable knowledge of medicine and pharmacology.
7. Political action	The Dugway Sheep Kill Incident	Congressional hearing obtains admission by Army that nerve gas tests killed 6000 sheep. Admission came after repeated denials by key army officials and involvement of a dozen different agencies.
8. Decision	NTA (Nitrilotriacetic Acid) in Detergents	Surgeon General acts to stop manufacturers from using NTA in detergents, based on environmental studies that were disputed by extensive manufacturer tests.

Source: Lawless (1977).

adequate. *Any perspective may illuminate any element.* It is inconceivable that a technical element can be understood without use of the T perspective. But the O and P perspectives may add important insights. Similarly, appreciation of an organization requires an O perspective, but much can be gained by use of the T and P perspectives. One person may be able to offer all these perspectives (T, O, and P) on a problem—the rational analyst's, his organization's, and his own. Or one perspective may dominate his thinking, blinding him to others. We strive for a balance among the perspectives, be they drawn from a single person or a battery of sources. We seek to avoid gross imbalances so often evident when technologists grapple with issues that are not purely technological.

Perspectives are also dynamic—they change over time. Even retrospectively we observe this characteristic: each generation reinterprets the past. Historians, writing in different generations, view a specific past event or culture in very different ways. Similarly, the 1955 impacts of a given technology as seen in a 1980 evaluation may appear much changed in a 1990 study. Different perspectives of the same future event at the same time may well imply contradictions, hardly surprising in a dialectic mode of inquiry (Section II D). We will find that the conscious, parallel use of multiple perspectives does not mean they are mutually exclusive. Rather, it facilitates interaction among them and the synthesis serves as recognition that, in complex systems, the whole is more than the sum of its parts.

1. The Technical Perspective

This perspective has been the dominant one in the systems, risk, and impact analysis literature. The first book on the subject of TA announced that:

> Technology assessment is a systems analysis approach to providing a whole conceptual framework, complete both in scope and time, for decisions about the appropriate utilization of technology for social purposes [Hetman, 1973:45].

The technology and its environment are viewed as a system in the now-familiar way sketched in Chapter II. The world is seen in quantitative terms, so popular with management consultants, such as curves (Phillips, Laffer, etc.) or computer models (econometric, system dynamic, etc.). Terms like *alternatives, trade-offs, optimization, data,* and *models* suggest the rational, analytic nature of the technical perspective. The "tools" include probability and game theory, decision and cost–benefit analysis, system dynamics, and econometrics. There is much interest in the classification and categorization of information, in preparing lists and matrices, in structuring organization charts and graphs. In TA, for example, the text of Porter et al. (1980), the tool survey of Coates (1976), and the structural modeling review of Linstone et al. (1978) exemplify the perspective: all focus on such techniques. Axelrod's cognitive maps (signed digraphs) constitute a T perspective technique to depict an individual's belief system or, more accurately, his assertions of causal links. A valiant effort has been made to apply this tool to political decision analyses of the deliberations of the British Eastern Committee in 1918, Gouverneur Morris' arguments on the U.S. presidency at the 1787 Constitutional Convention, and proposed international control of the oceans (Axelrod, 1976).

The United States as a culture is the most strongly T-oriented culture in the world. We love statistics and polls. A true baseball fan is awash in statistics, and a girl is a "10." We define quality of life (QOL) in terms of numerical indicators—so that it would be more precise to label it quantity of life. The bias toward the T perspective is seen in the Central Intelligence Agency:

> Technological cleverness is the pride of the U.S. intelligence. . . . But American supremacy in technical intelligence is profoundly misleading. It is not representative of the U.S. intelligence capabilities as a whole but stands in stark contrast. For in every other intelligence field—human spies, analysis of data collected, and ability to conduct secret operations—the U.S. intelligence community appears to be dangerously deficient [Toth, 1980:1].

It is probably not a coincidence that the means of obtaining input (personal contact) and the type of input obtained with the O and P perspectives are not those accessible to surveillance satellites and other high-technology sensors.

As the T perspective is such a well-mined lode, we will focus our attention on the other perspectives.

2. The Organizational Perspective

The organizational perspective sees the world through a different filter, from the point of view of affected and affecting organizations. There is great concern whether a new policy will threaten the organization's rights, standing or stability, whether it fits the current standard operating procedures (SOPs) and parochial priorities. In this perspective, we deal with power: Where is the real leverage? How can conflicts among units be turned to constructive use? There is no intensive search for analytic tools; in fact, often there is a mistrust of "academic" techniques. They are viewed either as unrealistic or as unpredictable and uncontrollable. For example, if a banking commission of senior civil servants and bank representatives was created to analyze the impact of electronic funds transfer, finding each member using an organizational perspective rather than a technical perspective would not be unexpected. Although uniqueness of the technical perspective is the rule, *each organization may have a different O perspective on the same sociotechnical system.*

For our purposes, "organizations" may be formal or informal, hierarchical or egalitarian, permanent or ad hoc.[5] They may be traditional structures (for example, corporations or bureaucracies) or they may be bound by substantive

---

[5]Permanence often becomes a top priority internal organizational objective. This may lead to perpetuation of the organization far beyond its raison d'être. For example, the U.S. Assay Commission, appointed each year since 1792 to ascertain that U.S. coins contain as much silver or gold as promised (a chore routinely duplicated by the Bureau of Standards), was abolished only in 1980 by President Carter.

activities or interests. The fact that a collective may not be formally organized does not invalidate its significance.[6]

Sometimes a postulated "public attitude" can alter (or sustain) an impact as if it were a powerful advocacy group. Alexis de Tocqueville (1966:261–262) eloquently described this condition:

> Time, events, or the unaided individual action of the mind will sometimes undermine or destroy an opinion, without any outward sign of the change. It has not been openly assailed, no conspiracy has been formed to make war on it, but its followers, one by one, noiselessly secede; day by day a few of them abandon it, until at last it is only professed by a minority. In this state it will still continue to prevail. As its enemies remain mute or only interchange their thoughts by stealth, they are themselves unaware for a long period that a great revolution has actually been effected; and in this state of uncertainty they take no steps; they observe one another and are silent. The majority have ceased to believe what they believed before, but they still affect to believe, and this empty phantom of public opinion is strong enough to chill innovators and to keep them silent and at a respectful distance.

The world seen from the pure O perspective in ideal form is an orderly progression from state to state, with an occasional minor crisis along the way, for which experience and the procedural manual have the answers. Rules and procedures are there to be followed: policy is quasi-sacred once it is promulgated.

With all human beings socialized into some sociocultural organization, this perspective influences all actions and decisions ("Is this right?" "Do I have a right to?"). Perhaps the strongest argument for inclusion of this perspective is the realization that, in the political arena, highly technical information is usually, and properly, discounted in favor of social interests and considerations of values involved—and these can never be adequately encompassed by a T perspective. Pressures emanate from institutions, regulatory agencies, special interest groups, and mass social movements. Illumination of the interplay of these pressures necessitates the O perspective.[7]

The O perspective also reflects the culture and myths that have helped to mold and bind the organization, group, or society as a distinct entity in the eyes of its members. Outstanding companies have strong cultures, which reflect their values. Myths and legends accumulate over the years to reinforce these values (Peters and Waterman, 1982). Later we shall see glimpses of such corporate

---

[6]Adelson has suggested that the O perspective might be split into two types, separating the *societal* perspective from the domain of organizations (Linstone, 1981b). This S perspective would then represent the diffuse decision-making process that pervades the social fabric. It embodies concepts such as morale, popular will, cultural values, and national character. Argument rages endlessly between those who feel that this kind of collective process is nothing but the sum of individual and organizational decisions and those who feel that society and culture have independent existence and force.

[7]For a discussion of the roles of policy analysts in government, see Meltsner (1976). Also note Meltsner and Bellavita (1983).

cultures in the case of a utility company (Section VI A 3), an electronics company (Section VI B 5), and an aircraft company (Section VI C 2), and find them essential in understanding their decision making. In the U. S. Army, the Western marksmanship tradition has had a profound impact on modern rifle procurement (Section V A 2). Engineering laboratories, too, have distinct cultures. Churchman (1982:128) recalls his experience during World War II at the Army's Frankfort Arsenal. Requests to 20 metallurgical laboratories to calibrate the hardness of a steel bar produced significant differences among them. The unique training pattern in each laboratory was probably responsible.

The social psychologist Kurt Lewin has posited that all actions have some specific "background" and are at least partly determined by it. Lewin (1948:145–146) insists that this background is of crucial importance for the perception of reality and is intimately bound to the need for security, that is, for "belonging." Often, we can identify individuals who create, amplify, or manipulate myths. In the case of Banc One of Ohio, innovation as a corporate value can be traced directly to John G. McCoy and John Fisher (Section VIII E 1).

In the political arena, Adolf Hitler almost singlehandedly presented the German people with the myth of racial superiority and national destiny to create a Thousand Year Reich. His charisma transformed a personal (P) perspective into a collective O perspective so successfully that his party won 37% of the popular vote in the July 1932 Reichstag election.

The power of O perspectives to create illusions is evident in the enthusiastic acceptance of ludicrous doctrines about Aryan physical characteristics and racial purity by millions of Germans (and even Austrians). The first major group of victims, German Jews, held its own distinct O perspective, which created a collective blindness to a clear and present danger—with tragic consequences for many of them (Bolkosky, 1975). Antisemitism was never absent from Germany, and Hitler's National Socialist goons as well as his *Mein Kampf* certainly had visibility in the 1920s. The German-Jewish O perspective was based on an idealized image of a Germany molded by Goethe, Schiller, and Lessing,[8] a Germany in which they saw themselves as fully assimilated into an enlightened, cultured, and technologically advanced society, which exhibited their own values. This meant a collective acceptance of a myth quite distinct from the reality of the Germany in which they lived. German Jews became 110% Germans; they were nationalists, proud of fighting and dying for their beloved country.[9] Only an understanding of this perspective explains the refusal to see the reality of the growing threat and to act.[10] The points we want to emphasize here are these: 1)

---

[8]Especially his play *Nathan der Weise*, reflecting Lessing's close friendship with Moses Mendelssohn, often labeled "the first *German* Jew."

[9]Example: at the close of World War I, Albert Ballin, the very successful Jewish director-general of the famous Hamburg-Amerika steamship line and a friend of the Kaiser, committed suicide rather than accept the nation's defeat (Bolkosky, 1975:45).

[10]Many German Jews agreed with the pronouncement of a German-Jewish member of the Reichstag: "No! It would be false to take these people [Nazis] seriously politically" (Bolkosky, 1975:166).

a group's O perspective is crucial as a basis for its members' decision making, whether or not it corresponds to outsiders' perceptions of reality; and 2) the perspective may be subtle and require more than superficial probing to bring to light.

There is another aspect of interest: future problems are discounted in contrast to near-term problems, that is, short-range consequences for the organization and its actions are given priority. Here this perspective deals with organizational or social time (see Chapter II H). Each organizational actor is cognizant of parochial priorities and interests; they are distinctive to his or her organization. The same applies to standard operating procedures; they go far toward limiting potential decision alternatives. Seen from the organizational perspective, a technology appears to create problems or solve problems for the organization. There is concern that the technology may disturb the functioning of an organization, that is, become a disruptive force. Interest in a technology also is a function of the amount of "noise" made about it (inquiries from "above," mention in the media).[11] There is a strong tendency to break down problems in accordance with organizational responsibilities. The Department of Agriculture may be interested in guayule as a new crop, but not in its potential air pollution.

Another characteristic common to many organization staffs is the fear of making errors. This is reflected in the utility curves of executives. These curves are typically asymmetric, that is, in absolute numbers the value (on a utility scale) of making x dollars for the company is not nearly as high as the value of losing x dollars. As a city manager pointed out, "Government can't accept failure" (Section X B 1).

In an era of transition, as experienced by today's advanced societies, this fear is deplored as a serious weakness in the organizational ability to adapt to changing needs. Complex sociotechnical systems cannot be adequately modeled, so that experimentation is vital and, in Michael's terms, we must be willing to embrace error (1973, Chapter VI).[12]

Hegel (1860:367) saw Machiavelli as a champion of a vital organization—the state:

It was Machiavelli's high sense of the necessity of constituting a state which caused him to lay down the principles on which alone states could be formed under the circumstances.

More recently, Jay (1968), an executive himself, noted:

Machiavelli . . . is bursting with urgent advice and acute observations for top management of the great private and public corporations all over the world [4].

---

[11]Factors such as these suggest how the O perspective affects technological forecasting (see Section XII B).
[12]Christine von Weizsäcker uses the German term *fehlerfreundlich*.

TABLE 7. Two Types of Collectives

Caste	Sect
Multiple issues	Single issue
Membership goal: high quality	Membership goal: high quality (goal rarely attained)
Organization: hierarchical	Organization: egalitarian (except for sect leadership)
Manipulates others collectively	Is manipulated by leaders
Stable when mature	Inherently unstable
National or global in scope	Local in scope
Willing to compromise and negotiate	Unwilling to compromise or negotiate
Does not recruit members	Recruits members
Science used in a conventional way	Science "facts" used only as they support issue; constant repetition as unquestioned slogans.

Source: Thompson (1980).

It means looking at the corporation in a new way: looking not through the eyes of the accountant and systems analyst and economist and mathematician, but through those of the historian and political scientist [x].

Machiavelli (1851) recognizes the difference between an O and a P perspective. He sees morality as necessary to guide individual conduct, but not to guide state conduct. Thus a diplomat as representative of the state is not bound by the moral code of its people: "No good man will ever reproach another who endeavors to defend his country, whatever be his mode of doing so." The modern executive faces the same dichotomy: he may recommend corporate actions that he would never condone in his personal life.[13] (See, for example, Section VI C 3).

Cultural anthropologists and sociologists have done much valuable work to identify the characteristics of O perspectives.[14] For example, Michael Thompson's (1980) study of castes and sects is highly relevant to any technology assessment of nuclear energy policy. In advanced countries, a debate on a new technology encounters two particular O perspectives, which may be labeled the *caste* and *sect*. Table 7 distinguishes their characteristics.

In the first century AD, the Jews were a caste and the Christians a sect. Today the Roman Catholic Church is a caste and the "Moonies" a sect. A second glance at the descriptors in Table 7 suggests that grassroots computer networks could well become the sects of the future. Communications technology has vastly

---

[13]Another work drawing such analogies between modern management and Machiavelli is Buskirk (1974). See Appendix B for some examples of Machiavelli's statements.

[14]In a sense, they have illuminated the O perspectives by applying their T perspective to them.

altered the power of a sect (actually of its leadership). The media can magnify the impact of a sect to an incredible degree. A miniscule sect can alert the media of a demonstration (time and place), and the small size and short duration are completely masked in the two-minute television evening news segment shown to millions. The resulting amplification of sect influence can create paralysis in the political establishment.

The value of this sketch of two O perspectives is readily appreciated when we consider the nuclear power issue. Thompson suggests that Scientists and Engineers for Secure Energy (SE_2) is a pronuclear caste, the Sierra Club an antinuclear caste, and Friends of the Earth (FoE) an antinuclear sect. His analysis leads to useful strategy recommendations. Suppose, for example, that SE_2 wants to defuse FoE. It can:

1. reveal the hypocrisy of the sect leaders, the "Porsche populists";
2. recognize that SE_2 can negotiate with other castes, such as the Sierra Club, but not with FoE—by seeking out antinuclear castes, it can begin a dialog;
3. correct the distortion created by the media coverage of sects (which tends to frighten politicians unduly by making the sect view appear to be a mass view).

In sum, the organizational perspective helps us with sociotechnical systems in at least the following ways:

• identification of the pressures in support of, and opposition to, the technology;

• insight into the societal ability to absorb a technology—organizational incrementalism is an important bound;

• increasing ability to facilitate or retard implementation of technology by understanding how to gain organizational support;

• drawing forth impacts not apparent with other perspectives, for example, based on realities created within an organization;

• development of practical policy (for example, new coalitions).

It might well be argued that reductionism, noted as a characteristic of the technical perspective, is in evidence also in the organizational perspective. The point to be made, however, is that it takes quite a different form. We are not concerned here with a reduced number of quantified variables, but rather with such "reductions" as application of a discount rate, fragmentation of problems, and use of standard operating procedures. All of these characteristics are simplifications, but fundamentally different from those associated with the T perspective.[15]

---

[15]Allison (1971) uses the word *rational* as a label for the first perspective. We avoid this term because it seems to suggest that the organizational perspective is irrational—a notion we reject. Rationality can only be judged from within, that is, in the context of a given perspective.

A list of characteristics of the O perspective as well as a comparison with those of the other perspectives will follow in Section C of this chapter. Representative statements illuminating the perspectives are presented in Appendix B.

3. The Personal Perspective

This is the most subtle and elusive perspective, the most difficult to define. Here the world is seen through the filter of the individual's eyes and brain. The P perspective should sweep in any aspects that relate individuals to the sociotechnical system *and* cannot be brought out by the other perspectives. Thus we exclude from this perspective the purely physical impacts of a technology on the individual as well as the impact of, say, farmers as a group on an agricultural technology. But intuition, charisma, leadership, and self-interest, which play vital roles in matters of policy and decision, may only be understood through the P perspective. The systems philosopher sees the "unique individual" (Section IIG), the clinician talks about "specificity of behavior."

Freud, in his epochal *Interpretation of Dreams,* perceived three layers: professional, political, and persona. He found the first to be the most current and accessible; the third to be the deepest, least current, and least accessible (Schorske, 1981:184). The analogy to our three perspectives is self-evident. As would be anticipated with Freud's psychoarcheological conception, we shall find most difficulty with the personal perspective.[16]

A T-oriented analysis of selected individuals' decision-making processes has clearly shown that their cognitive maps of causal linkages are remarkably free of feedback, that is, cycles. Axelrod (1976:244) attributes this to people's having more beliefs than they can handle. They simplify by considering the one-directional policy-consequence linkages and avoiding the complication of doubling back. Military planners exhibit this tendency in studying future enemy strategies and tactics: they develop our responses to them and then fail to consider what the enemy might do to minimize the effectiveness of these responses. Technologists start with a problem and develop a solution, but neglect to go the next step, that is, probe the problems created by such a solution (see Section II A).

Thus we have at least a partial rational explanation of the "irrational" behavior of the individual, as well as the group.[17]

---

[16]Maruyama prefers to distinguish two personal perspectives: the *situational–personal* and the *individual–personal* (denoted by P_s and P_i, respectively). P_s means that the behavior, choice, point of view, etc. reflect the particular situation rather than the characteristics of persons. Most individuals who are put in a similar situation would behave in a similar way. When different persons are put in different situations, they behave differently because of the situational differences. Here the situation does not mean organizational situation, but refers to personal circumstances.

On the other hand, P_i reflects unique personality, perceptual, cognitive, and emotional patterns, tastes, and preferences, etc. Different individuals in the same situation may act differently due to these differences. The same person would tend to act in similar patterns in different situations (Linstone et al., 1981b: Appendix B).

[17]As Hofstadter (1980:575) points out, the computer can be as irrational as the human mind. The notion that "irrationality is incompatible with computers" rests on a serious misconception. A computer working perfectly can be instructed to print out illogical statements. Similarly, a brain with faultlessly working neurons may support "irrational" human behavior, that is, a belief held in the software of the mind may clash with the hardware of a perfectly functioning brain. Meaning exists at different levels: the mind and the brain.

Identifying individuals. There are clearly many individuals who interact, directly or indirectly, with a sociotechnical system. There are beneficiaries and victims, entrepreneurs and users, regulators and lobbyists. There are the "hidden movers." These are individuals who, from a second- or third-level position, pull the strings that determine how things progress. (Attention is usually so keenly focused on the behavior of the puppets, which is overt, that the effect of the puppeteer, who is hidden from view, is ignored.) In the case of a very prominent power position, we need to look for the "power behind the throne," especially if we suspect that the ostensible power person is not operating under his own steam. This is difficult enough, but at least in such a case—because of the interest of historians, political analysts, etc.—the persons surrounding the power position are in the public eye and therefore subject to scrutiny. Still, the "gatekeeper," or person who controls the information flow in an organization, is often difficult to identify.

For less publicly prominent positions, the powers behind the throne usually remain obscure. They may not even appear on the organization chart. One way of possibly identifying them is to look for the individuals who do the writing in an organization (policy statements, position papers, standard operating procedures or regulations, etc.). Their writing frequently sets the tone for the organization or else becomes a point of departure for discussion within the organization. If such persons hold their position for any length of time, it may be assumed that they wield considerable influence.

Personal probing is essential in identifying key individuals. In cases of an emerging technology there may not yet be identifiable individuals. In such instances, types and their characteristics must be sketched. And here, too, the P perspective is of inestimable value. What makes a future Sammy run can often be predicted by analogy with past movers. In fact, an interview might elicit interesting insights on how to "beat the system" or outflank recalcitrant bureaucracies.

Intuition, leadership and self-interest. Intuition is a well appreciated trait in the world of business, as the following quotes suggest.

- R.P. Jensen, Chairman of General Cable Corp;

  On each decision, the mathematical analysis only got me to the point where my intuition had to take over [Rowan (1979):112].

- J. Fetzer, Chairman of Fetzer Broadcasting Co.:

  Walk through an office, and intuition tells you if things are going well [Rowan (1979):112].

- R. Siu, Management Consultant:

  Effective CEO's . . . are aware that rationality and the scientific method provide critical inputs to only one of three crucial questions overarching key decisions.

These are: (a) Does it add up? (b) Does it sound okay? and (c) Does it feel right? Logic and science contribute primarily to the first question, less to the second, and even less to the third [Siu (1978):85].

The typical T-trained mind usually balks at the mention of intuition. However, a few T-oriented, highly respected scientists have not been afraid to pay homage to intuition and accept it as an important concept. Consider Jacques Hadamard's classic, *The Psychology of Invention in the Mathematical Field.* Hadamard (1945:21) writes:

> That those sudden enlightenments which can be called inspirations cannot be produced by chance alone is already evident . . . there can be no doubt of the necessary intervention of some previous mental process unknown to the inventor, in other terms, of an unconscious one.

He quotes the German physicist Helmholtz, who observed that "happy ideas" never came to him when his mind was fatigued or when he was seated at his work table. "After the fatigue . . . has passed away, there must come an hour of complete physical freshness before the good ideas arrive."

Poincaré, another well known French mathematician, distinguishes 1) fully conscious work, 2) illumination ("happy ideas") preceded by incubation, and 3) the quite peculiar process of the first sleepless night. The unconscious appears to consist of several levels. Hadamard (1945:113) writes:

> It is quite natural to speak of a more intuitive mind if the zone where ideas are combined is deeper, and of a logical one if that zone is rather superficial. This manner of facing the distinction is the one I should believe to be the most important.

In the case of exceptionally intuitive minds, even important links of deduction may remain unknown to the thinker who has himself found them. Hadamard cites examples: mathematicians Fermat, Riemann, Galois, and Cardan. Cardan's invention of imaginary numbers ($i = \sqrt{-1}$) is a beautiful example of the use of the nontraditional to leap from one rational to another rational domain.

More recently (1980), Nobel Laureate Herbert Simon and associates explored the differences between experts and novices in solving physics problems. They find that the expert is mentally guided by large numbers of patterns serving as an index to relevant parts of the knowledge store. The patterns are:

> . . . rich schemata that can guide a problem's interpretation and solution and add crucial pieces of information. This capacity to use pattern-indexed schemata is probably a large part of what we call physical intuition. [Larkin et al., 1980:1342].

Each individual has a unique set of patterns that inform his intuition. In calling on the P perspective, we are thus augmenting the conscious, logical T process by opening ourselves to the deeper mental levels that store patterns of great potential value. Salk specifically stresses the need to cultivate both intuitive and reasoning realms—separately and together. Indeed the evolution of the human mind depends on this binary relationship (Salk, 1983:79).

Berlin (1967:70) insists that a superior P perspective affords a sense of greater vision, a more profound feeling for the flow of life in which we are immersed. It sees what can be, what cannot; it has an awareness of the interplay of the imponderables with the ponderables.

Leadership is a quality of recognized importance in science and business, as well as in politics and the military "He who knows how to summon the forces from the deep, him they will follow" (von Hoffmansthal quoted in Schorske, 1981:172). This applies not only to political demagogues and statesmen, but to influential academics and dynamic entrepreneurs. Courant in applied mathematics, Rabi in atomic structure, von Braun in rocketry, and Ford in automobile production were leaders; disciples, students, and imitators built on these leaders' innovative ideas and magnified their impact.

Self-interest motivates most of us, although it is usually hidden. It may take the form of prestige, profit, power, or pleasure.[18] The felt need to mask this energizing factor generates deceptions and illusions that may be difficult to penetrate. Successful technological innovation and policy change implementation require leadership; leadership is driven by self-interest.[19]

Effective organizations are those that have found successful ways of making the self-interest of the members work constructively and in unison to support the goals of the organization. And one guideline to pursue self-interest in organizations successfully is to:

> . . . provide others a personal perspective on what you are trying to accomplish and the importance it holds in terms of what matters to you [Culbert and McDonough, 1980:204].

And "what matters to you" is found in each person's unique reality, his or her "alignment."

> There is no way of comprehending the rationale behind someone's behavior . . . until you understand the alignment that underlies that person's orientation [Culbert and McDonough, 1980:204].

---

[18]For a P perspective on the engineering profession, Florman's delightful book *The Existential Pleasures of Engineering* (1976) is recommended. See also statement 67 in Appendix B.

[19]We recall Henry Kissinger's comment: "Power is the ultimate aphrodisiac."

The roles of the P perspective. Specifically, we see the P perspective in four roles:

1. Understanding of the total decision process is enhanced through the participating actors.

Political activity involves the interactions of organizations and individuals. Usually we cannot grasp the political process without knowing the characteristics of the individual players, and they are illuminated by the P perspective.

Voter attitudes may be better understood by selected in-depth interviews than by polls. The *Washington Post's* Haynes Johnson blamed himself and his colleagues for basing too much coverage of the 1980 campaign on polls, then writing learned analyses claiming to know what was on people's minds:

> As it turned out, reporters would have been much better served by relying on their own legwork, which in turn produces their own political instincts [*Time,* Dec. 8, 1980:101].

Insiders' books on the Kennedy and Nixon White Houses and works such as Truman Capote's *In Cold Blood* give us other examples of the insights dug up from the deep layer of the P perspective.

In many top-level corporate and governmental decision-making settings the staff is highly sensitive to the chief executive's P perspective. They therefore filter incoming information for him so that it conforms as much as possible to that perspective. This process has disastrous effects at times. The filtered intelligence provided to President Lyndon Johnson on Vietnam, Presidents Nixon and Carter on Iran, and President Reagan on the Falklands and Lebanon all reflect a kind of "sanitized groupthink" molded by loyal subordinates anxious to support and enhance their superior's P perspective.

2. It serves as a precursor to better understanding of the O perspective.

The affected persons may be considered as a group, but the impact may be comprehensible only by dealing directly with individuals and their perspectives on a one-to-one basis. By learning individual beliefs, we can separate those that are widely shared (that is, collective beliefs) from those that are not. For example, union reactions can be gauged better by knowing the attitudes of individual union members, the reaction of blacks to automatic teller machines could be fathomed by direct dialog, the understanding of the impact of television on children or of mobility on the aged benefits from personal contacts.

3. Individuals may matter, and this perspective identifies their characteristics and behavior.

It was the grand old man of forecasting, Bertrand de Jouvenel who observed that:

> . . . who sits up there makes a major difference . . . and it seems foolish not to recognize that individual decisions are historical causes in their own right [1967:108, quoted in Loye, 1978:32].

Individuals can bring about change more easily than can institutions. Salk (1983:120) sees this as a prime reason to focus on the individual.

Robert Goddard, Andrew Carnegie, and Admiral Rickover had recognizable impact on the course of technology. Yet, we have found that there is a strong temptation on the part of T perspective-oriented individuals to downplay the P perspective. Among the arguments are the following, each of which will be considered in turn:

a. only in rare cases does the individual make a difference;
b. there are too many individuals to be considered;
c. it provides a carte blanche for baseless claims;
d. the analysis would become too sensitive, that is, politicized.

a) The criterion as to whether an individual makes a difference is often difficult to apply. Would the American Revolution have had the same outcome if the roles of Generals Washington and Gates had been reversed? There are obvious situations, but more frequently it is possible to provide a meaningful answer only in hindsight.

"Crazy Judah" (Theodore D. Judah) was the brilliant railroad engineer whose enthusiasm—or fanaticism—galvanized the largest and most important engineering enterprise of America's first century, a transcontinental railroad. It was a technological project comparable in its challenge to the Apollo manned lunar landing in this country's second century. Not one man in 50 in 1860 believed that rails would ever cross the rugged Sierra Nevada mountain range. Judah was the conceptualizer, money raiser, engineering supervisor, and lobbyist. He convinced several Sacramento merchants—among them Huntington, Stanford, Crocker, and Hopkins—to form the Central Pacific Railroad Company. He wrote impact assessments, determined the route, and arranged to be on the staffs of both the House and Senate Committees dealing with the Railroad Bill to support the project. On July 1, 1862, in the midst of the Civil War, President Lincoln signed the crucial bill. Judah then had the difficult task of keeping the effort steadfastly directed at his long-range objective rather than becoming sidetracked for attractive short-term profits.[20] Undoubtedly, a railroad would have been constructed

---

[20]Judah died of yellow fever at age 37 (contracted in Panama on one of his trips from Sacramento to New York).

after the Civil War, but the changed timing and nature would have affected the course of California's development.

Suppose there had been no Wright brothers. Someone else would have initiated powered flight, possibly in Germany or France. Would it have made a difference? The American aerospace industry might have been a German or French one. It frequently does matter who is first.

Dr. Frances Kelsey of the U.S. Food and Drug Administration was a key figure in preventing the sale of thalidomide in the United States.[21] Did she make a difference? Had another, less stubborn person handled this New Drug Application, the ultimate result would have been the same, although a great deal of human suffering would have been precipitated. To argue that Dr. Kelsey's decision did not matter to the technology, because it would have been only a matter of time until the harmfulness of the drug had been established, is like saying that Galileo's recanting did not matter because eventually the truth would prevail. In the Kelsey case, public attitudes toward government regulation, toward the ethics of drug houses, and toward chemicals generally could have been significantly different. If we contend that anyone in Dr. Kelsey's position might have resisted the pressures equally well, we are saying that decisions do not matter, only roles do. And if decisions do not matter, what is the point of decision and policy analysis at all? Is not the purpose to aid the decision process? If decisions do matter, they must not be treated as though they do not; thus the people who make them also matter. Moreover, such analysis is concerned with the short and intermediate, as well as the long-term future, and the transient effects of individual decisions are of the essence as they influence the trajectory and its practical concomitants.

Holsti (1976:30) lists seven circumstances in which the individual decision maker may be of significance:

1. nonroutine situations where SOPs do not apply;
2. decisions made at the top of the organizational hierarchy by leaders free from constraints;
3. long-range policy planning, where there is wide variation among policy makers on "what is desirable," "what is important," etc.;
4. when the situation itself is highly ambiguous;
5. when there is information overload, and such strategies as filtering, queuing, and omission must be used;
6. unanticipated events unleashing individual initial reactions that may be decisive;
7. circumstances in which complex cognitive tasks associated with decision making may be impaired by stresses on decision makers.

---

[21]Thalidomide was a new drug introduced in Europe to treat headaches. It proved to have a most serious side effect in pregnant women: deformed children.

b) This argument assumes that a P perspective is useful only if a very large number of individuals with different perspectives is included. This is analogous to the contention that a decision maker cannot make a decision unless he has obtained input from every affected individual. Recognizing that this is impractical, the decision maker does not jump to the other extreme and argue that he should not talk to any affected party.

The most widely articulated argument among political scientists against cognitive approaches to foreign policy decision making is based on "theoretical parsimony and research economy" (Holsti, 1976:26). Not surprisingly, the T-oriented researcher is readily convinced that he can get more mileage from T than from P; in other words, with his very limited resources, the benefit–cost ratio of T appears higher to him.

c) It may be argued that our ability to analyze a sociotechnical system is very modest, even with the perspective that is most "scientific." After all, the T perspective involves conjectures about consequences, assumptions about models, and at best partial evidence. The lack of rigor characterizing P provides the analyst leeway for all kinds of gratuitous interpretations and attributions. When it comes to assessing, by way of anticipation, the influence of an individual actor on the development or implementation of a technology (or, more generally, on historical processes), the criterion of "reasonableness of conjecture" should be applied. Certain "wild" speculations should be eschewed, even though it can be demonstrated that there are historical precedents for the projected scenario. Because Caligula appointed a horse to the position of consul, we are not justified to spin out extraordinary possibilities of a similar nature. Unfortunately, history is a cautionary tale of the chameleon nature of the reasonableness criterion itself. Hitler seemed eminently reasonable to a plurality of German voters in the 1932 election.

One cannot pose an *a priori* argument that multiple perspectives are invariably superior to a single (T) perspective. Obviously, three poorly done perspectives will be inferior to one excellent T perspective. As in aerial photography, three overexposed shots from different angles will tell us less than one sharp shot. The answer lies with the quality of the multiple perspectives, that is, the integrity, appropriateness, and experience of the analysts. On a *ceteris paribus* basis, multiple perspectives should be preferred to single perspectives.

d) The argument assumes that the analysis can be apolitical and operate effectively at a macrolevel, where individuals are seen far below as so many ants. Those most comfortable with the T perspective are also most likely to be made nervous by the political sensitivity of the perspectives that are most appropriate to what Allison calls bureaucratic politics (Table 3) and what is shown as "political activity" in Figure 4b. They nearly always prefer to shun these aspects, although doing so may strip the work of much of its value and submerge some of the very things that should be brought to the surface. A noncontroversial impact assessment is also likely to be an assessment of very modest usefulness.

Some of the consequences of descending from the Olympian heights, where objectivity reigns and politics can be disdained, are as follows.

- the sponsor may be displeased and withhold further contracts or assignments from the analysts;
- other clients may withhold contracts or assignments;
- the report may be buried by the client;
- if care is not exercised by the analysts, confidentiality of input may be breached through attribution, with resulting embarrassment to informants;
- individuals and organizations may be helped or hurt.

Despite these concerns, we cannot escape the fact that a sociotechnical systems analysis, like any policy analysis, is inherently political.[22] It is therefore pointless to fear politicization.

    4. Communication of complex problems and issues may be made more effective by means of the personal perspective.

Novelists and playwrights successfully express social issues through the words of individuals. Shaw uses the unique Liza Doolittle and her father to portray class problems in England. Arthur Miller uses Willie Loman to describe the American urge to be well liked. Barbara Tuchman uses a single person, Enguerrand de Coucy, as the focal point of her sweeping survey of 14th-century Europe. Hauptmann's *Rose Bernd,* Ibsen's *The Wild Duck,* Solzhenitsyn's *Gulag Archipelago,* Burgess' *1985,* and television's *Upstairs, Downstairs* are other striking illustrations of the use of the P perspective to communicate social concepts. The enormity of the Nazi holocaust cannot be told at all by the T perspective (statistics of six million murders), but it is at least partly communicated by the P perspective *Diary of Anne Frank* and the TV production *Holocaust.*

Focusing on the business world, Peters and Waterman (1982:61) also find that:

> . . . we are more influenced by stories (vignettes that are whole and make sense in themselves) than by data (which are, by definition, utterly abstract).

Ruth Miller (doctoral dissertation in process) explores the use of "speculative futures fiction" to enhance impact assessment. The stress here, too, is on improving communicability through the P perspective.

The rare individual who can incorporate in his own thinking the appropriate balance among the T, O, and P perspectives can apply the multiple perspective

---

[22]Interestingly, some other languages do not differentiate between policy and political analysis. (For example, in German, there is only the word *Politik.*)

concept as a one-person effort. Burby's *The Great American Motion Sickness* is, in effect, a TA. It is merely necessary for a member of Congress to read this book (which the government did not need to fund) to be quite well informed about transportation technology. Another example is Mostert's *Supership*. It may at times prove more effective to support a good communicator for one or two years to write a book on a technology, approaching the subject from different perspectives, than to fund a conventional TA team.

Tolstoy's struggle with the P perspective is most revealing. In the epilogue to *War and Peace,* he addresses himself to the historian's eternal question: were Napoleon and Alexander the cause of the effects they produced, or was the movement of nations produced by the activity of all the people who participated in the events? His answer:

> Morally, the wielder of power appears to cause the event; physically it is those who submit to the power. . . . The cause of the event is neither in the one nor in the other but in the union of the two [Tolstoy, 1869:1335].

Tolstoy had a marvelous feeling for piercing the heart of a P perspective; he recognized the importance of each individual. He felt it was essential to present the invasion of Russia through the eyes of individuals, not organizations and abstract forces. His unresolved dilemma was his inability to integrate a vast number of P perspectives. He could not do what, say, the physicist does in dealing with the immense number of particles in a gas, that is, integrate the individual effects into a very meaningful gas law. Focusing on Napoleon is clearly *not* the way to integrate the individuals involved with the invasion of Russia. But neither does this mean that Napoleon as an individual is immaterial. As Isaiah Berlin (1967:34) observes:

> Napoleon may not be a demigod, but neither is he a mere epiphenomenon of a process which would have occurred unaltered without him.

Section C provides a listing of characteristics of the P perspective and a comparison with the other perspectives. (See also Appendix B.)

C. T + O + P: A SINGERIAN INQUIRING SYSTEM

As is evident from Table 2, our perspectives are close to those of Andersen, differing significantly only in the personal perspective. Andersen's third (cognitive) perspective includes small-group interactions, whereas our third (personal) perspective deals with the individual, and we include small groups under organizations. This is reflected in the placement of "socially constructed reality" in different perspectives by Andersen and ourselves. Table 8 summarizes the distinctive characteristics of our perspectives; Figure 5 relates them to our discussion in Chapter II and should be compared with Figure 1.[23] Once more we note that their usefulness extends beyond the strict confines of decision analysis.

The Multiple Perspective Concept may be seen as a Singerian inquiring system in Churchman's (1971) terms:

- it is a meta-inquiring system, that is, it includes all the other inquiring systems (data, model, dialectic, etc);

- it is pragmatic, that is, the truth content is relative to the overall goals and objectives of the inquiry;

- it takes holistic thinking so seriously that it constantly attempts to "sweep in" new components; it is, in fact, nonterminating and explicitly concerned with the future;

- it postulates that the system designer is a fundamental part of the system; his psychology and sociology are inseparable from the system's physical representation.

A subtle, but important, advantage in the use of such a pragmatic Singerian approach is the automatic reduction in the reliance on shaky theoretical analysis in decision making. The strength of the quasi-theological faith in models developed via the T perspective is awe inspiring and frightening. Multiple perspectives should minimize this self-delusion because the T perspective no longer dominates the analysis.

The schematic in Figure 5 shows a single vertex for the T perspective and multiple vertices for O and P. We do not consider the differences between disciplines (for example, aeronautical engineering, electronic engineering, economics) as reflecting different inquiring systems. They all use the same data/model-based paradigms (see Chapter II)—the same mode of perceiving—but they do look at different parts of the problem (for example, use different variables and mathematical models). The aeronautical engineer, electronic engineer, and economist may look at the same aircraft design and focus on different problems (for instance, lift, avionics, cost per mile). But they all use the T perspective: they develop models (wind tunnel or computer) and seek to quantify and optimize. This is denoted in Figure 6a by the use of a single vertex for all three. Putting it simply, their "how" is the same, but their "what" varies, whereas with the O or P perspectives the "how" itself differs.

This is not to deny the change, over time, of the accepted scientific paradigm and the simultaneous existence of conflicting paradigms (as with the Ptolemaic and Copernican cosmological theories). It is, however, the exception in the T perspective, while it is the norm in the O and P. Kuhn's *Structure of Scientific Revolutions* deals with this process in the hard sciences.

A striking current example of opposing T perspectives is the split among

---

[23]For statements which further explicate the characteristics of each perspective see Appendix B.

TABLE 8. Multiple Perspectives

	TECHNICAL (T)	ORGANIZATIONAL (O)	PERSONAL (P)
World view	Science-technology	Social infrastructure: Hierarchical (caste) . . . Egalitarian (sect)	Individuation—the self
Ethical basis	Rationality	Justice/fairness	Morality
Goal	Problem solving Product (study, design, explanation)	Stability and continuity[a] Process Action and implementation	Power, influence, prestige Status maintenance or improvement
Modes of inquiry	Abstraction and modeling Data and analysis	Dialectic/adversary Negotiated reality/consensual	Intuition, persona, individual reality Experience, learning
Time concept	Technological time	Social time	Personal time
Planning horizon	Far Often little breadth	Intermediate distance Intermediate breadth	Short distance Variable breadth
Discount rate	Minimal	Moderate	High (with rare exceptions)
Constraints	Problem simplification by limiting variables, relations	Fractionating/factoring problems Problem delegation to others or avoidance if possible	Hierarchy of individual needs (security, acceptance, self-fulfillment)
	Cause and effect	Agenda ("problem of the moment")[a] Bureaucracy often pervasive[a]	Challenge and response Each construes attributes of others

			Inner world (subjectivity)
	Need for validation, replicability (or "audit trail")	Political sensitivity and expediency[a] Loyalties, credentials Restricted access by outsiders (caste) or recruits members (sect)	Need for certainty, beliefs Creativity and vision of the few
	Objectivity emphasized	Reasonableness, common advantage	
Characteristics	Prediction	Recognition of partial unpredictability Long-range planning often ritualized	Cope with few alternatives or variables only Filter out images inconsistent with past experience
	Optimization (best solution)	Satisficing (first acceptable, rather than best, solution)[a] Incremental change, slow adaptation Parochial priorities	Game playing ("homo ludens")
	Feedback loops recognized		Focus on simplistic hypotheses rather than scanning many Leaders and followers, mystique
	Quantification Use of averages, probabilities Trade-offs	Standard operating procedures Compromise and bargaining[a] Monitoring and correction	
	Uncertainties noted: many caveats ("on one hand . . .")	Uncertainties avoided Fear of error[a]	Fear of change and unknown
Communication	Technical report, briefing	Directive, conference, interview Private language with insiders Hortatory language with public	Narrative (story), discussion, speech Importance of personality

[a]Usually applies to hierarchical structures only (see Table 7).

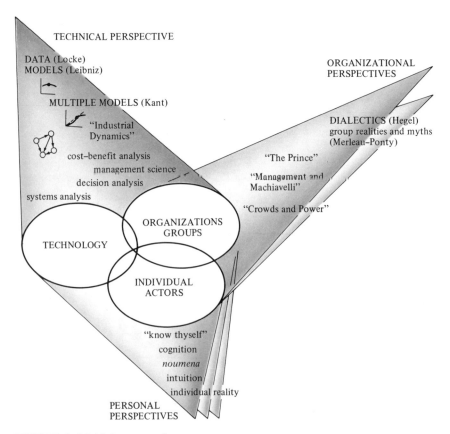

FIGURE 5. Multiple perspectives.

forecasters between technological optimists (for example, Herman Kahn and Julian Simon) and pessimists (for example, the Club of Rome and Global 2000 Reports). Dunlap (1980) sees them in terms of two sets of paradigms: exemptionalist and ecological. In the former, culture and technology enable *Homo sapiens* to adapt nature to human ends, that is, man possesses characteristics such as intellect and organizational capability, which make him an exceptional species "exempt" from the ecological principles which govern all other forms of life. In the ecological paradigm, man cannot evade ecological laws and is dependent on the continued stability of the global ecosystem (for example, on finite resources).

Another situation that may require multiple T perspectives is Third World development. China and India had their own science and technology prior to the dominance of the Western approach. In India, both native and Western T perspectives are still in evidence today: rural areas try to maintain and develop indigenous technology while urban areas pursue Western technology. Chinese acupuncture and herbal medicine contrast with Western medical technology.

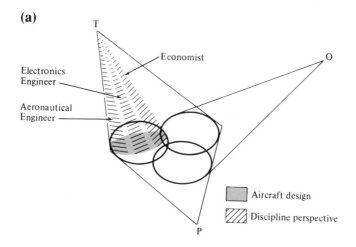

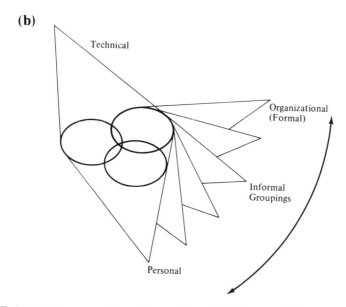

FIGURE 6. Multiple perspectives: **(a)** as distinguished from multiple disciplines—an example; **(b)** personal-organizational continuum.

The crucial differences between perspective T, on the one hand, and O and P, on the other, may be explored further. In Figure 6b we show (by a slight modification of Figure 5) the quasi-continuous range of perspectives between individuals and organizations. There are various individuals, informal groupings, formal small and large organizations, or social entities, Each has a unique *Welt-*

anschauung, a distinct perspective.[24] We have already noted that the O and P perspectives can be formally subdivided into various categories (societal perspective, individual–personal, situational–personal). We have chosen not to complicate the basic concept; to follow this path could easily lead us into a morass of semantic and sterile academic debates.

Looking at the sweep of history, we see that the popularity of the T perspective is a distinctly modern phenomenon. For millenia of human existence, the O and P perspectives were prominent. Western medieval man, for example, used the O and P perspectives almost exclusively: his society and religion were his world, and these "organizations" prescribed his perspectives. His space and time were finite: the world was 4000 years old and would soon end. The realm of knowledge was also assumed to be bounded. But the past years of exploration and scientific discovery have resulted in the ascendency of the T perspective to a level of importance unknown in any previous era. By no means, however, has it replaced the other perspectives. A look at Germany, the world's leading country in science and technology during the 1920s and 1930s, should make this very apparent (see Section IV B 2).

The perspectives may also be considered in an ethical context. The T perspective avoids involvement with moral concerns; it is neutral and sees any system through the eyes of an external, objective observer. It searches for cause and effect, for solvable problems.

The scientist/technologist, initiated into the multiple perspective concept, sometimes responds as follows:

- "In the decision sciences there are techniques for each perspective—cost-benefit analysis is a T perspective, social welfare theory is an O perspective, and decision theory is a P perspective approach." In examining such claims, we must, for example, ask: Does decision theory use rationality or morality as a guiding ethic? If the former, it is a T, not P, concept. Does decision theory rely on models and data? If so, it again indicates T rather than P. It is our belief that all three decision theories are T-focused. We will see this problem surface in Section X E.

- "The T perspective *ought* to have more normative force than the O and P perspectives; it is on a higher plane." This view is not far removed from the notion that the T perspective is *the* correct one and that the others simply reflect irrational human beings interfering with it. We do not share this quasi-technocratic attitude. Science's very modest level of understanding of the human brain suggests that the proposed reliance of *socio*technical systems on the T perspective, even if only for normative considerations, seems rash indeed.

The O and P perspectives sweep in human beings, their emotions and ethics.

---

[24]The dynamics of the shift from P to O suggested by Figure 6b recall Canetti's "enigma of enigmas," the dissolution of the individual in the crowd (1962).

The difference between O and P is exemplified ethically as that between organizational and individual dominance, between subservience to the society and personal freedom (Von Foerster, 1977). In a hierarchical, authoritarian society, P perspectives arc unimportant; only the O perspective matters.[25] In a heterarchical, democratic society, P perspectives are important; each individual is responsible for his or her own actions.

The technologist's preference for the T perspective commonly mirrors a natural bent: he feels more comfortable dealing with objects than people. It is, after all, the people orientation that most profoundly distinguish O and P from T. It has recently been suggested that in the business world, what truly sets the bootstrapping manager without an MBA apart from the stereotypical MBA and "what seems to account in large measure for his success is an almost passionate focus upon people" (Kiechel, 1982a:120). The MBA training emphasizes the technique-oriented, T perspective approach to management; it is much less effective in enhancing the ability to deal with people—and this is often where the degreeless executives excel. It is significant that Swiss banks and Israeli industrial enterprises draw many of their leaders from the respective military establishments. The demonstrated ability to lead and inspire people seems more important to them than a Harvard MBA. And this is precisely where the O and P perspectives come to the forefront.

Most individuals appear to constitute a dynamic mixture of perspective types. We rarely seem to deal with a pure T, O, or P-oriented person on the one hand, or with one exhibiting a perfect balance among the perspective types on the other. *The "norm" is apparently a presence of all three perspective types in an unbalanced way.* The ivory-tower scientist should be expected to have a dominant T perspective in the contacts we are most likely to have with him. We have already observed the presence of the P perspective in the scientist, in terms of intuition and prestige concern. The successful "organization man" (Whyte, 1957) should have a particularly well-developed O perspective, but should not completely lack T or P perspectives. Genetic as well as environmental factors may underlie the unique mix or dominance of perspective types in each person. Since we need diverse perspectives, research to improve our ability to identify the individual's characteristic imbalance would be most helpful.[26]

The preceding discussion raises an intriguing philosophical question: If the P perspective is defined as the individual's view of the world, does it not encompass whatever mix of T, O, and P types resides in the mind of that person? In other words, is it proper in our context to discuss an individual's world view in terms of T, O, and P balance and imbalance or is that world view indivisible? We postulate that a qualitative discussion of the individual's personal balance or bias in perspective types can be meaningful and useful. The characteristics of the types are usually distinguishable (see Table 8 and Appendix B). Freud's analogy

---

[25]Except possibly for the P perspective of the person at the top of the hierarchy.
[26]The T-O-P Profile Test in Appendix C is a modest step in this direction.

of the three psychoarcheological layers in the individual (Section IV B 3) assumes a similar separability of types. We do, in fact, often distinguish in our own decision making what is best objectively, what is best for our organization, and what is best for us personally.

We now address five aspects: choosing the team, differing time horizons, communications, changing perspectives, and their integration.

1. Choosing the Team

An individual steeped throughout his working life in one set of paradigms and trained to suppress the others will find it difficult to apply another in developing a new perspective. Thus the scientist or technologist is accustomed to T and may be unable to do justice to O or P. We find that a T-trained person will see, or assume, a world populated by rational actors and afflicted with problems to be "solved" by data and model based techniques. Such an individual often views the O perspective as mere detail and the P perspective as dirty politics. The O and P perspectives similarly have preconceptions about the T perspective—usually viewing it as naive. The mutual misperceptions are shown in Figure 7.

Consider the recent comments of Harrison Salisbury (1980:A23) on "De-Professoring Foreign Policy":

> If, as has been said, war is far too important to be left to the generals, is not foreign policy far too important to be left to the academics?
>
> The academic mind is trained at problem-solving, at presenting finite solutions to finite problems. Politics is the art of the indefinite. Its best practitioners know that no real-life problem can be neatly or permanently solved on squared paper. They understand that all questions—war, peace, foreign policy, domestic policy—are in the end constituency problems, issues of give-and-take, of fudgy language and accommodation. This year's solution is the basis for next year's negotiations. Academic perfectionism counts zilch. Neatness is the enemy.

FIGURE 7. Basis of miscommunications. *Source: Umbdenstock, 1981.*

Politics is a pragmatic art, not an exact or scientific one. . . .

The prickly pride of the Senate . . . broke the back of the only academic President of the United States and sent one of the finest scholarly constructs of its day, Woodrow Wilson's League of Nations, down the drain. . . .

Presidents need academics for their expert knowledge. But that expertise does not make scholars first-rate practitioners or gifted confidential advisers to statesmen, Mr. Kissinger's example to the contrary notwithstanding.

Salisbury tells us plainly that the academic's T perspective, held in high esteem by his peers, must never be the overriding basis for policy decisions.[27]

The situation suggests that great care must be exercised in choosing the team members: the familiar technicians or analysts are not ideal in developing O and P perspectives. Either team members must be chosen to balance the needed characteristics, or the available T-focused participants must be trained to develop the desired inquiring procedures and sensitivities.

On International Symposia

It seems to me that each of [the distinguished scientists] possesses a small fragment of the Truth which he believes to be the Whole Truth, which he carries around in his pocket like a tarnished bubblegum, and blows up on solemn occasions to prove that it contains the ultimate mystery of the universe. Discussion? Interdisciplinary dialogue? There is no such thing, except on the printed program. When the dialogue is supposed to start, each gets his own bubblegum out and blows it into the others' faces. Then they repair, satisfied, to the cocktail room.

Source: A. Koestler, *The Call Girls*

Let us first dispense with the idea of interdisciplinarity. In the scientist/technologist world view, dominated by reductionism, compartmentalization by disciplines is natural. Frequently, "interdisciplinarity" is interpreted as the participation of experts from several disciplines, for example, engineering, economics, and mathematics. Jantsch (1972) would label this approach "multidisciplinary." In any case, all such disciplines use the same T perspective, and so will their joint effort. We might next ask whether a systems analyst or operations analyst solves our problems. Such a person is, after all, interdisciplinary according to most definitions. The answer here is also negative. This individual may indeed be interdisciplinary, but he is still anchored in the same T perspective.

An effective team member, who naturally focuses on the O or P perspective,

---

[27]Dror has visited the rulers' offices in more than 30 Western democratic and developing countries and found that policy analysis is at present "an anomaly" for them. Usually, intuition and experience are relied on exclusively, augmented at most by some economics and traditional social sciences. There are deep doubts about any claims of "scientific" approaches [Dror, 1982:23–24].

often brings to bear a very different background than that of a T-oriented member, for example, law, journalism, politics, or administration. We know a lawyer is usually at home with dialectic inquiring systems, and an investigative reporter works on hunches. Such a person may be aided by having a high "social intelligence quotient" (Archer, 1980). Like Sherlock Holmes, certain individuals are talented at reading body language, that is, adept at picking up nonverbal signals. Archer reports that women are generally more adept than men in this regard and suggests that "female intuition" is not a myth. This observation is supported by Kaje (1977) on futures research, and by our own experience with male and female interviewers. We suspect that many male academics, particularly those with science or technology training, tend to be quite weak in social intelligence. This, in turn, is reflected in the bias toward the T perspective.[28]

Observations such as the preceding ones must not be interpreted as firm categorizations; we do, for example, find lawyers with a strong T focus. The choice of a well-balanced team will always remain an uneasy question of experience and judgment.

2. Differing Time Horizons

In Chapter I, we noted two "Catch 22" situations. We can now add a third. Many analyses in support of decision making must consider impacts and consequences that often lie 5 to 20 years in the future.

The multiple perspective concept leads us to the recognition of a predicament. Each perspective tends to have a different planning horizon (Figure 3 and Table 8). Combining this characteristic with our basic schematic (Figure 5), we can represent the dilemma as shown in Figure 8. Thinking of the perspectives as beams of light directed at the problem, we find that each beam has a different illuminating distance (like high- and low-beam headlights in an automobile). So we arrive at the catch:

- multiple perspectives are critical in developing insights on complex sociotechnical problems;

- the differential horizons of the three perspectives make it hard to deal with the long-term impacts and policy questions, which are vital to many problems.

Is it a wonder then that the T perspective dominates in long-range studies, such as strategic planning, and that in an O and P world long-range studies are viewed

---

[28]A booming field today is jury research, which concerns itself with the selection of the members, the best ways to impress a given jury, and similar problems. The approaches used by professionals in this area might well be studied with reference to our context (Lewin, 1982).

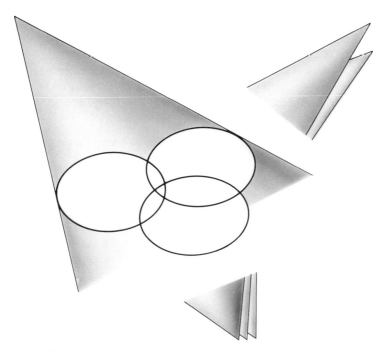

FIGURE 8. Different perspectives—different planning horizons.

with suspicion? The Japanese culture makes long-range planning somewhat easier. It handles the interaction between O and P perspectives in a particularly harmonious manner (see Section XII C) and encourages a longer range O perspective. Consequently there is often a more felicitous match between T, O, and P perspectives than in America.

Even the longest beam, representing the T perspective in Figure 8, is often overestimated. Consider technological and economic forecasting, for example. Ascher (1978:199), in his careful analysis of many academic, government, and industry forecasts, found a consistent pattern: the more distant the forecast target date, the less accurate the forecast.[29] He correlates this tendency with the core assumptions underlying the forecast. They are the major determinants of forecast accuracy and much more crucial than sophistication of the forecasting model. The core assumptions usually degrade with an increasing time horizon, so they constrain the T perspective horizon far more than the methodology-oriented "rational actor" generally assumes (see also Section XII B).

---

[29]Delphi forecasts have shown a similarly consistent pattern: the more remote in time the median date of the forecast, the wider the spread of responses (Linstone and Turoff, 1975:229).

We draw two implications:

1. Analyses are inherently difficult to do well when they must deal with long-term impacts and policies.
2. The most effective applications of multiple perspectives are likely to be in sociotechnical systems for which the focus is on near- and mid-range problems, that is, a time horizon encompassed by the O and P perspectives.

They explain the frustrations experienced by planners, forecasters, and impact assessors in the past decade. Point 1 finds its echo in Peter Drucker's admonition (1973):

> The future impact of new technology is almost always beyond anybody's imagination. . . . At the same time, a technology impact that the "experts" foresee almost never actually occurs.

On the other hand, he insists that:

> Technology monitoring is a serious, an important, indeed a vital task.

The difference is the horizon, predicting long-term system behavior versus monitoring what is going on now with a young technology.

The most important advice given on long-range analyses is to never consider your work complete; keep iterating or revisiting and "burnishing" it at subsequent time points. This advice can be interpreted as a means to deal with this dilemma. Referring to Figure 8, we recognize that the situation is dynamic. The O and P perspectives move in closer as time passes and will begin to illuminate the system jointly with the T perspective.

Point 2 is hardly a revelation to top level corporate and governmental decision makers. In fact, it is reflected in the discounting that is so pervasive in the business and political decision process (Figure 2). The corporate and governmental long-range planners are caught between a rock and a hard place. Either they conscientiously delve into long-range aspects via the T perspective only to find their reports unread and unused, or they concentrate on near-term policy and implementation decisions via T, O, and P perspectives, only to find their output becoming controversial and politically sensitive.[30]

At the same time, we draw some positive inferences:

1) There are in any society far-sighted individuals (who may as leaders also inspire organizations and social entities to be far-sighted). History has given us a Pericles, a Washington, a Lincoln, and a Churchill—men of vision. Churchill, for example, was thinking far beyond victory during the last years of World War

---

[30]We shall return to this subject in Section XIIC on Corporate Planning.

II. His planning horizon encompassed the post-War Soviet threat at a time when nearly everyone was concerned with the great ongoing war (see Section VA 3).[31] We also find men with vision as pioneers in industry—they "see" a new product line or company image before others in the organization. And they recognize the long-term impacts of their decisions. Ideally, the study leader should seek out such individuals; unfortunately, they are only rarely available. But he should certainly make a conscious effort to include, as team members or consultants, individuals with strong O and P perspective orientations *and* a longer-than-average horizon.

2) There are many situations where a near- or midrange time horizon provides a sound basis for policy decisions. The multiple perspective concept should ultimately leave its deepest imprint there as it bridges the gap between the model world and the real world.

3. Communications

Communication techniques for O and P perspectives (either for input or output) are by no means identical to those associated with the T perspective.

Input. Jay (1968:142) observes that standard documentation is not the place to determine the foci of power in an organization:

> Real power does not lie in documents and memos outlining your terms of reference and area of jurisdiction: it lies in what you can achieve in practice. The boss's secretary can wield great power, like the king's mistress, without any authority at all—or at least not the sort you can show anybody.

Interviews play a dominant role in O and P, in contrast to the reports and surveys used for T. Other methods such as participant observation, guided group dialogue, and open-ended simulation may also prove valuable in gaining an understanding of organizations and individuals. Future applications of O and P perspectives should explore these possibilities more fully.

The key to comprehending individuals in P perspectives is the empathic capacity of the interviewer or observer. No individual is capable of empathy with everyone. Psychosocial barriers between certain people are inevitable, no matter how skilled or naturally intuitive a given interviewer or observer may be.

Empathic capacity in the interview situation is, in part, a function of the respondent's perception of the interviewer as nonthreatening, and in part a matter of the interviewer's ego strength and self-sufficiency (in emotional terms). In

---

[31]Not surprisingly, some individuals, like Churchill, who use a lower-than-average discount rate in looking forward to the future, also apply a lower-than-average discount rate to the past. Hence, they have a more profound sense of history.

certain circumstances, neurotic behavior can produce close empathic feelings—especially if the neuroses complement each other—but, in such cases, the degree of comprehension will be distorted by the interviewer's own feelings and emotional reactions. Unless the interviewer can both gain insight and preserve the ability to dissociate himself from the client, the product will be a set of idiosyncratic projections on the part of the interviewer—not a useful understanding of the respondent. This is the classic psychoanalytic dilemma Freud noted years ago:

> It almost looks as if analysis were the third of those "impossible" professions in which one can be sure beforehand of achieving unsatisfying results. The other two, which have been known much longer, are education and government [Freud, 1937:352].

Freud's *Recommendations to Physicians Practicing Psychoanalysis* in 1912 deals with the need to learn how to listen and compares the analyst to the surgeon "who puts aside all his feelings, even his human sympathy, and concentrates his mental forces on the single aim of performing the operation as skillfully as possible." The analogy is appropriate because, as one psychoanalyst put it, gaining insight into another person's thought processes is as deep, radical, and complex a procedure as cutting out a tumor (Malcolm, 1980).

Thus we have a prescription nearly impossible to execute well in interviews. But some talent can go a long way, and our experience over the past five years shows that it exists most often in individuals who are not focused strongly on the T perspective.

Output. We take for granted the technical report format for systems, decision, risk, policy, impact, and other analyses. This format is standard for the T perspective, but not necessarily appropriate for the O and P perspectives. The latter in particular suggests a unique contextual point of view, which lends itself to experiential formulation and personalized presentation. A scenario, vignette, or story may crystallize the image or convey the tone better than a conventional format. It can also serve as a vehicle to communicate the main ideas of the entire output concretely to an audience that cannot deal with, or is not satisfied with, the abstract technical report format. For the importance of alternative means of communication see Meltsner (1979).

Table 9 suggests some of the possible matches of perspective and means of presentation. In the applications we have experimented with several of these vehicles for the O and P perspectives, as will be described subsequently.

The oral briefing, off-the-record conference and private discussion, need further explication, however. Almost any report can be transformed into one of these formats. They are included in Table 9 for O and P to highlight the problem

TABLE 9. Some Means to Communicate Perspectives

Perspective	Means	Example	Discussed in Chapter
T (technical)	Technical report	University of Arizona Guayule TA	IX A
O (organizational)	Technical report	National Commission EFT Report (see below)	VIII B
	Scenario		
	Transcripts of interviews	On-site solid waste	X B and C
	Summaries of interviews	Guayule interviews	IX B
	Oral briefing		
	Off-the-record conference		
P (personal)	Scenario/vignette	Perinatal health care scenario	VII D
	Transcripts of interviews	On-site solid waste	X D
	Summaries of interviews	Guayule interviews	IX C
	Oral briefing		
	Private discussion		

of the sensitivity of these perspectives. It may be possible to present important insights orally but not in writing. Unquestionably, these perspectives pose problems not of concern with the T perspective. They reflect the political nature of the work and must be faced just as they are by the journalist.

There are several alternatives:

1. partly oral and partly written report;
2. two-part written report (one part for distribution by the client, another for internal use by the client);
3. use of quotes but without attribution;
4. use of sensitive material by the analysts as input only, with implications presented in the report;
5. integration of insights obtained from different perspectives before the final report preparation;
6. transformation of sensitive material into fictional format.

4. Changing Perspectives

The balance of perspectives in the individual is, in considerable part, determined by his or her professional role. Figure 9 illustrates a typical relationship between the role and the dominant perspective of the person. The interaction of the perspectives suggests the decision-making process.

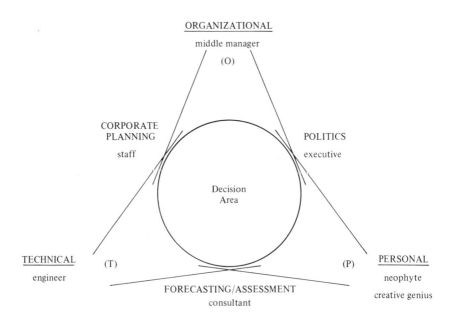

FIGURE 9. Perspectives and roles: a possible relationship. *Source: R. Miller.*

The individual, like a cut diamond, displays different facets under different light conditions. The balance among the perspectives should not be viewed as a fixed or rigid one. The manager's professional perspective may be dominantly O during the working day ("the organization man"), but recede into the background at other times. (If not, his personal life may suffer.) As an individual shifts jobs, say from engineer to department head, his dominant perspective may change from T to O.

A personal perspective may become an organizational perspective at a later time. This is particularly the case where a P perspective sweeps in "individuals who make a difference." As they gain support, they tend to become institutionalized and lose their status as individual actors. The name Roger Baldwin is not generally associated with the American Civil Liberties Union, although he was its first executive director and served in that position from 1920 to 1950. In a similar manner, Ralph Nader has become institutionalized as a consumer advocacy group and John Gardner as a watchdog group of congressional ethics. Such groups function as specific filters through which public behavior, such as legislation or environmental degradation, is screened.

Transformation of a P perspective into an O perspective may be the means by which an individual forms, gains acceptance of, or controls a group. An organization evolves that is bound together by a common perspective. The process often involves personal charisma and organizational tools, such as propaganda or "disinformation." Tsar Nicholas II's secret police fabricated the plot of "The Protocols of the Elders of Zion" out of 19th-century German and French fiction. Over the past 80 years, it has been used to fuel an antisemitic perspective by Henry Ford, radio priest Charles Coughlin, Adolf Hitler, and King Faisal of Saudi Arabia (*Time,* May 16, 1983:48–49).

British Tudor King Henry VII apparently used writers John Morton and Sir Thomas More to help pin the responsibility for murders he ordered on his predecessor, Richard III, of the rival House of York. These were, of course, the famous cases of the boy princes in the Tower of London. The image of evil was sharpened by saddling poor Richard with deformities he never had. Later, Shakespeare transformed this disinformation into a powerful play. As soon as the curtain opens, Richard proclaims not ony his lameness and deformity but also his treachery, falseness, and determination "to prove a villain." Thus a usurper's device for self-legitimation becomes the gospel of history for millions over the centuries.

A given perspective also shifts over time. As a corporate manager enters government service and becomes a federal bureaucrat, his O perspective is likely to change significantly. An interesting situation is created when an individual's dominant perspective, or mix of perspectives, varies strongly from that which is the norm of the organization into which he steps (for example, Jerry Brown as Governor of California). Thus the perspectives should be viewed as dynamic rather than static, and proper understanding requires considerable immersion.

In a technology assessment, for example, an important question is: how should the effort be apportioned to the different perspectives?

Emerging versus existing technology. A new technology requires a major T perspective effort to explore the technological implications; these are usually (but not always) well understood for a familiar technology. On the other hand, the O and P perspectives may be proportionately more extensive for a familiar, established technology as individuals and organizations have taken positions on the issues arising from the technology, resources have been committed, careers launched, and communications media involved.

Elite versus popular technology. Automobiles and television are technologies that involve the individual directly. However, with the exception of automatic teller machines, electronic funds transfer technology is largely hidden from the individual. The citizen is not concerned with the handling of checks among banks

A Multiple Perspective View of Scenarios

Roy Amara (1980) and Uno Svedin (1980) have suggested that scenarios may be usefully classified into three types as shown in the following table:

	Scenario typology		
	Probable	Preferable	Possible
Criterion	Analytical (reproducible)	Value (explicative)	Image (plausible)
Orientation	Exploratory (extrapolative)	Normative	Visionary
Mode	Structural	Participatory	Perceptual
Creator	Think-tank teams	Stakeholders	Individuals

It is striking that these three types can be related to our three perspectives:

- Probable (think-tank teams)   — T perspective
- Preferable (stakeholders)   — O perspective
- Possible (individuals)   — P perspective

It is reasonable to expect a T perspective scenario to be analytic and judged on its reproducibility. The O scenario is the product of organizational planning, hence participatory and prescriptive. The P scenario is significant only if it is imaginative or visionary, e.g., Hitler's *Thousand Year Reich,* More's *Utopia.* It contrasts with corporate planners' projections (O) and econometrics (T).

A Multiple Perspective View of Decision Styles

The varying decision styles have been subjected to study by Mitroff and Kilmann (1975) as well as Nutt (1979) using the Jung psychological types (see Table 1 of this work). Their four styles may be easily related to our perspectives:

Jung	Decision style	Dominant perspective
Thinking-sensation	Systematic	T
Thinking-intuition	Speculative	T
Feeling-sensation	Judicial	O
Feeling-intuition	Intuitive	P

and has no contact with an automatic clearinghouse. Similarly, the individual who flicks on a light switch usually does not know or care whether the electricity was generated by a hydropower facility or a nuclear power plant.

The P perspective covers very different ground in elite as contrasted with popular technologies. In the case of the former, it is usually much easier to pinpoint individual actors. Precisely because the public is not a direct user, the influence of individual actors associated with the technology, directly or indirectly, becomes a more important issue. These actors operate within a small circle of protagonists or antagonists, and their influence is not diluted by the pressures of the general public's behavior.

In the case of nuclear power, for instance, we can readily appreciate that it would make a great difference whether Herbert York or Edward Teller was the President's Adviser. It would also be important to assess the inputs of the relevant commission members in terms of their basic orientation, their views on how the technology should be promoted, and their relative power to have their views prevail. Societal ramifications are viewed from a T perspective: the engineer sees any conflict between the technology and the community as a form of societal maladaptation; he looks for the remedy in additional technology that will facilitate societal adaptation.

The citizen can have an impact on an elite technology only through the marshaling of considerable resources and organization (for example, environmentalist groups), whereas the normal marketplace mechanisms influence a popular technology. Thus the handling of the P perspective for large-scale solar energy development differs fundamentally from that for the personal computer.

The apportionment of effort among the three perspectives cannot be disposed of by a simple formula. It is a function not only of the technology, but also of the political framework of the task. *As a first approximation, an equal three-part split in effort among the three perspectives seems eminently reasonable.*

5. Integration of Perspectives

President John F. Kennedy (1963) wrote:

> The essence of ultimate decision remains impenetrable to the observer—often, indeed, to the decider himself. . . . There will *always* be the dark and tangled stretches in the decision making process—mysterious even to those who may be most intimately involved [emphasis ours].

"Ultimate decision" involves the final integration of input, usually of various perspectives. How should we deal with it?

Pro and con. We must address two basic questions:

1. Do the perspectives work at cross-purposes or are they complementary?
2. How are they to be integrated and by whom?

Consider a corporate executive faced with a complex sociotechnical decision. He obtains a T perspective from his engineers and systems analysts, an O perspective from his department heads, and a P perspective from workers and staff whom he informally queries. He may receive conflicting input as well as reinforcement. Similarly, the various witnesses at a trial provide different perspectives to the jury. The process of integration is not merely one of assembling a composite picture from jigsaw puzzle pieces, nor ironing out contradictions by some rules of thumb, nor arranging the information hierarchically. Integration resembles the task of conceptualizing a three-dimensional object from a series of one-dimensional descriptions and two-dimensional drawings. Alternatively, we can think of the process in terms of the integration of stimuli to the left and right hemispheres in the brain. *The perspectives cross-cue each other.*[32] Most decision makers find it quite difficult to describe this process explicitly, although they execute it every day. It is often just as difficult to reconstruct how a jury arrived at a decision. The fact that in both cases effective decision making does occur suggests that the integration process in our situation be left to the user or decision maker. Providing an integrated perspective to the client means weighting and interpreting, simulating closely held value judgments in advance—and this can be a hazardous exercise.

An even stronger argument against integration by the analyst can be made if there is *a priori* no well-defined user, as in the case of a risk analysis or technology assessment done for the National Science Foundation. Subsequent users will, indeed must, use different weighting and cross-cuing.

There are arguments for the other side also. One is the possibility that an inexperienced client may misuse the perspectives. For example, he might choose a "best" perspective and ignore the others. Or, the analysis might be thrown out because there appears to be disagreement among perspectives. (We recall that a technologist is not accustomed to dialectic inquiring systems.)

A second practical advantage of integration is the ability to "launder" or neutralize sensitive insights obtained from the O and P perspectives (see Section IV C 3).

It is our view that the disadvantages of integration outweigh the advantages, that is, that the decision maker may be poorly served by receiving only the integrated product. A compromise is to present the separate perspectives and one or more sample integrations of those perspectives.

---

[32]See Sections XIA3 and XIE for examples and further discussion of cross cuing.

The jury in a trial is presented with prototype integrations by the prosecuting and defense attorneys. They develop cross-cues and weave the testimony of different witnesses into a coherent pattern to arrive at a prototype decision. They do not make the decision, however, and the jury, which does, may ignore such prototype integrations.

Comprehensiveness and definitiveness? Two words that should be tabu in any discussion of the study of sociotechnical systems are *comprehensive* and *definitive,* as in "a risk analysis should be comprehensive" or "the described perspectives are definitive."

Only a T perspective mind is likely to use these words. Anyone who has tried to determine the number of interactions possible with a small number of elements in a system[33] will understand the unreality of comprehensiveness. So will anyone who has studied the impacts of technologies in history, for example, Lynn White (1974).

The changeability of perspectives has been noted. Individuals and organizations change perspectives over time, key actors enter and leave the stage. The image of a one-time "correct" analysis of the system is nearly always an illusion. The changing setting has been recognized by planners, for example, in the advice to periodically iterate their analyses and consider the iteration an ongoing activity.

The T, O, and P perspectives are not unique. Allison contemplated four models, and Appendix B of Linstone et al. (1981b) suggests other possibilities that, we hope, may stimulate further exploration.

6. Ruminations

We close this chapter with two thoughts.

A nagging worry. The Singerian inquiring system, implied by the use of multiple perspectives, understandably jars those (scientists and technologists) accustomed to Lockean (data-based), Leibnizian (model-based), and Kantian (data plus model or multimodel) inquiring systems. It also leaves us with the residual fear that the O and P perspectives may be unconsciously transformed into T perspectives (see Section XIII L). This concern is best alleviated by 1) creating an interparadigmatic, rather than interdisciplinary, team at the beginning of a project and 2) discouraging academic efforts to create formal (T perspective) theories for the application of multiple perspectives.

A different perspective on the perspectives. Our present limits of knowledge, as reflected in the state-of-the-art of science and technology, leave large voids,

---

[33]See Section IIC.

and multiple perspectives may help to fill a few of them. Evolution of life from the "primeval soup" to an information society has not relied solely on man's creation of science and technology. The process began—and proceeded admirably—long before the output of science and technology could have an impact. Replicating molecules were striving for negentropy (higher organization), range (expansion in space), and control through collaboration and Darwinian competition. The process has been stunningly successful (Marchetti, 1981). One can argue that much of this heritage (accumulated genetic knowledge?) resides in human beings (individually and collectively as a species) even though not yet encapsulated in formal science and technology. Thus O and P perspectives may automatically sweep in "knowledge" that augments the knowledge consciously developed by T perspective analysis.

V

ILLUSTRATIONS OF MULTIPLE PERSPECTIVES: THE PUBLIC SECTOR

H. LINSTONE, B. CLARY,
S. HAWKE, and S. J. WILL

By intervening in the Vietnamese struggle, the United States was attempting to fit its global strategies into a world of hillocks and hamlets, to reduce its majestic concerns for the containment of Communism and the security of the Free World to a dimension where governments rose and fell as a result of arguments between two colonels' wives. . . . For the Americans in Vietnam, it would be difficult to make this leap of perspective.

> F. Fitzgerald
> *Fire in the Lake*

In this chapter, we begin our look at the application of multiple perspectives. We first consider the public sector—the illustrations range from the Civil War to the 1980s, from local to national government, and from simple technology (rifles) to sophisticated systems (atomic bomb). In chapter VI, we will examine illustrations from the private sector.

A. MILITARY TECHNOLOGY AND OTHER NATIONAL DECISION AREAS

The T perspective has been extensively used in forecasting and assessing military technology since World War II. The study of the impact of a potential new U.S. weapon system on Soviet strategy may not have been labeled a technology assessment, but it essentially is one. In fact, the pioneering work of Allison (1969;1971) involved an application of multiple perspectives to a military–political problem.

We begin with three innovations in military technology and examine the significance of the O and P perspectives:

1. introduction of a new ship concept into U.S. Navy,
2. introduction of new rifles into the U.S. Army,
3. introduction of nuclear weapons into a war by the U.S. government.

1. The U.S.S. Wampanoag (H. Linstone, based on E. Morison, 1966)

The *Wampanoag* was 4200 ton "advanced technology" destroyer built for the U.S. Navy and commissioned in 1868. She had sails and a steam engine and was fast (over 17 knots). Sea trials proved her to be a magnificent technical achievement—ahead of ships in any navy at that time.

In 1869 all naval steamships were scrutinized by a board of naval officers. The mood of the Board is documented. The steam vessel, said the Board, was not a school of seamanship for officers or men:

> Lounging through the watches of a steamer, or acting as firemen and coal heavers, will not produce in a seaman that combination of boldness, strength, and skill which characterized the American sailor of an elder day; and the habitual exercise by an officer of a command, the execution of which is not under his own eye, is a poor substitute for the school of observation, promptness and command found only on the deck of a sailing vessel [Morison 1966:114].

The Board examined the *Wampanoag* and developed a bill of particulars leading it to the conclusion that the ship was "a sad and signal failure" and could not be made acceptable. The country was in a state of peace, and the Board opposed building ironclads, needed in war, to avoid unnecessary alarm. There was a large supply of timber in the Navy Yards "which the interests of economy demand should be utilized." They noted the familiarity of the workmen with wooden ship building and their dependence on it for a livelihood.

The ship was laid up for a year and soon sold by the Navy. Morison (1966:116–122) ponders this strange turn of events:

> Now it must be obvious that the members of this Naval Board were stupid. They had, on its technical merits, a bad case, and they made it worse by the way they tried to argue it. . . . [But after a time] I began to be aware of a growing sense of dis-ease. . . . Could it be that these stupid officers were right? I recalled the sagacious judgment of Sherlock Holmes. The great detective, you will remember, withheld the facts in the incident of the lighthouse and the trained cormorant because, as he said, it was a case for which the world was not yet fully prepared. Was this also the case with the Wampanoag?
>
> What these officers were saying was that the *Wampanoag* was a destructive energy in their society. Setting the extraordinary force of her engines against the weight of their way of life, they had a sudden insight into the nature of machinery. They perceived that a machine, any machine, if left to itself, tends to establish its own conditions, to create its own environment and draw men into it. Since a machine, any machine, is designed to do only a part of what a whole man can do, it tends to wear down those parts of a man that are not included in the design. . . .
>
> I don't happen to admire their solution, but I respect their awareness that they had a problem. . . . [It] is not primarily engineering or scientific in character. It's simply human.

In these passages Morison shifts perspectives, from T to O. A decision that appeared "stupid" when viewed from the former suddenly became reasonable when seen from the latter. Thus a new technological system was held back for reasons that would be exceedingly difficult to uncover with a T perspective.

As a postscript, the introduction of the revolving turret rendered all navies obsolete. The Naval Board could have rejected the *Wampanoag* on technical grounds.

2. The M-16 Rifle (H. Linstone)

Only joint consideration of T, O, and P perspectives can explain the complex decision process culminating in the selection of the technically superior M-16 rifle as the standard weapon in the 1960s. The attitude of a U.S. Army organization is shown to be consistent in the face of externally generated technological innovations over a 100-year period. Its actions in the defense of its position may have been extreme.

The rifle is the most basic weapon system in any army. Hence decisions to replace a rifle are a very serious matter. Since the Civil War the history of the U.S. Army rifle has been an interesting one, presenting us with technical, organizational, and personal aspects.

Figure 10 schematically describes the decision process that finally led to the selection of the M-16 rifle. It is based on the analyses of McNaugher (1980) and Fallows (1981), as well as discussions with former key individuals in the Department of Defense (Schwebs and Sprey, 1981).

The past 100 years can be seen as a struggle between marksman and citizen-soldier weapon proponents, or between the old Army Ordnance/Springfield Arsenal establishment and the newer Infantry Board/Secretary of Defense organizations.

The Civil War inaugurated the era of the bullet. A precursor to the M-16 story is told about the first reliable repeating rifle for military use (Fallows 1981:80). When the Civil War began, Union troops carried a cumbersome muzzle-loading rifle. A young inventor named Spencer, who came from outside the Army's Ordnance establishment, had developed the repeating rifle. When he could not get the Army's attention, he wangled an appointment with President Lincoln. They went behind the White House and the President, who was a good shot, test fired the rifle. The Secretary of War had been invited, but declined to attend. Lincoln liked the rifle and sent the Secretary a note ordering the Army to procure it. They bought the minimum amount, assigned the weapons mostly to the cavalry, and indicated that they were not suitable for infantry use. Several Union regiments, however, bought the Spencer rifles with their own money, rather than use the approved rifle. After Lincoln's assassination, the head of the Ordnance Corps quickly declared the Spencer rifles obsolete and ordered them sold. (Ironically many of these superior rifles were bought by the Indians and were used in the attack on Custer at Little Bighorn.)

After the Civil War, the myth of the Western sharpshooter and the formation of the National Rifle Association reflected the development of a uniquely American marksmanship tradition. A marksman firing in a long-range rifle competition needed a large, heavy round to maximize steadiness in flight and minimize sensitivity to wind. The Army Ordnance Corps, responsible for small arms, adopted the marksmanship concept as its own creed. Its Springfield Arsenal produced the first breech-loading rifle to fill this indicated need in 1867.

Again, in the Spanish–American War, Theodore Roosevelt's Rough Riders, with their ordnance-approved rifle, found themselves facing troops equipped with a superior rifle—the Mauser. When he became President, Roosevelt ordered the unenthusiastic War Department to buy Mausers.

Every modern conflict has raised doubts about the Ordnance Corps' criteria, that is, the appropriateness of the marksman's rifle for the citizen–soldier. World War I introduced the machine gun, and the semiautomatic rifle followed; suppression fire became an important consideration. In Europe, the smaller .276 semiautomatic rifle was introduced, and a specially appointed Army Caliber Board approved a similar version in 1932. But Chief of Staff General MacArthur sided with the traditionalists and disapproved. Instead, the .30 caliber M-1 became the standard Army weapon in 1936.

In World War II, assault tactics relying on volume of fire rather than accuracy became important. General Patton wanted "marching fire": several steps, then

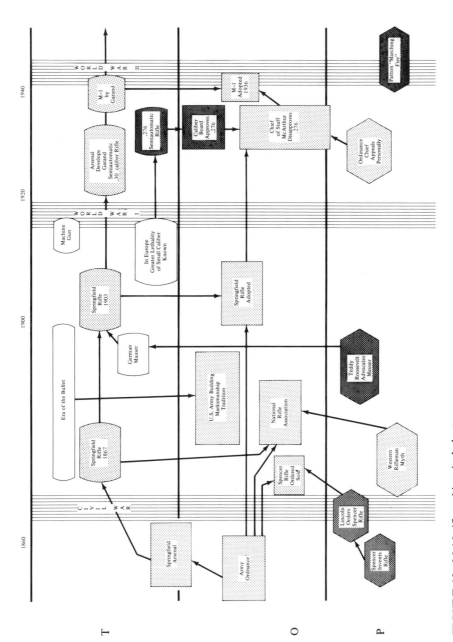

FIGURE 10. M-16 rifle: a historical chart.

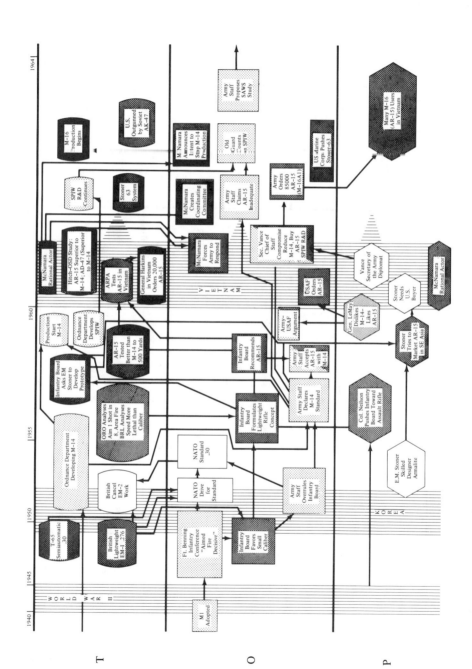

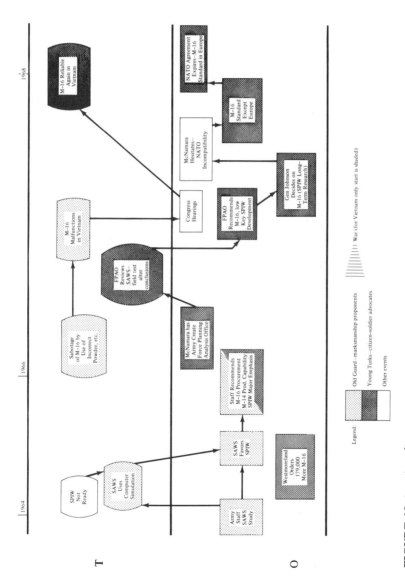

FIGURE 10 (continued)

a short burst, more steps, another burst. It was recognized that lethality is enhanced by bullet speed more than by caliber size, making a smaller caliber rifle clearly preferable as a weapon. It was also found that few soldiers in combat fired their rifles at targets over 300 yards distant. In fact, nearly 80% of the combat soldiers never fired their weapons at all during battles. The exceptions to this rule were those who carried the Browning automatic rifle—a portable machine gun that could spray continuous fire and "hose down" an area.

After the war, the British developed a small, lightweight, .276 caliber assault rifle. The U.S. Infantry Board tested and accepted the British weapon. There was the additional argument of standardization within NATO. Once again tradition overruled the recommendation, and in 1957 the Army Staff and Ordnance Corps (more precisely, the Army Materiel Command) responded with the M-14. It was an automatic-firing direct descendant of their .30 caliber M-1.

At this time Eugene Stoner of the Armalite Corporation completed design of the AR-15, which used the smaller, faster, and more lethal .22 caliber bullet as well as a plastic stock, thus weighing less. A soldier could carry nearly three times as many rounds as with the M-14.

Extensive Army field tests and analyses led to the embarrassing conclusion that the AR-15 was superior to the M-14. The organization men predictably applied the NIH factor ("not invented here"), ignored these results, and ordered full production of the M-14 and its round. One individual who did not go along with the "party line" was General Curtis LeMay of the U.S. Air Force. In 1962, USAF declared the AR-15 its standard and ordered the rifle.

Another individual now came onstage: Secretary of Defense McNamara, a "rational actor" *par excellence*. Tests in Vietnam conducted by the Advanced Research Projects Agency (not a part of the Army) concluded:

> In overall squad kill potential the AR-15 is up to 5 times as effective as the M-14 rifle. [The AR-15] can be produced with less difficulty, to a higher quality, and at a lower cost than the M-14 rifle. In reliability, durability, ruggedness, performance under adverse circumstances, and ease of maintenance, the AR-15 is a significant improvement over any of the standard weapons including the M-14 rifle [Fallows 1981:84].

The Ordnance establishment countered with its own tests and found the M-14 a "radically" better model. Later these tests were found to have been rigged (Fallows, 1981:85).

Secretary McNamara overrode the Army and sent more AR-15s to Vietnam; the reports coming back on their performance were enthusiastic. The AR-15 was renamed the M-16. Meanwhile the Army Ordnance hit on a diversionary tactic, development of a Special Purpose Infantry Weapon (SPIW). The Marine Corps, on the other hand, requested Stoner's type of weapon. To head off another confrontation, the Army Staff proposed a new study: the Small Arms Weapons System Study (SAWS). Since SPIW was not yet ready, computer simulation had to be used, and it "proved" SPIW to be superior to any other rifle. McNamara responded by creating a new Force Planning and Analysis Office (FPAO). It reviewed SAWS and concluded that the computer simulations were logically inconsistent. Its field tests again showed the M-16 to be superior.

Perhaps the most stunning phase in the organizational struggle was the sudden epidemic of malfunctions of the M-16 in Vietnam. The weapon that had been glowingly praised now jammed and misfired. The reason was found in the Ordnance Corps' "modifications" imposed on the M-16. A useless manual bolt closure was added, personally ordered by the Army Chief of Staff; the "twist" of the rifle barrel was increased, reducing lethality; most important of all, Stoner's ammunition was replaced by unsuitable ball powder that effectively increased the failure rate by 600%.

> The Army's modifications had very little to do with . . . warfare, but quite a lot to do with settling organizational scores [Fallows, 1981:77].

When more and more soldiers wrote letters home about the unreliable M-16, Congress went into action and conducted an exhaustive inquiry. Their report charged that the M-16 had been sabotaged by the Ordnance Corps.

> The most striking aspect of the testimony was its humdrum routine tone. When representatives of the Ordnance Corps were pressed to explain their decisions, they fell back on citations from the rule books, like characters in a parody of the bureaucratic temperament. They seemed to have a hard time remembering who was responsible for crucial decisions; they tended to explain things by saying, "the feeling was," or "the practice has been. . . ." They could list with careful bureaucratic logic the reasonableness of each step they had taken [Fallows, 1981:93–94].

The modifications that were so damaging were never properly corrected.

The O perspective is blindingly evident. Fallows adds a postscript to this tale. In 1980 when Army troops went on exercises in Egypt, unattributed comments began to appear: visibility is so good in the desert that a sharpshooter rifle is really needed, not a popgun like the M-16. The struggle of one organization to control the course of a technology may not yet be over.

We draw a number of implications from this illustration:

- The rational actor's selection of the "best" system hardly reflects the real-life decision process, that is, the T perspective does not suffice to understand the management of technological change. In this case the O perspective is central.

- The Army does not operate as a unitary decision maker. For example, the Infantry Board and Army Staff were on opposite sides of the argument.

- Individuals play a vital role in the process. For example, civilians in the Office of the Secretary of Defense—McNamara, Hitch, and Vance—as well as certain generals—LeMay and Wyman—were instrumental in shifting decisions.

- The overt and hidden motivations for actions must be clearly distinguished if the decision process is to be understood. Examples: the ordering of the SAWS project by the Army Staff and McNamara's creation of FPAO were indirect means to achieve certain objectives.

- The organizational actors may go to remarkable lengths to attain parochial objectives.

3. The Decision to Use the Atomic Bomb (J. Pearson)[1]

This illustration deals with the most influential innovation in military technology of modern times, the atomic bomb—specifically the world-shaking decision whether or not to use it. The T perspective dominates but is reinforced by the O and P perspectives.

On June 1, 1945, the situation was as follows: Truman had been President only seven weeks following Roosevelt's death. He had not only inherited a war but the organization, plans, and capabilities of winning it. Germany had tendered its unconditional surrender on May 8, and Japan had no prospects of winning. Unconditional surrender was being demanded of Japan; U.S. public opinion, ignited by Pearl Harbor and fanned by years of propaganda, would accept no less. Although its navy and air force had been destroyed, Japan was not yet ready to accept the humiliation of unconditional surrender.

The atomic bomb was being developed in an atmosphere of secrecy and uncertainty. Security had been a target throughout the weapon's development. On June 1, an atomic bomb had not yet been exploded; no one knew for sure that it would work.

Technical perspective. Henry L. Stimson's article "The Decision to Use the Atomic Bomb" is a model case of the technical approach to decision making. He portrays a unitary decision maker, President Truman, with Stimson as senior advisor.

---

[1]Since Pearson's study was completed, it has come to our attention that Davidson and Lytle have just published a book on "the art of historical detection" that also tackles the decision to drop the atomic bomb on Japan via multiple perspectives, specifically, using Allison's original models. They conclude that:

If historians based their interpretations on a single model, they would never satisfy their desire to understand the sequence of events leading to Hiroshima. . . . The use of several models allows the historian the same advantage enjoyed by writers of fiction who employ more than one narrator. Each narrator, like every model, affords the writer a new vantage point from which to tell the story. . . . Thus, as organizations grow more complex, models afford historians multiple perspectives from which to interpret the same reality [Davidson and Lytle, 1982:351].

The problem was bounded, and the goal was clear: "The principal political, social, and military objective of the United States in the summer of 1945 was the prompt and complete surrender of Japan" (Stimson, 1947:101). This objective was to be achieved as quickly as possible with the minimum of cost, physical destruction, and loss of American and Japanese lives. The alternatives were set out and their consequences assessed, as schematized in Table 10.[2]

Stimson (1947:106), as Secretary of War, found in his analysis total justification for the decision to drop the bomb.

> [These reasons] have always seemed compelling and clear, and I cannot see how any person vested with such responsibilities as mine could have taken any other course or given any other advice to his chiefs. . . . I believe that no man . . . could have failed to use it.

Whether these reasons provide full justification remains controversial. However, what they do not provide is a full explanation; so we turn to other perspectives.

Organizational perspective. If Stimson saw the use of the atomic bomb as the only logical means to end the War, P.M.S. Blackett, a British Nobel Laureate, saw it quite differently: "The dropping of the atomic bomb was not so much the last military act of the Second World War, as the first major operation of the cold diplomatic war with Russia" (Blackett, quoted in Amrine, 1959:232). The organizational perspective helps us to understand his statement and provides the second view of the decision.

The major Allied powers were the United States, Britain, and Russia with leaders Truman, Churchill, and Stalin, respectively. As long as their mutual survival demanded the defeat of the Axis, these nations were able to work together. But with Germany's surrender in Europe and Japan's retreat in the Pacific, their common goal was largely achieved. Attention shifted to new goals, reflecting each country's parochial priorities, perceptions, and interests.

Russia sought to ensure its defense and national well-being by imperialistic expansion in Europe (Rumania, Bulgaria, Yugoslavia, Czechoslovakia, Poland, and Hungary). It had similar goals in Korea, China, and the North Pacific. As old problems were solved and old goals achieved, new problems and new goals directed the search for new solutions.

Due to its closeness to the continent, Great Britain was most concerned about Soviet expansion in Europe. Churchill enthusiastically supported the use of the bomb. He saw it bringing ". . . a speedy end to the Second World War, and

---

[2]Some of the estimates in the table were still under security classification in February 1947, when the article was printed; they have been obtained from later sources.

TABLE 10. The Technical Perspective in the Atomic Bomb Decision

Unified decision maker:	Collective will unified in President Truman				
Bounded problem:	Japan's unconditional surrender				
Goal:	Obtain unconditional surrender as quickly as possible with minimum loss of Allied lives and (secondarily) with a minimum of cost, physical destruction, and loss of Japanese lives.				
Options:	Conventional Bombing and Blockade	Invasion	A-Bomb Japan without Warning	A-Bomb Japan after Warning	A-Bomb Uninhabited Island
Consequences					
Unconditional surrender:	Uncertain	Highly likely	Highly likely	Uncertain	Uncertain
Time to surrender:	Lengthy	November 1946	Short	Uncertain	Uncertain
Allied lives lost:	Moderate	1,000,000 +	None	None or few	None
Japanese lives lost:	Many	2,000,000 +	20,000–200,000	Few	None
Cost:	High	Very high	Low	Low	Low
Destruction:	Very high	Very high	High	High	Low
Other consequences:	Thousands of U.S. prisoners of war sure to die			Would use one of only two bombs, perhaps without the desired effect. If demonstration failed, then lower U.S. morale, higher Japanese morale, loss of international prestige. Japan might attempt to defend target. Japan might move POWs to target site	Would use one of only two bombs, perhaps without the desired effect. Shock effect reduced. If demonstration failed, then lower U.S. morale, higher Japanese morale, loss of international prestige.
Trade-offs:	Between lives, time, money, extent of destruction				
Choice:	As an optimum				

perhaps much else besides" (Churchill, quoted in Schoenberger, 1970:259). Far more than Truman, Churchill distrusted and feared the Russians.

American perceptions were changing, too. Russian entry into the Pacific conflict was still being sought by the allied military, but not by the diplomatic corps. The change in policy was incremental: the United States continued its official stance of welcoming Russian participation, but unofficially worked to avoid it. The United States wanted to contain Russian expansion in the Far East. And Russia's challenge in Europe was not forgotten. According to Leo Szilard (one of the top Manhattan Project scientists), Secretary of State James Byrnes argued that the bomb need not be used to defeat Japan, but rather to "make Russia more manageable in Europe" (Byrnes, quoted in Morton, 1957:347). The O perspective might therefore "see" a Soviet challenge—expansion in the Pacific—and the U.S. response—detonation of an atomic bomb—to demonstrate power and to accelerate the Japanese surrender before Soviet entry into the Pacific War.

An organizational perspective can also be applied on a different level. From this perspective, we view the nation as the organization and focus on several units within it: 1) the Executive Branch of government, including specifically the President, his advisors, the War Department, and the military; 2) the Congress; 3) the public, perhaps as represented by the press; and 4) the Manhattan Project scientists. Examining the relationships among these units, each with its own priorities, perceptions, and prerogatives, provides yet another view of the decision.

We begin with the relationship between the Congress and the Executive Branch. The checks-and-balances system gives Congress authority over appropriations. Yet secrecy required that the vast sums of money needed for the Manhattan Project be obtained without the informed approval of the legislators. The procedures employed can be characterized most charitably as highly irregular. That the Executive Branch was worried about possible postwar repercussions is clear from these statements:

> If we succeed, they won't investigate us at all; if we fail, Congress for a long time won't investigate anything else [General Leslie Groves, Head of Manhattan Project, quoted in Amrine, 1959:28].

> I know F.D.R. would have used it in a minute to prove that he had not wasted two billion dollars [Admiral William Leahy, Chief of Staff for Presidents Roosevelt and Truman, quoted in Schoenberger, 1970:5].

A student of the decision, Walter Schoenberger (1970:299, 105), has written:

> The halls of Congress might very well have echoed and reechoed with angry denunciations of the war's greatest boondoggle. . . . This was probably a consideration in quickly testing and using [the bombs]. Their successful use turned what might have been a political liability into what was a great political asset. What administrative foresight . . . [that] the atomic bombs had been produced just in time to effect the surrender of Japan.

Truman was a man who would have reasonably been sympathetic to arguments that the two billion dollars spent on the project should not prove to be a waste, and, more important, that it should not appear as a waste to Congress and to the people of the United States.[3]

A less forceful argument can be made that the agreement negotiated by Roosevelt with Churchill to jointly develop the bomb was a treaty that should have been approved by the Senate. Whether those still living were influenced to drop the bomb by this potential postwar problem seems unlikely but cannot be ruled out completely. The separation of powers required by the Constitution ran headlong into the secrecy required by the War. Secrecy won. The successful development and use of the bomb absolved the Executive Branch.

An important characteristic of organizations is their propensity to change only incrementally over time. This limited flexibility of organizations goes a long way in explaining the decision to use the bomb.

Statements by some of the major actors give a general sense of the strong momentum that the project assumed.

At no time, from 1941 to 1945, did I ever hear it suggested by the President, or any other responsible member of government, that atomic energy should not be used in the war [Henry L. Stimson, Secretary of War, 1947:98].

We always assumed if they were needed, they would be used. [J. Robert Oppenheimer, Manhattan Project Physicist, quoted in Morton 1957:335].

The decision whether or not to use the atomic bomb to compel the surrender of Japan was never even an issue. There was unanimous, automatic, unquestioned agreement . . . nor did I ever hear the slightest suggestion that we should do otherwise. [Winston Churchill quoted in Schoenberger, 1970:259].

The final decision of where and when to use the bomb was up to me. Let there be no mistake about it. I regarded the bomb as a military weapon and never had any doubt that it should be used [Harry S. Truman quoted in Schoenberger, 1970:25].

As a new President, Truman might have abruptly reversed policy; but his role in the organizational structure made that highly unlikely. He inherited a war and with it a winning strategy. Why increase uncertainty by changing the policies that were working? During the early days of his administration Truman told his Cabinet, the Joint Chiefs of Staff, Prime Minister Churchill, and the U.S. Congress that he planned to carry on the policies of Roosevelt. Although never a man to duck a decision, Truman freely delegated authority and responsibility to his advisors (the same men who had worked with Roosevelt). Roosevelt's and Truman's advisors included military men. In popular opinion, at least, the

---

[3]Truman had won renown in the Senate as Chairman of a Special Committee investigating the National Defense Program. The Truman Committee excelled in uncovering waste in war production.

military mentality is equated with tradition, maintenance of the status quo, and standard operating procedures. To the military mind, the objective of war is victory. That was U.S. policy, and the continuity of policy was not going to be upset by the new President.

Of the particular policies that Truman retained, none was more important than the demand for unconditional surrender. He probably had no choice:

- The attack on Pearl Harbor provoked a response of righteous indignation in the American people. Their hurt pride demanded revenge and retribution.

- Roosevelt capitalized on the emotional response to boost morale and rally the public to the battle cry.

- "Complete victory," "no compromise," "total elimination," "unconditional surrender,"—These phrases laced the speeches of U.S. leaders throughout the war.

- Suggestions for deviation from this policy were met by charges of appeasement in the press and from Congress.

Given the Japanese peace overtures during the summer of 1945, a more flexible stance on the terms of surrender might well have led to a negotiated settlement without the use of the atomic bomb. But a legacy of past policies and pronouncements permitted Truman only limited flexibility.

A type of Newtonian Law of inertia applies to organizations: "An organizational policy which is in effect stays in effect unless acted on by new information." In organizations, information flows only in certain channels. Secrecy requirements surrounding the atomic project inhibited information flow even more than normal. No information flowed outward to the public, press, or Congress. Outside opposition to the use of the bomb simply could not develop.

On the inside, among all groups involved with the weapon, only the scientists were not unanimous in supporting its use. The Frank Committee consisted of a group of scientists in the Chicago Laboratory that opposed an unannounced nuclear attack on Japan. The Committee prepared a report outlining its objections. This report did not reach Truman and probably was not seen by Stimson. Instead it was channeled to the bottom rung of the organizational hierarchy (Figure 11).

The scientific panel, which received the Frank Committee Report, found it unconvincing and concluded, "We see no acceptable alternative to direct military intervention" (Stimson 1947:101). Thus the only potentially effective counter-opinion to the use of the bomb was drowned in the communication stream.

The communication system also failed to deliver much of the available information regarding Japan's peace feelers. There was some awareness at the highest levels of government that the Japanese had initiated peace-oriented contacts with the Russians, but the intelligence of the OSS, Navy, and Foreign Morale Analysis Division—which emphasized the urgency and importance of the contacts—probably never reached Truman.

A new world political order, Constitutional violations, continuity of policy,

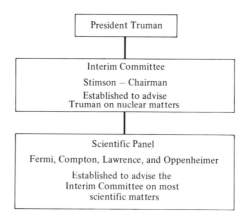

FIGURE 11. Organizational hierarchy.

mass psychology, restricted information flows—these are the factors the organizational perspective brings to the analysis.

Personal perspective. This perspective is most helpful in explaining how some of the results already discussed may have come about.

One of the reasons the information contained in the Frank Committee Report did not reach the President was the tendency of the human mind to filter out inconsistent images. The President was new and an outsider to the 12-year, F.D.R.-oriented executive establishment. He could not afford to challenge policies and fiefdoms so early in his presidency. Intelligence information regarding Japan's peace moves did not reach responsible U.S. government officials, in part because of their own and the system's limited information processing capacities. Stimson's article shows a willingness to focus on only one possible goal (unconditional surrender) rather than scan for alternatives (like negotiated settlement).

There is evidence that on several occasions members of the Joint Chiefs and members of the Interim Committee silenced their own personal disagreements in order to present a unanimous opinion to the President—probable instances of peer group reinforcement of the generally accepted view.

The earlier quotations from Oppenheimer, Churchill, Truman, and Stimson clearly indicate their strongly held belief that using the bomb was the correct decision. Their statements convey a sense that dropping the bomb was *really* right: "There was *unanimous, automatic, unquestioned* agreement" (Schoenberger 1970:259).

The P perspective may also explain Truman's continuation of Roosevelt's policies. Fear of change and of the unknown are present in his rather unguarded remark: "Boys," he said to a group of reporters the day after Roosevelt's death, "if you pray, pray for me now. I don't know whether you fellows ever had a load of hay fall on you, but when they told me yesterday what had happened, I felt like the moon, the stars, and all the planets had fallen on me. I've got the most terribly responsible job a man ever had" (Schoenberger 1970:107).

There is also the need of a new President to appear decisive and bold. Truman had a strong sense of history. We may speculate that a decision not to drop the bomb would later be viewed by historians as a sign of weakness.

Stimson picked the members of the Interim Committee that were to advise the President on matters of nuclear policy. It has been suggested that he picked them specifically because they would tend to agree with his views. Perhaps personal interests were at work.

One might also look to possible personal interests as the cause of the change of opinion by certain scientists to oppose the use of the bomb. Many were Europeans who had helped develop the bomb in a race against Nazi Germany. With Germany's surrender, the nightmare of Hitler vanished, and their motivation was gone. Yet we have seen that they had little real effect on the decision.

Lessons. This illustration shows how the three perspectives join to give a more fully rounded picture and higher degree of realism than the T perspective can provide by itself.

- The T perspective presents the decision as the only rational choice among alternatives because the strategy to use the bomb without warning virtually dominated all other alternatives, that is, this strategy was at least as good as any other on all important choice criteria then enunciated.

- The O perspective provides much of the motivation for allowing the unconditional surrender goal to stand unchallenged. It suited the international political needs of the United States and Great Britain: inhibiting the imperialistic expansion of the Soviet Union. The goal also suited the needs of the Executive Branch—justifying the constitutional breach and the "unauthorized" expenditure of two billion dollars. It was consistent with past government policy; dropping the bomb at this time was compatible with the propaganda of earlier times.

- The P perspective suggests that the key individuals believed deeply in the rightness of unconditional surrender. The new President was in a difficult position, succeeding a tremendously popular President who had in 12 years molded the Executive Branch completely in his own image. Truman had to make his mark quickly by decisiveness and boldness. The one effort in opposition to the use of the bomb was that of a group of scientists (the Frank Committee). It was probably influenced by the refugees among them, whose overriding motivation—fighting Nazi Germany—vanished with Hitler's death and Germany's surrender.

- Given the needs of so many people and so many organizational units, the organizational perspective suggests that they would create a socially constructed reality that made the decision appear rational, even inevitable.

- The personal perspective was used in several instances to show that the other perspectives were not exhaustive in their treatment of the decision; more was still to be learned. However, diminishing returns and the absence of first-hand commentary are reasons the personal perspective was not developed more fully.

- Each perspective was used, by itself, to explain aspects of the decision. Each proved useful and revealed features not captured by the others. This alone shows the value of adopting multiple perspectives. It is, however, only by weaving the strands of the perspectives together that the pattern of the whole cloth is revealed.

4. Further Comments (H. Linstone)

In moving from the first illustration, the *Wampanoag*, to the third, the atomic bomb, we have increasingly swept in higher levels of the federal government. In this section we augment the illustrations with a few vignettes that vividly bring into view the O and P perspectives in national and global contexts.

O perspectives as seen by observers of the Washington scene. In our exposition of the O perspective (Section IV B 2) we drew on Machiavelli. In the following comments on the operation of the federal government we see that such a perspective is as applicable to Washington in 1980 as it was to Florence in 1530.

PETERS

The Editor-in-Chief of the *Washington Monthly,* Charles Peters, gives us insights on "how Washington really works" that are far removed from the civics textbooks but would appear familiar to readers of *The Prince.*
On shadow organizations:

> Clubs are just part of a larger social bond that exists everywhere but is especially prevalent in Washington, where private life is so much an extension of professional life. This bond is the "survival network," and it is the key to understanding how Washington really works.
> Almost everyone in the government, whether he works on Capitol Hill or in the bureaucracy, is primarily concerned with his own survival. He wants to remain in Washington or in what the city symbolizes—some form of public power. Therefore, from the day these people arrive in Washington they are busy building networks of people who will assure their survival in power [Peters, 1981:5].

Peters quotes Nicholas Lehmann *(Washington Post):*

[Washington is] a place where every person you deal with is someone who is either helping you survive now or might conceivably later on [Peters, 1981:7].

On the use of delay:

Often delay will serve the client [company] just as well as outright victory [in fighting regulatory agencies] . . . The client could go on making money doing whatever he was doing wrong for those ten years. . . . But what about the $5 million to $10 million it would have cost the client?. . . . Legal fees are tax deductible [Peters, 1981:94–95].

On protection of turf:

The Firemen First Principle . . . when faced with a budget cut, the bureaucrat . . . chops where it will hurt constituents the most, not the least. The howls of protest will then force the cuts to be restored [Peters, 1981:40].

On power:

In a recent survey [lobbyists] rated the congressional staffs as their number one lobbying target (by contrast, the White House ranked sixth) [Peters, 1981:115].

On isolation:

Except for . . . rare occasions . . . the congressman's isolation is complete. . . . He shakes hands with hundreds of people every day, but he really talks to no one. . . . It is easy for those enveloped in this cocoon [the Capitol and its five satellite office buildings] to imagine that *it* is the real world. . . . This is the ultimate make believe [Peters, 1981:117].

On the irrational actions fostered by SOPs:

No [military] officer who wants to advance himself can afford a bad report.
From the moment the top officials at the Pentagon instituted the body count as the measure of success in Vietnam, commanders began to pressure their subordinates to produce bodies [My Lai was one result] [Peters, 1981:77].

On relations with the press:

The press, instead of exposing the make believe, is part of the show. . . . [the reporters] are too bound up . . . in the ease of being stenographers for government press agents [Peters, 1981:17, 32].

On this subject, Dieter Schwebs, in his review of Peters' work, adds an interesting organizational insider's view (Schwebs, 1981). This dedicated former systems analyst in the Department of Defense (DOD) and General Accounting Office (GAO) notes that the taxpayer pays the salaries of many thousands of employees (1500 in DOD alone, according to GAO) whose job is manipulating the press to make their bosses look good and to sell their programs. One effective tool of the bureaucracy is the judicious use of "sensitive," "confidential," and "secret" stamps. According to Schwebs, classification is readily used to cover up waste, declassification to fuel self-serving hype and help in the fierce competition for public funds. Declassification is even carried out illegally with impunity. For example, a controlled leak may be orchestrated by affixing a "top secret" stamp to a document and then providing it to an eager journalist who is delighted to print such apparently "hot" information.

Peters' publication has recently extended its penetrating O perspective to federal commissions. Besides blue ribbon commissions, the Executive Branch contains nearly 1000 ordinary commissions with 21,000 members. De Parle (1983) perceives ten kinds of advisory commissions and succinctly labels them by function: the lightning rod, the celebrity showcase, the rubber stamp, the bureaucratic endrun, the minority appeaser, the homage to utopia, the sacred cow, the retread, the stillborn, and—an embarrassing staff miscalculation—the runaway commission. In addition to the functions indicated, commissions confer credentials to, and provide contacts for, their members, and cheaply repay political campaign favors.

KISSINGER

On the federal government:

The problem of policymaking in our society confronts the difficulty that revolutionary changes have to be encompassed and dealt with by an increasingly rigid administrative structure [Kissinger, 1968:52].

On the State Department:

The system lends itself to manipulation. A bureau chief who disagrees with the Secretary can exploit it for procrastination. In 1975, the Assistant Secretary in charge of Africa managed to delay my dealing with Angola simply by using the splendid machinery so methodically to "clear" a memorandum I had requested that it took months to reach me. When it arrived, it was diluted of all sharpness, and my own staff bounced it back again and again for greater precision—thereby serving the bureau chief's purposes better than my own. Alternatively, the machinery may permit a strategically placed official's hobbyhorse to gallop through, eliciting an innocent nod from a Secretary unfamiliar with all the code words and implications [Kissinger, 1982:440].

On the Department of Defense, Henry Kissinger provides a fine example of astute political behavior on the part of the Secretary of Defense Melvin Laird:

Laird acted on the assumption that he had a constitutional right to seek to outsmart and outmaneuver anyone with whom his office brought him into contact. I eventually learned that it was safest to begin a battle with Laird by closing off all his bureaucratic or congressional escape routes, provided I could figure them out. Only then would I broach substance. But even with such tactics, I lost as often as I won. John Ehrlichman considered mine a cowardly procedure and decided he would teach me how to deal with Laird. Following the best administrative theory of White House predominance, Ehrlichman, without troubling to touch any bureaucratic or congressional bases, transmitted a direct order to Laird to relinquish some Army-owned land in Hawaii for a national park. Laird treated this clumsy procedure the way a matador handles the lunges of a bull. He accelerated his plan to use the land for two Army recreation hotels. Using his old congressional connections, he put a bill through the Congress that neatly overrode the directive, all the time protesting that he would carry out any White House orders permitted by the Congress. The hotels are still there under Army control; the national park is still a planner's dream. Ehrlichman learned the hard way that there are dimensions of political science not taught at universities and that being right on substance does not always guarantee success in Washington [Kissinger, 1979:32–33].

Ehrlichman's own perspective on Laird shows that such lessons were not lost on him.

Camp David's telephones went through an Army Signal Corps switchboard. . . . The Camp David operators were all Army enlisted men, and their supervisors were Army officers. The only question was: how closely did Mel Laird monitor the President and the rest of us at Camp David when we called someone on his Army telephone system? Did he just keep track of whom we called, or did he also know what was said? [Ehrlichman, 1982:96].

RICKOVER

Admiral Rickover was once asked by a Congressional Committee why so many "unqualified" officials rose to the top of the military structure. His answer:

The only rationale I can come to is that everything in life has been easy for these officials. They have been carried along by family, by wealth, by friends, possibly by political considerations. In a position requiring technical expertise for the first time in their lives, they believe themselves capable of solving these problems by their "personality" methods that have previously gotten them by [Rickover, quoted in Polmar and Allen, 1982].

In other words, the military academy ideal of the presentable, well-rounded, loyal defender of the service tradition is an important contributor to the O perspective and usually outweighs technical excellence as a criterion for promotion.

BORSTING

A recent thoughtful discussion of "Decision-Making at the Top" by Assistant Secretary of Defense (Comptroller) Jack R. Borsting (1982) also reveals the significance of perspectives other than the technical one. He notes that top level Department of Defense decision making is

- nonalgorithmic, creative, and free form (O, P);

- very data oriented (T);

- basically open loop, tending to give rudder directions but not looking at the wake (O);

- very short-term oriented (O, P);

- teamwork oriented (O);

- very personal—the judgment of one's close advisors is extremely important (P);

- creating a need to budget time for important decisions (O);

- demonstrating that external forces—Congress, the White House—are often more important than a rational systems analysis (O);

- subject to conflicting goals, for example, between public and private sectors (O);

- dealing with "messes" rather than well-structured problems; they must be treated holistically (T, O, P).

What makes this picture especially interesting is that it is drawn by a past-president of the Operations Research Society of America!

Due to its size and nature, the defense establishment offers a particularly rich lode for both O and P perspectives. Other excellent insights can be found in Art's the *TFX Decision* (1968) and Lewin's *Report From Iron Mountain* (1969).

ADDENDUM

There is, of course, nothing unique about the Washington scene. Vary Coates gives us an example of the importance of the O perspective from Bonn: the subject is technology assessment. The West German Bundestag seriously considered following the U.S. Congress' lead in establishing an Office of Technology Assessment. The proposal failed; it was repeatedly advanced by the opposition and fought by the party in control, which saw the concept as "an instrument of power in the hands of the opposition" (Coates and Fabian, 1981). The parliamentary majority clearly had an active interest in denying access to potential ammunition to the opposition.

Rachel Elboim-Dror (1982:183) brings us an O perspective from Jerusalem of Israel's parliament, the Knesset:

The recurring cycles of reforms that are never implemented resemble a ritual in their fixed repetitive pattern and expressive symbolic manifestations.

Like Sisyphus, the legendary king of Corinth, the members of the legislature are condemned to try over and over to do the impossible. But the process actually has significant functions—to divert and dilute conflicts, to release frustrations, and to create illusions of change. Each reform cycle has three stages: 1) rising feelings of inadequacy; 2) crystallization of these feelings into plans and proposals for change, accompanied by the rhetoric of reform; and 3) analysis, discussion, and dilution of the proposals. The fire of reform dies, and the difficulties of implementation mount until the proposals receive an honorable burial.

Multiple perspectives become critically important in international affairs. American perceptions of U.S.–Soviet relations differ drastically from Soviet government perceptions of these relations. The Russians do not exhibit a mirror image of American views of the "threat." Even today they cannot shake the legacy of their history: the invasions by Napoleon and Hitler have left their mark in an overriding concern with defensive capability. The United States has no such history. The Russians' awe of American science and technology translates for most Russians into:

> . . . the belief that if the U.S. wants to, it can change the military balance in its favor almost overnight—that it can pull some weapon-rabbit out of its technological hat at any moment and leave the Soviet Union far behind in the arms race [International Communications Agency, quoted in Marder, 1981:A14].

Thus understanding of the Soviet perspective on the "threat" must be at the core of any American preparation for arms limitation negotiations.

The State Department's view of Israel's concerns about Jerusalem cannot possibly capture the depth of Jewish attitudes.[4] Even closer to home, perspectives of the current struggle in El Salvador differ widely: the U.S. government sees the threat of Cuba–style, Soviet-encouraged communism spreading like a cancer in the Western hemisphere; intellectual idealists see the liberation of Central America from U.S.–supported right-wing dictatorships; the Salvadoran poor see a struggle between two power-hungry elites, intoxicated by their ability to terrorize them.

---

[4]Reflected in their familiar words of salutation, exchanged for nearly 2000 years—"next year in Jerusalem"—and in the powerful words of the 137th Psalm:

If I forget thee, O Jerusalem,
Let my right hand forget her cunning.
Let my tongue cleave to the roof of my mouth,
If I remember thee not;
If I set not Jerusalem
Above my chiefest joy.

P Perspectives. As already noted, the P perspectives are the most elusive and difficult to put on a solid footing. Yet, they can be a source of the most valuable insights. We consider four striking examples of national importance.

PERLMUTTER

Perlmutter (1980:21) is keenly conscious of the importance of the individual in decision making on national policy:

> Brzezinski's motivation for championing Iraq at first would appear to be puzzling, since hegemony over the Persian Gulf by a Soviet military client would hardly appear to help American interests.
>
> Brzezinski's stance, however, could have as much to do with professional jealousy as it would with the formulation of policy. It was Brzezinski's predecessor, Henry Kissinger, after all, who helped turn Egypt from a Soviet client into at least a nominal American ally. It would appear that Iraq is designated to be Brzezinski's Egypt.

Admittedly this is conjecture, but it offers a clue for further probing. The O and P perspectives do not disdain hunches the way the T perspective usually does.

DUGGER (1982)

Texas loomed large in Lyndon Johnson's psyche. Growing up the son of a tenant farmer in West Texas, pledging allegiance to the Lone Star flag in school, mythologizing the cowboy culture, and romanticizing his Texas ancestors left an indelible imprint on the man. And the man left an indelible imprint on U.S. policy. His words at a National Security Council meeting, "Hell, Vietnam is just like the Alamo," reflect this connection.

FALLOWS

Jimmy Carter appears to have had strong T and P perspectives but a comparatively weak O component. This mixture helps to explain both his failures and his successes. James Fallows points to "the lasting enigma of the Carter administration":

> . . . the President's indifference to the machinery of government . . . he seemed to find it distasteful, compared to the pure and lonely search for "rational" answers [Fallows, 1982:10].

A weak O perspective as this is unfortunate for situations where effectiveness depends on working through organizations, for example, the tactical ability to prevail in dealing with governmental bureaucracies. Conversely, Carter's strength in T and P seems to be instrumental in his successes:

> During the period of his public life in which he was politically most successful—
> the first six months of 1976, when he came from nowhere to win the Democratic
> nomination—Carter's appeal depended on his personality, rather than on any spe-
> cific policy he endorsed [Fallows, 1982:3].

And in the setting of the Mideast peace talks with Begin and Sadat:

> [Carter] was probably unexcelled . . . [in] his ability to understand the details of
> a problem and see his way to a rational solution. The clearest evidence is his
> success at Camp David [Fallows, 1982:8].

For an equally insightful explanation of the Reagan enigma, see Cannon
(1982).[5]

KELLEN

In many countries inflation is recognized as a top-priority national problem.
The economists' T perspective involving economic theory is given much attention. The perspective provided by Kellen is rare but possibly also significant.
He asks "Is Inflation Fun?" and answers in the affirmative for those not on fixed
incomes.

> The true secret of inflation is that it is pleasure at a price. . . . Inflation gives
> people a multitude of pleasures that were unknown to them in the past dec-
> ades. . . . Spending money is fun. And if there not only is no reason not to spend
> it, but every reason to get rid of it, it is even more fun, because the nagging feeling
> of guilt has been eliminated. . . . You not only spend more, you also earn more,
> or so it seems. The garbage man's son does not have to become a lawyer or doctor
> to make 10 times as much as his father did . . . [and finally there is] the unbridled
> materialism in our society. . . .
> One thing is certain. Economists will never solve inflation. . . . Poring over
> figures instead of looking into the human soul . . . they may be the last people to
> know what it is [Kellen, 1980:1–4].

A young urban real estate speculator with an annual income of more than
$100,000 confessed:

> Without inflation, I would have to be about 20 times smarter at my business and
> would have to work a lot harder to earn money instead of just making it [Time
> Jan. 19, 1981:67].

---

[5]In Carter's successor, the P perspective dominates both T and O perspectives. Reagan is seen as molded in
his youth by the prairie idealism of Dixon, Illinois—the self-reliance and the helpful neighbor—as well as the
simplistic high school history book view of America and the world prior to the Great Depression. And this image
was probably reinforced by the similarly simplistic pattern of heroes in the Hollywood films of Frank Capra and
John Wayne.

Kellen calls inflation a form of instant overindulgence—a collective vice. On this basis, his prognosis is devastating. Like individual vices—gambling, drugs, smoking—it offers both pleasure and harm. It matters little to the addict that his behavior is ultimately self-destructive. He discounts the future damage for the present ecstasy. Experience has shown that such a vice is resistant to almost any measure, as it has deep psychological roots. Hence Kellen insists that it may not yield to purely economic cures, although

> . . . it may have started as a set of adverse economic developments, just as a person may have started drinking because he was fired. But after several years of drinking, his alcoholism—not his having been fired—will be his problem. And so it is with inflation. The things that precipitated it are not the things that now feed it [Kellen, 1980:5].

National land management. The National Forest Management Act (NFMA) of 1976 calls for the U.S. Forest Service to develop comprehensive land management plans for each administrative unit of the national forest system. Extensive regulations have been promulgated to define and apply planning principles in the best T-perspective manner. Goals and sequential planning steps are specified

> . . . that resemble the rational decision-making approach of the professional planner. . . . The most common criticism is that the approach assumes conditions for decision-making that simply do not exist. . . . It [also] imposes crippling data demands and . . . becomes obsessed with techniques. . . . Land management planning allocates benefits to some and imposes costs on others, which makes the process inherently political. . . . [It] cannot be treated mainly as a technical process. . . . The tie between the political and technical aspects of planning must be strengthened [Cortner and Richards, 1983:79].

These observations constitute a clear call for the introduction of multiple perspectives into the Forest Service planning process. The technical skills of the professional resource manager are not sufficient and must be complemented by others.

Cortner and Richards (1983) point out that the Forest Service holds hearings to obtain diverse public opinions before selecting a preferred alternative.[6] However, once the decision is made by the Forest Service, the consequence is frequently a refusal by vested interest groups to accept that decision. The authors suggest that a broker is needed to negotiate a settlement among the interest groups by forcing mutual trade-offs, that is, political bargaining.

---

[6]We note here one of Sullivan's "Two Dozen Eternal Truths" in his "Public Interest Laundry List for Technology Assessment" (1976): "While agency officials are required to hold hearings for citizens, they are not required to listen."

An example is the concept of sustained yield, even-flow timber harvest mandated by NFMA.[7] It is seen by some as an obstruction to sound forest management, by others as protection against exploitive timber harvesting.

The Forest Service used a linear programming model (FORPLAN) for allocating and scheduling land use in its National Forests. The model requires the definition of production functions for different kinds of land. A soil resource inventory provided the basis for classifying land in accordance with the criterion that, if harvested, an area be capable of regeneration of seedlings within five years. The model capacity also requires a trade-off between geographic detail and the number of ways a given piece of ground may be managed. The Mt. Hood National Forest group decided in favor of the geographic detail. The planning effort was begun in 1979. The timber industry's concern with the classification procedure surfaced in 1980. Some soil classified by the Service as unsuitable (for example, above 4500-foot elevation or rocky) was considered by the industry to be quite suitable.

> We went out into the field and we started checking these things, and 90% of the calls [of unsuitability] we couldn't agree with.
>
> [Industry representative]

And some bitterness on the part of the civil servants was evident:

> We had many meetings with industry. . . . We talked about yield tables, restrictions, suitable land and acres. We took these people to the field . . . it was an open door policy. We supplied them with results of our [computer] runs—we even microfilmed them for them. . . . I think that is where we made a mistake because later on this information was used against us by people who didn't like the numbers.
>
> [a Forest Service technical expert]

> Industry has a better pipeline to their representatives in Washington than we do between our Regional Office and the Washington Office.
>
> [another Forest Service technical expert]

The controversy grew and came to a head with the publication of the preliminary findings in a March 1982 Service Newsletter. The projected annual harvest for the Service's chosen alternative was calculated by the model to be 100 million board feet below the current harvest. Opposition to the numbers was not confined solely to the timber industry; certain groups within the Service also echoed concerns.

The Regional Forester has now halted the planning process, but the controversy continues. The planning team leader concedes that early use of multiple perspectives could have avoided much of the difficulty. Both O and P perspectives

---

[7]We would like to acknowledge the assistance of David Nordengren in developing this example.

are essential to assess institutional barriers and opportunities, to know the principal actors and their motivations.

> Decision makers and planners must become comfortable working with the less rational, subjective nuances of planning. . . . While political feasibility may not be listed explicitly as a decision criterion in the regulations, it is an essential one, requiring a liberal use of seat-of-the-pants professional judgment [Courtner and Richards, 1983:81].

National planning, global solutions, and the futurists. Two recent administrations have initiated modest efforts to address national goals and thus facilitate long-range planning. In each case, T-oriented analysts plunged in with determination and went through the paces of producing a report. For President Nixon, the National Goals Research Staff, under Leonard Garment, wrote *Toward Balanced Growth: Quantity with Quality*; for President Carter, the Council on Environmental Quality and Department of State, under Gerald O. Barney, developed *The Global 2000 Report to the President.*

These massive undertakings had no visible impact whatsoever, providing merely textbook illustrations of ritualistic planning. The O perspective of the federal establishment obviously prevailed.

On the global stage, the saga of T-perspective futurists during 1970s seems reminiscent of the adventures of the brave, immortal Knight of La Mancha. Their computer models derive limits to growth and specify global collapses (Forrester, 1971; Meadows et al., 1972); their systems designs create global organizations (Laszlo); and their trend extrapolations show a per capita gross world product of $20,000 in 2176 (Kahn). It seldom seems to occur to them that their T perspective creates highly artificial models.

The pessimists underestimate human genius and creativity, while the optimists underestimate human greed and aggressiveness. An important source of error of the global thinkers evidently lies in their neglect of O and P perspectives. As an example consider the debate on world food supplies. The optimists argue that enough food can be grown to provide adequate nourishment to a global population more than twice that of today. The statement is true but unrealistic. Food distribution is not only hampered by lack of money, but by organizations with parochial priorities and by corrupt individuals. Maldistribution is profitable and rational from the perspective of many actors. The struggle between the haves and have-nots cannot be "solved" by equitable resource allocation systems optimized by mathematical models.

On the other hand, the pessimists' obliviousness to the human willingness to defy odds, to indomitable faith and hope, as well as to human complexity and adaptability, is also in evidence. Doomsday forecasts based on trend extrapolation have proven notoriously unreliable for the 1970s. Paul Ehrlich's 1968 statement that "the battle to feed all of humanity is over" and the Paddocks' 1967 call for triage in the case of Egypt and India ("can't be saved") should raise more questions of an ethical nature than pilpulistic arguments about the data base (Simon 1980). Equally significant is the fact that each cultural group sees the world very differently, and the concept of any global computer model as a basis for global decisions is, *a priori,* preposterous (Botez and Celac, 1981).

Thompson (1976; 1978) also sees a fatal flaw in the reliance of futurists on the T perspective. He insists that throughout history new cultures have begun with a strong P focus (animism, spiritualism, theocracy, myth). The ancient Egyptians labeled this first stage in a cultural development of the "Age of Gods." Their subsequent stages were the "Ages of Heroes," "of Men," and "of Chaos." (Today's equivalents are the several phases associated with a logistic or Pearl growth curve.) As one stage replaces another, the P perspective loses strength, and the O and T perspectives gain strength. This shift is reflected in growing concern with bureaucratization and methodology. Thompson specifically cites systems analysis as representative of the techniques of the mature stages of the culture and stresses that a new culture (or shift to a new logistic curve) can never be captured with a T-oriented systems analysis. Its tools (for example, computer modeling, trend extrapolation) are inextricably tied to the present and the recent past. They can only see tomorrow with today's eyes, and they lack the creative mode of thought, which is characteristically associated with the individual (see Table 8). A shift to a new culture requires a new perspective with new paradigms, just as a scientific revolution requires new axioms. And new paradigms do not readily issue from the exercise of tools appropriate to today's T perspective.

The one-sided emphasis on the T perspective may have something to do with the chasm between the futurists and the influential figures on today's world stage.

B. LOCAL CRISIS: THE MT. ST. HELENS ERUPTION
(B. CLARY)

Mt. St. Helens, one of the dormant Cascades Range volcanoes in the state of Washington, showed signs of life in March 1980 and became fully active with a dramatic explosion on May 18 of that year. The top of the mountain was blown off, reducing its height from 9700 feet to 8300 feet. The amount of energy released has been calculated as being equivalent to 500 times that of the atomic bomb dropped on Hiroshima. More than 44,000 acres of fir trees were leveled; stream flooding as well as mud flows caused extensive damage; and more than 60 persons were reported dead or missing. Sporadic activity continues at intervals.

Long-term watershed management has become a major concern. Communities in Southwest Washington, downstream from the volcano, face a constant flood hazard because of the unstable sediment produced by earlier activity, as well as the possibility of new eruptions.

1. T Perspective

Historically, the U.S. Army Corps of Engineers has responded to flood control problems with structural solutions, that is, building dams and levees or dredging river channels. In view of the suddenness and magnitude of the May 18 eruption, structural measures by a military agency were the only feasible short-term response. Emergency funds were authorized by the President, and the Corps began a construction and dredging program southwest of the mountain. Some nonstructural solutions, such as property acquisition, were examined and rejected on cost–benefit grounds.

The following year (1981), the situation changed. The crisis mentality faded, federal cutbacks reduced the Corps' allocation of funds for this operation, and a new Federal Emergency Management Agency (FEMA) report on hazard mitigation focused on nonstructural measures outside of large urban areas.

At this stage, the T perspective no longer suffices—there are more organizations and actors. Problems of politics, communication, and coordination come to the fore. It should be noted that White (1969) recognized the emergence of these problems in case of multiple mitigation approaches to flood control over a decade ago.

2. O Perspective

The first issue is historic: which federal agency is the lead agency—the Corps, the U.S. Forest Service, the U.S. Geological Survey (USGS), or FEMA? Interestingly, the O perspective affected technical as well as organizational questions. For example, the Corps and USGS continually disagreed on sediment estimates. Acceptance by the Corps of the USGS data would create a dilemma in justifying its decision to build debris dams on the Toutle River (the stream most affected by the eruption).

The National Flood Insurance Program (NFIP) has been in effect since 1968. A community which wishes to participate in NFIP is required to have a floodplain ordinance. Thus the communities west of Mt. St. Helens were spurred to develop at least minimal regulations. From their O perspective, the possible eruption of a long dormant volcano was certainly no stimulus for contingency action that would tie up potential industrial land. The societal discount rate eliminated any consideration of tectonic history and geologists' forecasts in 1975 of a major eruption before the end of the century (Crandall et al., 1975).

Even after the May 18 eruption, organizational resistance to change was widespread. The "crisis of the moment," which altered the five-century old topography drastically, forced little change in local floodplain ordinances. Cowlitz County was the one county that shifted its attitude significantly on land use control. Subjected to the most severe damage in the eruption, it alone placed a moratorium on building. Its officials exerted pressure to change existing federal policy. They noted that 1) 16 federal agencies had been given funds to assist the recovery, and 2) only one or two had fully spent their appropriations. The conclusion was obvious:

> If the money has been appropriated and we have legitimate needs to be addressed, then we should be able to pool our resources and direct them to these problems [Board of County Commissioners, 1980].

The County specifically wanted permission to acquire property in the floodplains of the Toutle and Cowlitz Rivers, rather than rebuild damaged structures. It would thus be able to exercise better control over development. Not surprisingly, this request was turned down; it ran counter to federal SOPs.

The societal discount rate also affected posteruption planning. A new flood warning and emergency preparedness program was considered—and forgotten when the winter of 1980–1981 produced below-normal rainfall and little flooding. Only the scientists with their T perspective maintained their concern over the possibility of another disastrous flood.

A local planner put it very plainly:

> Emergency planning is seasonal. It's ridiculous to emphasize flood prevention during the summer months. But on December 1 people start to listen. If you use the right timing, you can sell them on anything.

The familiar seasonal pattern of flood danger seemed to be the operative concern despite the nonseasonal nature of flooding caused by volcanic eruptions.

The Mt. St. Helens area clearly constitutes a long-term management problem: the geologic data prescribe continual dredging of the affected rivers. There are at least two obstacles: 1) the ideology of the Reagan administration, which militates against long-range funding of such local projects, and 2) the inappropriateness of current federal legislation, that is, the inability of the Corps to purchase land for dredge spoils. We see organizational inertia, problem avoidance, fractionization, and step-by-step problem solving in response to immediate crises. The county is weak in any confrontation with the federal government, and inequities result. In this case, we note that Mt. St. Helens lies within federally owned land, and the problems it has created are regional. Yet the burden of flood management responsibility is on local shoulders. Congress could, of course, declare the volcano a "continuing disaster" as a means to maintain the emergency funding flow, but there is no precedent. Furthermore, the affected parties do not have a well-established, effective lobby in Washington, D.C. Hence this alternative remains unlikely.

3. Conclusion

The eruption acted as a powerful stimulant to the scientists—Mt. St. Helens suddenly became a living laboratory, a rich lode for research papers, and a justification for conferences. In these activities, the T perspective prevailed. However, effective mitigation demanded an O perspective. The frustrations in getting action can be traced to traditional organizational characteristics that inhibit action. One positive development was FEMA's formation of an interagency Hazard Mitigation Team. The Team cut across organizational boundaries and was problem focused. Representatives from 11 federal agencies examined co-ordination, funding arrangements, and action implementation. More recently, Cowlitz County has formed an even more diverse group involving federal, state, and local officials, as well as scientists and private citizens, to aid in developing a floodplain management plan. Thus multiple perspectives are swept into the planning process.

The following quotes simulate the spectrum of views:

- T perspective
    - on technical aspects: "levee building is not a long-term cost-effective strategy";
    - on organizational aspects: "all we need is money and we can solve the flooding problem";
    - on personal aspects: "I don't know why they want to rebuild in the floodplain given the risk."
- O perspective
    - on technical aspects: "why should the county restrict building just because there was a mudflow 500 years ago?";
    - on organizational aspects: "even a massive eruption has not resulted in much change in floodplain ordinances";
    - on personal aspects: "doesn't Reagan understand that we have a critical problem?"
- P perspective
    - on technical aspects: "well, it didn't flood the first year after the eruption";
    - on organizational aspects: "the county can't keep me from building; it's my land";
    - on personal aspects: "I just can't move back there after what I've been through."

Exploration of the cross-impacts among these perspectives is a formidable task, as suggested by the myriad of possible relationships (Section II C). The use of digraphs for this purpose will be discussed in Section XI E 1.

There are 16 major volcanoes in the Cascades, and two have erupted in the past 70 years. The prevalence of volcanoes near populated areas throughout the world, as well as the richness of insights drawn from the different perspectives, suggests that this approach can be quite useful in the formulation of disaster policy.

C. EDUCATION: A NURSING SCHOOL IN TRANSITION[5]
(S.J. WILL)

1. Background

In the United States, the profession of nursing has a long history of struggling to attain recognition and status for its purpose and functions within the health care field. Traditionally, a profession comprised primarily of women, it serves its public under the shadow and overwhelming dominance of the largely male medical profession. In addition, until recently, most nurses were educated in a system also under the domination of a primarily male profession, that of the hospital administrator. Since the early 1900s, schools of nursing have been located in hospitals that "traded" education of women in the nursing arts for their own manpower needs. Through the end of World War II, hospitals were staffed almost exclusively with nursing students; practitioners were essentially independent and frequently unemployed and worked mainly in private practice for wealthy clients who could afford such a luxury. After World War II, however, increasing recognition of society's physical and emotional needs, coupled with a technological boom in terms of medical treatment techniques and diagnostic capabilities, made it impossible for hospitals, which were rapidly expanding, to continue to staff only with student populations. At about the same time, the government intervened in response to the overwhelming cry for health care providers and legislated support for the education of nurses and physicians, at all levels and in all specialties. The Nurse and Physician Training Acts were first implemented in 1946, and so the demand for increasing numbers of health care workers was to be satisfied.

Education of nurses, however, continued to be centered in hospitals and under the direction of hospital administrators and physicians, whereas physicians gradually moved from the apprenticeship model of education into the realms of the higher education environment. These changes, together with the concurrent boom in medical technology, resulted in significant advances for physicians in both power and status. These societywide gains, aided by the public's nearly blind faith in everything technological, assisted the physician in building a mythology about medicine that was beneficial in terms of both power and money.

By contrast, nursing education remained predominantly under the apprenticeship model until Mildred Montag, in the early 1950s, proposed a plan for the education of nurses in two years' time. Such education was designed to focus on the particular education and training needs of hospital-based nurses (a direct response to the shortage of hospital nurses at that time) and was to take place in an academic setting, the community college. Although touted as a step forward in terms of achieving professional status, this movement has, in fact, had serious

---

[5]Certain minor changes and deletions have been made to assure individual anonymity.

negative consequences for the field of nursing. In effect, one form of vocational education was substituted for another, providing an educational experience of even less time and lower quality (at least in some instances) than the derided hospital-based "diploma" programs. In terms of rapidly increasing the numbers of registered nurses available for the work force, perhaps the objective was met. However, in terms of increasing the profession's status and influence in the world of health care, the objectives were clearly not met by this change in educational form. In fact, these nurses were, and are today, not prepared to compete on the same level as physicians in a society in which educational credentials are so important.

Recognition of the adverse impact of nursing's currently accepted credentialing methods on the potential for nursing to advance as a profession prompted several actions in recent years designed to remedy the situation, at least in part. In 1975, the American Nurses Association voted to 1) no longer accept hospital-based diploma programs as legitimate educational settings for nurses, and 2) by 1985, to have designed and implemented the appropriate legal and educational mechanisms for accepting *only* graduates of baccalaureate nursing programs as "professional" nurses. As a result of these changes, diploma programs today have been nearly phased out. However, the proportionate number of baccalaureate programs and, hence, baccalaureate-prepared graduates, shrinks in proportion to the still-growing percentage of associate degree programs and graduates.

Concomitant with the conceptual shift in the profession from a vocational emphasis to an academic approach to nursing education, has been a shift in focus from the technical aspects of nursing practice to its conceptual components. An influential core of currently recognized leaders in the field for several years has had as its agenda the development of the "academic" base of nursing in an effort to legitimize the profession as a credible and scientifically certifiable academic discipline. To this end, growing emphasis has been placed on "nursing theory development," and a considerable amount of literature in the past five years has concerned itself with this aspect of the development of the profession. Crucial to such an effort in theory development is a body of recognizable and scientifically sound nursing research. Consequently, the bywords in nursing most recently, and growing in impetus for the past eight to ten years, have been *theory* and *research*. This emphasis is particularly noticeable in schools of nursing located in institutions of higher learning, and even more so in programs that offer graduate programs in nursing, at either or both the master's or doctoral levels.

2. The Problem

The current climate at the eastern university's School of Nursing with which this case study is concerned reflects this struggle toward recognition of nursing as a legitimate member of the so-called scientific disciplines. The current Dean of the programs, which include both baccalaureate and master's programs as well as plans for a doctoral program, *is* one of those nationally recognized nursing leaders striving to raise the status and power levels of nursing as a profession within the health care field. Changes for both students and faculty, particularly in the past two years, reflect this movement toward achievement of scientific credibility. Changes for the students center around course content requirements, entrance requirements and standards, research requirements and standards, and graduation requirements and standards. Changes for the faculty center around acceptable educational credentials at the varying academic ranks, faculty work load (particularly those activities recognized as "important" as opposed to those that are necessary but not important), promotion and tenure requirements, faculty organization (especially the articulation between teaching faculty and administration), and curriculum decisions (especially the long-term plans for the school's programs, which direction these should take and which programs have priority in terms of resource allocation).

Over the past two years, the Dean's vision for the programs has become increasingly apparent and changes have been implemented, which reflect movement toward achievement of this vision. Before these changes, the faculty's primary emphasis was on teaching. In addition, this teaching was fairly traditional, that is, highly technical and essentially apprenticeshiplike in nature. Large blocks of time were allocated for "clinical experience," and the faculty and students saw this endeavor, that is, the transmission of knowledge from faculty expert to student novice, as the primary goal of the experiences. Faculty members were rewarded for such behavior by the system as well. For example, tenure came to those who demonstrated loyalty to the school or who had demonstrated their devotion to students. Other activities, such as publishing and research, were welcomed but were certainly not demanded. Promotion and tenure standards for faculty did not exist in writing and were not so explicit that a certain set of activities or a specific academic credential was required for promotion or tenure. In the past several years, nearly all of this has shifted—if not totally in practice, then almost totally in concept. The emphasis in teaching is on "efficiency" and "teaching to objectives." No longer is clinical time devoted to "just being on the unit" taking care of patients. In addition, the faculty members are faced with new, stringent, and abruptly implemented promotion and tenure requirements, which demand first priority on research and scholarly activity, as evidenced primarily in publications.

The problem for the School of Nursing faculty and the school as an organization is one of weathering the transition. This evolutionary process can be examined retrospectively, and its directions understood. In addition, the consequences for both the faculty and the organization as entities can be pondered, based on the evolution of organizational goals, emergent organizational patterns, and current organizational norms and values. Finally, the consequences for individuals presently employed in the system, and the impact of these changes on individual persons, can be assessed. The following section will attempt to characterize this evolutionary process from the T, O, and P perspectives. At the conclusion, an effort will be made to synthesize the insights revealed by each of these perspectives into some gestalt, and to capture, and more fully explore, some of the underlying reasons for perceived difficulties with this shift. Finally, speculative attempts will be made to predict the overriding consequences of this evolution from the vantage point of each of these perspectives and to suggest possible alternative actions that might be useful in ameliorating the negative consequences resulting from this change.

3. The T Perspective

The T perspective is primarily concerned with the achievement of goals, matters of cost and benefit, efficiency and effectiveness, and other basically quantifiable processes. In this context, the goals of the School of Nursing and its faculty can be, and have been, stated in such places as the school of nursing's Ten-Year Plan, a national Nursing Self-Evaluation Report, and an affiliated accrediting agency Self-Evaluation Report. These documents testify to the purposes of the school of nursing, as follows. It is the role of the School of Nursing:

1. to prepare sufficient professional nurses for first-level positions in primary, secondary, and tertiary health care settings for the region;
2. to provide continuing education for those registered nurses living in proximate areas of the region a) who wish to continue their career development by obtaining a baccalaureate degree and/or b) to permit them to maintain their practice at a high level of competency;
3. to prepare nurses for leadership positions in clinical practice, teaching, research, and administration for the region;
4. to conduct nursing research individually and in collaboration with nurses and other health care professionals throughout the region;
5. to practice professional nursing in various health care settings to enhance quality of care as an integral part of the faculty role;
6. to work intensively with nursing services at the associated university hospital and clinics to achieve and maintain high-quality nursing care.

The substantive focus, that is, "what" is being viewed, clearly is organizational change.

From a T perspective, the goals of this transition period include 1) achievement of both the university and School of Nursing missions and goals and 2) achievement of these organizational goals via means or methods that reflect *higher levels of both efficiency and effectiveness*.

This second goal was, and continues to be, extremely relevant, because of the resource difficulties historically experienced at the university and in particular by the School of Nursing. Each unit is expected to contribute toward achievement of the overall missions and goals. However, the School of Nursing receives only a fraction of the overall budget of the university and suffers other shortfalls in areas such as faculty salaries, faculty appointment to nine-month as opposed to 12-month contracts, and inadequate support staff. For example, the School of Dentistry and School of Medicine faculties receive 12-month contracts as part of a standard appointment. School of Nursing faculty members, on the other hand, receive nine-month appointments, unless they are funded by a federal grant or are part of the administrative staff. Likewise, the School of Medicine has an average of one clerical employee for every three faculty members; in the School of Nursing, the ratio is half that, or one to six.

The efficiency and effectiveness issue for the School of Nursing faculty is consequently focused on the interplay between meeting these organizational goals and missions, and the nature and amounts of resources allotted to unit faculty with which to reach these goals. Based on the perceived deficiencies in the School of Nursing, strategies have been employed by the faculty and administrative staff to make it possible for the School of Nursing faculty to contribute toward these missions and goals on a more equitable footing with other university faculties. For example, efforts have been and are currently being made to reduce the work of organizational maintenance to a minimum. This includes streamlining decision making, without alienating or undermining the faculty's rights for input into the decision-making process in areas of concern. One change that is projected to accomplish this goal includes the consolidation of the faculty into fewer departments, decreasing the administrative structure somewhat and making the administrative decision-making group smaller and presumably more efficient. Likewise, Department Chairpersons rewrote their job descriptions to make themselves responsible for nearly all decision making at the departmental level. Such issues as faculty assignments, work loads, budget monitoring, projections of future needs, and so on, which had previously been overseen almost entirely by the Dean, were suddenly the total and final responsibility of the department Chair. The decentralization of decision making had several projected consequences: 1) to make decision making more efficient; 2) to increase the power and autonomy of the departments as independent units within the School of Nursing; 3) to reduce the number of decisions that would have to be made directly by the Dean; and 4) to make this group smaller, hence more cohesive and more loyal, both to one another and to the Dean.

Another strategy employed to achieve increased efficiency and effectiveness included an effort to increase the resources available to the faculty so they could begin to address missions of the school beyond teaching. These changes centered primarily on redistributing work loads, both among departments and among individuals. A formula was developed for "calculating" faculty work loads, and faculty assignments were made based on projected numbers of students per didactic class; the number of credit hours per class; the number of clinical students and credits carried by a faculty member; the number of thesis students carried by a faculty member at any one time; and so on. Other changes included faculty commitment to a standard 12-month contract and simultaneous development of what is known colloquially as the "practice plan." The practice plan is a commitment by the School of Nursing faculty to devote a minimum of 45 (eighthour) days to "hospital work," at the discretion of the hospital unit and personnel to which a faculty member is assigned, per calendar year. Such service assures the faculty member of a full-time, year-round salary; this commitment can be "negotiated" between the faculty and hospital personnel and has resulted in patterns as diverse as a faculty member working as a staff nurse on a hospital unit one day per week, to a full-time commitment (on a shift of the hospital's choice) throughout the summer months. Finally, a recent innovation, also designed to provide faculty members with resources for achieving these missions and goals, is the newly created Office of Research Utilization within the School of Nursing, developed jointly by the School of Nursing and the hospital nursing administration and staff. This office is specifically charged with focusing on the utilization of nursing research and has hired two nurse researchers from a large midwestern university who have just completed a federally funded project that had similar goals. In addition, a full-time psychometrician has also been hired as part of this staff. These individuals are specifically mandated to assist both the nursing faculty and the hospital-based nurses in designing and implementing practice-based research at the university. The implication is clear: all faculty members are expected to conduct research; all research conducted by faculty members will be practice centered; and all research will be conducted within the university's facilities, specifically in the hospital and in conjunction with the hospital nurses and patients.

A final strategy employed to increase the efficiency and effectiveness of the School of Nursing faculty is the proposal to move from a three-year undergraduate program to a two-year, exclusively upper division, program. It was assumed when the proposal was made that, by reducing the number of years students were in the program, the number of faculty members required to teach at the undergraduate level would also be reduced. Unfortunately, after a year of work by the faculty in designing a program that was sound from a curriculum point of view, the ultimate criterion for the change to an exclusively upper division program was efficiency. And the deciding variable was not, as originally proposed, the length of the program, but rather the number of students in the program. With faculty–student ratios for clinical supervision established by law, that is, by the State Board of Nursing, it is, in fact, not possible to reduce the number of faculty hours required *unless* the number of students is reduced.

From the T perspective, then, proposed changes in the School of Nursing structure and the addition of resources were primarily concerned with making the operation of the programs more efficient and more effective, in terms of both offering courses to students and providing avenues and resources for faculty members to meet the missions and goals of the School of Nursing and the university more effectively.

4. The O Perspective

From an organizational point of view, the picture appears somewhat different. Although the same or similar strategies have been employed, the goals and the vision of the organization vary considerably from that proposed in the T perspective. For example, the changes made in the organization over the past five years have evolved from the recognition that nursing, as a profession, is changing, and that, as the recognized leader in baccalaureate and especially graduate education in nursing in the region, the *program needed some overhauling to "catch up" with its university-based school of nursing contemporaries, and then to stay there.* Such qualities were sought in the Dean when the former head of programs retired. Consequently, when the current Dean was hired, it was with the understanding, at some level at least, that part of her mission was to upgrade the quality of nursing education and nursing practice both within the university and within the region.

One goal for this evolution, then, from an O perspective, is the establishment of new standards for nursing and nursing practice. What this has meant in organizational terms is first bringing the School of Nursing into line with what has been required of the university faculty in the Schools of Medicine and Dentistry: earned doctorates for the majority of faculty members and a commitment to research and practice as well as to teaching, for example. Changes, then, were implemented to meet this goal. For example, the promotion and tenure standards were changed to reflect this emphasis on research and scholarly activity. "System" activity, such as serving on committees, community or professional service, and so on, was no longer worth much. In addition, the evolution and implementation of the practice plan was presented as a method for faculty members to begin to "integrate" teaching, practice, and research. Faculty members were charged with assisting hospital staff to increase quality of care, through consultation and practice with the hospital setting. (By the way, the practice plan is limited to an agreement with the university hospital; faculty with other community-based interests or practices do not get "credit" on the practice plan.) A final strategy employed to bring the School of Nursing into line with the other university units was a proposal for offering a Master of Science degree to students, as opposed to the Master of Nursing degree, which has traditionally been offered. The rationale for this change was straightforward: an academic degree is better than a professional degree and is more respected in the scientific community. In addition, all academic majors (that is, specialty tracks) at the graduate level were to redesign their course work to "look" like academic programs. Currently each major requires both a different sequence of course work and a different number of hours for graduation (all of which exceed the standard number of hours required for other academic graduate degrees) and none of which is patterned after more traditional Master of Science programs. Instructions from the Dean included compliance with recognized state standards for masters' level programs, that is, a maximum of 45 hours, including 15 hours in a cognate minor.

A second goal from the organizational perspective is to increase the autonomy and independence of the faculty and to increase faculty responsibility for decision making. Closely aligned with this was a tertiary goal, to increase the homogeneity of the faculty in terms of status, academic rank, and overall responsibilities. Strategies employed to reach these goals included intense recruiting for faculty members with doctorates for all position openings. This has been operational for at least two years, and the number of doctorates and consequently the proportion of higher ranking faculty has increased dramatically during that time. In addition, the reorganization of graduate faculty throughout the departments was also proposed as a method to upgrade all faculty levels and to diffuse the concentration of well-educated "master teachers." Some effort was made to establish the norm of "teaching across levels." This meant that all faculty members would be prepared to teach all levels of students within the constraints of their particular specialties. This was also proposed as a method for decreasing the "elitism" inherent previously in the separation of faculty into undergraduate and graduate levels, and to increase the skill levels of all faculty members in areas such as thesis reading and advising as well as research skills in general. Finally, this strategy was employed to implement the ideal (eventually) of the "community of scholars" approach to faculty organization and administration. Department Chairpersons in recent years have been recruited with the understanding that this "community of scholars" is the faculty's goal, and therefore, the Chair position is not permanent. In most cases, the appointment was made with a time limit stated, with options for renewal and/or renegotiation based on faculty, Chairperson, and administrative input. At this time, projections remain that the School of Nursing faculty will convert within five years to a "rotating Chairperson" concept, depending on the status of faculty credentials and expertise at that time.

A final goal from the organizational perspective is the achievement of a new organizational vision. The impetus and focus for the organization now and in the future is *to establish a reputation at the national level for quality and excellence of the program,* based on the research emphasis of the faculty and on the specific areas of excellence in research the faculty builds. This vision is what spurred departmental reorganization. Previously, efforts had been made to "merge" departments. However, combining faculties and changing the names did not overcome the dynamic obstacles to integrating two traditionally separate specialty groups. Faculty members continued to offer courses and to function as though they and their courses were from separate departments. However, the specific mandate of the reorganization was that faculty define the "conceptual" basis of their nursing practice. The underlying assumption was that 1) faculty members were expected to build their research based on this departmental conceptualization, and 2) the research interests of faculty members within departments would, of course, be consistent with the overriding conceptualization as defined by the department. To avoid mismatches of faculty and departments, faculty members were encouraged to "shop around" and to negotiate for placement in a departmental "home" that was as nearly compatible with their own research interests as possible. They were also encouraged to define these departmental conceptualizations so their research and practice interests were reflected. Hence the graduate major in Nursing Management and Administration, when it merged with the Community Health Department, influenced the department so that it was renamed the Department of Community Health Care Systems. A final strategy employed to assist with the implementation of this goal toward establishing a national reputation for excellence was, and continues to be, an effort to recruit not only doctorate-prepared faculty members, but also "big names" in nursing education and research. This has proved inconsistently successful, because some "big names" have clearly not been compatible with the climate of the school, either as it was or as it is emerging.

5. The P Perspective

The personal perspective is significantly different from the previous two perspectives in that they are or can be goal oriented, but the struggles and fates of individuals within this system and within this problem context are impossible to generalize. What can be said, however, is that the goals from an individual point of view are survival, achievement of power and autonomy, and maintenance of stability or the status quo. Most individuals are not great risk takers and prefer to keep themselves and their environments as they are most comfortable, that is, unchanged. What is relevant from this point of view is 1) the significance of certain key players within the system, in terms of orchestrating this evolutionary process, and 2) the impact such changes have made on the persons required to live within these changes, where the rules are changing both drastically and rapidly.

First, the key players must be considered. The most significant players in this context are clearly the President of the university and the Dean and Department Chairpersons of the School of Nursing. They are significant both because they are by nature powerful individuals, and because of the positions they hold in the hierarchy. The President, by virtue of the power delegated to university presidents in the state, has virtual control over every element of university functioning. Consequently, when he made it clear that his designs for the university were to give it a national reputation, he also made clear that each unit of the university had to "measure up" in terms of academic standards. The School of Nursing was clearly behind in achievements, and changes were mandated that were designed to correct the situation. The Dean's position was as follows: "The President will no longer accept the promotion and tenure guidelines as they exist. Consequently, if you [as a faculty member] approve something less than I have proposed as acceptable, I will be forced to reject it and will consequently review applicants according to my own set of standards." It did seem clear that the faculty would either go along with the new guidelines or would be evaluated by them with, in essence, no other recourse.

However, the Dean is certainly not in disagreement with the President on these matters. Her needs for recognition as a leader in nursing are apparently no less great than the President's need for recognition, and the proposal for "areas of excellence" in nursing research seems not too different from the President's vision of a nationally recognized Biomedical Research Center. It is also increasingly clear, at least from the speed with which some of the implementations have been effected, that the Dean has a rather short time frame for making some of these changes. Already well established as a nationally renowned nurse researcher, she is eager to implement what she perceives as innovations in nursing education. This includes continued work in the area of research utilization, the community of scholars approach to faculty organization and responsibility, and most particularly the implementation of a "clinical" doctoral program in nursing, based on applied research and emergent nursing theory. The faculty is presently struggling with what all that means. Especially difficult is the notion of a "clinical" research degree; most programs in nursing at this time are either clinical (Doctorate in Nursing Science, D.N.Sc.) or research (Ph.D.) degrees. Also seen as an innovation is the merging of faculty and clinical roles, but in a manner different from the "unity" model that has been implemented at some schools. Particularly maligned is the "Unification Model" of Luther Christman at Rush University, which is criticized in many factions of nursing as imitating the medical model for teaching, and therefore suffering many of its faults. At any rate, the Dean is a most powerful actor within the School of Nursing and wields her influence through persuasion, rationality, and occasionally, ultimatum.

Other significant actors in this evolutionary scenario are the individual Department Chairpersons. As a group, they are significant because of their access to information and their role in decision making within the school. At a personal level, however, they are differentially influential, and, in the change process, they have seen their real power in the system either grow or diminish, depending on their relative positions to one another before the most significant changes. Currently, there are four departments: A, B, C, and D. As changes were implemented to build the power and autonomy of the individual departments, resultant changes occurred in the power bases of these individuals. Formerly extremely powerful within the faculty as a whole because of certain strategic duties assigned to him by the Dean and by virtue of the size of his department, the Chair of Department D saw at least some of his influence wane during the past year. This resulted not only from a relative decrease in the size of the department (that is, as other departments gained faculty the proportionate size of Department D decreased), but also from a new configuration of Chairpersons that effectively prevented him from exercising certain previously employed methods of influencing the decision-making process. Department A, on the other hand, through the acquisition of graduate faculty plus the addition of several newly funded positions, doubled its complement of faculty and for the first time in the history of the school numbered close to the mean for all other departments. In addition, a newly acquired Department Chair, highly favored by the Dean, quietly but firmly works behind the scenes to "move the department along."

Probably most significantly lacking in faculty expertise, in one year's time this chairperson has managed to replace, or is in the process of recruiting replacements for, the majority of her least well-prepared faculty. Her influence and power are evidenced in such nontraditional but nevertheless symbolic indicators as the space she has managed to garner for her faculty. The most highly prized space is on the floor that houses the School of Nursing administrative offices. This was previously allocated exclusively to faculty in Department D and to selected graduate faculty members. In the most current transition, Department D has managed to hold onto this prized space, but all others are being moved. Members of Department A will be sharing this coveted space with Department D and, in addition, have preempted both Department B and Department C faculty on the floor directly below. The rest of the faculty, that is, Departments B and C, will be located in the most objectionable space—a building that has been condemned by the state as being unsafe and that is a minimum ten-minute walk from the remaining faculty offices.

This sketch of Department Chairpersons includes two more, Chairpersons for Departments B and C. The Chair of Department B is also a recent arrival and is known as the system's prima donna. She is, however, awesome in her capabilities to work the system for her own and her faculty's ends. Having been at the school less than one academic year, she has managed to institute measures specifically designed to get the entire department "on line" with the goals of the reorganization. Visiting faculty have been employed, and a year-long program has been outlined that will presumably culminate in increased departmental cohesion and certainly a clearer idea of what the department's focus will be. In addition, this Department Chair has proposed several other significant involvements, for example, arranging with a local children's hospital for research space for her faculty's exclusive use. She has plans for generating additional faculty opportunities as well.

Finally, the Chairperson of Department C is a longer term resident of the faculty and has been the Chair of the department for the past four years. A nationwide search for a replacement for this position was conducted this past year, with no success. He states that he has been looking forward to stepping down from the Chairperson position for some time, although he was clearly ambivalent about this when the search began, and says he is eager to put more time into writing and research. Although many faculty members perceive him often as ineffective, it is clear that his ideas are generally sound, and that much of what he says has merit. Unfortunately, he is intimidated by others, and his increased levels of anxiety cause him to become circuitous in his thinking and less than articulate in his presentations. Being articulate is highly prized by nearly all faculty members, therefore the punishments for this lack of clarity are probably more severe than they otherwise would have to be. Nevertheless, the effect is one of continually decreasing power within the department as a result of the Chairperson's ineffectiveness in dealing with his peers on an equitable level. This is exacerbated by the fact that the content area represented by Department C is the least respected by the other specialty areas. For whatever reasons, nurses with specialties in other areas of nursing believe that, for the most part, this content is either nonessential or can be adequately taught by any nurse. This attitude is not unique to this setting; I have observed it as being fairly universal within the nursing community. Nevertheless, this perception by other departments, coupled with the generalized ineffectiveness of this particular individual, creates a situation wherein the department as an entity has consistently lost ground to the other departments in the system. As indicated previously, this is demonstrated in allocation of space, as well as in allocation of secretarial assistance (particularly in who gets the "good" secretaries), and in who is informed about events, opportunities, or other benefits in the system. A striking example of ineffectiveness and lack of knowledge by this Chairperson involved a visiting professor employed by Department B for a faculty development workshop. This visiting professor happened to be one of the most eminent nursing leaders in the specialty area represented by Department C. The Chairperson of Department B employed this individual and scheduled this course work around another national meeting to be held in the city in the near future. Members of Department C, however, were never informed of the fact that this renowned individual would be on campus, and even efforts to obtain information about the national meeting met with slow response.

As may be apparent from this discussion, much of the relevant politicking that occurs around these issues of power and territory is centered at the level of the Department Chair. Because of the nature of the decision making that the chairperson group performs, the informal network, although powerful in other ways, has little influence at the decision-making or resource allocation level. This fact is also what makes the differences among the Department Chairpersons as individuals so significant. What is gained or lost at the Chairperson's level will affect all others in the system, regardless of power or status. Few faculty are immune to these effects.

At the level of particular individuals in the system, the impact of this changing organizational vision and the focus on achievement of rational goals (such as increased efficiency in teaching and the demand for higher levels of output in historically foreign areas of concern, for example, research and publishing), is great. Of particular concern and frustration is the abrupt change in the promotion and tenure standards for persons "caught" somewhere between the old ways and the new. A common complaint of nearly all faculty members (except those most recently hired, with doctorate and publications in hand and well along in the development of their research skills), is, "How can faculty be expected to do everything all the time? It's just not possible to do research, clinical practice, committee work, community service, *and* teach all at the same time! And I'm going to school, too!" Less generally, individuals complain about the specific impact that the changes have had, or which they expect to have, on themselves and their careers. For example, an undergraduate faculty member from Department D says, "Around here you have to have your Ph.D. when you walk in the door—those new faculty they hired aren't as good as many of our (longer employed) faculty—but they have their Ph.D., so they're listened to!" Likewise, a faculty from Department C said, "It's not going to be possible to go to school *and* continue working here any longer. Either you have to be ready to do ongoing research, and be publishing every year, or you just won't make it."

Recent decisions about tenure have also been felt reverberating through the system. Said one person, on hearing about the decision not to tenure a popular and well-respected member of the faculty, "She didn't get tenure? I can't believe it! She's one of our most valuable department members." One of the individuals who was evaluated for tenure this past year and turned down said, "They told me that I didn't qualify for Associate Professor in *any* area. I can hardly believe that. Even worse, they said that in the area of scholarly activity, the reason I didn't qualify was because I couldn't demonstrate a history of five years' worth of scholarly production. That means I might as well not even exercise my option of reapplying next year—I'll have the same history again." More philosophically, some faculty members have been able to speculate on the consequences of this organizational behavior over the longer scene. "It's really too bad to see good faculty forced out of the system. Some people just want to be good clinicians and good teachers—and they don't need their Ph.D.s and they don't want to do research."

Faculty members also react to the extensive emphasis on achievement of the rational goals, especially the emphasis on "research only for research's sake" as a strategy for gaining recognition as a scientific discipline. Says one rather insightful faculty member, "It seems incredible to me that we should try to teach nursing from at least a partly humanistic base, with the system so clearly un-humanistic. It's become so masculine—all legalistic and rulebound. I don't like it at all." Along a similar vein, but expressed differently, a faculty member says of herself, "It's really something to see the effect on morale. These strategies have certainly had a negative effect on me. For the first time in my career I'm ready to make a real commitment—and it's the wrong place. . . . By the time I get my Ph.D., it will be too late."

The rapidity of the changes, as well as their extensiveness, has also precipitated some predictable, but generally not overt, hostility among traditional factions within the school as well as among departments. For example, undergraduate faculty members perceive those who teach exclusively at the graduate level as usually "not doing anything." This is primarily because undergraduate faculty members have spent so great a proportion of their time in the clinical areas supervising students, whereas graduate faculty members are not required to be present during students' practical experiences and consequently focus more on keeping up on the literature and advising students with their research. Said one undergraduate faculty member to a graduate faculty member, "Well, the graduate faculty may have to finally join the real world! Welcome to the world of the masses!" However, what is perceived as a chink in the elitist armor of the graduate faculty by one person is countered by the observation that another undergraduate faculty member makes about the doctorate-prepared group of faculty who are presently designing the Doctoral Program in Nursing for the university: "That group designing the new Doctoral Program is really designing our futures as well—we [the undergraduate program and faculty] will get what's left, you can be sure of that."

A final area of consternation, which is mostly overtly expressed in the system, is the disbanding of the Graduate Studies Department and the dispersal of these faculty members throughout all other departments. Faculty members who resided in this department in some cases had never had another clinical "home" and consequently were quite distressed at being uprooted from their friends and allies. Several significant events occurred as a result of these feelings, such as a two-day "retreat" by the graduate faculty to "review policies." No one admitted to the fact that the group had no power to implement or independently approve policies, so instead they "went through the motions" of viability, in a last attempt at denial of the inevitable. Most significant, much of this body of people frequently expressed their sorrow at the "death" of the department and perhaps of the program as it had been known as well. Representative of these concerns is the following statement by one of the graduate faculty: "The graduate program is just going to hell. Who's going to see to the things that need attention? The departments can't do it. Undergraduate faculty don't know anything about teaching graduate students—they think we don't do anything." Most significant of all is the final gesture made by one of the most staunch supporters of the "old" graduate program: a "wake" held for all graduate studies faculty members. This is likely to be the last remnant of concern so overtly expressed, but as a symbol of the feelings of this vested group of faculty, it is exquisite.

6. Integration and Implications

From the three perspectives emerges a picture of an organization undergoing a significant amount of change. Evolution toward a new organizational vision has combined with the rational goal of increased efficiency, and the effect is one of strident and sometimes incongruent messages that harass system residents to "shape up and keep moving." Like a prisoner chain gang, participants in the line who cannot keep up are mercilessly removed and others, younger and stronger, willingly replace them. Prisoners who once had joined the struggle out of a sense of devotion or humanity are now required either to walk faster to keep the pace or to sorrowfully join the casualties along the way. In either case, the tenor of the march has changed, and those who at one time joyfully sang along now shuffle and grumble and wonder at the change.

Perhaps this gestalt is too negative and too fraught with coercive overtones to be entirely accurate. Nevertheless, many faculty members are caught up in a situation that contains for them many conflicts between recognition of the "changing beat" and their not-so-ambitious goals in life. In addition, this recognition also contains in it appreciation of the irony of these conflicts, that is, that any individual who has devoted many years to developing excellence in the teaching of clinical skills, and who finds ultimate satisfaction in assisting young men and women to learn the science and art of nursing intervention, should be confronted with the demand to reassign priorities and put what has always been first, last. The conceptual rationale for linking practice and research to excellence in teaching is not lost; it simply is not understood, because the humanistic components of nursing practice cannot be understood from this rational frame. Likewise, the realities of dwindling resources and the need to become more efficient in the teaching of nursing practice is not lost to the prisoners of the system; these concerns are simply not understood in light of the apparent surfeit of resources available for beginning and bolstering a doctoral program, at the very time when the cry is to tighten one's belt.

Consequently, the view that emerges from the combination of these three perspectives is a kaleidoscope of images that frequently overlap and in which the themes are consistent, but which, in several constituent areas, sharply contrast. The goals of rationality are in direct conflict with the goals of the organization, particularly in the demands for efficiency, and the concomitant cry for larger vision. The goals of larger vision likewise fly directly in the face of the individuals in the system who were content with things the way they were. Even more painful is the discrepancy between the pace of these changes within the organization and the pace by which individuals will be able to change to maintain a place within the organization. It is increasingly clear, also, that many of those who desire to keep up, and who *are* willing to march to this new leader's drumbeat, will not be able to realize the necessary changes quickly enough and so will become unwilling casualties of the change.

So what does the future hold for the organization and its residents, from the perspective of each viewpoint? And what difference does this knowledge make after all?

With the climate and culture of the organization in rapid transition, it is likely that the School of Nursing will suffer and exhibit many of the effects that all cultures in transition exhibit. For example, when societal cultures change, or in recent times become "Westernized," individuals within the culture become depressed and disillusioned and the rise of traditional psychiatric illnesses is dramatic, particularly in psychosis, violence, and alcoholism. In addition, rites and rituals that formerly were significant from a cultural point of view are no longer enacted, or the society takes on some combination of old rites and new tradition. Former patterns of creativity and artistry are kept alive by only a handful of those who before were engaged in such activity. In Western takeovers, the original basis for contribution to the society is no longer viable, and frequently a large percentage of the population of the culture becomes the recipient of the "welfare state," that is, much of the population goes on welfare or social security, trading money for their former base of livelihood.

In an analogous way, the School of Nursing is exhibiting many of these symptoms. For example, since the Dean and the President have been in office at the university, they have made a concerted effort to develop allegiance to "new traditions." This includes formal awards ceremonies for students, whereas there were none previously; the eradication of what was known as "pinning" ceremonies for nursing students; and a new face for an old tradition, that is the Wassail, held around the Christmas holidays, for friends and faculty of the School of Nursing, for many years. Whereas this tradition previously had the overtones of a "high tea," it is now the rather elaborate, but no longer mandatory, gathering of faculty and School of Nursing supporters and has more political than social overtones.

In addition, faculty members are exhibiting many of the difficulties with morale that are often apparent in the breakdown of a long-standing culture. It is not evident that they are suffering such severe maladies as alcoholism or psychiatric illness. However, the increase in anxiety, and an apparent and overt reliance on hostility, aggression, and anger as the method for interacting with cohorts, is a real and palpable change in the climate during recent months. Likewise, some faculty have reverted to a "welfare state" attitude, that is, they are willing to simply bide their time until they are asked to leave the organization, or are hanging onto old duties in hopes that they "won't make a difference." This is apparent even in some of the faculty members who received tenure before the current rules and requirements became effective, and who are hoping that the posttenure review process takes a long time to become operational.

In the future, it is likely that the efforts of at least some tenured faculty members to retreat will continue, and that more and more frequently recent residents of the system will either stay a shorter length of time or will enter the system only when they are prepared to compete with the more powerful and favored ranks. From a T perspective, the goals of efficiency and effectiveness may not be easily attained. Teaching will become much less a priority, and perhaps the quality of teaching will decline as well. Since quality of teaching is rarely evaluated within the university setting, however, this seems, from a T point of view, a change that is or will be easily absorbed; the effect will be unknown and/or undocumented. In addition, with less emphasis on teaching and continuously increasing amounts of resources allocated to research and scholarly activities, it is also likely that the amount, if not the quality, of research produced by School of Nursing faculty will increase dramatically in the near future. This will undoubtedly contribute to the perception of an increase in the scientific nature of nursing practice and, hence, to the goal of raising the status of nursing as a scientifically grounded profession within the scientific community.

From an O perspective, current trends in the system also support continued advancement toward achieving national status as a quality nursing research center, and recognition as a center of excellence in nursing practice. Again, this will undoubtedly result from the increase in the number of publications by faculty members who are employed at this university, and by the increased visibility of faculty members as they venture out to present papers and deliver verbal accounts of these research efforts. It is more difficult to project the future success of such notions as the idyllic "community of scholars" approach to faculty organization. Said one faculty member visiting from another school, "Everyone will be so frantically scrambling to do research and writing, they won't have time to worry about matters of organization, and who is making which decisions in the school."

Finally, from a P perspective, the future is bright for those already finished with educational agendas, and bleak for those who are either less far along or whose ambitions do not lie in this direction. Persons who enter the system will clearly be required to compete more cleverly and more seriously than has been the mode in this system previously. Political savvy as well as professional competence will be mandatory to attain success in the future.

Given the balance between the negative and positive consequences of present trends in the organization, the question that must be addressed is: How can the negative consequences be ameliorated while maintaining the positive ones of movement in the organization in these present directions? Such a question assumes 1) that the rational goals of efficiency and effectiveness and the organizational goals of increased status and recognition, are worthy and 2) that the negative impact on individuals within the organization should be reduced, from a moral or humanistic point of view. Given these assumptions, it is clear that the negative consequences of these changes result from at least two sources: 1) the rapidity of the changes and 2) the nature of the changes. Strategies that might be employed to reduce the impact of these include the following:

1. slowing down the rate of implementation of such changes, such as the change in promotion and tenure requirements, and the time line for implementing the doctoral program;
2. immediately implementing a two-track system for faculty hire, so that a) faculty who desire to teach exclusively and particularly in the undergraduate clinical area may do so under a clinical teaching label and so not be required to devote large blocks of time to conducting research and b) "academic" faculty can be hired onto the tenure track, with a different set of expectations;
3. allocating resources that are devoted exclusively to faculty development, such as "scholarships" or reduced teaching loads, so those who desire education have the opportunity to obtain it without becoming a casualty of the system;
4. providing intensive workshops on conducting research and writing for publication, so faculty members will understand what has traditionally been a rather mysterious process to most nurses;
5. providing "mentors" or "apprenticeships" in nursing research, to prepare faculty members for conducting high-quality nursing research;

6. increasing resources devoted to teaching assistants, research assistants, and secretarial help, so faculty are free to devote time to activities that require thinking and writing.

Implementation of some of these strategies might indeed reduce the impact of the changes taking place currently within the university and particularly within the School of Nursing.

In sum, the simultaneous use of multiple perspectives in analyzing this transition within the School of Nursing reveals that the goals and the impacts of current trends in the system are indeed different and have differential consequences from any or each of these perspectives taken individually. The gestalt of the perspectives reveals where interventions may be targeted for making the consequences less severe, particularly in this case from the individual point of view. Knowledge from each of these viewpoints is critical to understanding the total impact of current changes and reveals a picture quite different from one that focuses exclusively on any one perspective. Particularly enlightening is the view from the individual perspective and the significant impact of this change in organizational culture on the individuals who reside in it and, indeed, comprise it. Clearly, in this case, had the analysis been limited to only the rational view, the pathos of the impact on persons in the system would never have become evident. Such knowledge may prove instrumental in the development of successful strategies to attain the T-perspective goals.

VI

ILLUSTRATIONS OF MULTIPLE PERSPECTIVES: THE PRIVATE SECTOR

P. COOK, S. HAWKE, and H. LINSTONE

You can't be rational in an irrational world. It isn't rational.

J Orton
What the Butler Saw

The simple have something more than do learned doctors, who often become lost in their search for broad, general laws. The simple have a sense of the individual. . . . The Franciscan teachers considered this problem. The great Bonaventure said that the wise must enhance conceptual clarity with the truth implicit in the actions of the simple.

Umberto Eco
The Name of the Rose

In Chapter V, we viewed the decision process in the public sector in terms of multiple perspectives. Now we turn to the private sector for illustrations, specifically the utility, electronics, and aircraft industries.

The first decision involves construction of a hydroelectric facility, the second a corporate acquisition to develop applications of an advanced electronics component, and the third the manufacture of commercial wide-body trijet aircraft.

A. THE WILLAMETTE FALLS HYDROELECTRIC PROJECT (S. HAWKE)

Portland General Electric's recent proposal to build an additional hydroelectric facility at Willamette Falls in Oregon City involves a decision process that can be illuminated through our multiple perspectives. At the time of this writing (December 1980), the decision to build a new facility in Oregon City had not been made. However, a postscript indicates the subsequent action.

1. Historical Background

Since the early days of pioneer settlement in Oregon's Willamette Valley, power from the natural waterfall on the Willamette River near Oregon City has been used for industrial purposes. Early industries at the Willamette Falls included a flour mill, saw mill, woolen mills, and a dry dock. In later years, these industries were replaced by paper mills.

River traffic to and from the upper Willamette towns bypassed the falls overland until construction of the government's large lock was completed in 1874. In 1889, the Willamette Falls Electric Company tapped the falls for a hydroelectric power plant described as a "dynamo house" with rock-filled wooden bulkheads. This new plant generated 32.5 kilowatts of power, which was then transmitted 14 miles to downtown Portland, where it powered lights to illuminate the city's streets. This was, interestingly enough, the first instance of long-distance transmission of electrical energy for commercial purposes in the United States. Known as "Station A," the plant is still in use today as part of Publishers Paper Company's facilities.

In 1892, the Willamette Falls Electric Company and several other small utilities merged into a new company, Portland General Electric (PGE). By that time, demand on the Willamette Falls facility far exceeded its output. Consequently, as one of its first generation ventures, the new Portland General Electric began construction of a larger plant at Willamette Falls—"Station B." The concrete power house was erected on the west side of the river, on ground between the ship canal and the river. In 1894, three 400-kilowatt alternating current generators were installed. Some of this plant's original equipment is currently on display at the Smithsonian Institute.

In 1953, the plant was completely reconstructed and automated, and today it is known as the T. W. Sullivan plant. Generating 15 megawatts of power, it is a contributing part of PGE's hydroelectric system.

Principal industries at Willamette Falls today consist of the paper mills of Crown Zellerbach Corporation and Publishers Paper Company. These companies' past use of water power in the wood-grinding process has now largely been replaced by purchased electric power.

2. The T Perspective

To adequately understand PGE's "technical approach" to the Willamette Falls project, it helps to place it in the context of earlier, similar PGE decisions. In a company that has been staffed by large numbers of engineers, most major decisions on generation followed well-defined guidelines. Land and water rights would be secured, applications would be made for permits, consultants would be hired to design a facility, and contractors would be hired to build it. There was comparatively little public interest in these projects.

The beginning of the latest Willamette Falls proposal was following the same track. It has been known since the early 1920s that additional generation capacity was available at the Willamette Falls site. In the late 1950s, the economics of the location became attractive. A list of the major studies since that time follows:

- 1958, Bechtel: investigation of methods for increasing spillway height—broad analysis of the Station A/east side site;
- 1971, Bechtel: broad analysis of using the existing Crown Zellerbach site, update of the analysis on the Station A/east side site—east side channel excavation study;
- 1978, PGE: cost update of 1971 study—Stage II channel excavation study;
- 1979, Bechtel: cost update of 1978—fish facilities options investigated,
- 1980, Bechtel: broad analysis of west side site—detailed analysis of turbine types.

Through these studies, the technical alternatives were reduced to four major possibilities:

1. Build a 60-megawatt (MW) facility on the Station A/east side site.
2. Build a 60-MW facility on the west side by raising a portion of the existing Crown Zellerbach facility already scheduled for decommissioning by Crown Zellerbach.
3. Build a 75-MW facility on either the east or west side and close Sullivan. This would mitigate certain fisheries problems, and the existing turbines could be sold advantageously on the market.
4. Install 20-MW additional capacity in the existing Crown Zellerbach facilities.

All of the options would involve an amendment to an existing federal license, which would simplify some of the permit applications. The water rights issue was clarified in a study done for PGE by a local legal firm in 1979 and resulted in PGE's filing for a preliminary water certificate. This assured priority status on the water usage should the project proceed. The fish issue was, and continues to be, extremely sensitive, and negotiations with various state agencies were an ongoing process. Recreational improvements were required under the licensing process, and these were coordinated with the appropriate local and regional governmental agencies.

Economic analyses of the technical options showed the 60-MW east-side option to be the most attractive. It would generate electricity for considerably less cost than new or planned thermal generation facilities. Unlike thermal facilities, a hydroelectric plant is almost completely insensitive to rising fuel costs, transportation charges, and oil prices. A detailed cost–benefit analysis showed the benefits exceeding the costs by over $70 million over the first 20 years of the project.

In terms of financing, the planning and construction would extend over five years at a total cost of $70 to $100 million, depending on the cost of fisheries facilities. Long-term low interest industrial revenue bonds could be sold for this type of hydroelectric project, and significant tax benefits could accrue. In the peak construction year, the project would represent no more than 10.5% of PGE's total construction budget. At this point, with favorable reports in most areas and continuing negotiations with the fisheries people, PGE historically would have decided to proceed with the project. However, as will be discussed in the organizational perspective, the project did not proceed along the historical lines. Major additions to the process were made.

First, the PGE Public Affairs Department was consulted about the project's probable impact on the attitudes of the residents and elected officials in the Oregon City area. This was somewhat of a first for PGE—asking for public reaction in the initial planning process in order to make the program proactive rather than reactive. It reflected an increase in sensitivity to public input in major community decisions in general, and to the Oregon City area's concerns in particular. A Citizens' Task Force was selected, based on the recommendations of a local consultant. It represented a cross section of community interests, and its input carried a majority of the weight in the decision on whether to build or not.

Additionally, a government coordination plan was worked out by the Public Affairs Department to assure that local, regional, and state officials were kept informed of developments on a timely basis. Informational packets were prepared for distribution to these officials and to the news media.

In general, a change in the decision-making process had been made during this project. The traditional concerns had to be supplemented by additional considerations of public and political impacts and effects. The technical, economic, legal, financial, public relations, and political aspects were addressed by various organizational components, and the process proceeded in an orderly and rational manner. To see the impetus for the change in the process, however, one must view the underlying organizational and personal perspectives.

3. The O Perspective

At least three levels of organizational interactions are indicated in the Willamette Falls Project: 1) PGE as an organization composed of many subunits that must interface with one another, 2) PGE as an organization interfacing with other organizations, and 3) PGE in a special organizational relationship with Publishers Paper and Crown Zellerbach.

The general trend in the area of PGE interfacing with other organizations has been one of increasing complexity. Although legally the Federal Energy Regulatory Commission (FERC) has sole responsibility for approving the project, in practice it has systematically brought other agencies into the process in ever-increasing numbers. As many as 16 individual state agencies and bureaus must approve a project before FERC will consider the application. Many of these state bureaus defer to input from several regional and/or local agencies. In the case of federal agencies, the company goes through established procedures and works on an informal level with the federal staffs. On state and local levels, PGE often devotes far greater planning and development resources to a decision than do the corresponding agencies. Informal rivalries often develop, based on the respective interest each group feels it represents. For example, fisheries is one area where federal and PGE staffs have far greater resources than the Oregon Department of Fisheries and Wildlife. (In general, these kinds of organizational relationships are further distorted nationally, where much larger, multistate facilities are matched against small state bureaus.)

The O perspective is even more noteworthy in the Willamette Falls decision as it relates to the departmental subunits within PGE. In this case, the P perspective is also particularly important. By the time the Willamette Falls project started, there had already been a long-established organizational structure for decision-making processes. Frank Warren, Chairman of PGE at that time, had been in control since the early 1950s and had established a fairly clear-cut hierarchy for decision making. Under his leadership, the initial Bechtel studies were commissioned by the Generation Engineering Department, which also undertook the economic analyses with input from the Rate Department. Planning was done in each department as deemed appropriate.

By the mid-1970s, many changes had taken place that substantially changed the complexion of the company. Some of the more significant changes included Warren's retirement, the expiration of long-term Bonneville Power Administration contracts and subsequent construction of the Trojan nuclear facility, a drastic increase in oil prices and subsequent electric rate increases, and an accelerated public interest in major decisions. The result was that organizational adjustments were made within PGE that were designed to reflect the increased importance of the large generation projects that began to dominate the company's efforts. Complexity increased dramatically.

Among the first major changes were the formation, in 1977, of a Corporate Planning Department and the addition of a staff of 70 to support it. Although this new department did not abolish the older Generation Engineering Department, it did considerably diminish its original planning stature by assuming many of the responsibilities for resource and long-range planning, which the Generation Engineering Department had formerly held. Other departments saw many of their responsibilities changed as well, and short-term interdepartmental jealousies naturally ensued. In the beginning, then, cooperation between the Corporate Planning Department and some of the older departments was not necessarily an easy task.

The new Corporate Planning Department was just one example; similar situations were occurring elsewhere in the company. Other new departments were being formed, and previously small departments were increasing in size to accommodate new external requirements and the new management's priorities. For example, as new, more sophisticated employee programs were added, the Human Resources Department staff increased in response. As the financial performance became a priority, new departments were formed to monitor, plan, and guide financial activities. In 1970, the company had about 1800 employees; by 1980, the number exceeded 3000.

Complexity was increasing, and interdepartmental relationships were constantly changing where once they had been stable. As a result, the imbedded decision process had to adjust to meet these new conditions. No longer could the simple hierarchical chain of command handle the decision making. The Willamette Falls Project, for example, was administratively set up to be run by a 12-member intercompany task force that would meet periodically to review progress and coordinate activities. This system would not necessarily have been considered in simpler times. In addition, an executive oversight committee was set up to provide general policy guidance and to handle high-level political contacts where necessary. These were major changes by PGE standards and were instituted by many new people. Their individual contributions can readily be seen through the personal perspective. But before proceeding to the P perspective, one additional organizational consideration should be mentioned.

A third organizational aspect emerged, which was peculiar to the Willamette Falls project, involving the relationships of PGE with both Publishers and Crown Zellerbach. A project at this location is attractive no matter who builds it. In owning the land and filing for a preliminary water certificate, PGE put a lock on the ability to build from the start. But the relationships with large customers, particularly those in strong financial positions, do not lend themselves to clear-cut decisions. When both became aware of the latest activity at the Falls, they expressed interest in joint participation. Discussions occurred over a year's time as to participation schemes that could prove financially beneficial to PGE and to the general rate payer, and at the same time benefit Crown and/or Publishers. With the high levels of return required in today's market, these two conditions could apparently not be simultaneously achieved; and, while there is still some activity in the negotiations, the situation appears to be skewed in favor of a solely owned PGE project. The deference on the organizational and personal levels afforded customers of this size is a reality that cannot be ignored, and its impact on the decision process was tangible.

4. The P Perspective

In a project of this magnitude, there are numerous visible instances where distinct personalities influence the decision process. And, as in the organizational perspective, we recognize at least two phases.

Frank Warren was President and Chief Executive Officer of PGE for 30 years. In the 1950s, 1960s, and 1970s, he personally made the final decision in the company. With comparatively few employees, his decision hierarchy was fairly flat. There was easy access from several levels below him. The company promoted almost exclusively from within and was managed primarily by engineering-type managers who had come up through the ranks. Under these conditions, the organization was stable, and the decisions followed orderly, well-established procedural guidelines.

In the 1970s, as the complexity increased on all fronts, many changes occurred simultaneously. Robert Short was elected as Warren's replacement. His previous experience was in public relations and the political arena, with a solid background in finance. Under his influence, things changed appreciably.[1] William Lindblad was elected President at this time. Lindblad came to PGE in 1977 as a Vice-President from Pacific Gas and Electric in California. Short then chose three Senior Vice-Presidents. James Durham was previously Deputy Attorney General for the State of Oregon and had been with PGE since 1978. Ken Harrison was an officer with a major bank and had been with PGE since 1975. Chuck Heinrich, who had been with PGE since 1956, progressed through the Rate Department ranks.

In general terms, the upper management after Warren's departure was somewhat the opposite of that during his Presidency. The newer executives were generally younger, had considerable nonutility experience, and were specialized in areas not necessarily specific to a power utility. Not surprisingly, these rapid changes created some uncomfortable feelings. Existing long-time middle managers perceived that not only were executive slots filled that they otherwise might have sought, but these positions were filled with young individuals not likely to leave soon. Entire departments were being created and staffed with young individuals with limited experience. The experience and decision base, which was once so solid, was changing almost daily.

The Willamette Falls project was of such a magnitude that an executive oversight committee was formed, which included Lindblad, Durham, and Harrison. As mentioned earlier, they were to provide policy guidelines and high-level

---

[1]This change is apparently quite typical. Steiner (1981) recognizes "The New Class of Chief Executive Officer." He is becoming "a public figure, a spokesman for both a company as well as the business institution."

political contacts in an effort to make an "informed decision." In this case, public reaction was to be integral to that decision. This group also viewed the fisheries and viewed public reaction as integral to that decision. Additionally, they considered the fisheries negotiations very sensitive and did not want to push the State Fisheries and Wildlife Department into making decisions at a speed not commensurate with its staffing. Finally, they wanted to be certain that appropriate attention was given to input from both Publishers Paper and Crown Zellerbach.

The project was considered by the 20-member Citizens' Task Force in the Oregon City area.[2] Their input plus the final outcome of PGE's staff negotiations with the Oregon Department of Fisheries and Wildlife became pivotal points in the project. If input proved favorable, the project would have reverted to the traditional decision-making processes and standard operating procedures. If their input was not favorable, the project was to be cancelled or altered appreciably.

Again, to the casual observer, the decision-making process appeared quite orderly and rational. Only when overlaying the organizational and the personal perspectives can one gain any appreciation for the behind-the-scenes motivations and impacts that influenced the Willamette Falls Project.

Anglers Concerned: PGE Hydroplant Plan Blasted (Headline)

We're acting like drug addicts in this panic over energy.

A member of Santiam Flycasters

Positioning the powerhouse at the falls would be the worst place in the Willamette River to build.

A member of the Isaak Walton League

Do we want to look like LA or like Oregon?

Another Santiam Flycaster

Article reporting Citizens' Task Force hearing, *The Oregonian*, January 15, 1981.

---

5. A Postscript

The Citizens' Task Force was active for eight months. Numerous meetings and public input sessions were held as the Committee gathered facts and gained sensitivity to community opinion. Questionnaires were distributed to all customers by mail. A temporary office was opened in the community to supply speakers or information to local groups and citizens. Local, regional, and state

---

[2]At one recent hearing, half the 80 persons present spoke to express their objections to construction of the 60-MW plant. Although several impacts were addressed, the opposition focused time and again on the protection of game fish (*Lake Oswego Review*, Jan. 18, 1981:1).

community leaders and politicians were kept informed of developments. The end result of the process was a report from the Committee to PGE. In late 1980, two criteria had been established for project construction: 1) that the plant be economically justified, and 2) that the Citizens' Advisory Committee confirm community acceptance and support. On March 3, 1981, PGE's Robert Short announced that the company would not build the Willamette Falls hydroelectric plant (*The Oregonian*, March 4, 1981). The cost-effectiveness criterion was satisfied; the community support aspect was not. As Short stated to the Task Force:

> You pointed out that the project has little or no approval from either local or statewide fishermen, and the public just doesn't want any further development in this location which might disturb its present or its future. We determined our social and environmental responsibility must be given more weight in this particular project [*The Oregonian* March 4, 1981:B3].

Editorial comment praised the decision:

> Portland General Electric deserves praise for the process it used in deciding not to build a hydroelectric project at Willamette Falls.
> . . . above all, PGE has demonstrated an environmental awareness and responsibility in using the citizens' committee to determine what people want. If other potentially controversial projects are proposed by corporations, PGE showed that the advisory committee is a good thermometer to take the public's temperature on how the project will be received [*Oregon Journal* March 18, 1981].
> While the Willamette Falls hydroelectric project will not see the light of day, the community participation process is expected to survive. The corporation appears committed to it at this time [paraphrased from *The Sunday Oregonian* March 8, 1981:B8].

It is evident that the O and P perspectives can contribute significantly to the total picture. A change in leadership of the corporation contributed to a change in its organizational structure, and, as a result, the attitude toward the planning process shifted significantly. The analyst's position permitted an insider's view and facilitated the interviews held within the corporation. The influence of an intense single interest group was magnified by the new procedures. Clearly, the future of the project was more strongly dependent on organizational and individual factors than on technical considerations.[3]

---

[3]Perhaps the most fascinating case for the O and P perspectives in recent hydropower developments is "minihydro." The 1978 Public Utilities Regulatory Policies Act (PURPA) requires utilities to buy energy from small producers at a reasonable rate. As a result, small "mom and pop" entrepreneurs have sprung up to develop small-scale hydropower across the country (the number of applications for such projects to FERC grew from 18 in 1978 to 1800 in 1981). For an excellent example of a P perspective on this subject, see McPhee (1981).

B. ELECTRONIC SYSTEM MARKET: FAILURE OF A STRATEGY[4]
(P. COOK)

In the spring of 1977, the Manager of Business Development at the Data Re-
duction Group of Acousticon, Inc. proposed that Acousticon acquire Gramma
Corporation, the third largest source of Generalized Acoustic Survey (GAS)
Systems in the United States. Acousticon was Gramma's largest supplier, selling
Surface Acoustic Wave (SAW) filters to Gramma.

Much preparatory work and analysis led to negotiations that reached agreement
on the conditions for the sale (including a price of approximately $12 million).
The proposed deal was rejected by Acousticon's Board of Directors.

Gramma was sold to another company for $20 million in 1978 and resold to
General Electric for $110 million in 1981. Acousticon entered the GAS market
on its own in 1978. Two years and $6 million later, it withdrew.

We apply the T, O, and P perspectives to fathom a decision that seems difficult
to explain on the basis of the T perspective alone.

1. Historical Background

Acoustic filters were invented in the mid-1950s as a way of discriminating the
individual frequency components of the waves picked up by ground microphones,
or geophones. These waveforms contain information that enables trained geophysicists to determine potential locations for oil exploration, but the information
is difficult to extract. The filter permitted the user to look at specific narrow
frequency bands from the wide range of noise returned when dynamite explosions
were recorded through the geophones.

International Business Machines (IBM), working in conjunction with the Exxon
Research Laboratory, introduced the 225 Geological Acoustic Survey System in
1958. Although Exxon used it in its pioneer GAS-I system for automated data
reduction, the product was a business failure for IBM. With a monthly rental
of over $4000, less than 500 were sold or leased.

The high cost of the early acoustic filters was due to their filtering technique,
adapted from radar technology. The data had to be filtered by making use of the
nonlinearity of tetrode vacuum tube characteristic curves.

The result was that the monthly cost of a work station, which could generate
the output of four to six manual analysts, was about $10,000, including the
computer time to execute the analysis software. As that cost in the late 1960s
was equivalent to five fully burdened analysts, only the large oil companies had
both the heavy analysis work load and the innovative attitude required to use
computer GAS techniques.

In 1964, the Acoustic Device Research Department of Acousticon was trying
to develop a technique for capturing low-level acoustic waveforms. Acousticon
was (and is) the world's leading manufacturer of geophones, a device for cap-

---

[4]The names of the product, companies, and individuals have been changed for obvious reasons.

turing acoustic waveforms for recording on magnetic tape. By refining the SAW technology, Acousticon scientists discovered a technique that made it possible to record the various frequency domains independently, greatly simplifying the waveform analysis process.

The vision of a commercial market for the SAW acoustic filter outside geophony was the work of J. Crawford Pinkston, who headed a small group working on crystal structure analysis, determining faults in crystalline materials. When his optical input device failed to work, he took the acoustic filter to the market as the F5002, selling for $10,000. Pinkston was later to found the very successful Digital Filter Systems, but his venture into acoustical analysis did not satisfy the business needs of Acousticon. He was replaced by Ralph Willsaw, a rapidly rising design engineer and manager who had recently completed a tour at Acousticon Holland. Willsaw saw the need for a lower cost product and software to accompany it. He initiated a low-cost filter design program and hired an experienced software development manager.

The Acousticon 5010 was a major breakthrough when it was introduced in 1972. With a purchase price of $4000, and accompanied by the Accu-10 software package, it made possible an order of magnitude reduction in the cost of an analysis work station and opened up the acoustical survey market to a large number of applications. In addition to geophysical surveying, GAS analysis was found to be justifiable in testing the crystal structure of forgings, analyzing the internal operation of moving machinery, and forecasting the weather using GAS analysis techniques on satellite data.

The most successful analysis product in Acousticon's history was the 5015, follow-on to the 5010. It used a larger filter that could handle more discrete frequencies, permitting faster and more accurate analysis.

Two major application areas emerged: ultrasonic analysis of cast parts and immediate field evaluation of geophysical exploration results. For foundries, acoustical survey made it possible to detect flaws in the crystalline structure of cast parts before any of the cost of machining was incurred. In petroleum exploration, geophysicists in the field could evaluate the results of each shot before the equipment was moved and without sending the data back to corporate headquarters. Bad shots could then be repeated at once, reducing the cost of keeping the crew in the field. Quick to match up the new filter technology with a market need, a number of companies were formed to supply acoustic analysis systems. By 1976 there were four major contenders and numerous minor ones, as shown in Table 11.

2. Current Situation: Spring 1977

In the spring of 1977 the Generalized Acoustic Survey Systems market seemed poised to explode. Numerous articles had appeared, documenting savings of 4 : 1 to 7 : 1 in manpower expenditure to accomplish a given analysis, and numerous specific applications had stable and proven software packages avail-

TABLE 11. Generalized Acoustic Survey Systems Market Shares (1976)

Vendor	Sales (millions of dollars)	Market share (%)	Orders for Acousticon filters (millions of dollars)[a]
E	16.0	24.6%	1.78
F	13.0	20.0	1.72
G(Gramma)	10.0	15.4	0.82
H	8.0	12.3	1.21
J	4.0	6.2	–
K	4.0	6.2	1.49
L	3.0	4.6	–
M	1.5	2.3	0.55
N	1.5	2.3	0.72
P	1.0	1.5	0.10
Q	1.0	1.5	
S	1.0	1.5	0.72
T	0.5	0.8	–
U	0.3	0.5	–
	0.2	0.3	–
Totals	65.0	100.0	9.11

[a]Note: Acousticon *orders* are not directly comparable with customer's sales, as they reflect anticipated growth. In some cases they are inflated to insure delivery or to obtain greater discounts.

able. The GAS vendors, of course, were mounting major sales campaigns aimed at early and even late adopting organizations.

As can be seen from Table 11, Acousticon had been getting a significant proportion of the money expended even though it was only a supplier to, rather than a participant in, the GAS market. The costs of computers on a chip (microcomputers) and memory (RAM) had been coming down very rapidly. Several of the GAS vendors were now looking at building their own filters, based on digital Fast Fourier Transform (FFT) technology, rather than buying them from Acousticon. By doing so they could increase their own value added and offer lower priced work stations to their customers.

These filters had the unfortunate characteristic of being based on digital software FFT technology, with a series of narrow frequency ranges, rather than the wide ranges available with the SAW filter. In addition, the data resolution was not as precise, and the time required to generate it was much longer. Some customers, it was felt, would continue to pay a premium for the higher quality of the SAW filter. The anticipation was that rapid growth in the market would lead to continued growth in sales of SAW filters to these vendors, for whom Acousticon was the sole source, although market share would be lost to the rapid growth of digital FFT filters.

The Acousticon Acoustic Data Reduction Group (ADR) was organized into

into three Divisions: Systems, OEM, and Products (Figure 12). The operation was headed by Ralph Willsaw, who had been responsible for the growth rate of 45% per year since the introduction of the 4010. Willsaw had made the initial contacts with Gramma and felt strongly that the acquisition would greatly strengthen the position of ADR in the acoustic analysis market.

The Information Display Systems Division (IDS) had responsibility for two products that combined processing capability with filters and peripherals to make a functioning system. The IDS Division was also responsible for investigating opportunities for Acousticon as a vendor of applications packages. The OEM Division was responsible for sales to original equipment manufacturers of products to be built into their systems and resold. This Division interfaced with the GAS vendors, including Gramma. It was headed by Jerry Grass, a former SAW design manager, who was open minded about the acquisition, but very concerned that it be handled in a way that would not jeopardize his relations with OEM customers.

The Information Display Products Division (IDP) was responsible for the bulk of the product line: graphic terminals, hard copy units, plotters, and peripherals that were nonintelligent (had no processing capability of their own). Many of the IDP customers were buying terminals as components for their own in-house GAS systems or for use on time-sharing systems. Ray Martin, Manager of this organization, was not involved in planning for the acquisition.

The IDS division was headed by Tom Tinker, brought in from Honeywell by Ralph Willsaw to provide computer industry experience to the organization. Tinker was primarily an engineer and was finding his first experience with general management something of a problem: he lacked the vision and insight to plot a course for his group. His management style was to manage the ongoing business and let his subordinates generate the plans for the future of the division. As a result a number of possible market venture products were under consideration, but none had caught the fancy of Ralph Willsaw, who had to approve them. He

FIGURE 12. Acousticon Data Reduction (ADR) Group organization.

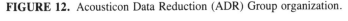
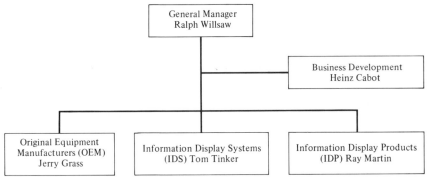

was interested in the acquisition of Gramma as a means of obtaining an established position in the market.

The strongest proponent and champion for the move was Heinz Cabot, recently brought in from Filcomp, the leading vendor of output plotters, where he had been Vice-President of System Development. Cabot was a business strategist who saw several strategic possibilities in the acquisition. The first was the one obvious to the other participants: establishing a direct marketing channel into the GAS market. Another was the idea of extending the market life of the acoustic filter by reducing Gramma's selling prices to the point where the storage tube volume would justify the new manufacturing facilities needed to produce a truly low-cost version of the device. The third was tapping Gramma's software expertise in acoustic analysis system design and using that to go into new markets. Above all, however, was the prospect of a major role in the management of the newly acquired business, which he viewed as a major career opportunity.

Gramma was a likely target for acquisition by someone. It was having trouble generating adequate cash flow to sustain the growth that was essential for retaining a market share in this rapidly growing market. Equity funding was almost nonexistent for companies such as Gramma, and its existing debt made further borrowing impractical. Its current position was marginally profitable, but its projections, based on adequate capitalization, were for good profits in the next several years.

Electrosight had initiated litigation against Gramma, claiming $25 million in damages and penalties for theft of trade secrets. Electrosight claimed that a group of programmers, who left to go to work for Gramma, took proprietary software with them. Gramma claimed that the group did original work that was not proprietary to Electrosight.

U.S. Department of Justice guidelines indicated that the acquisition of Gramma by Acousticon would be viewed as a case of forward integration, in which a large vendor takes over a smaller customer. That move would have violated proposed new guidelines, but those currently in effect did not appear to prevent the acquisition. Adding to the concern was the fear that the newly appointed Carter administration officials showed signs of vindictiveness in their intent to prosecute mergers they opposed.

3. The Acquisition Decision

After extended negotiations, a tentative deal was struck. Acousticon would trade one share of Acousticon stock for every 3.25 shares of Gramma stock in a merger of interest acquisition. The effective sale price was $12.3 million, roughly equivalent to one year's sales. The principals of Gramma agreed to hold their stock for one year following the merger and to manage the company for that length of time. The basic tenor was friendly, and both sides assumed that the Gramma management would be integrated into Acousticon with little turmoil.

Gramma would be run independently of the Acoustic Data Reduction Group, but would coordinate closely with it. It was the expressed intent of both parties to use Acousticon products in Gramma systems as a way to maintain the SAW filter as a major factor in the market.

An elaborate proposal was put together by the group working on the project. The acquisition was represented as an implementation of the XYZ Consulting Group Model, advocated by corporate planning, and a major business opportunity for Acousticon. The proposal concentrated on the technological perspective and ignored the position of Joe Towers, who had been instrumental in the decision making of the Board of Directors.

The proposal was rejected by the Acousticon Board of Directors on the basis of the contingent liability represented by the Electrosight lawsuit, and because the ADR group was not sure that the acquisition could be integrated and managed properly. Indications were that the Board did not spend much effort on the merits of the business case, on understanding the GAS market, or on an XYZ-oriented portfolio-management consideration.

As a result of this decision, Tom Tinker was given the charter to build a petroleum exploration GAS system and take it to the marketplace. Rights to an existing software package were acquired from a software developer who failed to live up to his promises. After a few disastrous benchmark competitions, it was obvious that a great deal of further developmental work was needed to compete effectively. Additional software people were hired, and a VAX computer system was purchased from a leading computer manufacturer.

With an investment of somewhat more than $6 million and a product starting to win some of the competitive sales situations, a top management planning session came to the conclusion that Acousticon's share of the GAS market would not become substantial in the next few years. Following the business portfolio concepts of the XYZ group (which said the market leaders control a market, and only participants with large market shares could be profitable), the group was shut down and the products were removed from the product line.

4. The T Perspective

The acquisition made sense on the basis of objective consideration of both the technical and business aspects. Acousticon's products were already designed into the Gramma product line and had attained a good reception in the marketplace. The software supporting the system had been designed to make full use of the characteristics of the SAW filter and made an effective tool. Gramma's business was good, but growth was restricted by the availability of cash to fund the growth that would result from aggressive marketing. Acousticon, on the other hand, had a cash surplus without obvious business opportunities to pursue.

The SAW filter had not only been the basis for Acousticon's success in Generalized Acoustic Survey Systems; it had opened up the market, and made feasible an investment of hundreds of man-years in software development. But with the cost reduction of the semiconductor industry, digital filters could be designed by individual system vendors. This type of filter, in spite of its marginal resolution, is used because of its low cost and relatively high value added. In addition, the proliferation of home computers has given the industry a new low-end standard of "quick and dirty" filtering.

The SAW filters are made using commercial fused silica substrates in the form of ground and polished Vycor plates made from Corning 0120 glass. Because commercially available plates are used, they require a large amount of reworking. Because the typical volume of a glass plant is so high, glass companies are unwilling to entertain production runs of special plate types when a year's supply requires more setup than run time. Several studies have shown that a substantial increase in plate volume is of enormous benefit to Acousticon, but the required market and pricing strategies have never been seriously entertained (Table 12).

Acquisition of Gramma has the potential for building the volume of SAW filters because at least one major GAS vendor will have the incentive to stay with that technology over the long run. If that volume could provide the incentive to invest in the special design and in Cathode Ray Tube (CRT) production facility automation, the reduced price will keep other customers with the storage tube for the present.

On the business side, Acousticon had a good financial position, with the filter business generating a substantial amount of cash, and all major product lines profitable. Most investments for new product development and additions to facilities are internally funded, although a line of bank credit has been negotiated to provide for future needs.

Gramma, on the other hand, is finding some difficulty in funding its growth. The GAS systems have the characteristic of requiring a significant investment in work-in-process because they contain major purchased components, including computers and filters, which have to be paid for long before the end customer's payment is received. Although absorbing cash, Gramma is profitable, and is projecting growth rates of 35 to 45% for the next several years.

The Corporate Planning Group at Acousticon was a strong advocate of the philosophy of the XYZ Group, whom it retained as consultants. The XYZ Group holds that the business in which a corporation is involved should be managed as a portfolio of investments, where each opportunity is funded or dropped based on the merits of its market position. It further advocates division of the market into distinct market segments and holds that any business must be larger than the competitors and grow faster in order to control pricing in the market segments.

TABLE 12. Plate Cost versus Design Type

Design type	Raw plate cost	Reworking cost	Total plate cost
Commercial	$18.00	$432.00	$450.00
Special[a]	$67.00	$113.00	$180.00

[a]Note: The special design involves $170,000 of tooling charges. Amortization over the first 100,000 plates (minimum order) is included in the raw plate cost.

The XYZ Group suggests that growth can come from two sources: 1) taking the market share from competitors, and 2) preempting their growth. The latter tactic is normally accomplished in rapidly growing markets by aggressive marketing and preemptive pricing. In this case Acousticon's financial strength would permit market strategies by which Gramma could overtake market leader E in three to five years of growth in the 45 to 55% range.

Based on the XYZ-oriented corporate investment strategy, the case for the Gramma acquisition is a favorable one.

Three major negative factors exist, which can be viewed as quantifiable risks in the technical perspective. One is that the move would require approval by either the Federal Trade Commission or the U.S. Department of Justice. There are no other producers of the SAW filter, but there is clearly a risk associated with a detailed review of this natural monopoly by either of those agencies.

The second is the litigation that has been filed by E. Acousticon planned to have an independent consultant look at the source code for both Gramma's and E's software packages and evaluate the degree of similarity at that level of detail. Common law doctrine states that a craftsman cannot be prohibited from practicing his craft, but the protection of trade secrets and proprietary information is critical to the computer business, where software cannot be patented. Working with the consultant, corporate attorneys can estimate the degree of risk associated with the lawsuit.

The third factor is the damage to relations with the existing customers because an Acousticon subsidiary would compete directly with them. Evaluation indicates that this point is moot, because they will continue to use the acoustic filter displays if the cost-cutting strategy is pursued, and will develop their own digital filters otherwise. Analysis indicates that the competition factor does not significantly change the GAS customers' probability of developing their own display, although it may have some effect on the timing.

5. The O Perspective

Acousticon was founded in Midland, Texas, shortly after World War II by a group of individuals who believed they could build a better geophone than any then available on the market. The surface acoustic wave geophone is a device that detects sound waves and converts them to voltage waveforms with a high degree of accuracy. The excellence of their product, and their timing in catching the wave of geophone applications, led them to very rapid growth for the first decade of their existence.

During that decade, when it appeared that they could do no wrong, a number of organizational characteristics, which originated as ad hoc solutions to operational problems, developed into an immutable corporate culture, much of which exists today. Individual decisions made by managers to solve immediate operating problems quickly became "the way things are done at Acousticon."

On the boundary between the personal perspective and the organizational perspective is the operation of individuals in the nascent organization. In the process of managing the business, they take actions that evolve from solutions to precedents to practices, and finally mature as corporate policy. Although these policies may be actually inappropriate in the larger, more mature organization, changing them becomes difficult and requires the conscious effort of an individual. So the practice goes full circle, from the personal action of a founder to solve a problem, to corporate policy, to another individual operating under the motivational structure that drives individuals in organizations.

Acousticon was the result of the work of two men: Bill Hunt, a brilliant electrical engineer, and Jack Shaw, a talented businessman and humanitarian. Early in their efforts they hired Joe Towers, a conservative and risk-averse young lawyer, as corporate secretary.

From their efforts emerged a successful company with a unique culture; a culture that embodied several unusual characteristics, because the long period of strong growth permitted many practices to solidify into custom without the normal test of practicality and economic reality.

Among these characteristics are the following:

- The concept of an "Acousticon Family"—no layoffs, no firings, very low turnover.

- Profit sharing—employees are paid a base pay, and corporate profits are shared with employees as a percentage of base pay, usually around the 20% level. Employee cost consciousness is a result, leading to completely open stock rooms where employees help themselves to the supplies and equipment they need.

- Decision making by consensus—most decisions are made in meetings where lengthy discussion of issues is much more the practice than is management fiat. Decisions take a long time to emerge and can be reopened at a later date by almost anyone.

- Preference for building in-house rather than purchasing—Acousticon winds its own transformers, forms its own sheet metal and plastic, wraps its own cable, and manufactures resistors, capacitors, and integrated circuits—components that most companies buy on the market. The general feeling is "we can do it better," which is often true, but does not take economics into account.

- Reluctance to change—the organization is slow to innovate in all areas except the technical ones. The way things are done is particularly slow to change, although new technical ideas are incorporated into products ahead of competitors. The company is totally unable to react quickly to changes in the market other than those it creates through product innovation.

- Caution—in any decision with legal implications, Acousticon will defer economic considerations to a conservative approach. Fear of litigation is a major concern of the corporation and affects its flexibility in pricing, acquisition consideration, factory operation, accounting, and a number of other operating areas. For years it preferred not to build militarized products for the U.S. Government, because of intrusive federal regulations such as the Renegotiation Act of 1951.

- The "Acousticon window"—to be accepted by management a new product proposal had to fit the market characteristics of existing products. The selling price should be between $1000 and $10,000, and annual sales between 300 and 8000 units. Low-cost, high-volume items and big-ticket systems did not fit the manufacturing process, the sales practices of the field force, or the market understanding of management.

In this environment the proposal to acquire Gramma had a difficult path at best. Acousticon didn't buy things, it developed them. With one special exception, Acousticon had no operations other than field sales outside Midland. Top management had no "feel" for the Acoustic Survey System market, and GAS systems selling for $100,000 to $300,000 were outside the "Acousticon window." The pending lawsuit with E was frightening, as was the perceived threat by the antitrust forces.

So, in spite of the fact that the acquisition fit all the guidelines set by Corporate Planning's XYZ model—that the market prospects were very good for Gramma and that the strategy held great promise for extending the life of the acoustic filter—it was rejected by the Board of Directors. Joe Towers was the leading opponent of the move on the basis that the business opportunity, as he perceived it, was overshadowed by the risk involved.

6. The P Perspective

Five individuals were the prime actors in this situation:

1. Ralph Willsaw. Willsaw was a talented and multifaceted individual who had risen to the position of Group Vice-President in the upper management of Acousticon. He had a good sense of the market and an excellent set of managerial skills in addition to being an electronic engineer by training. He was the primary proponent of the acquisition because of the value he felt it would bring to Acousticon. He had confidence that the organization could be managed after it had been acquired and believed it was a good business decision. He was the most objective of the individuals involved, operating almost entirely on the basis of the technical perspective.
2. Heinz Cabot. Cabot had recently been brought in from Filcomp, where he was a Vice-President. Cabot was both a skilled negotiator and an intellectual. He had been chartered by Willsaw to find one or several acquisitions Acousticon could use to build on its base in acoustical survey to emulate the performance of Hewlett–Packard in the computer market. Cabot ran

the day-to-day progress of the negotiations and generated a team spirit among the participants. He gave seminars on how to keep secrets, warned against IKBICTY (I know but I can't tell you) actions that might compromise the secrecy, and obtained a great deal of effort and cooperation from the group. He was motivated both by the potential business opportunity and by the prospect that he would be likely to play some management role in the new acquisition. Cabot was very astute in his consideration for all three perspectives, and he operated very effectively at organizational levels below Willsaw. Although he had no direct access to the Board of Directors, he and an associate did a great deal of research work with the outside corporate attorneys to investigate the potential impact of the pending lawsuit and the antitrust implications of the merger.

3. Tom Tinker. Tinker was a professional engineering manager, brought in from General Electric by Willsaw to add experience to the organization. He functioned well in that role as long as the scope of the work to be done was well defined. In the unfamiliar role of General Manager, he was unable to develop techniques to test the validity of the recommendations made by his young and ambitious Marketing Manager. The result was that he operated with a short-time horizon, concentrating on the accomplishment of existing goals rather than setting new ones. The Gramma situation appealed to him because it was in existence and could be evaluated using familiar management methods rather than the judgmental evaluation of future proposals, which he found difficult. When the acquisition was turned down, he proceeded to implement a development program to enter the market, depending largely on his marketing manager to provide direction. A number of major errors in management judgment were made by his organization, including underestimation of the competition, overestimation of the capabilities of the purchased software package, and expenditure of a great deal of money to take the product to the market with a major announcement, rather than a slow entry to test the product's viability.

4. Jerry Grass. Grass, an excellent Manager, made clear the potential impact on his business of the acquisition, but indicated that he could operate effectively either way. If Acousticon came into the end-user market as a direct competitor, either through an acquisition or in-house development, it would hasten the conversion of the other OEM customers to digital FFT technology. His approach then was to open up new OEM markets where the SAW filter could still be effective and to emphasize OEM opportunities for other display group products, including copiers and desk-top computers. Grass occupied a key position because, from an organizational perspective, his group effectively had a veto on the proposal. His personal perspective was that new opportunities would open up as a result of the expected growth, and he had high personal regard for Cabot and the work he did. So rather than oppose the plan, his personal self-confidence led him to

support Cabot. Grass now (1981) occupies the job then held by Willsaw as general manager of the whole organization.

5. Joe Towers. Towers was a very powerful individual who maintained a low profile. In an organization dedicated to open offices, he had the only office in the executive suite. A lawyer by profession, he approached all the corporate management decisions from a legal point of view. His impact on the culture was such that the organization was close to paranoid about potential violations of law or the prospect of lawsuits. It is impossible to estimate the impact on the growth of the corporation his decisions had over the years, but the relative growth of Acousticon and the competition indicate that Acousticon could now be twice as big as it is, if it had been more aggressive. On the other hand, Towers' conservative policies have kept the company out of legal problems and remarkably free of direct government influence in light of the large volume of government business Acousticon does. Because he was an early and influential employee of the company, Towers has built an interesting position in the organization. He often finds it unnecessary to take personal action on decisions he opposes, because he has had such a strong influence on the development of the corporate culture that subordinate organizations tend to follow policies that implement his views.

7. Implications

An advanced technology organization, like any other human organization, does not behave in a strictly "rational actor" mode. Hence the T perspective fails to describe its decision process adequately. The history of the corporation, its "family tradition," and its unique personnel mix are important determinants of its actions.

In the Acousticon case we have seen an example of a solid technological case rejected by the organization, with some individuals proponents of the move and others opponents.

Several individuals were very interested in completion of the deal, as it would result in prestige for them and perhaps a career move to a position of responsibility in the new venture. The atmosphere of secrecy surrounding such a project carries its own aura of excitement, increasing the energy level of the participants. A great deal of work was done to substantiate the move, integrate the two companies, and prepare management presentations.

Opposed to the move were certain influential power agents at the top of the corporate hierarchy. Acting as curates of the corporate culture, they were concerned with federal antitrust implications, contingent liability from a trade secret theft suit by a litigious competitor, and integration problems with previous acquisitions. In addition, Acousticon had long pursued a "do it yourself" philosophy regarding technical development. There is no indication of ethical impropriety on either side, but the failure of the proposal has had a strong deterrent effect on other such technological opportunities that have been presented. It appears likely that this move, and one or two others like it, has had an inhibiting effect on Acousticon's long-term growth.

C. COMMERCIAL AIRCRAFT: THE WIDE-BODY TRIJETS[5] (H. LINSTONE)

1. The Competition

As John Newhouse (1982) so aptly put it, commercial aircraft manufacturing is a "sporty game." Since World War II, the U.S. aircraft industry has dominated the world's airliner business. Until the jet age, Douglas was the leader with its DC-3, DC-6, and DC-7. After World War II, the newly established U.S. Air Force chose its prime supplier of bombers, the Boeing Company, to develop a jet-powered tanker—the KC 135—in support of its jet bombers. Boeing had been out of the commercial aircraft business since 1950 when its clumsy, underpowered Stratocruiser failed. It was the KC-135 that brought Boeing back into the commercial aircraft business. This aircraft became the progenitor of the first successful commercial jet, the 707.[6] Douglas tried hard to catch Boeing with its own DC-8 but never quite succeeded. From 1957 to 1960 Douglas sold 42 DC-8s, compared with Boeing's sale of 170 707s. Lockheed, whose Constellation had been a worthy competitor to Douglas' DC-6, was convinced that there was room for another propeller-driven airliner (actually a prop-jet) before the jets took over completely. It produced the L-188 Electra, an efficient aircraft but a dismal failure.[7]

Boeing soon surpassed its 707 success with the smaller three-engine 727 for the midrange market. Douglas went after the short-range market with its twin-engine DC-9 but had to suffer competition from Boeing's 737. The military once more set the stage with its competition for a gigantic cargo aircraft.

Boeing and Lockheed competed fiercely—and in 1965 Lockheed's C5A won. Boeing shifted at once to the design of a commercial wide-body jet—the huge 747. The U.S. lead airline was Pan Am, which had also been Boeing's supporter of the Stratocruiser. The 747 was a great achievement, but too large for its time; it became a status symbol as 66 airlines ordered it (three-fourths of them non–U.S. airlines). The airlines soon recognized the desirability of a smaller wide-body jet, analogous to the 727 in the narrow-body generation.

We shall now point up some highlights of the ensuing development of the wide-body trijet and note the relevance of the various perspectives.[8]

---

[5]This illustration is based on the reportage of Newhouse (1982), Boulton (1978), and Godson (1975), as well as the author's own experience at Lockheed.

[6]The crucial role of federal policy on the commercial aircraft industry, in particular the impact of the military on commercial aircraft innovation, is discussed by Mowery and Rosenberg (1981).

[7]Abnormal propeller rotation induced wing vibrations causing a number of Electra crashes, and structural modifications were necessary.

[8]The letter refers to the perspective characterizing the comments following.

T. American Airlines took the lead in 1966 and sent specifications for a twin-engine jumbo jet (250 passengers, 1860-mile range) to Boeing, Douglas, and Lockheed. At the time Boeing and Lockheed were still in competition for the supersonic transport (SST). When Boeing won its pyrrhic victory, Lockheed immediately threw its engineering resources into the American Airlines proposal.

O. A major reason for Lockheed's supreme effort was pressure on its management to diversify and move away from its almost complete dependence on defense contracts. The proposed wide-body jet was now "the only game in town," that is, the only new commercial jet business in sight. It should also be noted that the three U.S. manufacturers were so intently competing with each other in the commercial aircraft business that they hardly noticed a spot on the horizon, the European Airbus Industrie consortium, which was also studying a twin-engine, wide-body jet under the brilliant leadership of the French engineer Roger Beteille.

The year American Airlines initiated its proposal was also the year Douglas faced mounting difficulties. With bankruptcy looming, the company's bankers insisted on a merger.

P. Lockheed was interested, and its dynamic Chief Executive, Dan Haughton, later reflected on the opportunity:

> We considered the merger, but I didn't pursue it aggressively enough. We could have put the money together [Newhouse, 1982:135].

He calls this failure one of the two biggest mistakes of his life. The smaller McDonnell Corporation, a military aircraft builder, did accomplish the merger in January 1967. Its founder, James McDonnell ("Mr. Mac"), was a strong willed and able man totally inexperienced in dealing with airlines.

O. The difficult adjustment of the Douglas "division" in Los Angeles to its new leadership in St. Louis, as well as the SST decision, gave Lockheed an initial advantage in its pursuit of the new wide-body jet. By summer, Mr. Mac had decided to compete, and the race was on. American Airlines was obviously not going to have its own way with the specifications, as other airlines had to provide orders to make any new jet a reality. The range was extended and three engines rather than two were agreed on. The key players in this game were now established: Lockheed's L-1011 and McDonnell–Douglas' DC-10 as proposed aircraft, and the "Big Four" domestic U.S. airlines—American, United, TWA, and Eastern—as initial buyers.

T. A 1967 corporate analysis at Lockheed (Linstone, 1968) considered the consequences of alternate L-1011 strategies, for example, a go-ahead on the basis of two (or three or four) Big Four orders totaling at least 60 (or 100) orders. A basic costing quantity of 350 units was used, with an average cost of $13.7 million. A representative result of the analysis is shown in

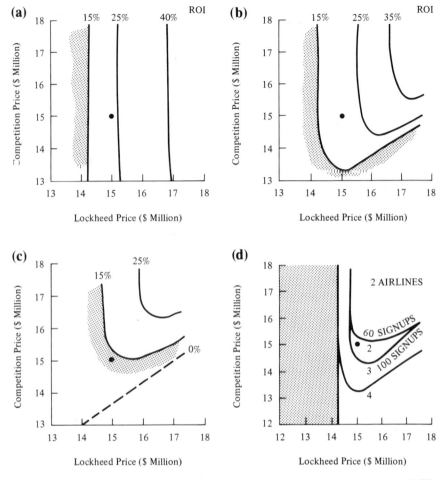

FIGURE 13. Corporate risk analysis: a,b, and c—50/50 chance of reaching stated DCF ROI level: **(a)** strategy I, 4 airlines/60 signups; **(b)** strategy II, 3 airlines/60 signups; **(c)** strategy III, 2 airlines/60 signups; **(d)** minimum number of "big four" airlines, which must be signed to achieve 50/50 chance of 15% DCF ROI.

Figure 13a, b, and c, which reveals contours of constant discounted cash flow return on investment (DCF ROI), based on a 50/50 chance of attaining the percent value shown. Figure 13d integrates the results into one diagram. It shows the number of airlines that must be signed up at the time of the go-ahead decision to yield an adequate DCF ROI. The calculations confirm that a go-ahead with 60 sign-ups by two airlines has less than an even chance of achieving the desired earnings level at a $15 million unit price. The conclusion? Looking at it from the airlines' point of view, the emerging strategy is evident: They should force the competing manufacturers into the lower prices (that is, lower left corners in Figure 13) to the point where the program would be barely profitable for one manufacturer with all Big Four airlines—and then eliminate all but one manufacturer. Compare, for example, strategies I (four airlines) and III (two airlines), that is, Figures 13a and c, at the low prices. Knowing this to be the airlines' strategy, the manufacturers could continue to underbid each other to this point and accept a break-even program on the assumption that all but one manufacturer will be eliminated. However, they run the risk of a very bad loss if the airlines split between two manufacturers. Unfortunately, this early analysis hit close to the mark!

T: As the competition progressed it became obvious that the differences between the two designs progressively shrank. The airlines' own engineers expressed a slight preference for the L-1011. Its third engine was mounted on the rear fuselage, whereas the DC-10's was perched on the vertical tail fin. The L-1011 had four hydraulic systems compared with the DC-10's reliance on three. The L-1011's hydraulic lines were positioned on the trailing edge of the wing, the DC-10's on the leading edge (with subsequent fatal results). The L-1011 also had the more advanced avionics and an all-weather landing capability. A crucial aspect of the competition centered on the choice of engine—Lockheed preferred the more sophisticated Rolls–Royce, whereas McDonnell–Douglas offered both General Electric and Rolls–Royce engines. All in all, the L-1011 appeared to have an edge in terms of technology.

O: On the other hand, several key nonengineering executives made their judgments on the basis of confidence in the company rather than the design. This group included American and United Airlines, both having had decades of good experience with Douglas airliners. TWA, on the other hand, had a similarly long relationship with Lockheed (that is, the Constellation).

American Airlines had started the ball rolling two years earlier and now, in February 1968, wanted to be the first to order. As the deadline approached, the two bidders' supersalesmen, Dan Haughton of Lockheed and Jackson McGowen of McDonnell–Douglas, put on the "full-court press." Lockheed's price was slashed from $15 million to $14.4 million and then to $14.25 million.

P: C. R. Smith had been the driving force behind American Airlines since 1934. After being its Chief Executive for 34 years, he was asked by President Lyndon Johnson to be Secretary of Commerce, and George Spater replaced Smith at the airline's helm. Smith had developed a strong dislike of Mr. Mac and, according to Jackson McGowen, would have ordered the L-1011. But Spater was a different case; he had confidence in Douglas-built aircraft and was ready to announce an order for 25 DC-10s at $15.3 million each, confident that the other trunk airlines would have to follow suit and order the same aircraft.

O: When American's blow fell the game took a surprising turn. The logic of the analysis (Figure 13) and the similar realization of many participants in the game, that is, the importance of avoiding a destructive split by ordering both aircraft, went unheeded. TWA and Eastern announced orders on March 29 for 94 L-1011s. In addition, Haughton achieved a master stroke by obtaining 50 L-1011 orders from the British Air Holdings organization.[9] A few days later Delta Airlines ordered 24 L-1011s so that the total in this momentous week was 168 Lockheed trijets. American and McDonnell–Douglas seemed to be out on a limb.

P: When United Airlines' President George Keck called Haughton to ask whether he could have the L-1011 with the General Electric engine, Haughton made the second of the two biggest mistakes of his life: he answered no. As Newhouse reports (1982:156), Haughton now says:

> We should have designed the airplane for alternative engines. We didn't do it, for financial reasons. The costs of developing a second engine would have been around a hundred million dollars. But we'd have had enough orders to write off that money.

O: United had a long-standing relationship with Douglas; therefore, it is uncertain whether a positive response to the engine question would have turned the tables. In any case United went for the DC-10 with an order of 60 and McDonnell–Douglas was back in the game. The 2/2 split of trunk airline orders was now a fact. And, as forecast, both companies have lost substantial money on their programs. Lockheed, for example, garnered only another 76 orders in the 14 years since that unforgettable week in Spring 1968!

The implications have been serious indeed. Boeing remains the foremost aircraft manufacturer. But both McDonnell–Douglas and Lockheed have now lost their place in this market. We recall that American's original proposal in 1966 was for a two-engine medium- to short-range wide-body jet. While Lockheed and McDonnell–Douglas were battering each other, the European Airbus Industrie consortium moved in with its twin-engine A-300 Airbus and derivatives (500 orders and options to date from 45 airlines). The United States' prospects for the future are further dimmed by the possibility that Japan may become a strong competitor in the aircraft manufacturing business and thus continue the pattern set with automobiles and consumer electronics.[10] Southeast Asia is expected to be the fastest growing commercial aircraft market for the next 20 years.

---

[9]A hastily assembled consortium involving Rolls–Royce, the British government, and Lockheed.
[10]See Section XII C for a discussion of Japan's MITI.

2. *The Bankruptcy of Rolls–Royce*

Lockheed began work on the largest jet aircraft ever designed, the C5A military transport, in 1965. To win the fierce competition with Boeing it had to propose a price that assumed the best of all engineering worlds, that is, a project in which everything goes right. This is standard procedure in contracting with the U.S. Department of Defense. The hope is that the usual overruns can be later "taken care of" by claims and higher price follow-on orders. However, Secretary of Defense Robert McNamara instituted a total package procurement system (TPP) designed to improve the process. Under this concept, bidders were required to submit one bid covering research, development, and production. The winner's contract fixed the total price, as well as specifications and delivery dates. In essence, the risks and uncertainties were shifted from the U.S. Department of Defense to the manufacturer. The revolutionary C5A was the first major test of TPP and Lockheed's inevitable overruns were now to be made good by the company, not the Pentagon. Further, the expected follow-on orders did not materialize in the wake of the Vietnam debacle. There was growing opposition to U.S. Department of Defense requests, particularly huge transports designed to carry American troops to remote locations and facilitate United States involvement in distant conflicts, such as Vietnam.

O: The Company faced a $750 million claim by the U.S. Department of Defense just at the time it was moving forward full force on the costly development of the L-1011. After prolonged discussions, Chairman Dan Haughton flew to Washington in January 1971 to settle the claim with Deputy Secretary of Defense David Packard. Haughton reluctantly agreed to accept a loss of $480 million. From Washington, he flew on to London to meet with the Rolls–Royce management on progress and problems with their engine for the L-1011. On his arrival he was informed that Rolls–Royce would declare bankruptcy the next day. It was a terrible shock to the British public and to Dan Haughton. As a British government official put it, "the news of Rolls–Royce was like hearing that Westminster Abbey had become a brothel." As Lockheed had selected the Rolls–Royce RB-211 jet engine (more advanced than that of General Electric) to power its L-1011, the implications for Lockheed were severe: the entire L-1011 program—a billion dollar investment—was placed in jeopardy. A switch to the General Electric engine at this late date would delay and raise the cost of the program. But so would salvation of the RB-211 program. And Lockheed was just made $480 million poorer by the settlement with the U.S. Department of Defense.

It is interesting to speculate the effect if these two events, separated by a few days, had been reversed in time. If the U.S. government had had full knowledge of Lockheed's dilemma with Rolls–Royce prior to its meeting on the C5A with Haughton, a settlement more favorable to the company would have been a strong possibility.

P: At this point Haughton's brilliant management capability came into play.[11] He realized that the British government was willing to help Rolls–Royce's survival by providing a share of the needed funds. He had to keep the six airlines that ordered the L-1011 from bolting, and he had to satisfy the 24 American bankers who were increasingly nervous about their Lockheed loans. The British government was willing to advance $250 million to keep the RB-211 work going but wanted assurances that Lockheed would complete the L-1011 program; the U.S. government wanted its $480 million C5A reimbursement. Haughton persuaded each of his L-1011 customers to pay $640,000 more per airplane and the banks to extend their line of credit. But this was contingent on a $250 million government loan guarantee. The U.S. government had a justifiable concern in avoiding the collapse of Lockheed—a prime DOD resource and a leader in aerospace technology. Its engineers believed deeply in the company slogan "Look to Lockheed for Leadership."[12] The Administration proposed the guarantee and Congress approved it—by three votes in the House of Representatives and one vote in the Senate. In hindsight the guarantee was a complete success. The banks received their loan repayments and the U.S. Treasury collected $31 million in fees.

Much of the success of this cliff-hanger can be attributed to Dan Haughton himself. Born in 1911 to a poor Alabama farmer's wife, he started to supplement the family's income when he was eight. In school he was good in mathematics and graduated from the University of Alabama in accounting and business administration. His rise at Lockheed began with a $3300 per year job as a systems analyst in 1939. Ten years later he was president of two small Lockheed subsidiaries. John Newhouse (1982:49–50), in his book *The Sporty Game,* gives this description of Haughton:

Lockheed had a vivid style. . . . In (Haughton's) day, it was a bold and exceptionally innovative company, more worldly than its competitors but somewhat less rigorously managed than Boeing or the engine manufacturers. Haughton is perhaps the most interesting figure his industry has produced. He is sometimes described as a red-clay aristocrat, both because he has a naturally gracious and modest manner and because his beginnings in rural Alabama, were modest too. Yet he was also an inspirational leader, and was often said to be evangelical in promoting Lockheed's interests.

---

[11]Chairman Courtlandt Gross had perceived Haughton's talent early: "I first met Dan Haughton in 1939, soon after he came to work for us. It was evident then that he had managerial and leadership qualities, loyalty, and very good judgment" (Meyers, 1969:78).

[12]The brilliance of just two technical achievements—the Polaris missile program led by Eugene Root and the YF-12 reconnaissance aircraft program led by Clarence (Kelly) Johnson—amply support this claim.

I, too, have been exposed to the Haughton style and have been similarly impressed. When he spoke one was invariably reminded of his fellow Alabaman, Governor George Wallace. His complete dedication to his company was always in evidence. With regard to a controversial consultant, he once said, "I would hire the devil if it will do the company some good." He would typically spend a day at the Marietta, Georgia, plant, fly the company jet back to the Burbank headquarters at night, and be in his office at 5 a.m. It was general knowledge among his staff that the best time to see him was before 7 a.m.

3. The Grease Machine

O/P: Haughton not only drove himself mercilessly but also inspired remarkably intense levels of effort by his people. We recall that Haughton had garnered 168 L-1011 orders in the Spring of 1968, but this was still far below the break-even number of 250 (which itself kept rising inexorably). Haughton was determined to try for a miracle—to sell enough L-1011s to make the program profitable despite the market split. The key was overseas sales—and marketing in most countries was a sporty game indeed. As Haughton's right-hand man, Lockheed's President Carl Kotchian, explained marketing expenses of $4.6 million in Japan in 1972:

If you want to sell airplanes in Japan this is the way that you do it. It is a normal practice outside the United States. There are only certain countries where you do not have to make such payments: one is the United States and another is England. In the rest of the world, generally speaking, you must practice this kind of thing in order to sell airplanes. You must have a man who has connections and give him money [Boulton, 1978:7].

Two Japanese airlines were in the market for DC-10s or L-1011s: Japan Airlines (JAL) wanted 12 and All Nippon (ANA) wanted six. Of these, the ANA order was the more attractive because of follow-on potential. Kotchian was in charge of the Japanese marketing task. He recalls:

If U.S. products were to be imported by Japan, the Nixon administration would be happiest if Japan purchased Lockheed planes. These were the plausible rumors which we were going to circulate. It was the main feature of our strategy. [Boulton, 1978:240].

He knew that the procurement decision would be made by the Japanese government, not the airlines themselves. On August 21, 1972, Kotchian suggested to Lockheed's official representatives in Japan, Marubeni Corporation, that its head meet the new Prime Minister, Kakuei Tanaka.

According to Boulton, the next day Marubeni's Managing Director proposed "a pledge to pay money to Prime Minister Tanaka." Kotchian asked, "How much?" The reply: "The customary amount to ask for a favor in connection with a major transaction is 500 million yen." If Lockheed could come up with the cash, Marubeni associate Toshiharu Okubo would look after arrangements for transferring the cash, because he was "very close to Mr. Enomoto" (Tanaka's secretary). "It was at this point" says Kotchian, "that I was convinced that the money was going to the office of Japan's Prime Minister."

Kotchian then went to see Lockheed's influential agent Yoshio Kodama and there meet Kenji Osano, the single biggest private stockholder of both airlines and an old confidant of the Prime Minister. He also needed 500 million yen. Kotchian:

In the morning I was made by Mr. Okubo to promise 500 million yen intended for Mr. Tanaka and in the afternoon I was asked by Mr. Kodama to pay an additional 500 million to Mr. Osano. It occurred to me that 500 million yen seemed to be a figure frequently used in Japan [quoted in Boulton, 1978, 243].

Thus in one day Lockheed's President had committed the corporation to $3.5 million in payoffs. Subsequent disclosures indicate that the competition was also making "questionable payments" in Japan.

This was not the end. To clinch the ANA order Okubo needed another 120 million yen in cash for ANA President Wakasa and six Japanese politicians. Okubo:

If you ready the money first thing tomorrow morning, we can formally get the ANA order during tomorrow without fail. I would like to have the whole sum ready by 10 a.m. [quoted in Boulton, 1978:249].

The timetable was too tight, but 30 million yen was delivered before 10 a.m. Six hours later, Kotchian was asked to be at ANA's head office at 6 p.m. There Wakasa told him:

Congratulations, Mr. Kotchian, your company has got our company's contract [Boulton, 1978:249–250].

Kotchian:

If, in a situation where high government officials have influence on matters pertinent to a private company, money is requested as pay-offs for those officials, can that private foreign company, which wants its products to be bought at all costs, realistically decline the request on the grounds that it is not a good thing from the ethical point of view? [Boulton, 1978:252].

The Senate Subcommittee investigating the payoffs found that Lockheed had paid out $22 to 24 million to spur overseas sales of its L-1011, Starfighter, and C-130 transport between 1961 and 1972 [*Time*, Feb. 23, 1976]. Few Lockheed employees voiced criticism when these revelations hit them through the media coverage (quoted in the *New York Times*, Feb. 17, 1976):

Barbara Alexander, Senior Secretary:

Everybody's doing it. That's the name of the game; that's the way business is done all over the world these days. Why do they have to pick on Lockheed?

George Crozier, hydraulic specialist, with the company nearly 40 years:

Everybody else does it—not just in aerospace, but throughout business. . . . Mr. Haughton's been responsible for keeping this company on its feet; we need him; it's too bad he has to be the scapegoat

Mae Woods, Secretary:

We're not angry; we're scared. I told [my 14-year-old idealistic son] that what the company did wasn't right, but that it had no choice. And he said: "How could you say that?" I told him that "you wouldn't be asking me these questions if you were 44 and had to pay bills."

4. The DC-10 Cargo Door Case

Marketing is certainly not the only industry activity for which the O and P perspectives shed insights. An engineering problem[13] may also require these perspectives for more than superficial understanding.

T: On June 11, 1972, an American Airlines DC-10 enroute from Detroit to Buffalo experienced an explosive decompression over Windsor, Ontario. Although most control cables were disabled, it landed safely at Detroit. The trouble was quickly traced to a rear cargo compartment door that was not properly locked and had blown off.

This was in fact, not a new problem. In 1969, Nicholas Schipper of the Dutch Civil Aviation Authority had voiced his concern to the Federal Aviation Administration (FAA) over possible loss of control of the DC-10 if a collapse of the floor between passenger and cargo levels occurred. In April 1970 the subcontractor for the cargo door, Convair, recognized

---

[13]One of the two major problems with the DC-10. The other was cracks in the engine pylon resulting in engine separation (responsible for the American Airlines crash in Chicago, May 25, 1979, with 271 deaths). Improper engine installation during maintenance appeared to be a prime contributing factor.

that the cargo door locks were inadequate and conducted a "fault analysis" of the problem. This analysis also showed that, following a cargo door blowout, the floor of the passenger cabin would collapse.

A month later in the standard "pressure vessel test" of the DC-10 at McDonnell–Douglas, the forward cargo door exploded open and part of the floor buckled. An engineering fix was made: venting between the passenger compartment and forward cargo hold (Godson, 1975).

O: The FAA has at its disposal two means of effecting change in aircraft systems: 1) issuance of recommendations incorporated in the manufacturer's service bulletins and 2) issuance of air worthiness directives. The former are advisory, the latter have the force of law. Manufacturers inherently dislike directives and strongly prefer to deal through service bulletins.

O: Within five days of the American Airlines incident, the Los Angeles office of the FAA had prepared a directive ordering a fix of the cargo door locking system. The Washington FAA office promptly released the directive on June 16, 1972.

P: Douglas Division President McGowen contacted FAA Administrator Shaffer personally immediately after the incident and reached a "gentleman's agreement" to go the Service bulletin route.

O: The Los Angeles and Washington offices were not aware of the agreement when the directive was issued. On June 19 an order went out from the FAA to its regional offices to destroy the directive. In its stead McDonnell–Douglas issued Service Bulletin A52-35, which strongly recommended a quick fix—a viewing window in the cargo door so the cargo loading crew could check whether the door was properly locked (using a flashlight to peer in if needed).

O: The National Transportation Safety Board (NTSB), an agency independent of the FAA, is charged with investigation of accidents. It makes recommendations to the FAA on the basis of its examinations. The existence of two such organizations has inevitably generated bureaucratic animosity between them. The NTSB claimed at one point (1970) that it had made 121 recommendations for correction and improvement based on its accident investigations, yet only 45 were either "complied with" or "essentially complied with." In response the FAA insisted that it had received 115 recommendations from the NTSB and complied with 105, rejecting only 10.[14]

---

[14]Significantly, the same organizational animus still persists a dozen years later. In the case of the B-737 Air Florida jet crash into Washington's 14th Street Bridge January 13, 1982, NTSB recommended on-ground wing deicers or an increase in take-off speed. By November, the FAA concluded that it was premature to order either change. In January 1983, NTSB went public with a response letter rejecting the FAA conclusion and urging immediate action for the current winter season.

By June 23, the NTSB had prepared its recommendations (A-72-97, A-72-98) with respect to the DC-10 cargo door problem: 1) an effective locking mechanism, and 2) venting between passenger and aft cargo compartments. The FAA ignored these recommendations, and no directive was issued. The FAA merely told the NTSB that "additional modifications are being considered." On July 3, a more substantial modification in the locking mechanism was recommended in Manufacturer's Service Bulletin 52-37 by McDonnell–Douglas. The airlines made the modification gradually (for example, United averaged 90 days for its DC-10s and American Airlines, 268 days. Presumably the corrective measure was also incorporated in DC-10s not yet completed or delivered to the airlines.

T: In fact, not all DC-10s received the modification. On March 3, 1974, 20 months after the issuance of the service bulletin, a Turkish THY DC-10 rose from Paris on its way to London, lost the rear cargo door 12 minutes later, and crashed with a loss of 346 lives. The correction had never been made on this aircraft. As in the American Airlines case the passenger floor collapsed into the cargo area below and crippled the flight control system (severing the cables imbedded in the floor).

O: McDonnell–Douglas records showed that the modifications stipulated in Service Bulletin 52-37 had been made on this aircraft prior to delivery to the airline (and on another found subsequently to be defective). Apparently the quality-control records were inaccurate (Godson, 1975:238).

5. Summing Up

It should be apparent that the O and P perspectives illuminate facets that are central to the decision-making process in the commercial aircraft business.

The O perspective tells us:

- Headquarters management may be inclined to weight the O more heavily than the T perspective and override engineering advice:
  There was a characteristic split at some airlines: engineering departments preferring the L-1011; headquarters favoring their old Douglas relationship.
- Logical analysis may easily succumb to other deep-seated corporate needs:
  The disastrous effect of splitting the market and building two similar trijets was recognized in advance; there is almost an aura of Greek tragedy to the game.
- Bribery is a standard operating procedure:
  It is virtually forced on the manufacturer overseas in a competitive market.
- The pervasive organizational reaction "don't rock the boat" can have deadly long-term impact:

The DC-10 cargo door could have been a minor matter if handled forcefully at the outset by all concerned. (The automobile industry has shown a similar tendency.)

The P perspective suggests:

- One person's leadership, charisma, and negotiating skill can save an organization:
  The Rolls-Royce bankruptcy involved Lockheed, 24 U.S. banks, and two governments in an incredibly complex situation. Dan Haughton personally was the key to its successful resolution and saved Lockheed.
- Matching a leader to a situation (or P to O) is crucial:
  Mr. Mac had been an outstanding aircraft industry pioneer, but his lack of familiarity with the commercial side of the business had a serious impact on the organization at crucial moments.

In general, such insights can be developed prior to the decision point, albeit not by confining ourselves to the traditional T-oriented "analysis." Indeed, recognition of the implications of such insights may be used to good advantage, for example, pointing up a specific need to match the key person to the situation.

However, we also are made acutely aware, from both O and P perspectives, that:

- Unforeseeable events can prove critical:
  The selection of C. R. Smith by President Johnson to become Secretary of Commerce may have been pivotal to American Airlines' choice of the DC-10.
  A reversal of appointment days for Dan Haughton to settle the C5A claim with the Pentagon and fly to London to meet with Rolls–Royce might have substantially helped Lockheed.

TABLE 13. Summary of the Policy Studies Presented in the Next Four Chapters

Subject	Nature of effort	Scope	Technology	Chapter
Health care—perinatal regionalization	New study—social system strategy development	Local–urban	Social	VII
Electronic funds transfer	Retrospective look at National Science Foundation (NSF) TA	National	Physical–contemporary	VIII
Guayule commercialization	New perspectives on NSF TA in progress	Regional	Physical–old	IX
On-site solid waste treatment	New perspectives on NSF TA in progress	Local–nonurban	Physical–old and new	X

D. COMMENT

In this chapter, we savored a varied menu of corporate decision problems in terms of multiple perspectives. In the next four chapters, we focus on four policy studies (three of them formal technology assessments). In each case, the question is the same: does the use of multiple perspectives add significant insights and thus improve the basis for decision making? The four cases are summarized in Table 13.

VII

HEALTH CARE SYSTEM: A CASE STUDY[1]

L. UMBDENSTOCK

It is not the outsider with a "better" system that becomes king, but the insider who most thoroughly masters the internal system.

Gerald M. Weinberg
An Introduction to General Systems Thinking

In the previous two chapters, we sampled the use of multiple perspectives in a wide range of contexts—from the U.S. Civil War to today's electronics industry. We now examine several applications in greater detail. The first concerns social technology: the design of a perinatal regionalization system. Like the School of Nursing case (Section V C), it deals with health care; however, the allocated effort permitted deeper probing and evaluation of the present one.

The region is part of a large metropolitan county where over half of the population is Black and Hispanic. It leads the county in fetal, neonatal, and infant death rates and has the highest teenage and total birth rate, as well as the lowest median family income in the county. "Perinatal" refers to the period surrounding birth—prenatal, natal, and postnatal care, family planning, and genetic counseling. "Regionalization" refers to coordination of institutions and personnel providing perinatal care services in a given area (both private and public). The aim is to match health risk level with appropriate services to ensure the best outcome for mother and infant, while maintaining an efficient use of resources. The O and P perspectives shed light on the difficulty in accomplishing so rational an endeavor. They also provide clues for courses of action to be pursued.

A. BACKGROUND

For years the American medical profession has been concerned and embarrassed over the United States' standing in the world in birth-related mortality rates: we rank 17th! The perinatal regionalization project was conceptualized in the 1970s to alter this situation. This assessment may help determine the further evolution of this sociotechnical system.

The study consists of two parts: a multiple perspective policy analysis of the project and a decision Delphi to aid in participative policy formulation for the future of the system. The former is condensed here; the latter is briefly discussed in Section XI E 2. Both are fully described in Umbdenstock (1981). Perinatal regionalization now commonly includes the following features:

- methods to coordinate and communicate medical services;

- programs of continuing education for all providers in the system;

- methods for monitoring cost and effectiveness;

- standardized medical records, often computerized for reporting and research;

- patient referral and transport;

- consultative services and diagnostic laboratory;

- interdisciplinary peer review;

---

[1]This chapter is a condensation of a doctoral dissertation by Linda Umbdenstock, done with the guidance of H. Linstone and completed in June 1981.

- early identification of high-risk mothers;
- assessment of facilities (designation of hospitals based on equipment, staff, and expertise);
- follow-up of high-risk mothers and newborns.

Common problem areas observed in reports on perinatal regionalization programs are:

- fear of regimentation and bureaucratic entanglement negating professional autonomy;
- fear of relegation to normal care management and exclusion from high-risk (higher status, more interesting) case management;
- inability of smaller hospitals to compete and subsequent loss of physicians and patients to more extensively equipped facilities;
- distance to be traveled by physicians;
- fear of change in the physician–patient relationship;
- lack of admission or referral policies, methods of financing;
- lack of admitting privileges (acceptance of physician to admit patients at a given hospital);
- lack of definition and estimation of patients (high versus low risk);
- lack of clear definition, increased expectations and complexity in medical standards as well as their potential effect on malpractice litigation and revenues;
- threat of increased government interference and licensing requirements;
- ambiguous role of the general practitioner and the family practice specialist as related to the provision of perinatal care;
- social–religious aspects of referral hospitals (for example, sterilizations and abortions);
- economic nature of hospitals and the differences between public, private, nonprofit, and private profit institutions.

Health professionals involved in perinatal regionalization in the project under study include physicians, nurses, administrators, planners, research and data staff, and support and clerical workers. The types of facilities or provider sites include:

- Hospitals
  a tertiary level countywide general hospital,
  a secondary level private/nonprofit hospital,
  a primary level private/profit hospital,
  a primary level private/profit hospital in reorganization;

- Ambulatory facilities
  10 county locations,
  two free clinics,
  several private group practices,
  many private physician offices.

The types of medical specialities or subspecialties included in perinatal regionalization are obstetrics and gynecology (perinatology, genetics), pediatrics (neonatology, genetics), family practice, and general practice. We now present abbreviated versions of the three perspectives applied to this social technology case.

B. THE T PERSPECTIVE

1. The Rationale

The concerns and approaches found in national statements of perinatal regionalization are reflected in the local area under study. In fact they are found in the initial planning and organization statement used to solicit consensus among key potential participants even prior to obtaining the grant. The purpose of regionalization is:

> . . . to establish a cooperative network for provision of perinatal services in the. . . . Region . . . to improve the outcomes of pregnancy by assuring all patients access to the facility or resource which provides the services most appropriate to patient needs, continuously improving the quality of institutional and professional services, increasing intraregional communication, and maximizing the efficient and appropriate utilization of all participants in the Regional network.
>
> To assess and document the impact and effectiveness of such a network on pregnancy outcomes; on professional, paraprofessional, and institutional performance; on patient and professional satisfaction; and on efficiency of resource allocation. [Proposed Statement of Philosophy and Objective.]

Efficient use of resources and effectiveness of methods to improve the quality of care, through a network of services meeting every level of patients' risk, was at the heart of the proposed effort.

In addition to providing support to these efforts, grant funding was sought to demonstrate that an urban minority, high-need area with a newly established medical school and tertiary level hospital was capable of establishing a system meeting the area's specific needs.

2. The Key Decisions and Implementation Strategies

Initially, efforts to organize a regional network brought together doctors, nurses, and administrators from both the public and private sectors to increase the quality of care in the region through mutual cooperation. This group supported the decision to seek grant funding to provide staff for augmenting regional resources both directly and indirectly. With many regional projects forming throughout the country, a variety of alternative approaches was available. Knowledge of regional providers, along with the basic goals of improved health care delivery, shaped the particular philosophy and principles of the organization (formalized in November 1974 as a Regional Perinatal Committee). Decisions regarding the general objectives of the regional network laid out the program components to be developed.

Time lines, staffing patterns, and budget allocations delineate the original plan to implement the objectives. Changes in them point to decisions to adjust and refine priorities and strategies. A detailed "Plan of Action" is a virtual map, over 70 pages long, of the original implementation strategies. The proposed and actual organization charts and budgets show changes in the scale and specific components of the regional plan as staffed. Figure 14 indicates significant project milestones.

3. Cost–Benefit Indicators and Performance Measures

The basic questions to consider are: What has been gained by $2.5 million over five years? What ongoing costs need to be picked up, and are they worth it? The project has generated many contributions to the region. The outputs of these efforts can be measured on several levels—first, the number of specific activities, and second, the changes in patterns of resources, procedures, mechanisms in place, and results. An example of the latter is seen in Table 14.

Overall, dramatic changes in the pattern of care have resulted in large part from the impetus provided by the project working with county and private agencies. High-risk perinatal care became twice as available, and the waiting time for the first visit decreased by 50%. Current areas of need are staff and space in the public sector (or load redistribution), physician in-service policy formulation, patient education in the private sector, and high-risk infant follow-up in both public and private sectors.

There are no available measures of long-term benefits for disabled children, changes in litigation costs for malpractice, and system savings in perinatal costs versus cost to raise the standards. The closing of several hospitals does, however, represent cost-effective concentration of efforts in large obstetric services more capable of producing positive results (generally said to be those with over 1000 deliveries per year). Undoubtedly, the remaining hospitals faced increased costs to upgrade their staffs and equipment. Some of these represent one-time costs; others represent improved management through staff reorganization—the long-range cost of which is measured by decreased malpractice costs. Ongoing costs to maintain project assistance include in-service education and data processing as means of maintaining and developing the quality of care and to monitor results and developing problems. Patient costs reflect the rising institutional costs, with

FIGURE 14. Major project milestones.

	1974	1975	1976	1977	1978	1979
Liaison with state, county, regional agencies established	X					
Regional perinatal committee organized	X					
Special medical record implements (policy)		X	X	X	X	
Regional conference on perinatal health care		X				
High risk diagnostic services available to region		X				
Classes and meetings accredited			X			
Data system operating				X		
HSA agreement and privacy and confidentiality agreement				X		
JCAH and Medicaid approval of forms					X	
Agency profiles completed					X	
Pediatric follow-up assessment forms developed and used				X	X	
Neonatal modules completed					X	
Infant follow-up conference						X
First mortality and morbidity conference						X
Workshops for office staff						X

Record Orientation	Classes at Center	Classes At Sites On request	Training of Hospitals' In-Service Instructors emphasized. and Self-Instructional Program	Consultation on Nursing Service Organization and Hospitals' In-Service Program Development Conferences for Office Staff
75/76	76/78	78	79	80

the closing of certain hospitals. There is no longer a choice of low-cost delivery for self-payers. The alternative, the county hospital, is higher in cost than private care.

What impact did this great amount of effort have on perinatal outcomes, as measured by perinatal mortality and morbidity? A major research project by Johns Hopkins University compared the results of regional births in 1977 and 1979 as part of a major project, which included seven other regions and control areas. Birth weight-specific disability was measured on the basis of one-year follow-up studies of all babies residing in the region, irrespective of where they received care. The results showed no significant difference within this period.

Another major study in 1977 based on an approach of comparing observed versus expected outcomes for birth weight- and ethnicity-specific categories showed a poor ranking for the hospitals when compared with hospitals statewide.

A number of research issues are involved in these findings—perhaps most significantly, the rapidly and radically changing conditions during the time of the intervention and measurement.

TABLE 14. Key Project Interventions and Results

Intervention by project			Results		
Identification of patients at risk					
Pub[a]	Pri[b]	Protocols implemented	Pub	Pri	Screening is an integral part of prenatal intake
Pub	Pri	POPRAS in use	Pub	Pri	Consistent identification of high-risk prenatal
Pub	Pri	Nursing in-service for ID	Pub	Pri	Intrapartum risk assessment
Pub	Pri	Screening staff trained	Pub	Pri	Neonatal risk assessment
Identification and management of resources					
Pub	Pri	Provide in-service to increase quality of care	Pub	Pri	Increase resources
Pub	Pri	Negotiate levels of hospitals	Pub	Pri	Hospitals categorized
Pub	Pri	Augment resources through planning, grant seeking, and consulting services	Pub	Pri	Continuing education in-service for nurses
Pub	Pri	Provide quality of care feedback	–	Pri	Attract new physicians to area
Matching patients and resources					
Pub	–	Protocols, in-service and auditing for high-risk mothers and infants	Pub	–	Routine referral of high risk to special clinic for diagnosis
–	Pri	Protocols and in-service for high-risk patient transfer	–	Pri	Same referral of high risk for antenatal diagnosis
Pub	Pri	Insured routine and emergency transfer	Pub	–	High-risk patients seen at high-risk clinics
Pub	–	Public Sector	–	Pri	Some intrapartum transfer
–	Pri	Private Sector	–	Pri	Some increase in early neonatal transfers

Source: Gore (1979).

[a]Public sector.   [b]Private Sector.

A number of specific results indicate program potential. Perinatal mortality among the highest risk group, who had used the special obstetrics diagnostic laboratory, was 8 per 1000 in contrast to 14 per 1000 for nonusers. Low birth weight, a prime indicator of perinatal mortality, was 3% for laboratory users versus 8% for high-risk nonusers. Similarly, women in a comprehensive program for high-risk pregnancies had fewer perinatal deaths and other indicators of morbidity. A concentrated education program for low-risk women with fewer physician contacts also showed better results than did a comparable group. Special programs for pregnant adolescents yielded better outcomes for their participants as well.

4. Analysis of Changing Input Factors

A number of factors greatly affected the progress of regionalization in a negative way: population changes, decreases in public sector funding, regulatory pressure, and changes in professional work force.

Population changes. Both the number and distribution of patients in the region changed over the course of the project. Most significantly, the increase in the Spanish-surnamed population increased not only the birth rate but the redistribution of patient load into the public sector, because many of these patients are "self-payers" and as such are unacceptable for private hospital admission (Figure 15). An estimate of impact can be gauged by the size of the shift from 23% Spanish-surnamed births in 1970 to 48% in 1976, and from 41% Black to 36%. Overall minority births increased from 64 to 85%. In the public sector in 1980, minority women comprised 99% of deliveries—about 90% being Spanish surnamed. The population shift brought with it medical and management concerns as well—increased high-risk pregnancies and deliveries; different types of problems such as hypertension, sickle-cell anemia, and high multiparity (number of previous deliveries); and patient behaviors, including poor diet, increased lack of care seeking, etc. (see Table 15).

Decreased public sector funding. While public sector births (see Figure 15) and the associated risk were increasing, funding from state and county sources declined dramatically. The increased work load at the county hospital can be seen by comparing the number of births with the number of staff. Staffing depends not only on availability but on budgeted positions and hiring freezes. In com-

FIGURE 15. Actual and projected deliveries—county hospital, 1973–1980.

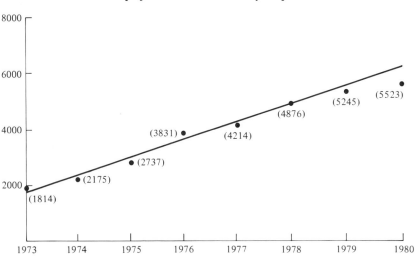

TABLE 15. Comparison of Births with and without Prenatal Care

Category	Prenatal care (%)	No prenatal care (%)
Total	91.6	8.4
Low birth weight	2.6	9.5
Low APGAR	2.2	4.8
Maternal complications	10.5	14.3
Infant complications	24.9	52.4
Born out of asepcis	3.1	5.0
Neonatal intensive care unit	7.0	5.0
Difficult delivery	8.3	9.5
Stillbirth/neonatal death	0	9.5

Source: Spanish Surnamed Study (1979).

parison with other county facilities, this hospital has 23% of the public births, 15% of labor and delivery registered nurses (RNs), and 0% of critical care nurses in labor and delivery. The number of budgeted RNs has remained 11 despite the doubling of births in five years. According to professional standards, 32 RNs are necessary for this case load. According to a productivity study performed by the Arthur C. Young Co., a total of 79 staff (all levels combined) are necessary for the current work load: the total staff numbers 32. In addition, cuts in other support areas increased nonnursing functions, such as cleaning, stocking, errands, meal distribution, etc.

Various political measures produced funding changes. In 1976 an initiative passed by voters drastically cut property taxes and consequently various services. The 1980 elections brought a wave of budget-slashing politicians to office, including a majority on the County Board of Supervisors who had campaigned to cut medical services for "illegal aliens." At the state level, a special program for high-risk mothers and infants cut out pediatric services for high-risk infants and decreased support of prenatal services in the region.

Work force changes. The late 1970s saw a great nursing shortage develop. For many nurses, hospital work required the greatest work effort and the fewest rewards. In strictly monetary terms, one could work a registry for selected days (similar to substitute teaching) and make as much as in full-time hospital work— with more independence. Vacancies became extremely difficult to fill (many were filled with foreign-trained staff), and turnover was high. The cycle of overload is suggested in Figures 16a and b.

Not only nurses but physicians and administrators changed. Of the 21 partic-

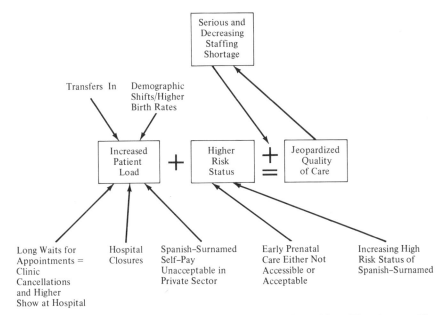

FIGURE 16a. Overview of county obstetrics overload. The problem: There is a steadily increasing patient load, a high risk status of patients overall, complicated by a serious staffing shortage. All of these variables work together to affect the quality of care.

ipants in the 1974–1975 planning sessions, four represented institutions that are now closed and 14 no longer in the region. The remaining three were the project directors and administrator.

Regulatory pressures. The 1970s saw a dramatic rise in malpractice insurance, in fact an insurance crisis, and an increase in government-mandated attempts at cost containment—Health Services Agency (HSA) Planning and Certificate of Need requirements for capital expenses. Both produced some impetus for co-operative self-regulation and planning. The region produced an agreement with the local HSA acknowledging the region's interest in and capability to plan in the area.

5. Summary

Despite the achievements and unfulfilled expectations of the project, the true extent of its impact remains unknown, because without the program the impact could not be measured: there is no other region to be matched on critical dimensions; key conditions of patient inputs and regular levels of support did not remain constant but, in fact, changed drastically. The stabilization of the number of births in the early 1980s seemed to be accompanied by a significant drop in

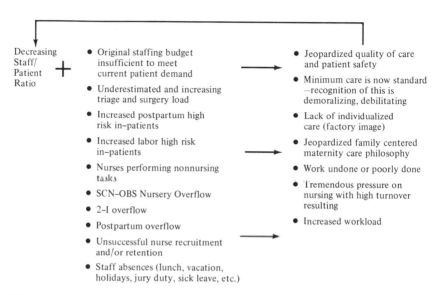

FIGURE 16b. Overview of the labor and delivery staffing problem. *Source: Labor and Delivery Overload Study (1980).*

mortality rates. Several areas of activity are still in the process of development, hinging on changes extraneous to the system. Nevertheless, current assessment of need and areas of success suggest directions for the future.

C. THE O PERSPECTIVE

1. The Organizational Elements

The county hospital is the largest provider of obstetric and pediatric services and the pivotal institution in regionalization. It also serves as a resident training center, that is, a postgraduate school. The role played by private practitioners in the private hospital is represented by faculty in the public hospital, with an important difference. The public hospital is a training facility, and as such must be prepared (in terms of equipment, high-level support staff, etc.) to handle any perinatal problem. These special demands are set against the county funding crisis and an especially severe nursing shortage in the public sector. Management of this crisis is viewed differently by the training- and service-oriented faculty on the one hand, and the cost-containment-oriented administrators in the public hospital on the other.

The hospital, being the only multistory, multiacre structure in the area, is claimed as a symbol of the Black Community effort. This status is rooted in the fact that the hospital bond measure was rejected at the polls by the larger, non-Black populace, and its construction represents major political maneuvering.

Much is at stake in its successful operation, both on the part of the powers that brought it into being and those who voiced the demand on behalf of the community. The day-to-day operation of the hospital reflects these currents.

As in any institution, there is a disparity between the one that exists on paper and the one that is a functioning reality. As a county institution, this discrepancy is evident in many ways and reflects the nature of county institutions. For example, the county persists in basing its planning and projections on 90 post-partum beds, whereas there are fewer than 60, because one-third are allocated to gynecology and antepartum patients.

There is also a disparity in the professionally defined nursing role and actual nursing practice in the overcrowded, understaffed hospital. People come and go, but the unique institution remains recognizably the same. For all the internal hassles, staff from the top down switch into a proud mode when addressing the role of this hospital vis-à-vis other medical institutions and talk of becoming a model and possible training site for others.

The region also has a private nonprofit hospital, religiously affiliated and long established in this community. The third hospital in the area is a small community hospital operated by a national hospital corporation. It is the newest of the three and the most beautifully appointed. The feeder clinics and private physicians complete the list.

2. The Organizational Dynamics

Within each organization, the dynamics center on professional roles, power distribution, and socialization of front-line workers. Understanding these is the key to understanding the dynamics of accepting regionalization and its implementation.

For example, doctors give orders and expect to be assisted. If, while the nurses are busy, one doctor pulls rank with an unreasonable request, such as having a nurse order his supper, she may intentionally keep him waiting by staying busy with other doctors or patients requiring attention. She can also let a new intern, who is practicing the status of "doctor," sink for lack of information; conversely, a nurse may subtly advise, "Doctor, we usually give this medication . . . to a patient in this situation. Do you wish to do the same?"

Points may be scored by doctors in other ways, such as case conferences. The primary purpose of case reviews is to provide education, with the aim of improving the quality of care. This is one place where the variety of cases becomes an attractive recruitment tool. An intern presenting a case in front of his peers, faculty, nurses, and technicians is on the spot. Not only is he publicly reviewed for the way in which he handled the patient, but he is also on the firing line as part of the initiation required to join the fraternity. He may escape censure if he can blame an identified problem on a nurse. It is a battleground where nurses have no position and, thus, have ceased to participate.

Another subtle result of these conferences traditionally is team identification. Party lines are established between obstetrics, pediatrics, and anesthesiology, and the behavioral protocols are hammered out.

The Computer: Threat to Doctors, Benefit to Nurses

Since 1969, Dr. Larry Weed and his colleagues at the University of Vermont Medical School have been developing the computer-based Problem Oriented Medical Information System (PROMIS). It contains 45,000 tree branching displays of medical guidance and information. The group has also created the Problem Oriented Medical Record (POMR), which structures a patient's medical information (i.e., history, diagnosis, treatment plans, progress notes) logically. The patient, assisted by a nurse, can input symptoms and answer questions himself by means of a touch sensitive screen. The system thus becomes more patient oriented. Of course, such systems also serve the physician as powerful tools to guide him through the complexities characteristic of a field in rapid technological evolution. With PROMIS, the physician touches the appropriate line on a display, and the system presents the next choice or needed input for him. The physician no longer needs to rely as heavily on his memory—the computer becomes a prosthesis of his brain. Although a considerable number of physicians have become users of the POMR, the majority of physicians resist this challenge to their mystique, territory, and economic privilege.

Gordon Cook (1979, 1982) reports that

> nurses love [the system] because [it gives] them access to the electronic record of the physician's decision-making process, the *complete* process, for the first time ever.

Cook quotes anthropologist John Pfifferling on one case:

> Nurses were able to audit the care of the patient, since they had access to the same store of information that the physician had. The nurses' questioning of the logic behind diagnostic and therapeutic plans, made so apparent by the computer, was considered by some physicians as highly insolent. The computer was voted out of the ward by a meeting of the senior medical staff. . . . The new roles and responsibilities that emerged through the "compulsiveness" of the computer were, in my assessment, "territorially" unacceptable to those in power.

Cook adds:

> The nurses, in their own meeting, voted unanimously to keep the computer on the ward. It was nevertheless removed. After a decade . . . Dr. Weed had gained the reputation of a charismatic iconoclast and had challenged so many entrenched interests that he was getting nowhere.

Yet another dimension of the system is the relationship between nurses, more specifically the relationship between RNs and licensed vocational nurses (LVNs). The RNs supervise and are accountable by virtue of their training and responsibilities. Because RNs have more career opportunities and are generally overextended due to severe nursing shortages, they have a much higher turnover rate. The LVNs generally have the greater longevity and have used it to develop a system of their own.

There are initiation rites in which the mythologies of the place, the proper attitudes and roles, priorities, and channels are learned so one can know his place in the system. When a new nurse comes in he or she is tried in various ways to determine his or her willingness to perform group-assigned (as opposed to supervisor) tasks without questioning or causing trouble for others by making waves within the system. Someone sensitive to these internal dynamics and cuing methods can be easily integrated, whereas one who does not understand the game will not last long.

Among the hospitals a number of dynamics are evident. The traditional dominant relationship has always been one of competition between the private hospitals—competition for doctors. This is set against a lack of interaction between the private and public sectors. The competitive stance between private hospitals is primarily an administrative one, because about 90% of the doctors in the area practice at both hospitals and their patients may be admitted to either one.

Regionalization seeks a complementary relationship and, thus, distinguishes among three levels of hospitals based on the level of risk they are capable of handling. There is a natural basis for this three-level distinction in the size of the hospital, number of deliveries, staff expertise, and numbers and types of equipment. Nevertheless competition persists. Another dynamic militating against regionalization rests in the attitudes of front-line staff in how they perceive other hospitals in the region. These attitudes may be shaped by rumors traveling along the community grapevine or may be based on personal experiences of staff when the hospitals interface with one another. For instance, transferring sick babies to another, perhaps more "capable," facility provides an opportunity to compare procedures, attitudes, and protocols, as well as interface on the matter at hand.

Two main forces affect the relations between the environment and the internal operations of the medical providers: a rapidly changing social demographic situation brings with it changes in the ratio of self-paying patients to those covered by insurance or Medicaid. A concomitant change occurs in the ethnic distribution of patients and is attended by a shift in the types of risks to be considered.

3. Organizations as Interlinking Networks

Certain aspects of organizations can best be seen through their relationships at various levels and the ways in which they interconnect. They include:

- turf—the arena of action and decision defined by formal or informal prerogatives;

- standard operating procedures—the ways in which actions are taken;
- messages—the images developed and the context for interpretation in this system;
- external operating positions—the stances of the organization in relation to others and within its environment;
- boundary spanning—connecting activities, especially between organizations.

Together, these topics constitute what may be called protocols. Over time, they define an institution and become its inherited repertoire. They form its unique pattern of constraints and potentials.

As an example consider *turf*. Organizationally, nurses report to administrators through a nursing hierarchy. Doctors are a parallel source of authority when it comes to patient care. In one hospital, the established domains of doctors and nurses came to light in the course of the regionalization effort. A new head nurse received support from the doctors when she approached the administration, requesting sufficient nursing staff to provide a given quality of care. The doctors stood with her despite the administration and despite the recommendation, in the report of the corporation's efficiency expert, that the nursing staff be slashed. Yet, when she again, in line with the concept of regionalization, suggested to doctors that her staff was not yet sufficiently trained to handle high-risk babies that another hospital could handle, they dropped their support. She had overstepped her bounds. The choice of where a patient delivers is the doctor's, and the hospital's capability is but one factor. He may also consider where the bulk of his admitted patients are for that week, the privileges offered by the administration in pursuit of non-Medicaid patients, whether he has been temporarily suspended for incomplete records, or whether the woman wants a tubal ligation at the time of delivery.

Turfs were also manifested in the regional education and training sessions. One of these involved orientation to the Problem-Oriented Perinatal Risk Assessment Medical Record. Another concerned fetal monitoring. It was appropriate for these to be taught by nurses most qualified in these areas. Interns and residents, however, failed to attend these orientation sessions because the sessions were taught by nurses. When their presence was mandated by the Chief and roll call was taken, they would show up late and be disruptive.

Another example of conflicting turfs concerns doctors and administrators, both of whom claim ultimate responsibility for the quality of care. Their positions are clear but overlap. Doctors claim ultimate authority by virtue of their professionalism. They maintain that only personal and professional integrity and peer review are necessary to maintain quality standards. Administrators, on the other hand, stand legally liable and exercise their control through quality assurance programs, standards for medical practice, and admitting privileges. But, in reality, most of these are administered by doctors themselves. As an effort to raise standards through peer consensus, one of the first means to involve physicians in regionalization was through the development of protocols. Generally, these were designed by faculty at the medical school and were discussed in meetings by the regional physicians. When, after several years, they were asked about their methods of risk assessment and procedures, many doctors commented that they had their own, based on their medical training and experience. The only physician to mention regional protocols commented that in any possible litigation, they could prove too restrictive, because a doctor may have had a good reason for deviating in that particular case.

The SOPs form the "rules of the game," until some power moves to change them. For example, a conflict among several SOPs occurred in the Regional Center's Pediatric Intensive Care Unit (ICU) regarding staffing patterns. The Unit's Medical Director used national professional standards to determine the desired staffing pattern. These standards specify the number of RN and LVN hours per intensive and intermediate care patient. The Director of Nursing, however, insisted that the unit be staffed according to county standards, which did not differentiate between the hours per patient spent by RNs and LVNs or by aides. In addition, the county standards stipulated a lower number of nursing hours per patient overall and diluted the actual RN hours per ICU baby, because these nurses actually covered both intensive and intermediate care infants. Both practices, however, were in accordance with state standards, because the state did not specify the type of staff required.

With regard to *external posture,* any organization adopts a certain stance or strategic position vis-à-vis the others in its field. In the case of the hospitals under discussion here, it is possible to look at them as entities relating to one another and to the environment. Their interrelations involve competition, co-operation, and adaptation. Each organization seeks its own piece of the medical "pie" by virtue of its particular mission, goals, and functions. The "pie" itself is seen somewhat differently by each organization; and each perspective on the "pie," in large part, determines what entitles one to a piece of it. The project staff sees the health care system as serving patients. In that respect, the staff serves in an auxiliary role, facilitating the operation of a *regional* system. For them, regionalization *is* mission, goals, and functions. The hospitals, on the other hand, see the "pie" as a service industry or sector in which they claim a unique place. In so doing, they must maintain themselves as members of the industry and show a profit in the process. The hospitals under discussion in this region, to assure their unique position, must define and distinguish themselves in type or approach. One hospital provides an industrial accident facility, designated under the State Workman's Compensation Act, which brings in a significant amount of money. Additionally, it is attempting to upgrade its emergency room as a trauma center. The second hospital prides itself in building a community image. It promotes family-centered medicine and does fund raising in the community on this basis. The hospital has an established obstetric service and, in addition, a neonatal ICU.

Providers, that is, the doctors themselves, exist as independent organizations and as such they are, of course, more directly concerned with developing a profit-making business. They are heavily in demand due to the relative shortage of obstetric and pediatric practitioners in the area, but it is not a particularly lucrative field, and relative to other specializations it demands more time and is less adaptable to scheduling. For this reason many obstetrics and gynecology specialists emphasize the gynecology side of their practices, which is amenable to scheduling and is income producing in terms of surgical procedures. In view of these factors, the ideals of regionalization are seen as having more academic than practical interest. Like hospitals, doctors see regionalization as more interference than assistance to them in their practice. This point will be reinforced subsequently through the P perspective. Table 16 summarizes the characteristics and important features of the interrelationships.

D. THE P PERSPECTIVE

The age-old storytelling tradition hands down a way of communicating human insights. The fictional form is simply a medium for a point of view at once highly personal and deeply common—evolving recognition of the human dimension, shaping facts and experiences.[2] Each of the following "stories" should be read on its own terms. Each seeks to present some of the nuances to the question: How do you see regionalization fitting into your ways?

"THE DOCTOR IS IN"—A VIGNETTE
i It was almost 12:30 p.m. when I arrived at the doctor's office and introduced myself to the receptionist. I had called earlier to ask the best time to come on business, explaining that I was one of several people working in a regionalization project. We were interested in learning how the project's objectives were being perceived: How might doctors such as this one, who is established and influential, "hook into it"? How might we be of service to him—make our project more effective in coordinating available resources?

From her window, the receptionist waved me toward a small waiting room across the hall. I sat down near the door. The waiting room was plain, rose and beige plastic covered the furniture. There were a few well-thumbed magazines on a small table to one side. Sitting in the room were several women with children. I wondered about my timing. Across the hall I could hear the doctor's voice. "Who? From where? No. I don't want to be bothered. Get rid of her." There it was, I thought, the answer to my question; still I waited, curious to know how I would be handled.

While I continued to wait, the receptionist came to the door to call one patient after another. Not once did she look my way. After nearly an hour, I got up and approached

---

[2]Cf. Peters and Waterman's comment on page 61.

her window. "When will the doctor be able to see me?" I asked. "Maybe I could return after office hours."

She flushed. "The doctor is very busy."

"Yes, I can see that he is."

"Today isn't a good day. Especially right in the middle of everything."

"I see. I'm sorry. I was told that this would be a good time to come. But, things go that way sometimes. May I make an appointment for a better time?"

"All right," she said, hesitantly. "But you can't see him tomorrow. Wednesday's his day off you know. Could you come on Thursday?" I nodded assent. "Office hours begin at 11:00 a.m. so come before then."

"I'll be here by 10:00 a.m.," I assured her and asked her name. I thanked her for her help, and left the office, aware that I was learning the hard way what medical salespeople learn fast about getting in to see a doctor on business. Come in an hour ahead of time.

ii On Thursday I arrived at 10:00 a.m. The doors were locked, but inside the office was bustling. I rang the bell. The receptionist recognized me and let me in. I sat in the same chair near the door of the dim waiting room. After about 30 minutes a woman arrived with a small child in tow. They settled on the other side of the room. The little girl gingerly sat at a child's chair and table. The receptionist followed them in and turned on another bank of lights. The day of patients had officially begun. Soon a second woman arrived, and then another. They spoke as if they had run into each other before. The first woman picked up one of the two magazines and leafed through it, watching her child distractedly, her mind on the door. Soon a patient was called. Then a second. I began to worry but reasoned they would be waiting in the examination room for some time, and so I continued to wait. More patients arrived, in ones and twos. The waiting room was filling quickly with women, some with patient faces, others harrassed or anxious, some with children. One child was flushed and sleepy. Another began immediately to crawl under the table, like an earth-moving machine. His mother smiled apologetically at the women across from her who stared past the child. Suddenly I was aware of the doctor coming down the hall from his office. He was strolling casually toward the outer door with a man in a three piece suit. My attentive ears picked out bits of their conversation. Gold. One of them is taking a trip. They joked easily with one another. The man exited. The receptionist called the doctor into her office. Again I could hear some muffled conversation. "No! I told you earlier. I'm too busy. I don't have time for that stuff."

I continued to wait. Another patient was called. A tired looking woman followed the nurse to the examination room. The first patient was out now, ready to leave. I waited behind her at the receptionist's window. "Oh, you're still here," said the receptionist.

"Will the doctor see me today?", I ask.

She didn't look at me. "I'm sorry. The lawyer took up all his time today. He had some important business to discuss."

I persevered, "Could I reschedule for tomorrow?"

She glanced back over her shoulder to an older woman in the office who shrugged and nodded. I smiled at her, feeling I was catching on to the game. "Are you Mrs. Brown? I spoke with you on the telephone, didn't I?" She rose and came to the window. We exchanged pleasantries and exclaimed over busy days. I left with another appointment for the following day.

iii Once more I arrived at 10:00 a.m. and took up my post near the door of the waiting

TABLE 16. Organizational Perspective: Keys to Understanding

	Areas	Means of development		Constraint/danger	Potential/opportunity
		External	Internal		
Turfs	Layout of social system, power system, reward system and punishment	Postures in territories	Access via connections or dual turfs or recognition or multiple levels	Subversion of creativity by survival mechanisms Lowest common denominator	Creation of nonzero-sum games, connection of pride and group expectancy, and realistic goals
SOPs	Internal rules of the system	Authority and reinforcement	Practical, *personal* benefit to sufficient extent limited	Subversion of positive change by crisis SOPs, habit as mainframe, limited expectation by the tried and true, legitimated exercises	Can humanize the means by which tasks are done as well as accomplish them: forms of organization as mutually beneficial; make life easier
Messages	Communication patterns	Marketing image; self-evident context	Medium is the message Self-generating link Internal context	Can never say just one thing so can result in double bind of two levels, which leaves one helpless and immobile	Can create an image that is provocative and charismatic; creates its own need and motivation that once triggered is self-generating and expanding; small change has great potential

Internal posture	Stance	Strategic position in relation to others, to the environment, that is, cooperation, competition, adaptation	Persistence	Switch system level at juncture	Status quo stalemate—see other organizations stereotypically	Beyond opposites; conflict or cooperation, free enterprise or socialized medicine
Boundary spanning	Connection	People who are links between organizations creating cooperative ventures	Position of spanner	Interest of spanner	Alignment with wrong one—a troublemaker—can lead to deteriorating relations; with too powerful seen as threat of expansionism; with too weak seen as sign of lack of understanding of the system	Can produce changed alignments between organizations: conditions, network of growing interests for the organization

room. It was 50 minutes later, almost time for office hours to begin, when I was finally ushered into the doctor's inner office. As I entered I saw him seated behind an ornate desk, flanked by large windows. Opposite him against the interior wall a bank of aquariums bubbled and gave off a soft light. In one corner the statue of a nymph spilled water from a perpetual urn into a small stone basin. The doctor was on the telephone. I could not escape hearing some of his conversation. He was evidently talking to his broker. "Shall I sell now, or next week?" he asked. "What effect is that going to have on my taxes?"

Finally he hung up and looked my way. Rising, he leaned forward to shake hands. I introduced myself and explained that I had come to hear his views on regionalization of health care, since his views in this area were very important.

He prefaced his answer by explaining that he was a long-time friend and associate of the physician who headed the project. They had traveled together to many conferences. He told me the head of the regionalization project was a man for whom he had great respect, who had shown his strength of leadership on many issues, and was recognized throughout the country."

"How do you see regionalization yourself?" I asked.

"Well, it increases the quality of care while decreasing the overall costs and eliminating duplication of services. Who can be against it? Why in this area . . ." he stopped mid-sentence and buzzed the other office.

The nurse entered. "I can't see through these," he said, handing her his glasses.

She pulled a tissue from the box on his desk and wiped the lenses while he continued. "I hope you understand why I couldn't see you the other day. There was the business with my lawyer—and besides the girls didn't tell me you were waiting. I'm very busy, you know." The nurse handed back his glasses. He took them, held them at a distance for a moment, then put them on and waved her away. Rising, he leaned over the desk and looked directly into my eyes over the rim of his glasses.

"You know," he said, "regionalization will work, when we doctors want it to. We've got the power to make it go. Maybe the time is coming."

CHORUS: VOICES OF THE PEOPLE—ANOTHER VIGNETTE

Apart from the formal interviews with hospital staff—the ways in which people present themselves and their situations for the record—there is an undercurrent of attitudes and feelings that comes out only informally in the commonplace of everyday talk. As one moves, works, and becomes familiar with the region, the community, and the people, a sense of place emerges that cannot be expressed in any better way than through the voices of people. These are presented in a dramatic form that seemed appropriate to the situation. Imagine a stage—theater in the round. There is a chorus representing the most commonly expressed views of the community speakers—nurses, doctors, staff, patients—all these voices in their own words. The speakers are Black unless otherwise indicated.

CHORUS: Blacks are different. We have special medical needs. Take sickle cell, for example, or hypertension. We have our own ways of doing things. White folk don't understand. What we need is sensitive health care. What we need is people who understand.

SPEAKER: A while back there was a private university (White and generally conservative) tried coming in here to set up a program. Black doctors here didn't trust them. They protested and tried to keep them out.

SPEAKER: At the dedication of a health center here, every politician in town showed up to give a speech. We'd never seen any of them here before, but they all wanted credit.

GROUP: Now the politicians say, let them do it themselves.

GROUP: The politicians can wash their hands of it.

SPEAKER: We got our hospital.

CHORUS: Out of the ashes of the riots, this place was built. It's a symbol of commitment to the Black community.

SPEAKER: When the bond failed one politician supported us. He got the initial funding. Now they call it his "plantation." His reputation's at stake so he keeps a tight rein on the place.

CHORUS: Politics, politics, politics.

MAN SPEAKER: Now it's fiscal politics.

WOMAN SPEAKER: Infantile politics.

GROUP: Now dollars come first, not health needs. Even Black administrators play the game. They try to prove to the "Man" downtown that Blacks can manage. Prove that we can take care of ourselves.

GROUP: The politicians can wash their hands of it.

CHORUS: Out of the ashes of the riots this place was built. It's a symbol of hope, of commitment to the Black community.

SPEAKER: This center is built on race, not competence.

SPEAKER: It's designed to fail.

THREE GROUPS IN UNISON: The doctor's offices here are not better than the County.

WOMAN: They're crowded day in and day out.

MAN: You wait for hours.

GROUP: And Medicaid pays for it just the same.

SPEAKER: This is the only hospital in the County where patients have to pay for the building in just 10 years.

CHORUS: The politicians say let them do it themselves—the politicians can wash their hands.

SPEAKER: But Blacks don't trust each other.

SPEAKER: Blacks don't want to go to Black doctors. They don't think they are as good.

GROUP: It's the old brainwashing. Unless you're a number one, you're no good at all and when something bad happens, people say I knew it all the time.

SPEAKER: A lot of older Blacks don't go to Black doctors.

SPEAKER: Well, for some people, the young ones, maybe.

CHORUS: Martin Luther King, Jr. was the only one that ever pulled Blacks together.

BLACK DOCTOR: There aren't any partnerships among Black doctors here. They're too suspicious.

BLACK DOCTOR: Black professionals discriminate against those Blacks who come from prestigious White schools. Most of the doctors here graduated from two Black medical schools.

SPEAKER: People raised in this community have to go somewhere else for an education. In order to become a doctor, you have to give up your Blackness.

SPEAKER: When a Black leaves for training, he never comes back to the community he left. He goes away to gain skills. But his attitude and values change, too. More than he could have imagined. He doesn't fit in anymore.

SPEAKER: He's not the same old guy.

SPEAKER: But you can't fight ignorance with ignorance. For those with the motivation, there's no choice. You have to get out.

SPEAKER: And you end up different.

SPEAKER: You can't cover it up later with beads and dashikis.

SPEAKER: If you're going to be a professional, you better look like one.

FACULTY: I'm proud to say many of our residents are now serving right here in the community.

WHITE SPEAKER: Some years ago there was a racial problem, but due to the changing character of the area, it's not a problem any longer—it's not White flight. Whites just don't like to be treated by Black doctors.

SPEAKER: Blacks have a hard time relating to Blacks in an authority position. You're always underestimated. You always have to be overqualified. So there's a lack of respect for superiors and more insubordination.

BLACK DOCTOR: There used to be more problems with the administration because the administration is White—it's a difference in orientation. Not a conscious desire to obstruct.

CHORUS: Maybe we are a little paranoid, but we've learned you have to be.

SPEAKER: There's a terrific race consciousness here. Some people don't understand that.

CHORUS: Our community fought hard to build this hospital. Out of the ashes of the riots. It's a symbol of hope to us. A commitment to the Black community.

GROUP: But the hospital isn't serving the population for which it was built.

VOICE: And for which Medicaid would pay costs.

NURSE: Most of the Spanish-speaking are self-payers. That is, they have no insurance. Not even Medicaid. That means. . . .

CHORUS: They don't pay. They're crowding us out.

(SCENE: *Latino couple in the billing office.*)
  Man: But $837 for three visits? The nurse at the clinic said to come to this hospital if there was bad pain and discharge when the clinic was closed.
  Billing officer: Yes. A vaginal infection it says here. Well there are the emergency room charges and they apparently sent you upstairs to the obstetrics ward and then there were all these tests . . . blood type, ultrasound . . .
  Woman: But I had all those tests at the clinic already.
  Officer: But of course the hospital didn't know that. Now if you'll just sign here, at least $10 a month . . .

SPEAKER: You've got to understand. There's hostility toward Mexicans because in the Civil Rights days they didn't stick their necks out and join with us.

CHORUS: They should learn English. They're crowding us out.

NURSE: There's hostility to the Spanish on all levels—to preserve one's own job.

(SCENE: *In a recovery room. A group of nurses joke together loudly around a table. Someone enters. "May I speak with you?" Then, noticing a patient at the end of the room, "Excuse me." "Oh, don't worry about her. She can't understand English anyway.")*

(SCENE: *In a ward corridor. Many people, patients, and professionals coming and going.)*

Doctor to pregnant woman: Go home, Vallase. You're not ready yet.

Woman in hospital robe: Habla español? Donde esta mi baby?

Pregnant woman with bottle of medicine: Habla español? Que decis de medicina me tomo?

Man: Habla español? Como esta mi esposa?

Doctor to first pregnant woman: It's too late. Es muy tarde. If you had been here I could have helped you.

Small group, mimicking: Habla español? Why don't they learn to speak English?

CHORUS: This place was built for us.

WHITE DOCTOR: All this race stuff! It doesn't make any difference. Competence is what counts. Take that nurse, for example. She gets along fine. . . . She's worked here a long time. She really knows her stuff.

WHITE SPEAKER: Besides, most of the nurses aren't Black. They're Asian now.

BLACK RN: She knows her stuff alright, but she's well, pushy. You know what I mean. She doesn't understand that you don't come walking in here as if there's nothing worthwhile going on and just take over. She's nice enough, but they talk about her.

BLACK RN: The Project is, practically speaking, just about all White, you know.

SPEAKER: The Center is just a stepping stone. Professionals come in here and do their research or get their practice, then go on to more prestigious places.

SPEAKER: You've almost finished your paper, haven't you? When will you be leaving?

GROUP: You see everything here. It's a great place to get experience.

FACULTY: I'm proud to say that many of our interns are serving right here in the community.

GROUP: Our docs can't go elsewhere. They resent the community. They resent being told they don't know something, being told they need to update their knowledge.

YOUNG WOMAN IN CROWDED ELEVATOR: I know some people call this hospital a killer. But you can't tell me that. . . . Do you know who I am? I'm the very first patient this hospital ever had—and they saved my life. I was 13. Everyone thought I was a goner. I had been stabbed in the leg, and I hid it from my mother. I hid it for three days. When she found out, the infection had set in and it was almost too late. They brought me here to the hospital. I don't even remember coming in, I was so far gone I was out of it. But I'm here today, and I tell you truly it's because they saved my life.

CHORUS: Out of the ashes of the Riots this place was built. It's a symbol of hope. A commitment to the Black community.

---

1. Commentary

What do these two stories mean? A good story puts something before us to work with, respond to, and engage in. To this extent these stories are "good"; their meanings reside in the process by which the story meets the reader. Even in highly crafted stories, the fullness of what is caught and to be shared is not always conscious. It's what makes each storyteller at once unique and in touch with something identifiably real.

This storyteller, an amateur, would like to share some of the shaping of the stories, some reflections on them, and some responses to them. As always, stories should speak for themselves—or they don't converse at all.

Story shaping: Contextual Research. The portrait of the doctor in his office (the first vignette) is a vivid image in my mind. If I were a painter, I could frame the pose and expression. The reason the picture is powerful is because I *felt* what I had heard from others—the presence of one in charge of an orderly world at his command. I felt it, in part, because as a woman I identified (I see now) with the other women in the waiting room and with the nurse in the office. I felt it because I was new to the scene and did not yet take for granted the way this little world operates (I didn't yet fit). The presence is not, however, uncaring, simply "other." The doctor is not "typical," but I recognized something of "doctorness" that is hard to put one's finger on in that situation. His office portrays his world. His world frames regionalization.

In the Chorus (the second vignette), the form has several sources. The Greek chorus represents very classical, myth-laden drama. Black voices, for example, from the Civil Rights demonstrations, represent extremely powerful resonances. They hold special meaning for me from a certain time in my life. The dramatic line develops and comes back on itself in reinterpretation of the theme in a way congruent to how I was taught about this particular community. Its members, my friends, co-workers, challengers—to the extent they trusted me and I fit in— fostered my understanding. It was a developmental process, one recognized as obviously incomplete to anyone on the inside. In fact, I am leery of exposing myself and my understanding because I do not have a sense of the end point and how far I am from it. I sense being in and out to varying degrees. At the same time, these same learnings exposed me to the different voices and the contradictions in the situation—a tumultuous context laden with intense feelings shaping the path of regionalization.

SOME RESPONSES TO THE FIRST VIGNETTE.
1. A doctor I don't know who read another's copy: "Yeah, that's exactly the way it is. She caught it."
2. A woman friend: "That's the problem I feel with my gynecologist. There's a certain attitude."
3. Another friend, intrigued with people and settings: "Who *is* this person? Does he make a difference?"

SOME RESPONSES TO THE SECOND VIGNETTE.
1. A Black graduate student, friend of a friend: "It fits what I know of the area and the place. I've heard some other stuff. That's why I'm here instead of there."
2. A friend, minority, who formerly worked in the area: "You don't have the sense of the language right. What people say to each other and what is understood when repeated to 'outsiders' is quite different. You've got to be careful of context here. Your audience for this paper will not understand it the way your co-workers do. For example, 'Blacks are different,' your opener, can be taken as condescension."

E. SUBSTANTIVE CONCLUSIONS

This section conveys the issues in developing a regional system and the strategies for continued development suggested by the analysis.

1. From the T Perspective

The issues in developing a Perinatal Regional System:
- How can the system be made more effective in the outcome of care, and more accessible to patients?
  Should the focus of education efforts be the unusual and interesting topics, or the most frequently seen basic problems?
  Should arrangements be made within the system for transfer and referral of mothers as well as babies, or should individual facilities be upgraded and neighboring regions be used, based on patient preference, space, and county arrangements for payment and liability?
  Should the system operate as a kind of quality-assurance group in monitoring case outcomes?

- How can the system be made more efficient and cut needless duplication? How can hospital wide forms be eliminated when they duplicate the POPRAS record?

  How can hospitals desiring growth and upgraded services do so without duplicating existing services?

  How can quality control committees be assisted with existing data?
Strategies for continued development:

- Develop an ongoing master plan with carefully selected emphasis and commitment of resources.

  Gradually, this plan and the associated resources should become the province of a "Board."

  In the interim, it is essential for system management to provide direct and systematic coordination of service components and direct contact with agencies on all levels.

- Provide a formal surveillance system for a finer analysis of problem areas and plans to address them. This includes analysis of sources of mortality and morbidity by providers, type of patient, type of problem, level of resources, changing environment, etc.; follow-up communication, and proposals for improvement of monitoring of needs and progress; high-level mortality/morbidity conferences, including only top administrators; and a faster turnaround time in response to requests for assistance, data, etc.

2. From the O Perspective

The issues in developing a Perinatal Regional System:

- How to assure the economic viability of subsystems (hospitals, doctors, etc.) as an inducement to regionalization?

- How to foster an increase in quality of care without "meddling" and violating independence?

- How to foster relations between the private and public sectors when politically sensitive program instability affects the type of care, attitude toward patients, and capability in the public sector?

- How to foster positive relations among professionals that facilitate movement toward a common goal?

- How to foster continuity of care between prenatal and intrapartum providers in the public sector, given the history of the relationship?

- How to focus on the level of patient care when the basic orientation is one of fragmentation ("my patients") and the noninsured patient is discriminated against?

- How to foster regional consciousness despite entrenched conservatism?

- Are the most significant measures of achievement the ones set at the start of the program—or the measures of involvement, attitude change, desire for continuity, etc.?

TABLE 17. How the Three Perspectives See Aspects of Regional Development

	Technical	Organizational	Personal
Goals	To develop mechanisms for action necessary to effect change	To be in an advantageous position	
Focus	Decrease mortality and morbidity based on level of risk and level of care—cost efficient	Cooperative functional interorganizational health care delivery system	Roots Unique shaping of system
Expectation of change	Relatively smooth and systematic Planned outcome per effort	Long time, takes patience Also the opportunity—now or never in its own time frame	Unpredictable, self-generating yet timing is of the essence Understanding develops slowly
Implementation approach	Serial effort via action ties organized by budget and staff patterns Based on goals—normative Interactive and self-correcting from evaluation, impact	Constant effort repetition, reinforcement or "fit" within existing system: extrapolative, force of tradition, habit	Spark—not too pushy, demanding, insistent unless power to back it Leadership and persuasion, peer pressure is leavening to raising of standards People who are "in's" to system ensure balance, however because of interplay of situation and personal dynamics change is "breakthrough"
Involvement role of staff	To support good (rational) ideas in action	To gain access in order to change processes through authority channels or informal effective networks As an interinstitutional partner	To shape, inspire, model through personal contact
Success depends on:	A good plan managed well	Threshold effect in organization	Personal interest and motivation of each and of key leader

Strength and stability	Powerful because logical Rightness of cause	Powerful because works within own system, self-reinforcement of multistable system aspects; organization as territory	Powerful because personally satisfying/inspiring—prestige direct or indirect—self-fulfilling gratifying Volatile "forces"
Non-match points at system interfaces	Details to be manipulated (outcomes are unknown) to fit the whole plan by establishing an umbrella organization seen as possible in a relatively short (that is, conceivable) time frame	Different strokes for different folks Go different routes—pathway is the essence—break habits Complex time relationships/habits are essential for routine details so that energy can be devoted to crisis demands	Main concerns to be negotiated (outcome uncertain) Persuasion (based on respect, image)
Withholding enthusiasm	Seeking better options	Resistance to change Inefficiencies in bureaucratic organization Holding onto what works	Fear of change Power plays, self interests Bargaining for the best, working through
Image of regionalization effort of those not yet part of it	Goals are great: you have the money and you want x so you give staff . . . etc. and do it	Try it: life goes on Wait and see	Doing it for self-aggrandizement: prestige, papers
Types of issues raised	Efficiency Effectiveness Access	Relationships in organizational upheaval, economics, cross points Opposition to change	Context, image, patterns, uniqueness, key movers
Type of recommendation	Activities of project based on demonstrated effectiveness or need assessment	Role of project: model, involve, orient, assist, recognize multilevels, look for switch points	Role of project in relation to others: Develop image to others Develop initiative of others

Strategies for continued development:
- Recognize the opportunities inherent in overlapping interests, for example: professional and economic;
  job satisfaction (including control, manageability, respect, and performance);
  independence and team needs.
- Market special services appealingly.
- Develop the nonprofit registry of highly trained nurses and contract at local hospitals for staffing and training—a resource that would cut across many types and levels of system needs.
- Assist the public hospital in compensating for its decreased resources and negative regional image through its improved competency, involvement, and image development; assist it in the development of arguments for increased resources. Do not use it as a tertiary facility until more settled.
- Find an external focus to join forces "against" in addressing internal common needs (malpractice insurance companies, etc.).
- Assist doctors by providing programs for office staff.
- Model team work among obstetricians, pediatricians, RNs, data staff, etc.
- Improve attending physician coverage backup for relief and on-site availability because the presence of this group contributes to a sense of security and order as well as performance.

3. From the P Perspective

Issues in developing a Perinatal Regional System:
- Who are the key movers and how do they relate to regionalization—including partial and contradictory types of support, other personal priorities, and styles of operating?
- How can the image of regionalization be developed by various interests and help to congeal them (marketing?)?
- How can "enculturated" patterns and attitudes shape regionalization?
- What is the role of the consumer in perinatal regionalization?
- In what way is regionalization unique to this time and place?

Strategies for continued development:
- Develop the initiative of participants through encouragement, support, and linkages, assisting them to fit into group context, for example:
  assist A with coordination of clinics and hospital service;
  give recognition to X for his support of new physicians;
  involve Y in Center mortality and morbidity conferences;
  send reports routinely to F so she feels recognized;
  spur D to meet with R regarding some strategies for coordinating participation;
  enhance the positions of B and C, who have more developed conscious-

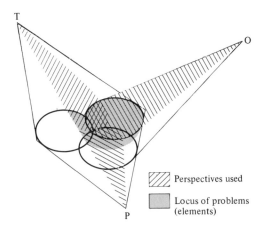

FIGURE 17. Schematic of perspectives: Perinatal Regionalization Case.

ness and enthusiasm regarding regionalization while maintaining balances of power in their groups.

- Develop an image of regionalization:

    as a unique resultant of personally useful and professionally advanced cooperation specific to these participants;

    as sensitive to Black professionals and their unique and controversial role in the community;

    as simultaneously noble and pragmatic;

    as a desirable way to avert outside interference and socialized medicine.

- For orientation and review, use an updatable medium (slides) with pictures of participants in specific activities, especially those unique to this region.

- In policy discussions, support a positive and unique image.

- Develop consciousness in expanding nursing roles.

F. THE ROLE OF MULTIPLE PERSPECTIVES

The multiple perspectives perceive the perinatal regionalization situation as summarized in Table 17. It is seen that the perspectives yield quite distinct images of an emerging social technology. Referring back to our Figure 5 schematic, we can depict this application as shown in Figure 17. The substantive focus and the perspectives used are both suggested.

The lessons learned from this case study in the use of multiple perspectives—both evaluative and procedural—will be addressed in Section XI A after descriptions of the other case studies.

VIII

ELECTRONIC FUNDS TRANSFER TECHNOLOGY ASSESSMENT: A RETROSPECTIVE LOOK

A. MYSIOR, J. SHUMAN, and H. LINSTONE

What is essential is invisible to the eye.

> Antoine de Saint-Exupery
> *The Little Prince*

What is laid down, ordered, factual, is never enough to embrace the whole truth: life always spills over the rim of every cup.

> Boris Pasternak

In this and the following two chapters we bring multiple perspectives to bear on three technology assessments undertaken with the support of the National Science Foundation. In looking back over a decade of NSF involvement in TA, Nehnevajsa and Menkes (1981) see the evolution of technology assessment in terms of several stages. Stage I enlarged the systems analysis, specifically cost–benefit evaluation, to encompass concerns beyond economic feasibility. Stage II was more ambitious, aiming for "comprehensiveness" in identifying and evaluating the full range of social, economic, and environmental impacts. Stage III recognized the futility of this goal and retrenched to the development of "good risk" contingency plans and policy options. Thus technology assessment is linked much more intimately with the decision-making process. Nehnevajsa and Menkes suggest that multiple perspective use may move us into stage IV of the evolution of technology assessment.

The first and earliest of the three TAs, performed by Arthur D. Little, Inc. (ADL) (1975) and widely considered a superior example of the genre, falls into stage II: "The goal of this assessment . . . is to be as comprehensive as possible." The organizational element of EFT was the object of most attention. The T and O perspectives were utilized, with the former dominating. The approach presents an interesting counterpoint to the contemporary work of the National Commission on EFT, which was much more strongly oriented to the O perspective.

In contrast to both the ADL study and the preceding Perinatal Regionalization case, our level of effort allocated to this retrospective look was quite modest. Hence our own additions can only be suggestive of the possibilities in introducing multiple perspectives.

A. THE ADL STUDY

In 1975, Arthur D. Little, Inc. undertook a technology assessment of Electronic Funds Transfer. The study was done under contract to the National Science Foundation and directed by Martin Ernst. Funding was about $500,000.

Electronic funds transfer is taken to include the following functions:

- automated teller machines (ATM),
- automated clearinghouses (ACH) (direct deposits, automated bill paying, telephonic bill paying),
- check safekeeping,
- corporate-to-corporate transactions,
- point-of-sale terminals (POST).

ADL had previously conducted studies for a banking industry that was becoming increasingly concerned over the expanding volume of paper transactions (about 7% annual growth). One such study concluded that the existing modus operandi would be able to handle the expected growth until at least 1980—but this time point was fast approaching. In the foreseeable future, the volume would likely exceed the processing capability of the present system. In the course of investigating the issue, ADL gained a comprehensive overview of the payment system. In particular, the study recognized that the nature of the technology was not the heart of the EFT problem.

The work plan called for three iterative analyses of the problem, culminating in a final report. The first phase of work was to be based largely on information already available to ADL, supplemented by a limited series of interviews and a fairly extensive literature search. This phase was devoted to background development and question formulation rather than to the development of answers. It was limited to an examination of first-order impacts.

The next phase was devoted to restructuring the task and consolidating the information developed in the first phase. For example, over 70 significant participant groups and some 80 areas of immediate concern to one or more of these groups were identified. To make the output comprehensible, these had to be clustered into a conceptually manageable number of themes. This restructuring went hand-in-hand with the development of a set of questions that were to provide the focus of the investigation. The questions were divided into four areas covering the following issues:

- the (then) current operation of the system:
    how it works,
    what it costs,
    how the different participants perceive it in terms of satisfactions and
        concerns;
- functions and elements where change may occur:
    experiments in progress,
    institutional plans,
    expressed intentions;
- proposals for change:
    as viewed by change agents,
    as viewed by other participant groups;
- potential impacts of change:
    on depository financial institutions,
    on business,
    on user groups.

The third phase consisted of a more sophisticated analysis of all the collected data. The significant components and trends were identified and the relationships and interdependencies of the components, as well as the independent strands of development, were analyzed.

Unlike Congressional creations—such as the EFT Commission and the Office of Technology Assessment, which generate studies specifically as an aid to administrative policy formulation and in the legislative process—the NSF sponsors TAs on the basis of existing or potential public concern. The latter TAs have been characterized by Joseph Coates as "off-the-shelf supermarket items." Thus the ADL product is designed for a different audience than the report of the EFT commission.

The TA was atypical in important respects. The most interesting characteristics were the focus on the organization elements (Figure 18a) and the heavy use of interviews (over 200). The technology was considered state-of-the-art; advances in peripheral computer and telecommunications technology were largely ignored because the EFT concepts evaluated did not require them. There were also relatively few explicit quantitative forecasts (for example, transaction volume and detailed costs). The basis for the TA was seen as an existing, not emerging, technology. Characteristic of the T perspective was the concern with developing an "audit trail" to assure replicability of the work.

Both T and O perspectives were used in focusing on the organizational aspects. The T perspective was more heavily used (Figure 18a) and was quite sophisticated. Not only were organizations and institutions considered per se, but overarching regulatory constraints, advocacy barriers, and problems of the culture–technology interface were seen as significant. For example, how much EFT technology can this society absorb in a given time? Thus several levels of the organizational setting were included.

The T perspective also saw EFT in terms of the allocation and distribution of "value" via the medium of "payment." Billions of exchanges of goods and services between social entities (organizations and individuals) must be managed, and the complexity is evident. A system for managing and controlling these transactions had been worked out and was functioning fairly well. What happens when an innovation is introduced? In this case, a tangible medium of exchange is being converted into intangible information. How will this innovation affect the functioning of the economy? More specifically: How will the various participant groups fare as EFT is introduced into the system? And how can undesirable consequences be avoided?

The O perspectives involved primarily consumers, regulators, and financial institutions. The stress on interviews is characteristic of the O perspective. Team members had to have interviewing skills, and care was taken to make the interviews productive.

Both the T and O perspectives will be further discussed in Section VIII C.

There was some concern with the individual as an *element*, again from the T and O perspectives (Figure 18a). However, no attempt appears to have been made to throw a P *perspective* on any element. It is a matter of conjecture whether its absence was due to 1) the common rational actor/analyst conviction that personal perspectives are immaterial to the assessment of a technology such as EFT or 2) the political sensitivity of this perspective (for example, that its inclusion might adversely affect chances of future work by the contractor for the banking industry).

Viewed in hindsight (from 1980) the implicit forecasts in the study appear

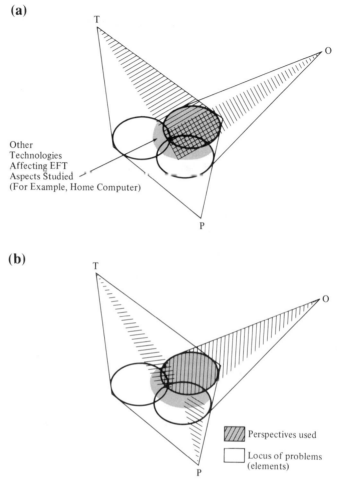

FIGURE 18. Schematic of perspectives: Electronic Funds Transfer Reports: **(a)** A.D. Little Technology Assessment; **(b)** National Commission Report.

very reasonable and appropriate. However, the transformation of the EFT system was initially slow and is only now accelerating. There were reasons for the slow initial pace:

- it was not an issue of national urgency;
- it required considerable investment of private funds with only long-term profitability;
- in the short run, monetary institutions were satisfied with the existing system;

- consumers were content with the existing system and there was nothing in EFT to excite their imagination;
- business and wealthy users wanted to maintain the float concept;[1]
- consumers feared computer errors;
- low-income groups with minimal reserves and credit, and often no checking account, must depend on cash;
- older consumers liked the social intercourse in the bank.

When the study was initiated, EFT was an emerging application of an existing technology. Had a popular book been written about EFT along the lines of Rachel Carson's *The Silent Spring* or Robert Jungk's *The New Tyranny* (which tied energy issues to political structures and the centralization of power), the evolution of EFT might have been affected. With the popular imagination unstirred, it is not surprising that little change in development occurred in the initial period. However, if we were to make an assessment of EFT for the next five or ten years, the picture would look quite different. In the interim, other social processes have undergone significant development, which can be expected to affect EFT soon.

B. THE EFT COMMISSION

As we have noted, the perspective of the TA on organization matters was more technical than organizational. In this respect it is interesting to compare the ADL report with the work on the contemporary EFT Commission (Figure 18b).

This Commission was created by an act of Congress and began work about the time ADL completed its TA (1975). In the enabling legislation, $2 million was allocated for the Commission's activities, about four times the funding of the TA.

The Commission, established as an "independent instrumentality of the United States," was to "conduct a thorough study and investigation and recommend appropriate administrative action and legislation necessary in connection with the possible development of public or private electronic funds transfer systems. . . ." The following were to be taken into account:

- the need to preserve competition;
- minimization of government regulation and involvement (for example, avoidance of a system competitive with the private sector);
- prevention of discriminatory or unfair practices;
- facilitation of user or consumer convenience;
- preservation of the right to privacy for the user;

---

[1] The benefit of the delay between check writing and account debiting.

- the impact of economic and monetary policies;
- the impacts on the availability of credit;
- the implications of expansion of EFT internationally and into other forms of electronic communications;
- protection of the legal rights of users.

Although copies of ADL's highly readable TA were provided to the Commission, its use was quite limited. The executive and research directors had originally been on a team bidding unsuccessfully against ADL on the NSF TA study. Now, the Research Director felt they had the opportunity to do "exactly what we wanted to do." That perception lasted about three weeks. The 26 Commission members were far more politically conscious than the typical TA team and promptly squelched the initial work proposals that would emphasize the T perspective. In the words of the Research Director, "We had to do something that was way down to earth; we could not do what you and I would be very comfortable with" (Boucher, 1979).

The Commission members represented various bureaucracies and other vested interests and quite naturally emphasized the O perspective. As would be expected, their planning horizon was different from that of the Research Director. They were committed to preparing a basis for legislation and administration action that would accommodate each organization's concerns. And there were many concerns. For example, with banks, credit unions, and savings and loan institutions experimenting differently in EFT, "somebody was going to get hurt." An indication was the introduction of a Bill in Congress for a two-year moratorium on EFT. The bill died, but the Commission was born. The members distrusted ready-made recommendations from the available studies. They wanted to wrestle with the issues themselves to create answers. If such answers were the same as conclusions or recommendations in, say, the TA by ADL, it would be a lovely coincidence, but irrelevant. The important point was that the answer was their product.

The O perspective might have recognized that an unofficial aim of the Commission was to buy time and gain two years of public policy discussion in a "goldfish bowl." It was a very rational approach from that point of view. Non-experts in Congress had to develop a policy, and the Commission was an appropriate vehicle for doing so. The staff reported on current EFT installations throughout the United States, compiled key documents, listed issues, and organized informal workshops. It is important to understand that the Commission, once created, was an independent instrumentality of the United States and not, like the Office of Technology Assessment, a captive agency of the Congress. Of course, through the funding mechanism Congress had considerable influence. But the independence of the Commission made it possible to gain active and meaningful participation of diverse vested interests.

The O perspective might also have noted that the short time horizon common to the banking establishment conflicted with the long time horizon needed to manage the implementation of EFT and the need to consider its consequences.

There were 105 Commission meetings, and 65 papers were produced. Town Hall meetings were run where public response was solicited and obtained. There were also many informal meetings with Congressional staff and others. Commission meetings involved intensive argument, confrontation, negotiation, and arbitration over a two-year period. A set of 135 recommendations was hammered out and included in a final report, addressed to the President and the Congress. A portion of the set of recommendations has, in fact, been enacted into law.

The Commission's effort presents us with an alternative balance of perspectives on EFT when compared with the ADL study (Figure 18). Both applied the perspectives primarily to the organizational element of the EFT system. Both used T and O perspectives, but ADL favored T while the Commission emphasized O. Characteristically, the T perspective in the ADL study brought out the uncertainties, whereas the dominant O perspective in the Commission tended to develop a consensus. The Commission had a very different kind of membership than the ADL TA team and was closer to the decision-making process—and these facts go hand-in-hand with the shift in perspective balance.

We had this interesting thing happen; I learned a lesson from it. By law we had to submit an interim report to the Congress. In the interim report we had 50 or 60 recommendations; we were that far along the process. When we came to the final report, we had another 80 or so recommendations and one of the Commissioners said at our final meeting where we were voting finally on these issues: "What about those early 50 or 60, shouldn't we revote them? After all, a year has passed. Shouldn't we revote all those so everything has a current stamp of approval on it?"

And there was one statement made on the Commission level in response to that: "If you revote any one issue, I will insist that we reopen every other issue and not just look at the proposition and revote it but reexamine all the arguments." That ended that right there. What the Commissioner who said that was trying to point out was that it was a package at this point. They had given so much on particular issues and the compromises were subtle, that to reopen that whole decision-making process would have been cataclysmic, catastrophic, because they would find it exceedingly difficult to reconstruct the original arguments. Let's just get on with it. That was all approved in one vote on the earlier recommendations . . . .

That doesn't happen in TA's that I'm familiar with.

Source: Wayne Boucher, Research Director of the Commission (1979)

C. UPDATING THE IMPACTS ON ORGANIZATIONS: 1980

Viewed from the T perspective, the organizational element involves primarily the mechanics of implementation, that is, the matching of the technological and social systems. From this point of view, the full development of EFT is first of all a matter of economics. The total substitution of EFT for paper (checks) and money transactions produces cost reductions, so the system inexorably moves in that direction. Progress will be incremental because of the high initial cost of installing the system and because of the deficits (compared to the paper and cash system) until economies of scale are reached. This is inevitably going to happen because the system is already in use, and those who have invested in it are going to want to protect their investments. Advertising campaigns, the pressure of competition, and the slow phasing out of the old system will do the rest. Such fears on the part of participants as potential loss of privacy, computer errors, etc. are not viewed as critical and are assumed to be amenable to correction by technological intervention.

An interesting T-perspective approach to technological-social system matching analysis is the process developed by Fried and Molnar (see Section IVA). It was applied to the ACH part of EFT on a demonstration basis in Linstone et al.'s (1978, volume 2:1–33 to 1–54) study on the use of structural modeling in TA. Interviews were used in 1977 by Fried and Molnar over a one-month period in one city. These formed the basis for codings of 27 variables that were then compared for match or mismatch.[2]

The O perspective is of major significance. The effort of the ADL study was initially directed toward identification of all the groups that would be differentially affected by EFT and, second, at specification of the concerns these groups had about EFT. An analysis was then made of the balancing of forces produced by the social pressures exerted by the various groups. This led to an assessment of how people behave and of the consequences of those behaviors. Five years later, it seems that little needs to be added to, or subtracted from, this analysis.

Today (1980) the engineer/technicians focus on this year's semiconductor and

---

[2]The 1977 conclusions:

> The ACH system as presently constituted is neither cost effective nor viable. Clearly the problem is not in the Technical Zone per se. . . . The codings of both the Managerial and Political Zones are markedly below those necessary to maintain and fully develop a national ACH network. That it works at all at a local level is due to the fact that ACH is considered as a research and development effort by both the banks and the federal government.

Three scenarios for the future were developed to show alternatives for viable EFT development:

1. Private enterprise: all financial institutions use the same EFT system but there is functional specialization.
2. Bank monopoly: banks have attained regional control of the EFT system and monopolize financial transactions.
3. Publicly controlled EFT system: a quasi-public corporation (like AMTRAK and COMSAT) controls all EFT operations.

equipment improvements. Bankers and regulators tend to be concerned with this year's costing out and possibly next year's purchasing and budgeting; "next fiscal year" is a common phrase used by these people. The promoter/researcher types are interested in 5- to 15-year marketing analyses. Consumer advocates and marketing personnel tend to look at the two- and five-year competition for the market.

There is widespread recognition in the U.S. banking industry that it has become technologically obsolete. For example, European and Japanese banks are generally ahead in exploiting computer technology (Boucher, 1979). However, the takeoff point finally seems to have been reached. The current acceleration of the pace is reflected in the dramatic increase of bill paying via telephone (from zero to two million transactions per month in the past two years) and direct deposits (15 million government payments per month to individual accounts). The number of ATM users has increased 55% in the past two years and usage itself 243% in the past three years. Between February 1977 and October 1980 Citibank alone installed 468 ATMs in New York City (*New Yorker,* Jan. 5, 1981:41). By the latter date, 870,000 customers used them for more than six million transactions per week.

Most machines are still installed on the outsides of banks. Little by little, more of them are being installed away from the banks. The courts have ruled that machines away from the banks are to be treated as bank branches. Banks favor them for three reasons: 1) by going into a new area, a bank can develop a new clientele; 2) teller machines cost much less to establish than new branches; and 3) banks can reduce their business hours by having these 24-hour devices. On the other hand, banks dislike the emphasis on withdrawal transactions (70% of all ATM transactions).

Legislation has been introduced in Congress to overrule the courts' definition of ATMs as bank branches, but no action has as yet been taken. The McFadden Act of 1927 binds national banks to the restrictions imposed by states on state banks. However, most states have passed enabling legislation, less restrictive than branching legislation, for the installation of ATMs. But there is still variation between states in the degree of strictness. The slow progress in this area is believed due to public indifference. The primary advantage of ATMs, as far as the public is concerned, is their 24-hour availability. Location becomes an issue if it significantly affects convenience.

Under the rubric of ACHs, three functions can be subsumed: 1) direct deposits, 2) automatic bill paying, and 3) telephonic bill paying.

Individuals can authorize employers to deposit pay, or pension funds to deposit pension payments, etc., directly to their bank accounts. The largest advance in this area has been made by the government, which now deposits social security and other routine funds electronically. (Many people still believe that the government sends checks to their banks for deposit to their accounts.) Some 26% of social security recipients are participants in the system, and the number is expected to rise to 40% by 1981. A reason for this relatively rapid progress is that participants do not have to take the trouble to deposit their checks; they also need not worry about theft or holdups.

The second function coming under the heading of ACH is automatic bill paying. This is simply a preauthorization to a bank to make certain recurring payments (for example, mortgage payments or insurance premiums) automatically at specified times of the month. This has not caught on as rapidly as anticipated, probably because it appears to be a surrender of financial control on the part of the individual. This perception of reduced control, produced by the absence of immediate feedback, causes the reluctance to have someone else make one's payments and debit one's account.

The rapid increase in telephonic bill paying is an example of how an existing technology can have an amplifying effect on an emerging technology. The touch-dial telephone makes electronic bill paying from the home possible. A touch-dial telephone can be used to communicate with a computer in a bank. Subscribers are given a list of code numbers referring to the most common creditors (utility companies, insurance agencies, mortgage companies, etc.), and this enables them to punch in amounts and the creditors' code numbers on the touch dial. In fact, a computer tape gives oral instructions for a step-by-step procedure. This is not the only way telephonic bill paying works; in many situations instructions are given to a bank clerk who is at the other end of the line. In any case, the subscriber, in effect, conducts the transaction, and this gives him the subjective feeling of being in control. It is to be noted that the largest amount of advertising has gone into this part of EFT.

Although the ADL study envisaged EFT primarily as a tool of financial institutions, the history of banking functions would suggest a different prognosis. Credit cards were innovated not by banks, but by department stores and other institutions (American Express, Diners Club, etc.). Banks got into the act subsequently by initiating such multicharge cards as VISA and MasterCard. This credit performed the same function, but in a more general manner. Functions originally the province of the banks—deposit and checking services, loans, and extension of credit—are now performed by other organizations under different headings and subject to different regulations.

Again, regulations passed in response to the pressure to protect the privacy of EFT users made it unlawful to use universal account (or identification) numbers for participants (the social security number for credit cards, bank accounts, etc.). Assuming a national, interlocking computer network for EFT, the regulation is not only ineffective, but unlocks unique opportunities for the computer expert to gain customer information (and potentially develop a market for it) through pattern analysis or generation of a personal cross-indexing program.

It would appear that law and regulation, far from being an external overseer of a technology, have to be viewed as an integral part of its development. And where there are differences between federal and state, foreign and U.S. control arrangements, opportunities for unanticipated (and sometimes unwanted) evolution occur. One example of such an organizational development is the expansion of foreign influence through control of U.S. banks. As of March 31, 1980, foreign-owned banks accounted for 26 of the 300 largest U.S. banks. In seven years, foreign banks doubled their market shares of business loans. During this time the total assets of their U.S. offices increased 600%. At first this does not seem to have any relationship to EFT. However, there are ramifications that will eventually converge with the development of EFT.

The fact that the consequences of this activity are extremely difficult to assess is borne out by the differences of opinion about it among the members of Congress. In a television broadcast on November 18, 1979, one Senator, two Congressmen, and the President of the Chamber of Commerce expressed themselves on this issue. The following are quotes from the transcript of the broadcast:

Senator Heinz of Pennsylvania (member of the Senate Banking and Finance Committee and head of the Senate move to place a six-month moratorium on foreign acquisition of U.S. banks):

There's a tidal wave of foreign takeovers of U.S. banks; it threatens the stability of the banking system, and the Federal Government is deaf, dumb and blind to the consequences.

Congressman Reuss of Wisconsin (Chairman of the House Banking Committee):

We should welcome foreign investment. It makes jobs, it fights inflation. That's good—I think it would be foolish to barge in and tamper with it.

Congressman Grassley of Iowa (primary author of the Agricultural Foreign Investment Act):

It's a growing concern of mine. Yes, there's too much investment at this point— and particularly in the area of agriculture and banking.

It seems highly likely that these international developments in the financial field are going to impact, and be impacted by, the continued development of EFT. The difficulty of assessing those impacts is indicated by the controversy surrounding both the foreign investment and the EFT question. Assessments have raised intriguing questions about the effect on EFT on domestic power centers and their control capability. The disagreement surrounding the results of foreign investment emphasizes the multifaceted relationships involved. The confluence of these two developments has to date been unexamined.

In performing a TA, one has to draw boundaries around the territory to be covered. One could simply decide to pursue the ramifications of a technology until the funding runs out. This was not the ADL approach. The area of investigation was very carefully circumscribed and the decisions made by ADL about what *not* to include were as a significant as those made about what to include.

D. HIGHER ORDER IMPACTS

Although, as Figure 18a indicates, the T perspective was dominant in the TA by ADL, it was directed at the organizational element and not the technological element. Consequently certain technological impacts were omitted. For example, the impact of computer technology and telecommunications technology on EFT was not developed (Colton and Kraemer, 1980). An increasing flow of information may swamp the system or lead to illusions of control. The ability to handle more volume in less time may have profound effects on the monetary system beyond increased efficiency. This concern is embodied in several questions.

For instance, what happens when the blood circulation of a social system (money) is swallowed by its central nervous system (computers *cum* telecommunications)? Can the economy be controlled if money moves through it so quickly? Can a crisis occur with much less warning time than at present? Does the rapid flow accelerate or restrain inflation? What is the effect of money movement speed on bank profits? Is there an optimum speed of money flow to maintain control? We might speculate that money, as medium of exchange, can be controlled only if it flows through the system at a rate of speed the system can react to in a timely manner. Our own conjecture is that it should be possible, in principle, to associate an optimal range of money velocity with a stable economy.

The value of the gross national product can be conceptualized as the product of the total quantity of money and the velocity of its movement, that is, the average number of times per year the money is turned over or spent. This means that, as long as production capacity is not strained, an increase in either money supply or velocity will raise the GNP without lowering the value of money and creating inflation (Kahn, 1982:94). The management of money velocity would seem to be just as important as that of money supply. A rapid acceleration of money flow can have surprising effects. One might conceivably assert that the stock market crash of 1929 was at least partly due to the rapid acceleration of credit buying, which generated money supplies that had no representation in reality and which moved through the system with increasing velocity.

The money volume of the Clearing House Interbank Payment System (CHIPS), handled by the Federal Reserve Bank of New York, has increased from a daily average of $4.5 billion to a one-time daily high of $188 billion in just nine years (1970–1979). Each CHIPS dollar is assumed to pass through the system many times a day, generating considerable earnings for the banks making the transactions. This entails two possible dangers: 1) the accelerated earnings, which represent no growth in anything of real value, generate destabilizing pressure; and 2) the failure of a few major banks may have such reverberations as to cause the collapse of the system with lightning speed.

Potentially significant impacts of EFT can be imagined in part by studying a society in the throes of a high inflation rate, for example, Israel, with an annual rate in 1980 of 135%. Companies are taking advantage of this situation by delaying payments, such as employee withholding taxes and social security contributions, by purposely making "mistakes" on checks so they are returned for correction, and by other clever schemes. It is conceivable that EFT could be used to diminish the profitability of high inflation rates (*Los Angeles Times,* Jan. 3, 1981:1). It is even possible that EFT, combined with an all-pervasive computer communications system, may do more to minimize inflation itself than today's monetary policies (Hiltz and Turoff, 1978:205).

Another interesting possibility is the introduction of electronic mail, which may well replace the postal system. One forecast estimates that half of all telephones installed between 2000 and 2010 will have terminals (Hiltz and Turoff, 1978:429). In such a setting it is difficult to visualize anything other than the complete takeover of EFT. At the same time the nature of the transactions conducted may change dramatically when the home terminal takes on the functions of an ATM, shopping mall, and market to bring together buyers and sellers, accountant, tax advisor, checkbook, and file cabinet.

Another higher order impact requiring a T (and P) perspective is the advance of innovative computer crime on the part of technologists. A computer security consultant in Los Angeles diverted $10 million from the Security Pacific Bank and almost succeeded in diverting $50 million from the Union Bank to his own account. More recently, several individuals pulled off a $21 million computer bank fraud at the Beverly Hills branch of the Wells Fargo Bank. The use of EFT makes possible virtually instantaneous transfer of billions of dollars. Thus the January 1981 transfer of $7.9 billion in Iranian funds from American banks to the Bank of England took less than 10 minutes. Today federal officials indicate that the average loss in a nonelectronic embezzlement is $23,500, whereas the average computer fraud is $430,000. The National Center for Computer Crime Data tells us that 99% of electronic swindles go totally undetected (*Time,* Feb. 16, 1981:64-65). Burns International Security Services estimates an average loss of $667,000 per incident, with a total for 1981 between $1.2 and 1.8 billion.

Theft of information may prove to be an even more insidious type of computer crime than theft of money. A company may be outbid or new pharmaceutical and chemical formulas stolen and patented. Usually, criminals are not prosecuted, as the victimized banks and corporations shun the publicity. Teenagers are becoming so adept at computers that they love the challenge of tapping computer systems—the "414 gang" commits crimes for fun rather than for profit. Donn Parker of SRI International fears that "by the end of the 1980s computer crimes could cause economic chaos" (*Time,* Jan. 19, 1981:76).

An organizational element that would have benefited from the addition of an O perspective is the shifting turf of banks and high-technology companies. Citicorp is buying telecommunications and computer capabilities; International Telephone and Telegraph (ITT) is buying financial institutions and computer capabilities; IBM is buying satellite capabilities.

More questions are raised: will competition among small banks be eliminated?

Will new oligarchies and cartels be formed? What happens within banking and other institutions as software experts play a larger role?

The takeover of world financial control by an oligarchy need not imply a deliberately organized conspiracy, nor would it necessarily be done for the pursuit of nefarious ends. Such an oligarchy may be a natural outcome of the development of EFT management. Operating like a group of ordinary business executives, this "incidental" oligarchy would not easily be subject to public scrutiny, while it would wield extraordinary power. The "gnomes of Zurich" refers to a concept of such an oligarchy, although on a much lesser scale of importance or power.

Finally, like other facets of information technology, EFT is likely to contribute to the draining of power from labor unions. It is evident that the higher order impacts may be far more significant in the long term than the local first-order impacts.

E. THE INDIVIDUAL PERSPECTIVE

1. Individual Actors

The ADL study did not focus on individual actors: the influence of personal (as opposed to organizational) interests on the development of EFT, on political power plays, bargaining, and compromises.

Would investigation along those lines have turned up any significant insights, that is, insights that would have implications beyond those generated by the other two perspectives? One way of approaching this question is to imagine a scenario in which an individual actor, playing a specific role, could have a significant effect on EFT. Next, one would investigate whether or not such a role (or position) exists in reality. Finally, if such a position is discovered, one would determine whether the incumbent is exerting influence in one direction or the other, or if it can be estimated what sort of influence will likely be exerted by those who will hold the position in the foreseeable future, provided logical candidates for that position can be identified.

In this instance, no idea along the lines of such a scenario could be elicited from the initial circle of respondents to our inquiry. It was claimed by the respondents that neither the President of the United States, nor the Chairman of the Board of the Federal Reserve System, nor any banker, business tycoon or consumer advocate, could have any appreciable influence on the development of EFT.

However, further probing suggests that this view is by no means unanimous. It is pointed out that Dale Reistad is a pioneer and entrepreneur in this area. He was the first Director of Information for the American Bankers Association, and it was his task to keep the bankers on the leading edge during the 1960s. He became interested in the concept of "the checkless society" and formed a com mittee to stay abreast of it. In 1968 he formed his own company, Payment Services, Inc. (PSI). Fifty percent of his clientele is in commercial banking, the rest loan companies, oil companies, communications companies, etc. His clients represent 16 or 17 countries. Nearly every talk he gives includes a scenario and forecast. His company publishes a newsletter with items such as "Providence, R.I., YMCA uses ACH for Dues Payments," "N.Y. City Fire Department Pension Fund Adopts Direct Deposit," and "Virginia Legislature to Permit Payment of Taxes Via Credit Card." These publicize potential new uses of EFT to an ever-increasing array of clients.

We have another interesting example of individual movers in the evolution of Banc One Corporation of Columbus, Ohio. Table 18 shows a chronology of the organization, beginning with the assumption of the presidency of City National Bank of Columbus by John H. McCoy in 1935. A solid, stable bank was forged. Twenty-three years later, son John G. McCoy succeeded him, and things began to happen: John Fisher was hired, money was set aside for research, and there was commitment.[3] Creativity was soon reflected in a series of innovative activities: credit card processing (1961), ATMs (1970), POSTs (1971), and in-

TABLE 18. The Banc One Chronology

Year	Event	Comment
1935	John H. McCoy becomes President of City National Bank of Columbus (CNB); deposits of $40 million	Sound foundation laid.
1958	Son John G. McCoy becomes President of CNB; deposits of $140 million	"Hire the best and delegate."
1959	Hires E. Reese (formerly American Bankers Association President) and John F. Fisher (former ad man)	"Find out what the customer wants."
		J. Fisher: "McCoy has been willing to bet. Once a track record is established, he's willing to keep laying more chips on the table. And he's willing to give reins to the horse . . . . so I've had lots of freedom."
	McCoy starts research and development for bank Can customer needs be satisfied at a profit? Before competitors?	McCoy: "I asked the Board of Directors—my father's friends, not mine—to approve setting aside 3% of earnings annually for research, and they said, 'We're a bank. Why do we need research?' And I said, 'I don't know. That's what I want to find out'."

(continued)

---

[3] In concrete terms, about 27% of the stock of Banc One Corporation today is owned by officers and directors.

TABLE 18. The Banc One Chronology (*continued*)

Year	Event	Comment
	DEVELOPMENT AREA A: CREDIT CARD PROCESSING	
1961	• Construction of data processing facility begins	
	• Checks printed with computer readable codes	
	• American Hotel Association proposes BankAmericard concept to CNB; venture not profitable	
1962	• Data processing facility opens	
1966	• CNB franchises BankAmericard in Ohio—*first outside California.* 100,000 users and 800 merchants signed	
1967	• CNB intensifies focus on "processing for a fee" for others	
1968	• Polaroid pictures on credit cards, card user education	
1969	• Two-story data processing plant opens—350 employees	
	• 200 banks in 3 states offer Bank Americard processed by CNB	
	• Master Charge added by CNB	
1971	• CNB one of top ten credit card processors in U.S.	
1975	• CNB introduces Bank of America's debit card; limited success	
1977	• CNB's card processing business second nationally; most profitable part of bank's business	
	• Start of check and credit card transactions for Merrill Lynch's Cash Management Accounts (CMA)	Merrill Lynch rep: "{CNB} was creative. We were concerned that bigger banks might not see this as important enough to use their best people."
	• This part of CNB renamed Financial Card Services (FCS)	
1981	• Data processing for 168 other organizations; $14 million in fees	

TABLE 18. (*continued*)

Year	Event	Comment
	• Banc One one of three largest VISA processors; currently processing for over 2 million cardholders (of which 3/4 million are brokerage firm customers)	
1967	First Banc Group (FBG) formed	Three strengths stressed:
1969	Fisher goes to Colorado, returns to CNB after 18 months	1. "uncommon partnership" with affiliated banks; 2. expansion by affiliation with financially strong banks; 3. development of noninterest rate dependent sources of revenue

	DEVELOPMENT AREA B: AUTOMATED TELLERS	
1970	• CNB *first* to install automatic cash dispenser in bank lobby	
1973	• CNB *first* to install 24-hour drive-in cash dispenser	
	• CNB opens nearly automated branch; 12 ATMs, 4 human tellers; proves premature	
1978	• CNB builds first autobank: ATM and human teller	
1981	• Banc One operates 9 autobanks, 45 ATMs	

	DEVELOPMENT AREA C: POINT OF SALE TERMINALS (POS)	
1971–72	• CNB runs 9 month experiment with POS terminals; not enough advantage over credit card for merchant	
1976	• CNB installs 60 check and credit card verification machines in stores; loses $400,000; disbands system	

1977	FBG has 16 members; deposits $1620 million	
1979	Name change: Banc One Corporation; affiliated banks become Bank One of _____	

(*continued*)

TABLE 18. The Banc One Chronology (*continued*)

Year	Event	Comment
	DEVELOPMENT AREA D: IN-HOME BANKING SERVICES	
1973	● Fisher visits France, sees home Videotex terminal in operation	
1979	● Fisher convinced home banking must be part of larger system of home services	
1980	● Southeast First National Bank of Miami, AT&T, and Knight-Ridder run 6-month experiment	
	● Bank One of Columbus and Online Computer Library Center of Columbus (OCLC) launch 3-month "Channel 2000" Videotex experiment with 200 participants. System includes access to videocard catalogs in public libraries and to Deaf Community Bulletin Board, permits payment of bills presented on screen and review of bank account statements, as well as other functions	
1981	Of $39 million in net operating earnings, $2 million are allocated to research and development	1981 Annual Report: "Change will be a way of life for the financial services industry."
	Banc One comparison with 100 largest banking organizations: fifth in return on average assets 13th in return on average equity 10th in average equity to assets	
1982	Banc One achieves all-time high annualized return on average equity capital of 18.5%	
	Assets doubled in last three years; Banc One prepares for interstate banking through acquisitions	

Sources: Harvard Business School (1982); Banc One (1981, 1982); J. Fisher (personal communication).

home banking services (1978). McCoy provided a steady, supportive setting, and Fisher pursued promising ideas and leads.

How important are Reistad, McCoy, and Fisher in the framework of an EFT assessment? One view is that the specific mover or experimenter should not be treated as an "individual actor." The rationale is as follows: EFT is a nationwide (and possibly worldwide) enterprise that comprises a number of innovative features, most of them requiring the participation of the population at large. Under these circumstances, the natural course of development requires experimentation, evaluation of the experiments, modification of procedures or of technical features, and so forth. The pressure of the technology itself makes experimentation inevitable. It can be claimed that if Banc One (or McCoy and Fisher) had not experimented, some other bank (and its executives) most certainly would have done so.

The other view is that the consequences and conditions associated with a technology are closely related to the particular trajectory it follows. The electronics, computer, and optical devices industries, for example, have one of their centers around Route 128 outside Boston. This is the result of the post–World War II initiatives of a group of MIT and Harvard professors and the support of local bankers—a combination that did not occur in many other places, although it might have eventually if it had not happened there. And the fact that they are where they are can be expected to influence future developments.

Similarly, the U.S. aerospace industry has one of its centers in Southern California because of early decisions by Donald Douglas and other industry pioneers. Much of the growth of that region is traceable to that industry and would probably have been anticipated in a successful TA if one had been done at the time. But for the specific initiatives of individuals these industries might have been located elsewhere; they might even have been eclipsed by their German, French, or British counterparts.

The importance of the individual in the world of banking generally has been recognized from the days of the Rothschilds to those of the Rockefellers. Consider the words of Arthur Sampson [1981]:

> Behind all its global responsibility and impersonal style banking is still a 'people business'. . . . Economists may talk about the macroeconomic functions of the international capital market, but down in the marketplace itself there are real people trying to impress and persuade other people. . . . It may be the most personal business of all, for it always depends on the original concept of credit, meaning trust. However complex and mathematical the business has become, it still depends on the assessment of trust by individuals with very human failings. . . . The history of banking remains the history of individual people each making their own judgment—vulnerable to hopes and fears, flattery and persuasion, moods of optimism and pessimism. (17, 20)

One banker described the fashioning of syndicated international loans in London to Sampson [1981:128] as follows:

> When I first started I was amazed how casual it all seemed. When I first signed a loan agreement for twenty million dollars for a country I hardly knew anything about, I thought 'we must be crazy.' Syndication depends on the personality cult. There's no greater fun than to know that everyone wants to talk to you at cocktail parties and to be part of the world of big BMWs and parties at Annabel's. When an ambassador rings up to suggest you join a loan, you want to be part of it: the Americans are specially vulnerable to flattery. Syndication depends on only about a hundred people in London, and you soon get to know them all.

It is evident that, even as banking becomes increasingly global and electronic, the individual who understands "the system" may exercise much indirect control and influence—possibly more power than ever before. That makes the P perspective both difficult and crucial.

2. Impacted Individuals

Although impacted individuals can usually be considered as a group, that is, from the O perspective, the impact often can be grasped only by communicating with individuals.

For example, personal contact elicited the view that Blacks like EFT because the machine is color blind and does not discriminate: "I put my card in and nobody says 'no' to me or hassles me." Blacks say that with EFT, they can cash checks in a southern city grocery store where they felt they would not have been trusted before. Other minorities may also benefit. In New York the Citibank ATMs communicate in Spanish, as well as in English.

Many people exhibit a generalized anxiety about ATMs until a bank employee "walks" them through the procedure. Then they are "hooked." While not everyone likes the system, almost everyone reacts to it in a curiously personal and

TABLE 19. Three Approaches to EFT Assessment

	TA by ADL	National Commission	Multiple Perspectives Potential
Elements studied	Primarily organizational (types of change, impacts on banks, business, other groups) Secondarily individual	Organizational (needed administration arrangements, EFT legislation) Secondarily technology, economics, etc.	Technological (for example, impact of telecommunications, higher-order impacts) Organizational—gaps in other studies (for example, crime, foreign influence on EFT) Individual (for example, key actors)
Perspectives used	Primarily T	Primarily O	T, O, and P
Aim	Comprehensive T look at organizational impacts	Recommendations satisfactory to major stakeholders Gaining time for development	Develop well-balanced insights for decision making through multiple perspectives Improved communication of insights (using P)
Client	Concerned Public	President and Congress	NA

The P Perspective in Action: Another Example

One of the most interesting examples of "computer misunderstanding" that I have been exposed to is the reaction of the people in our manufacturing plant to ACT—Automatic Cash Transfer of their payroll funds.

When we first introduced it about five years ago, it seemed like a logical extension of the fact that all check postings were being made by computer anyway and the only written instrument was the paycheck itself, which was also computer prepared in our case. To send our payroll tape to the bank for same day distribution to individual accounts seemed like a real advantage to our employees. And although it cost the company some "float," that would be made up by the lower cost of getting out the payroll.

I was surprised by the depth and vigor of the resistance to this idea. One of our best employees made a stirring speech decrying it as a bankers' and company ploy to disenfranchise the employees and conjured up all kinds of problems with a "faceless bank." Another took a religious tack and viewed it as the work of the devil and longed for the gold talents of Biblical times. We still only have about 30% of our employees on ACT as we have left it voluntary.* We have had little technical problem; and, as I travel a lot, it has proved to be a great convenience for me.

Few things have less intrinsic value than the piece of green paper in a pay envelope, but many of us seem to need some small tangible reassurance of what we have always held to be "reality." Maybe when we get all of our people up on terminals we can deliver their checks in living terminal green on payday and let them query the "computer in which they trust" themselves.

Douglas Strain
Chairman of the Board
Electro Scientific Industries

From: a comment made in EIES Computerized Conference on "Computers and Society," October 3, 1982.
*reduced to 18% by May 1983.

---

emotional way. Those who dislike it stress the malfunctions (not danger of theft or complexity); those who like it point to the 24-hour use (although most transactions occur during regular business hours). The general popularity of ATMs may have its roots in the same ground as that of electronic games—the man–machine love affair (*New Yorker*, Jan. 5, 1981:42).

Moving beyond ATMs, we find that senior citizens are pleased with telephonic bill payments because they no longer have to depend on someone to take them to the Post Office or elsewhere. On the other hand, tax dodgers and corporate manipulators are made nervous by the possibility of easier audit trails with EFT.

Obviously, intensive personal contact is required to do justice to the P perspective with regard to individual actors or impacted individuals. This can be achieved either through deep personal immersion, as in the Perinatal Region-

TABLE 20. A Comparison of Insights Derived from the Three Perspectives—EFT

TECHNICAL PERSPECTIVE (1975–1977)

1. The U.S. banking industry is technologically obsolete.
2. The security of the direct deposit process is a clear advantage.
3. The 24-hour availability of ATMs is a clear advantage.
4. Economics dictates EFT implementation (that is, the volume of paper flow and cost of handling make the shift imperative).
5. There is a mismatch between the technological and managerial aspects of EFT implementation.
6. The combined impact of vastly greater velocity and quantity of money flow possible with EFT is still unclear (for example, on international finance or on crisis management).

ORGANIZATIONAL PERSPECTIVE (1976–1980)

7. Commissioning a study project buys time.
8. It is important to provide a means for all vested interests (for example, affected federal agencies or banks) to interact in developing the basis for new legislation.
9. A vote on a set of recommendations is the result of complex compromises by vested interest representatives and is revised only with great difficulty.
10. EFT may create new opportunities for oligarchic arrangements and developments.
11. EFT plays a significant role in shifting the turf between financial institutions and high technology companies (for example, Citicorp, ITT, and IBM).

PERSONAL PERSPECTIVE (1980)

12. ATMs are color blind, a fact perceived by a non-White person.
13. Instructions can be given in the client's native language by an ATM, avoiding embarrassment of the customer in a bank.
14. Automatic bill paying seems like a surrender of personal financial control.
15. Dale Reistad (PSI) and John Fisher (Banc One) are pioneers who have had important personal influence.
16. Computer crime has a promising future.

alization Project described in Chapter VII or through a large number of personal interviews (or participant observation) as in the On-Site Solid Waste Management case presented in Chapter X.

3. Communications and the P Perspective

The usual scenarios do not go very far in providing vivid images or holistic visions of the future that would stimulate more than superficial discussions of EFT (Coates, 1977). The P perspective, executed by a writer or other effective communicator, could fill this void.

F. SUMMARY

In Tables 19 and 20, we summarize the key points of this chapter.

IX

GUAYULE COMMERCIALIZATION

M. ADELSON, H. LINSTONE,
A.J. MELTSNER, and R. MILLER

I received One Hundred Peanuts.
(signed) Hiroshi Itoh

(Aircraft Company Marketing Expense Receipt)

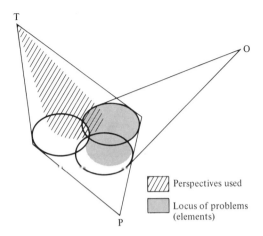

FIGURE 19. Schematic of perspectives: Guayule Technology Assessment.

Guayule is a rubber-producing plant suitable to growth in semidesert areas such as northeastern Mexico and the southwestern United States. This rubber, when processed, is a potential substitute for Southeast Asia's hevea rubber, the source of natural rubber since the latter part of the 19th century. Guayule rubber has characteristics very similar to those of hevea and was already known as another potential commercial source before the beginning of this century.

The University of Arizona's Office of Arid Lands Studies (OALS/UA) is a recognized center of expertise in the technology of guayule and was chosen by the National Science Foundation to undertake a technology assessment on the *commercialization* of guayule.[1] Unlike the electronic funds transfer case, the guayule TA was still in progress at the time of most of the work reported in this chapter. In view of the academic setting and research focus of OALS/UA, a strong T perspective was natural, as was concern with the technological elements (Figure 19—linear shading). The final report (Foster et al., 1980) presents an excellent T perspective of the state-of-the-art and prospects of guayule.[2] It also addresses the economics in considerable detail. However, only about 30% of it deals with commercialization impact and policy analysis (11% with the latter).

Section A of this chapter summarizes the TA by OALS/UA as the T perspective. Sections B and C summarize our own O and P perspectives, respectively. The disparity in resources[3] precludes a full-scale comparison of output. Our scope did not take O and P much beyond the commercialization question

---

[1]The TA project leader was Dr. Kennith Foster. Midwest Research Institute was a subcontractor supplying TA experience.
[2]Our contacts with the OALS/UA team revealed a considerable presence of O and P perspectives in their work; these did not find their way into the final product, however.
[3]In terms of person-months, less than 10% of the effort devoted to the T perspective.

itself to the "what-if?" However, the initial trajectory does play an important role in any impact assessment. The fundamental question is: Are there any indications that complementary insights can be generated by the introduction of the other perspectives?

A. THE T PERSPECTIVE (SUMMARY OF OALS/UA TA) (FOSTER ET AL., 1980)

1. Background

The United States, the world's major user of automobiles, is also the world's major consumer of natural rubber (in 1970, accounting for 20% of the world consumption). Malaysia has been the foremost supplier of natural rubber (in 1970, 1.1 million tons of the total production of 3 million tons). World War II saw the cutoff of rubber from Southeast Asia and an enormous twofold U.S. substitution effort: 1) synthetic rubber, pioneered by Germany in World War I, and 2) the Emergency Rubber Project (ERP) to develop a new source of natural rubber. The guayule plant was a prime candidate, having been long recognized as a source of natural rubber similar to Southeast Asia's hevea rubber, and native to northeastern Mexico and the southwestern United States. The ERP planted 32,000 acres of guayule (Strain No. 593), which yielded three million pounds of rubber.

After World War II (1946), the ERP was disbanded, due to the success of synthetic rubber development and the demand for agricultural land for food crops. A low level of research and development on guayule persisted until 1959. In the early 1970s the oil embargo revived U.S. interest in guayule. Mexico also became active, primarily through the activities of its Applied Chemistry Research Institute (CIQA) in Saltillo. International conferences in 1975 (Tucson) and 1977 (Saltillo) focused on improving guayule yield and processing. In 1978 the U.S. Congress passed a Bill authorizing $30 million for guayule research and development as well as creation of a guayule commission. However, as of this writing (1980), the funds for research and development had yet to be appropriated. Some plant-breeding studies are in process, test plots have been established, a pilot processing plant has been established in Saltillo, and radial tires containing 30 to 40% guayule have passed U.S. Department of Transportation tests. Among tire and rubber companies, Firestone has been the cautious leader in guayule experimentation at Ft. Stockton, Texas. It has been spending about $1 million per year on a modest program. Its plantings cover 100 acres.[4] It is estimated that, to be economically viable, 50,000 acres or more are needed to support one processing plant (with an annual output of 12,000 tons of rubber).

The use of rubber increased by 6.4% annually between 1948 and 1973 (natural

---

[4]Since this was written we have learned (1982) that Firestone is giving up its small guayule plantation.

rubber 3.3% and synthetic rubber 9.3%). By 1973 synthetic rubber supplied 69% of the total world demand and 77% of the U.S. demand. The price of natural rubber is now highly unstable: in the first two months of 1980 it rose 35% despite declining world demand and world oversupply; in 1981 it dropped 66%.[5]

About 70% of U.S. rubber use (75% of synthetic rubber) was for tires in 1970. The second most common use was latex products (12%). In terms of tonnage, one-half the total U.S. consumption is for road vehicle tires (passenger cars, trucks, and buses).

An entirely separate factor is the declining water availability in the southwestern United States, making such conventional crops as cotton increasingly marginal and such semidesert crops as guayule more attractive.

2. Rubber Forecast

Even in a low-growth future (double the current demand in the year 2000) the combination of synthetic and natural hevea rubber will fall short of world demand between 1990 and 2000 (by some eight million metric tons in 2000). Assuming natural rubber demand to be a constant fraction of 30%, the hevea shortfall in 2000 is projected to be 2.4 million metric tons. With high growth, the hevea shortfall is estimated as 4.9 million tons.

The shortfall in rubber may be met by:

- new supplies
  increasing hevea stands in Brazil, Liberia, and Ghana,
  oil from new sources (for example, Mexico) for synthetic rubber,
  polyisoprene;
- reduced demand
  smaller cars,
  gas rationing;
- new processing methods
  development of a cast tire (using less synthetic rubber),
  reclamation of rubber;
- guayule.

3. State-of-the-Art of Guayule

The guayule plant yields 10 to 15% rubber by weight during its fourth growth year; one acre yields one ton every four years.

Guayule requires rain in late winter, spring, and early summer, dry weather at other times, and well-drained, moist soils. The function of rubber in the

[5]The International Natural Rubber Organization, (INRO) created in October 1980, now buys and sells hevea in an effort to stabilize prices (*New York Times*, February 6, 1982).

guayule plant is not known. Guayule uses less water than alfalfa, cotton, corn, and sorghum; hence it can replace these crops in the water-short southwestern United States.

The state of development of guayule is summarized in Table 21. Research on guayule has been extensive—over 1000 scientific papers have been written on the plant. It is estimated that a strain with twice the yield of No. 593 is attainable.[6] In five to ten years of breeding, a 20% rubber content (by weight) is a reasonable goal. A crude rubber yield of 1500 lb per acre has been obtained in Arizona in three years (500 lb per year) and 2800 lb in five years near Bakersfield, California (560 lb per year). North American potential growth regions include most of California, Arizona, New Mexico, and southwestern Texas.

4. Economics

- U.S. import–export trade balance: currently (−) $674 million in natural rubber.

- Price: about 300% increase in natural rubber since 1972, serious price instability has existed since 1980, stabilization mechanism is now operative through INRO (at least until 1984).

- The depressed U.S. tire and rubber industry is a negative factor.

- Capital: there is a shortage of investment capital currently (1980), because a shift to radial tires requires new plant investment.

- Basic innovation time: there is a period of new capital investment in innovations anticipated on the basis of the Kondratieff cycle in the 1985–1995 period; this would apply to guayule agriculture—a "basic innovation" rather than an improvement innovation as a commercial product (Mensch, 1979; Graham and Senge, 1980).

- Acreage: in the potential guayule growth area 1.5 to two million of 7.5 to ten million acres could be planted by 2000.

- Guayule is a net energy producer.

5. Environmental Constraints

- Water: this is the limiting factor rather than land—18 to 24 inches per year is required.

- Air: turpines found in the guayule plant create haze (for example, as in the Great Smoky Mountains); the effect of large-scale guayule planting is not clear.

---

[6]Battelle Columbus Laboratories has recently reported a new extraction process yielding up to 55% more rubber from guayule (*Chemical and Engineering News*, January 18, 1982:56).

230

TABLE 21. State of Development of Guayule Technology

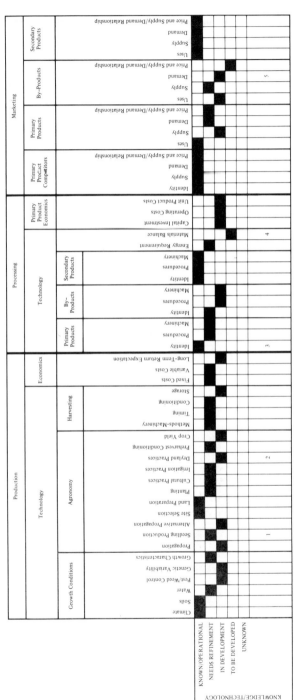

Source: Matrix conceptual design by Mortensen, Foster et al. (Foster et al., 1980).

1. Economics of seeding production needs refinement.
2. Texas dryland farming of guayule needs further research.
3. Agricultural costs need field demonstration.
4. Supply relationships between primary rubber product and by-products.
5. Bagasse demand as an energy source for processing is reasonably well known. Demand for other by-products needs more research.

6. Scenarios

Scenario A: surprise free. For the year 2000 a worldwide natural rubber shortfall of 4.88 million metric tons is predicted, with the corresponding U.S. figure 508,000 metric tons (559,000 short tons).
The U.S. situation will lead to:

- more U.S. purchases from world natural rubber supplies, raising prices further;
- more purchases of eastern European synthetic rubber;
- continued inadequacy of the U.S. rubber stockpile.

Guayule development can meet 100% of the projected natural rubber shortfall by 1991. By then, 1.3 million acres of guayule would be planted. After that date, guayule could be appreciably below the projected world natural rubber price, if the production cost is the determinant of price ($0.60 to 1.50 for guayule compared with $1.60 to 2.80 per lb for world natural rubber in 2000). Yield per acre is expected to double between 1985 and 2000. By 2000, 1.5 million acres would be cultivated: 42% in California, 32% in Texas, 19% in Arizona, and 6% in New Mexico. The principal by-product will be resin.

Scenario B: rapid commercialization. Substantial governmental involvement occurs following a 50% reduction in U.S. natural rubber imports. By 1990, 60% of the U.S. demand for natural rubber is to be met by U.S. guayule production (10% shortfall plus 50% hevea import replacement). At least nine processing facilities will be needed in 1990 to exploit the 1.25 million acres planted with guayule, and 16 plants by 2000. Research and development will increase substantially, resulting in a yield per acre 73% greater than that under Scenario A.
By 2000, 68% of the U.S. natural rubber will come from guayule (1.07 million short tons). Seed production by state and federal programs, as well as by rubber companies and private entrepreneurs, at a level of 8700 lb in 1979, will be expanded to 303,000 lb in 1981 and to 15 million lb in 1990.
It is suggested that a quasi-governmental corporation be organized to provide coordination and management of the accelerated program.

7. Impacts

Agriculture in three of the four potential production states—California, Arizona, New Mexico, and Texas—is of declining importance because of water shortages and population growth.

Jobs. The number of jobs in rural counties would increase slightly with Scenario A and modestly with B. For example, in Kern County, California, 19% of the total employment is in agriculture (28,000 persons). By 2000 the projected guayule acreage in the county under Scenario A would require 285 farmers or

1% of the agricultural employment (or 0.2% of the total employment). Non-agricultural employment created (for example, in a guayule processing plant) would amount to less than 0.3% of the 1978 county labor force. The impact would be somewhat more pronounced with Scenario B, with at least two processing plants and possibly a tire manufacturing plant in the county. The effect in Pecos County, Texas, would be more significant under both scenarios, because the area is presently more rural and sparsely populated. Under Scenario A, agricultural employment would increase 26% and total employment (agricultural and other) 12%. Guayule would bring back into use land earlier planted with cotton and now abandoned. Scenario B would yield correspondingly larger increases.

Environment. Large tracts of guayule will have effects on the ecological balance. The significance of impacts on air pollution and animal life are not known at this time. Replacement of a conventional crop, such as cotton by guayule, would ease the water availability, but create a greater fire hazard due to its high flammability.

Processing plants may engender respiratory or dermatological problems for workers, but the magnitude is not known. Bagasse, generated during processing, can also be a safety hazard because of the fumes it produces.

Land use. A benefit is the ability to keep agricultural land, largely in California and Texas,[7] in production when it may otherwise be lost to such activity because of low water supplies. Thus disruption of farm communities could be avoided for many years. The prospects for water-short Arizona and New Mexico are very limited.

Economy. The California Department of Food and Agriculture views guayule as a crop of importance when water shortages cut back current crops. Until such time, it expects to continue funding demonstration projects. Texas is less concerned with guayule commercialization at this time. The issues are not as well crystallized as in California. Arizona, a much poorer state, cannot provide major governmental support.

Table 22 provides a listing of the impacts.[8] Internationally, there may be both markets and competitors in the guayule industry. Potential new growth areas include Australia, Israel, and northern Africa.

8. Public Policy Analysis

Three kinds of goals are posited: stimulate guayule development, regulate its development, and mitigate adverse side effects. In addition, there are the strategic aspects (military/economic), to which Scenario B offers a response.

---

[7]For example, the Colorado desert in California and southern Texas.
[8]The TA does not include in-depth analysis of the impacts or issues.

TABLE 22. Sectors and Parties Impacted by Guayule Commercialization

Economic sectors, including parties-at-interest	Impact or consequence	
	Scenario A	Scenario B
Local focus		
Unemployed agricultural workers	Localized benefits from newly created jobs	Same
Unemployed semiskilled workers	Very limited benefits from newly created processing jobs	Same
Environmental, safety, and health effects	Limited impacts	Potential adverse effects in the short term
General business community	Benefit from increased farming and processing revenues and tax base, multiple effects	Potential construction of tire or other rubber-product fabrication facilities in Southwest, multiplier effects
Regional focus		
American Indian and other minorities	Limited positive effects	Probable economic gains for Indians through lease of land and water
Undocumented farm workers	Limited effects	Probable increased migration patterns
Marginal farm operations and economically displaced farmers	Benefit by shifting to less water-demanding crop	Benefit from Small Business Administration assistance and risk absorption
Banking and financial institutions	Uncertainty related to financing four-year crop	Moderate impacts regarding risk absorption, loans to small holders, probable futures market
Communities-at-large	Increased needs for social goods including housing, health, roads, police, fire protection	Same
National focus		
Environment-at-Large	Minimal impacts over near and middle term	Possible new patterns of insect infestation, moderate pollution potential in processing, moderate fire hazard
Guayule black market	Probable, especially for seeds and unprocessed shrubs	Same
U.S. tire and rubber companies	Slight gain in supply stability, little effect on prices	Gain in control of supply and counterforce to cartel activity

(*continued*)

TABLE 22 (*continued*)

Economic sectors, including parties-at-interest	Impact or consequence	
	Scenario A	Scenario B
National focus (*continued*)		
Guayule research and development efforts	Minimal budgets and expenditures by research groups including industry and academia	Maximum budgets
By-product values, including resins, wax, etc.	Limited positive impacts	Large impacts due to research and development efforts, possibly depressed older resin and wax markets
Fertilizer and pesticide manufacturers and sellers	Neutral to limited benefits	Same
Recycling–reclamation of rubber	Limited effect on/by guayule development	Same
U.S. rubber stockpile	Potential fulfillment in the long run, short-term market potential	Probable permanent shortfall
Various governmental and state agencies	Minimal potential conflicts of policy	Probable conflicts of individual policies on land and water use for agriculture, industry, and communities and environmental quality
International focus		
Balance of trade for U.S. rubber imports	Minimal effects over near and middle term	Moderate effects over the middle to long term
Mexican–U.S. relations	Probable strains if black market appears	Improvement through greater research and trade agreement and cooperation
Mexican government	Benefits limited to development and employment in rural, economically depressed communities	Benefits by shared technology and research-and-development advances
Hevea growers	No loss of U.S. markets for short term, some loss over long term	Loss of U.S. markets, gain in other world markets
Relationship between U.S. rubber companies and Mexican governments	Mexican land-ownership laws prohibit large-scale plantation ownership	Same

Source: Foster et al. (1980).

An inventory of policy issues. The questions and issues identified have been classified as 1) strategic or nonstrategic and 2) social, economic, or other. Table 23 provides a statement of the key points using this classification.[8]

Potential conflicts.

- federal resource allocation policies (land, water, labor);

- leadership in initiating guayule development (government versus private);

- environmental protection policies versus guayule development;

- self-sufficiency in natural rubber versus U.S. State Department objectives to increase international cooperation;

- antitrust policies versus vertical integration of guayule into rubber products industry;

- U.S. versus Mexican interests;

- small farmers and Indian communities versus agroindustry and rubber industry.

Table 24 presents a full listing of the potential conflicts at both national and local levels, together with possible resolution mechanisms.

B. THE O PERSPECTIVES (A.J. MELTSNER AND M. ADELSON)

The nonuniqueness of the O perspective has been noted (Section IV B 2). Two views are developed here; they reflect both the subjectivity of the viewer and the diversity of the organizations and groups involved in guayule commercialization.

1. Coalition Formation

At present (June 1980), the commercialization of guayule seems to be hardly moving; some would say it is immobilized. Guayule represents a classic case of a few interested and committed partisans, mainly researchers and scientists, with insufficient political and economic resources to fulfill their objectives. It is not, for the most part, a situation of deeply vested opposing interests, but more a matter of conserving—a wait-and-see defensive behavior on the part of the organizations, which are in, or might come to, the public arena. Thus one central question in assessing guayule's prospects is how to get it started, how to get it to move off dead center.

Assuming that market forces do not overtake political action in the next few years, an appropriate place to start would be in the federal arena. By its action, the federal government can signal the private sector, including farmers' groups, unions, financial institutions, and the rubber companies, that there indeed is a

TABLE 23. Policy Analysis in Guayule Commercialization

Critical questions regarding guayule commercialization	Identifiable issues
SOCIAL POLICY—NONSTRATEGIC	
1. What social groups or regions may benefit or suffer adverse effects? 2. Should this development be predominantly labor or capital intensive, or a mix? 3. Do potential benefits flow to targeted groups and communities as the result of minimum federal investment? 4. What are costs/benefits/risks to the public and private sector as the results of capital-intensive development? 5. What work practices and standards will be required? 6. What additional social goods will be required? 7. How may illegal immigration patterns be affected?	1. Benefits and possible adverse effects on American Indians, Hispanics, small-scale farmers, unemployed agricultural workers, economically depressed southwestern communities 2. Agricultural employment, including farm and processing operations, as function of costs and benefits 3. Uneven flow of costs/benefits/risks to targeted groups and communities 4. Spillover effects (positive and negative) 5. Individual safety and health; community health 6. Social welfare 7. Illegal immigration
SOCIAL POLICY—STRATEGIC	
1. Should the United States be dependent on foreign sources for meeting elastomer needs? 2. Who is displaced in the agricultural sector when guayule is commercialized? 3. Will nation's special needs constrain the development of a critical material need? 4. Will target groups and regional social needs be "lost" because of strategic material needs? 5. How much federal control is required to minimize perceived negative social consequences?	1. Interdependence versus self-sufficiency 2. Equality 3. Social needs versus strategic needs 4. Potential subservience of social needs 5. Cost/benefit/risk analysis
ECONOMIC POLICY—NONSTRATEGIC	
1. Is guayule development a regional "pork barrel?" 2. Does guayule development represent a new or replacement crop for the southwestern United States?	1. Political expediency; favored treatment accorded lobbyists 2. Agricultural business diversification-conservation 3. Income redistribution; favored treatment of minorities

3. Do economic benefits flow to targeted groups and regions, for example, substantial employment opportunities?
4. Will Indian tribes and landholdings specifically be involved?
5. Who, besides the industrial sector, benefits from guayule development?
6. Is any federal investment required/justified to offset perceived risks?
7. What is the appropriate scale for production/processing unit?
8. Is a centralized, large-scale operation desirable?
9. How do energy costs affect guayule development?
10. Is the four-year harvest cycle too risky for private investment and the small landholder?
11. Do by-product values significantly reduce investment risk?
12. Will U.S. guayule development foster a Mexican guayule black market?

4. Economic opportunities for Indians
5. Accrual and flow of economic opportunities and benefits
6. Uncertainty/risk to small landholder (that is, farmer) and to U.S. tire and rubber industry, private versus federal investment
7. Microeconomics; economies of scale; centralized versus decentralized
8. Economies of scale
9. Energy conservation; biomass development
10. Risk assessment of commercialization effort
11. Maximization of return on investment
12. Differences in local economies at the international border

ECONOMIC POLICY—STRATEGIC

1. Is it essential for the United States to establish a domestic rubber supply, and if so, in what time frame?
2. How would a 50% reduction in hevea rubber supply affect current demand for elastomers until guayule rubber is made available?
3. Will guayule rubber be used to bolster the natural rubber stockpile?
4. What is the impact of a "cartel" pricing policy?
5. How will foreign governments view U.S. guayule development; will United States be viewed as becoming isolationist?
6. How will guayule development affect U.S. balance of trade?
7. What happens if the natural rubber stockpile is depleted in the absence of alternate plans and programs?
8. What incentives will be needed to move the private sector into a cooperative guayule development program with the federal sector?
9. Are ERP or COMSAT viable routes to develop guayule?
10. Will guayule take priority over other agricultural commodities?
11. What happens if important food and fiber crops, for example, grains and cotton are displaced?

1. National security and self-sufficiency
2. Consumer, industrial, and military use patterns for natural and synthetic elastomers
3. Technological acceptability of guayule rubber and products
4. Loss of competitive pricing of elastomers
5. U.S. foreign relations
6. Strength of U.S. dollar abroad
7. National security and self-sufficiency
8. Risk absorption
9. Cooperative efforts by public and private interests
10. Food and fiber production
11. Relative economic importance of various crops

Source: Foster et al. (1980).

TABLE 24. Policy Conflicts—Potential Failures

	Conflicting Policies	Potential Problems	Potential Institutional Failures	Potential Resolution Mechanisms
a.	Water for agricultural use; water for municipal and industrial use	Value of water for agricultural use; value of water for municipal and industrial use	Market may not allocate water in socially desired manner	Governmental priority setting via economic incentives, disincentives to particular types of uses
b.	Land for food production; land for "other" production	Value of food production; value of fiber/material production; desertification	Conflict in policy—governmental failure to establish priorities	Limited policy statement with evaluation program to measure effect/intent
c.	Government investment; private investment	Scale of venture and anticipated costs/revenue	Each evaluating what others might do before making investment	Joint U.S.–industrial guayule investment group
d.	Government risk; private risk	Perception of degree of risk	Private risk structure (banks, other financial institutions) not capable of handling four-year risk project	Use of government to guarantee loans and insure investment; establish guayule futures market
e.	Federal; state; local agriculture policies	Value of various crops produced	Intergovernmental cooperation	Joint commission to oversee development
f.	Current crop patterns; new crop patterns	Value of crops produced; alternative crop production	Governmental monitoring/priority setting	U.S. Department of Agriculture (USDA)/stockpiling agency/states agreement
g.	Target groups: small business (farmers); American Indians	If strategic need, then social equity concerns may be overridden or ill considered	Inability of government to assist groups in equitable way	Use of lands/water as capital formation mechanism; use capital for other investment programs
h.	Strategic-materials policy; agricultural policy	Food and materials production	Inability of government to agree on policy stance where conflicting outcomes are sought[a]	May not be resolvable

i.	Strategic-materials policy: land-use policy	Alternative economic land use, for example, industrial development	Inability of government to minimize interference in market mechanism where conflicting needs are expressed	May not be resolvable
j.	Strategic-materials policy: water policy	Human consumption versus agricultural versus industrial water needs versus strategic need	Inability of government to minimize interference in market mechanism when conflicting needs are expressed	Will not be easily resolved
k.	Strategic materials policy: environmental policy	Land, air, water, safety, health, aesthetics ignored because of strategic need	Inability of government to set criteria and limitations in policy conflicts	Policy to minimize environmental impact
l.	Foreign policy: interpendence in world economy; independence in critical materials	United States versus hevea-producing countries	Inability of government to articulate single coherent policy	May not be resolvable
m.	Farm policy: family; corporate	Family farm versus corporate production	Inability of government to resolve basic policy conflict	Does not appear to be resolvable
n.	Strategic-materials policy: antitrust policy	Degree of vertical integration or horizontal cooperation	Government policy may inhibit efficient production method required to meet another governmental role	Government monitored oligopolistic structure

Source: Foster et al. (1980).

[a]Also market may not allocate resource use effectively, although it may do so efficiently.

stable demand for guayule rubber. It could also encourage state, regional, and local agencies, not just to promote experimental production, but to develop actual markets.

The present coalition. Up to this point the coalition of sectors that has been formed has had mainly a research experimentation orientation. For the most part the products of this coalition of the National Academy of Sciences, the NSF, and their colleagues from other federal agencies (such as the Bureau of Indian Affairs, Congressional supporters, and the rubber companies), have been research, and not commercial rubber. This coalition had the wherewithal to get the Native Latex Commercialization Act passed in 1978, but not to see that its authorization of $30 million was appropriated in subsequent years.

The $30 million was to be used to develop a domestic guayule industry to the point where the private sector would take over both production and processing. The private sector (for example, tire and rubber companies) is still waiting for that point to arrive. Experiencing a slump in demand for tires and saddled with a supply of hevea and synthetic rubber, they have been mainly pursuing "just-in-case" activities: testing tires for performance and endurance, experimental planting (particularly Firestone), and developing some processing patents.[9] As mature and well-established firms, the major tire and rubber companies have taken a defensive posture with respect to guayule. Thus Goodyear Tire and Rubber Company supported the Native Latex Commercialization Act and saw it as essential (Riedl, 1978), but at the same time expanded its rubber growing acreage in Brazil and Sumatra (Foster et al., 1980:289–290).

As a multinational industry, the rubber companies are certainly aware of the potential for instability in their supply of natural rubber because of international upheavals in areas where they have plantations. For example, the recent situation in Liberia has placed certain limits on supply; and for some companies, such as Firestone, international political instability has pointed out the need for a domestic supply of natural rubber. Taking the industry as a whole, however, the companies feel relatively safe and have confidence in the security of their sources. If one country collapses, they can always grow more natural rubber in another.

Even if the rubber companies were willing to assume the risk and become a major participant in the development and use of guayule, which at present they may not be, some of them would probably have difficulty in making the transition. From their own research, it seems that the rubber guayule produces is practically the same as hevea, but most of the companies' experience and organizational procedures are with the cultivation of hevea. To the extent that the companies would want to be involved in the growing and processing of guayule, they are likely to do so initially with a hevea orientation. For some corporate managers, natural rubber is natural rubber, regardless of its source. Yet cultivating and

---

[9]Goodyear had only 40 acres of guayule planted in Arizona, and Firestone has 100 acres in Texas (*New York Times,* November 4, 1980).

growing hevea is not the same as guayule, as one company discovered when it assigned a hevea person to grow guayule. That person made a number of mistakes and underwent considerable learning. For the short term, such negative experiences can only reinforce the corporate managers' reliance on hevea and synthetics.

Firestone is spending about the same modest amount of money as the federal government on the development of planting and on a processing plant for guayule.[10] Goodrich has a number of employees who were active in the World War II ERP and are now promoting guayule. Goodyear wants federal officials to push Congress for funding. But what does this behavior mean for the commercialization of guayule? It does not mean, at present, that the rubber companies, who traditionally do not appreciate governmental intervention, will go it alone without the help of government. The companies are experiencing too much financial distress (for example, Firestone recently cut its dividend); they are worried about their proprietary rights to protect their investment; and there are still questions of costs and some uncertainties about the growing and processing of guayule. All these concerns argue, from the perspective of the rubber companies, that the government should assume most of the risk in getting guayule off the ground. In the words of T. F. Minter, Goodyear Executive Vice-President of Research and Development:

> At the moment, we have a classic case of the egg and the chicken and which comes first [*New York Times* Nov. 4, 1980].

Thus the rubber companies seem to be willing to be a member of the coalition, but not to lead it.

One of the common characteristics of well-established bureaucracies is a tendency to emphasize the routine over the innovative. Thus it is not surprising to find that the USDA, established in 1862, has also been slow with respect to guayule. As one long-time observer of the Department expressed it during our interview:

> It's an organization that doesn't show a great deal of initiative. It's an organization that's living in the past and continuing projects that have been handed down since the Civil War. . . . Their money is nicely put into pockets all the way around, and they are afraid that if they take on something new that some other little station . . . is going to be cut on funds.

No doubt the USDA's reluctance has complex origins. Some members of the department may still remember the World War II Guayule Project and feel that they want to avoid "another black eye." Others may prefer food over fiber production. Whatever the reasons, and despite some minor efforts of economic

---

[10]See Footnote 4, p. 227.

and other research, the Department has put more of its energy into raising questions than into answering them. A case in point was the Department's opposition to the enactment of what became the Native Latex Commercialization Act of 1978. David G. Unger, Acting Deputy Assistant Secretary of Agriculture for Conservation, Research, and Education, testified at a Congressional hearing on the need for more study "before a Federal commitment of resources is made to develop and commercialize native latex rubber" (Vietmeyer, 1978).

The Native Latex Commercialization Act of 1978 created as its main organizational vehicle the Joint Commission on Guayule Research and Commercialization. The Commission is joint in the sense of being chaired and staffed by personnel from both the Departments of Agriculture and Commerce. Its first Chairman and Staff Director were from the USDA. At the Third International Guayule Conference held in Pasadena, California in the Spring of 1980, the Chairman reported on the Commission's progress. The Report was an excellent summary, mainly of the activities of other agencies, but it also indicated that the commission was still at a planning stage and had not launched its own program or obtained the necessary funds from Congress to do so.

A positive interpretation of this progress would give weight to the time and effort it takes to build up a staff, coordinate with relevant agencies, design future projects, and insert funding requests into a lengthy and constrained budgetary process. A somewhat more negative interpretation is that the implementation of a guayule program was not a very high priority for the organizations involved.

Having seen that the USDA and the rubber companies have not been as active participants in promoting guayule as they might have been, let us now briefly look at the scientific and research community that has kept interest alive and worked hard on promoting guayule. The prospects for the commercialization of guayule, at present, are in the hands of scientists and researchers.

Scientists have known about guayule since the 18th century. Our World War II experience with the ERP has provided not only knowledge but, more importantly, some scientists and researchers, who make up an informal network. Some of these are advocates for guayule, while others are skeptical and think that trying to commercialize guayule is a waste of time because the federal government will drop it again. In any event, newly interested scientists join these old-timers; they socialize, exchange views, hold conferences (for example, the three International Guayule Conferences), and develop into organizations such as the Guayule Rubber Society and Los Guayuleros. This network is a central part of the scientific and research element of the present coalition.

Other elements include the National Academy of Sciences, particularly those parts that have an incentive to probe overlooked areas. As Noel D. Vietmeyer (1978) explained in Congressional testimony:

> My program is set up at the National Academy of Sciences for lesser known areas of science, neglected areas of science, that seem important. We have had a lot of success in talking to botanists and finding crops that are not getting recognition.

Guayule came to attention in one of these studies. It seemed to have so much promise that we decided to gather a panel of people from the old program and some devil's advocates . . . and let them work it out. . . .

In addition, there has been the participation of the NSF, which has funded a number of research projects, including the TA by OALS/UA on guayule rubber commercialization (Foster et al., 1980). The NSF also has a representative on the Joint Commission on Guayule Research and Commercialization.

One of the difficulties with the centrality of scientific interests in the supportive coalition for guayule is that it tends to lead to minor funding for research but not to major funding for commercialization. No doubt this research is useful and some refinement in cultivation and processing is necessary to improve latex yield and profit potential, but as the National Academy of Sciences (1977:29) report said:

. . . there are no fundamental barriers to be overcome before production can begin.

Currently, there seems to be a displacement of goals, with more attention given to research and scientific interests than to actual commercialization efforts such as developing markets and designing processing plants.

State support without money. There is support for guayule at the state level, but it is likely not to be too aggressive and, in any event, heavily dependent on federal financing and action. Although there is also guayule activity in Texas and Arizona, what is going on in California provides a good example of this federal dependence. California has already passed legislation (Assembly Bill 3651, Thurman) and established a pilot program to determine whether commercialization of guayule makes sense in California. It did this, however, with federal funds.[11]

There is interest in guayule in a variety of California state offices. The Office of Appropriate Technology, for example, sees small-scale guayule production as a possibility for increasing the economic opportunity of Indians on their reservations. Other offices see their role as mainly providing information and facilitating the development of guayule. The Department of Food and Agriculture, which is in charge of the pilot program, believes that California farmers do not require much encouragement to grow new crops. What they need is information to consider guayule in a context of increasing costs and diminishing supplies of water. Conflict within the state government is likely to be over water, scale of production, and alternative uses of land—familiar enough topics of controversy.

---

[11]A report by the California Department of Food and Agriculture on this effort has now been published (1982). It concluded that guayule has an excellent potential to become established as a commercial crop within the next two decades.

At present (1980) the State Legislature is considering new legislation that would keep the guayule program in California going. But if that legislation involves state funds, it is not likely to pass. For example, a recent Bill (AB 3464) submitted by Assemblyman John Thurman called for $3.5 million; but the money was eliminated in Committee, with the substitution that the director of the California Department of Food and Agriculture was to be encouraged to look for funding. This revised Bill is at present on the consent calendar of the Assembly and will soon be considered by the California Senate. In any event, the Proposition 13 mentality, so pervasive in the state, is likely to exclude any program that makes a visible drain on the general fund and state revenue sources. It is likely that California will be in a good position to take advantage of federal financing initiatives, such as matching arrangements, but will not completely finance its own programs.

Needed: a new coalition. It should be apparent that what is needed is a new coalition at the federal level if the commercialization of guayule is to proceed. It should also be clear that guayule is a fairly low-priority technology when it comes to political support. Like many policies in American politics, it must ride piggyback on some other policy or interest. Guayule did so before, when the passage of the Native Latex Commercialization Act of 1978 required joining forces with eastern tobacco interests in the form of a rider to the legislation.

The most likely source of such support comes from our concerns with national security, as it has come in previous emergencies such as World War II. While instability in the supply of natural rubber might cause the rubber companies to take unilateral action, it is more likely to develop motivation for federal intervention. Thus at the core of a new coalition would be the Department of Defense and the Federal Emergency Management Agency. Interest in having control of a vital resource and in building our stockpile reserves to 500,000 tons should provide sufficient motivation for their participation.[12]

In the new coalition, the Joint Commission with its leaders from the Departments of Commerce and Agriculture will have to be given support and encouragement if this action is to have much effect. Consequently, a top-down strategy, working through the White House, is required. Such White House action should not be expected until there is an improvement in the country's economic situation. Another possible member of the coalition might be the Department of Energy with its policy of encouraging conservation of oil: less reliance on synthetic rubber through the use of guayule is an obvious motivation. In any event, without the leadership of the Department of Defense, the coalition will just not get off the ground. Leaving guayule solely in the hands of researchers, such as the

---

[12]The policy of the present administration (1982) seems rather schizophrenic from a long-range point of view: major increases in the defense budget but lack of interest in attaining independence in energy or strategic materials such as rubber.

National Science Foundation, will only produce more research and not necessarily lead to commercialization. The importance of the role that the scientific community has played in keeping guayule alive, of course, would diminish as commercialization efforts take hold.

Some of the required ingredients for coalition formation are already present. For example, there is excellent communication among many of the possible members of a new coalition, if we can judge by the numerous conferences, informal networks, and dissemination devices such as a newsletter. The main missing ingredients are organizational leadership and resources. Although there are several individual entrepreneurs who have been promoting guayule, their organizational sponsorship has been inadequate to promote coalition formation. Too many of the organizational members of the present coalition have adopted a wait-and-see mentality and behave more as followers than as leaders.

Even if organizational leaders would emerge, they do not have enough resources to ensure the maintenance of the coalition. To be sure, most coalitions are inherently unstable, frequently threatening to break up due to policy and other differences. In the case of the present guayule coalition, policy differences over small versus large production and processing facilities are likely to emerge as guayule commercialization is further defined. The desire of the rubber companies for some measure of vertical integration, for example, is likely to conflict with a policy of those organizations that see guayule as a cash group for Indian reservations. The current tenuous cooperative relationship with Mexico could also be jeopardized by differences over scale of production and method of processing. With such instability likely, it is essential that organizational leaders have sufficient resources to make side payments to keep the coalition together and to sustain the implementation of the program. Such resources obviously include money, but organizational leaders should also have the ability to make adjustments in policy and organizational arrangements, not only in the arena of guayule, but also indirectly through immigration policy, oil and natural gas agreements, etc.

Some consequences. From an organizational perspective, a number of consequences might follow the exploitation of guayule as a source of natural rubber. The imposition of the program on the USDA, for example, might encourage more flexibility and innovation within the Department. When an old-line department gets a new mission, such as the Department did with the use of food stamps, the new mission can act as an agent of change.

The rubber companies will have to adjust to new market conditions. Initially, they may not be able to control their sources of supply as they would like, because there may be too many small producers of guayule to achieve centralized coordination. The rubber companies may attempt, therefore, to stabilize their environment by asserting control at the point of processing. Because of their research and access to capital, they are likely to build large plants and thus discourage a middleman processing industry from emerging, and at the same time encourage the consolidation of farming into either corporate entities or into independent cooperatives.

The dominance of the DOD on the demand side, either for stockpile purposes or for military hardware application, should also have an effect on the characteristics of the market. One conjecture is that such a demand might encourage stability, or more accurately predictability in the market, and thus make the four-year growing cycle more palatable to the producers of guayule.

2. Scale and Trajectory

Business phase of companies. An O perspective sees organizations dynamically in terms of age or phase. In Chapter II we discussed the concept of organizational time (Figure 3). Here we have a variation on that theme.

According to Mensch (1979) and Graham and Senge (1980), industry goes through phases of conservatism and risk taking. There are phases where organizations are fully committed to carry out existing plans or carry on existing patterns of activity (steady state); phases during which they anticipate or experience increases in available resources and search for new commitments and opportunities (expansion); and still other phases during which retrenchment and cutting back occupy their attention (contraction).

During retrenchment phases, the future tends to be discounted most heavily because immediate survival is at stake. Longer term commitments are regarded as discretionary and are deferred in favor of short-term expedients. Organizational strategies focus on accessible payoffs and preservation of a floor under attrition. During full commitment or steady state phases, the future is discounted slightly less heavily on the average than in retrenchment, because a sense of organizational adequacy allows attention to some longer term prospects. (Sometimes, however, discounting of the future is heavier during full commitment because there is no arguing with success, and current modes of behavior, which emphasize day-to-day operations, dominate any suggested departures that might be implied by debatable arguments for future change.) During periods of expansive search and opportunity-seeking, the future is discounted least, and in some cases the discount rate may be negative (for example, the present may be discounted in favor of a future that carries the prospect of a higher price–earnings ratio).

Individuals in organizations are directly affected by these forces in their organizational environments and may, for various reasons, even exaggerate them in their own behavior. During retrenchment and equilibrium phases in organizations, individuals are more constrained in their behaviors and choices by the perceived expectations of the organization than in search phases. Individual characteristics matter more in search phases, as individuals are freer to exercise their discretion and creativity. Another way of putting this is that there is a shift from O toward P and T perspectives as things get organizationally looser, and the other way around as they get tighter.

In short, factors inside and outside an organization contribute to its reluctance to accept a new technology. Consider the tire and rubber companies. They are used to dealing with hevea rubber—both in growing it and in using it in manufacturing tires. Their procedures are geared to hevea and not to guayule. At the same time their environment has historically been fairly stable; there are few perceived reasons to take risks by taking the lead in the commercialization of guayule.

Right now (1980) the tire and rubber companies appear to be in anything but an opportunity-seeking phase. Their executives are consequently exhibiting caution and restraint beyond their usual conservatism. A comment heard at the Third International Guayule Conference was, "Uniroyal is in worse shape than Chrysler." General Tire and Rubber has recently been denied licenses for its television stations as a result of unacceptable business practices of the parent company. Firestone is subject to federal government contract denial because of failure to install an adequate Affirmative Action Program in one of its plants. Demand for U.S. rubber products is currently low and problems in the U.S. auto industry do not presage major improvement soon. The industry as a whole is probably best thought of as in a retrenchment phase. Impetus for innovation is therefore not likely to arise in their quarter; it will have to come from elsewhere. In fact, there is an opportunity here for new organizations to take on guayule.

Issues of scale and trajectory. The TA performed by the OALS/UA (Foster et al., 1980) distinguished between two major scenarios, one based on a business-as-usual approach, the other predicated on a strong governmental spur to development (see Section IX A 6). Acknowledgement was also given to another dichotomy, that between a highly centralized form of development and a more decentralized form. The decentralized approach was dismissed as unpromising, so the dichotomy received little attention.[13] Now, there is no question that, to make a palpable difference to the strategic rubber supply, balance of payments, and reduction of oil demand, the implementation of guayule technology will have to occur on a large scale. Those presently involved in guayule understand this to mean a need for a highly centralized system of guayule cultivation and processing, utilizing large plantations, a few dependable suppliers engaged in mechanized farming, and large processing plants capable of realizing economies of scale.

That is essentially the view of the major tire and rubber companies. It is their views—and natural preferences—that tend to prevail because until and unless the government (or some other major buyer) enters the market, they occupy a powerful oligopsonistic position and are therefore perceived as indispensable to commercialization. Their economic analysis is generally accepted as determining where the point of prospective profitability lies, what the probable price structure

---

[13]This dichotomy is, however, at the heart of much recent controversy about alternative energy supplies, other technologies, and political philosophies.

for natural rubber will be, on what socioeconomic-political futures its estimate(s) will be based, what production efficiencies are therefore demanded, and what processes are therefore feasible or even thinkable. These views have dominated not only the strategies of the companies themselves, but the activities of both researchers and government sponsors of research on guayule, and of other participants. As a consequence, no serious attention is given to devising or evaluating alternatives.

It became evident at the Third International Guayule Conference (1980) that for the rubber companies to become ready to proceed with guayule commercialization, the area under cultivation would have to exceed x acres, a processing plant of more than y lb per day capacity would be required, the yield from harvested shrub would have to exceed $z\%$ dry weight, and the cost of planting (or transplanting) must be less than $s\phi$ per seedling, etc. While x, y, z, and s are subject to some disagreement, this kind of calculation sets goals for research, influences investment decisions, and creates expectations of officials and the public. Given that the rubber companies are the key decision makers, these numbers describe the minimum conditions for the "change of state" to adoption of the new technology. Presentations by their executives set the parameters that control the decisions of most actors.

The tire and rubber companies do represent the most obvious candidates to institutionalize the new technology, which is analogous to, and a direct substitute for, the one they now operate and direct. Yet the history of technology contains many examples of companies and whole industries that missed such opportunities and were successfully invaded. Trucking and air transport overcame the entrenched railroads. The telephone outdistanced the telegraph and has itself now been effectively encroached upon by other industries.

Tire and rubber corporate management in the United States has shown its conservatism through its loss of leadership in radial tire technology to foreign producers.[14] It is precisely this kind of organizational inertia that Allison referred to in his model II (O perspective) discussion. Their approach—and there seems to be little disagreement among them in attitude, only in willingness or ability to invest—is clearly rational, given their perceived opportunity structure. It would be difficult for any of their executives—line or staff—to propose any other approach, especially now during retrenchment. He might shade the numbers a little to reduce or raise the decision threshold, depending on his degree of optimism, but the general line of argument that is acceptable is perfectly clear and resistant to change. For example, the argument that political instability in hevea-source countries could jeopardize supplies is met by a T perspective re-

---

[14]Since the mid-1970s, for example, Japan's Bridgestone Tire Company has vaulted from seventh or eighth position among the world's tire companies to fourth, and by 1985 it could be third. It is planning to take over Firestone's Nashville plant and start production there in 1984. (*Fortune*, March 22, 1982:136–146)

But there are also earlier indications. A T-type factor analysis clearly confirms the low standing of the U.S. rubber products industrial sector in the matter of technological innovation. Using 1960 to 1970 data, Blackman et al. (1973) found that this sector has been consistently lagging aircraft, communications, auto, machinery, and chemical product sectors.

sponse: whatever group comes to power in any such country needs to maintain the stability of an industry that provides income, hence the probability of supply cutoff is very low. This type of argument has enough basis in reality to be acceptable to those with a high stake in believing it. But it makes the extreme assumption that governing powers are generally able to act, and to induce people and organizations to act, in what *we* perceive to be their own best interests. Allison has shown this model I belief to be false even in highly organized and powerful nations (see also Dror, 1980).

The assumptions that appear to be the only reasonable ones to the U.S. guayule community about the need for large-scale centralized approaches may not be as self-evident to everyone. Research is needed on their validity. Such research would concern, among other things, what it would take for various groups to involve themselves in aspects of guayule culture and processing and in arranging for financing, formation of cooperatives, and other system design steps.

Many people and groups who could be involved, depending on the trajectory of implementation, do not presently participate in the dialogue and decision process, except indirectly (by reputation) and occasionally (and not very effectively) by proxy. These include farmers (presumably of diverse views and locations, etc.), certain Indian tribes, farm workers, labor leaders, landowners, rural community and town leaders, and certain social, ecological, and political theorists. At this stage, the chance of their having much effect is too low to motivate much participation. None of these groups for example, attended the Third International Guayule Conference.

Consequently, no strong views about possible *diseconomies* of scale, about effects on these groups, or about how large scale might be achieved by decentralized means have been effectively represented, or perhaps even formulated. There has been little or no research on ways to combine guayule planting with other crops to mutual advantage to small farmers; on the use of guayule to prevent or retard desertification or reclaim unusable land; on ways in which guayule culture might affect the flow of Mexican migrants to the United States; or on how the possible changes in northern Mexico, that might be brought about by U.S.–Mexican cooperation around modest-scale guayule culture, might enhance U.S.–Mexican relations around other issues, such as natural gas. Yet some such notions were presumably behind the wording of the Domestic Latex Commercialization Act that mandated U.S. cooperation with the Mexicans. In other words, the very nature of research being done is overwhelmed by the conventional T perspective.

For organizational/institutional reasons, clients for *this* class of research are invisible, and the decisions that are made cannot benefit from what such research might have produced.[15] The fact that it seems to be of negligible interest to most

---

[15]The newly formed Analisis de Sistemas en Zonas Aridas (ASZA) Project at northeastern Mexico's CIQA could be a partial response to this need.

of the Americans concerned may account, at least in part, for what appears to be a growing disaffection by the Mexican guayule community.

Is there any reason at all to question the established view on guayule commercialization prospects? There is. Recent analyses of two important industries by the International Institute for Applied Systems Analysis (IIASA), Laxenburg, Austria, show that, in at least some industries, as scale increases there may come a point at which the diseconomies of scale overtake the economies. The reasons include the need to assure a continuous supply of raw materials, the inefficiencies attendant on operating at less than full capacity, the overhead costs of managing large installations well, the increased sizes and numbers of parts and consequent increased probabilities of failure or malfunction, the special character of some parts and the special engineering challenge they present, and the inherent risks in increasing scale beyond the limits of past experience. In addition, there are costs associated with vulnerability to attack and sabotage, strikes, local political unrest, and natural disasters. And finally, there is the sociopolitical vulnerability that exists whenever control of a vital industry is lodged in a few hands. Of course, many of these social costs look like benefits to specific organizations (O perspective) and individuals (P perspective). The point here is that the putative *economies* of scale are not unmixed with significant *costs* of scale, and that their relative magnitudes depend on who is doing the estimating.

The issue of mode of implementation. The issue of centralized versus decentralized implementation could provide the key to an important transitional strategy. Groups such as certain Indian tribes and small-to-intermediate farmers are not now active, but they have an interest and could become important forces. How many farmers would rather switch to guayule than leave farming altogether? Which Indian tribes might seek in guayule, properly implemented, an acceptable economic base, consistent with their values, capable of keeping some young people from defecting to the cities or turning to alcohol or suicide? Could milling of moderate amounts of guayule be profitably time shared with milling of other crops, such as cotton or jojoba, at least during an extended transition phase? Might the income from guayule milling permit mill operators to invest later in guayule-specific processing facilities when the plantings assure a dependable supply? What would be the advantage of intercropping? How can starting small be made to lead to eventual achievement of needed scale, without what some think of as "undue" centralization? What consequences are there for Arizona or New Mexico?

Strategically, the groups mentioned could provide a way to start implementing both guayule cultivation and processing activity at the modest scale needed to provide a good transition to larger scale implementation.[16] As long as they are

---

[16]According to the magazine *Rubber World* (Nov. 1982), the U.S. Naval Air Systems Command has now indeed awarded a contract to the Gila River Indian Community at Sacaton, Arizona, to cultivate 5000 acres of guayule. The first harvest will be in 1987; a processing facility may be built there also.

considered superfluous, however, they will be excluded. Recruiting them into the guayule community will be seen as either incidental or essentially inimical to the need of the major companies to control the process, and the present stalemate will have less chance of being overcome. Were they to be brought into the field early, its future course might be somewhat different than if they were to enter it after the major producers had become established. If they understood that delay might permanently disadvantage them, they might take a more active stance. A much more moderate approach by federal officials than is now demanded by the major companies might be able to trigger commercialization.

A strategy involving selected tribal leaders and small farm organization leaders together with small millers, a state official or two, and perhaps farm labor leaders, could make possible a number of modest plantations and one or two small pilot processing plants. One might be located on an Indian reservation located strategically near a state border, another in some other politically appropriate region, perhaps connected with a university. The existence of two processing plants could provide needed assurance to farmers that processing capability for their crops would be available within a reasonable distance, while allowing quite distinct research and development approaches to be applied. An arrangement between a state agency and the federal government to share the cost of such a facility could be the key step. Informal talks among key officials about such a move show that it is quite reasonable in principle.

They would undoubtedly have to convince the major corporations that such a trajectory could help the corporate interests in both the short and long run. Otherwise, they would be exchanging a powerful group of well-organized companies, who could provide strong political support, for a much weaker and controversial political faction. The important feature of the appropriate O strategy is to transform what now appears to be an "either/or" approach into a "both/and" one. (The consonance of such an approach with the interests of Mexico could be a significant factor.) The transformation of what appears to be an irreconcilable choice into a collaborative synthesis is well known as a characteristic of creative leadership.

The multiple perspectives make it evident that many interests might be better served by a commercialization trajectory that passed through a phase of small to moderate-sized, decentralized implementation. For instance, a recent study reported in *NSF Science Indicators* found that small firms generate innovations at a higher rate per dollar invested in research than do large firms—a factor that might encourage exploring alternative trajectories. A paper presented by a Goodyear executive at the Third International Guayule Conference contained some interesting statistics. Seventy-five percent of hevea-producing acreage is worked by small farmers using relatively inefficient methods: they produced 60% of the total rubber, as against the 40% produced by those larger plantations that occupy only 25% of the land. These data lead readily to conclusions supporting the superiority of the large-scale operation, but they could also be interpreted to indicate that smaller farmers do not need to reach the same return as corporate investors. They can keep marginal farm land productive while the market permits them to remain viable as part of a mix of suppliers.

It seems likely then that smaller producers using different efficiencies may coexist with more centralized, predictable growers and processors and provide an important part of the supply. Further, these smaller producers may ease the transition to eventual large-scale production because their economics may require less government pump-priming action. A TA that included adequate O and P perspectives would have to examine carefully the set of prospects associated with this trajectory and to assess attitudes, constraints, predicaments, and aspirations of a very different set of actors than have been considered so far.

The Goodyear representative also argued that natural rubber will lose its market share to synthetic rubber unless guayule "takes advantage of its near-term opportunity." Then there is the importance of the U.S. balance of payments. Yet neither his company nor its competitors will move ahead unassisted by government, whose intervention they ostensibly deplore.

To some, this may sound like the argument of a man who (or an organization which) is trying to induce the federal government to underwrite a high risk, which his company and its opposite numbers are unwilling or unable to underwrite themselves. It ignores the attractive entrepreneurial prospects implied in the same presentation: that guayule grows faster than hevea and uses less labor. Also, the supply of petroleum feedstocks for the manufacture of synthetic rubber is prospectively a source of increasing cost for that product. This apparent contradiction suggests the possibility that significant underestimates of land cost for guayule culture in the United States have been made by the rubber companies, leading to understatement of the true costs of production in the near term, to make the desired federal underwriting of the scenario more attractive.

There are many ways of ducking an entrepreneurial challenge, for example, by arguing that advantages are nonprotectable or that guayule processing costs are higher than hevea, but these may be more rhetorical than real. Much modern entrepreneurial advantage depends more on lead time than on formal protection. Initial processing costs (which are used for analysis) are certainly subject to subsequent reduction, as the history of virtually every technology shows. So it is really the transitional risk taking that is at issue rather than ultimate profitability. But nowhere in the rubber companies' scenarios, or in those of the TA by OALS/UA for that matter, is there any mention of possible provisions for repaying the taxpayers for the risk reduction to which they are being asked to contribute. Nor is there any attempt to rationalize the requirement for government assistance with the ideological position that virtually every corporate representative contacted expressed at one time or another: that government intervention is anathema. From a public policy point of view, it seems important to disclose these curious inconsistencies, which are visible only from the O and P perspectives, and not the T perspective.

C. THE P PERSPECTIVE (M. ADELSON, H. LINSTONE, AND R. MILLER)

The personal perspective operates in all human endeavor. It may even at times be the dominant perspective in the interaction of the technological, organizational, and individual elements. In Figure 9 we illustrated a possible relationship between perspective and role. Identification of the role provides clues to the nature of the balance among perspectives and hence the decision process.

1. The Actors in Guayule

When we attempt to describe the situation in P terms, we must focus on specific individuals and how they might interact—with each other, or with the plant, or with the commercialization process itself.

There is a big difference between 1) those whose fortunes and careers are tied to guayule development and 2) those who must make decisions about whether to proceed with it. The former include some researchers, growers, seed collectors, patent owners, investors, publicists, and entrepreneurs. Their socioeconomic futures can be made or broken depending on what happens to the technology. Their status leads them to emphasize P and T perspectives. They therefore see guayule commercialization as obviously important and promising and as being held back by the indecision of bureaucrats, managers, legislators, and others who, if they would only move, could provide the needed "push." They see the needed push as modest, and its consequences as major and irreversible.

Category 2 consists of people whose roles require them to choose among competing demands for limited resources. Guayule is one of the demands, and, on balance, the wisdom of moving it forward against the competing claims is not yet sufficiently well established. They are using O and P perspectives. The T perspective alone is not convincing, either to them or to those whom they must convince. They are involved in O-level games in which the advocates have no great stake. The natural conservatism that was a factor in their selection for their posts leads them to demand arguments that are convincing beyond the advocates' ability to examine prospective consequences (for example, via a TA), and to operate, even when they are attempting to support the development, through organizational means.

As a result of these contrasting points of view (the advocate versus the judge), the judges see the advocates as self-interested, pushy, impatient, unreasonable, annoying, insensitive to the obvious realities of their roles, improperly attempting to influence what should be dispassionate decision processes, and overoptimistic. They see themselves as being constrained by their need to account for their decisions, dissipate some of the risk, sustain commitment to ongoing programs and people, and serve other responsibilities that are equally important, while trying to acquire the support needed to make appreciable progress possible. Of course, they tend to attribute to themselves judiciousness, perceptiveness, good timing, good will, and other positive attributes that account for their successful careers. By contrast they are seen by the advocates as unduly conservative, indecisive, temporizing, uninterested, devious, insincere in their promises (which otherwise they would keep more promptly and more directly), vacillating when under pressure, protective of their careers rather than dedicated to public service or corporate welfare, and excessively concerned with defending their decisions rather than taking action. The advocates see a tide in the affairs of guayule cresting now; the judges see another ripple on a very large and turbulent sea. Each sees the others' perceptions as distorted.

Because of all the claims made on the attention of each side, each can devote only so much attention to the claims of the other and tends to believe that it can understand the other side without additional effort or information. There is no mechanism readily available for reconciling opposing perspectives, nor is there much incentive for any third party to intervene to do so. Each frames the situation in terms of its own value structure and strategy types and is unsympathetic to those of the others.

2. Interviews

Following are excerpts from several interviews:

AN ENTREPRENEUR

Q: You're an attorney?

A: Yes.

Q: How did you get into guayule?

A: I had a client whose estate I was administering, and it was agricultural. . . . In handling her affairs I ran into some articles about guayule and the promise of guayule, and the need for seed. I got a publication that talked about the plant and its recommendations. It said that seed was very essential to its development, so I went to Mexico and I gathered seed. But I first had to learn about mariola [a similar plant]. . . . I went out to see [a university scientist] and he showed me the different plants. . . . I went first to _____ (in Mexico) almost by chance. In the small hotel I talked to the night clerk and he said his family lives in an *ejido* out here; this place has lots of guayule. So I went out the next day in a truck to an area where he was from and . . . found the guayule. The flower wasn't ready yet. This was in July and I planned to go back in August or September. So I arranged to occupy a little adobe place. . . . I came back a few weeks [later] and I lived there and every day I went out with the people on a wheel-drawn cart up into the mountains. We brought some food and then picked guayule. I had to make certain people didn't pick mariola. I didn't know really how well they knew the difference but they actually knew it well. . . . Now the question was how to clean it, so once again I talked to _____. The people and I just worked on various things, made some screens in Mexico, and we tried pushing it through the screens. . . . Finally, we had, I think, about ten pounds . . . and [the tire and rubber company] bought it.

Q: What did they pay for it?

A: One thousand dollars a pound, I think. Maybe $800 for the rest . . . I was coming out OK at that time. They were amazed but they didn't tell me. . . . The whole industry was amazed how clean the seed was and [how] fertile. I guess they felt that I would raise the price if I knew that. So I went to a dinner at _____ and the . . . people from [company] headquarters were there and one man in particular all evening kept saying to me: "Now tell me . . . , why did you really do it?" They were warned by [a guayule expert] not to buy it and by other people who said I didn't know anything and [they might] invest a lot of money and [get] dandelions maybe. So I just kept saying to the [company]: "All I can say is I was there and watched it and I saw it with my eyes—it has to be guayule." At this dinner everybody kept saying to me: "Your seed was very pure and very fertile and no mariola." So I said, "Well, I have a daughter who is a horticulturist and I have a son who is a geneticist and, I guess, altogether I got interested in plants." Then I said, "I want to know why you plowed all this plantation if you didn't have some seed?" I was mystified—where were they going to get the seed? They were mystified where on earth I could find the seed and know it when I saw it.

Q: You maintained your law practice during all of this?

A: Yes, I just won a case, so I'm going to China. I didn't expect to win it, it just fell out of the sky. They do have some horticulture.

Q: Will you introduce guayule in China?

A: Yes.

Q: Suppose that Arizona and California and Texas went into [guayule] in a big way, what would happen to you?

A: I think I would move on.

Q: So you're kind of a starter-upper.

A: Yes, I don't think there would be any place for me when it gets going. It will be all experts and nothing left for a small entrepreneur.

A STATE ADMINISTRATOR

A: I sense an almost alarming analogy to the automobile manufacturers who really did not take the 1973 oil boycott seriously, it really didn't sink in. I have the same kind of reaction to the tire and rubber industry. . . . There seems to be not the slightest concern about cutoff, about . . . instability.

A: I think you are right there. I've talked to these people in the rubber industry and I get the same feeling. Liberia is one example. I don't think [the upheaval there] is going to bother them. They were not worried about it.

Q: Do you coordinate with Chavez [the farm worker union organizer]?

A: No, it's very difficult [to do]. I think all the issues where Chavez comes into the picture . . . have to do with union busting or pesticide application or something like that. Now cotton sometimes needs eight or ten applications of insecticide to control insects. Here [with guayule] you don't even have a major insect problem. So, to me, he might even want to say, "Look, let's switch from cotton to guayule because it doesn't need that much pesticide."

AN INDUSTRY REPRESENTATIVE (COMMENTS PARAPHRASED)

[The speaker] said the wrong things in front of the wrong people. The Mexicans are not the important people here, the Americans are. To make himself so obviously different [not wear a tie so he would not be mistaken for an American], to separate himself so thoroughly from the decision makers in the crowd, is a tactical error.

A FEDERAL ADMINISTRATOR (COMMENTS PARAPHRASED)

The law that was passed by Congress establishing the Guayule Commission was regarded in four different ways. It was regarded first in terms of economic development, second as strategic supply, third in terms of technological innovation. But it was sold to the President almost entirely in terms of U.S. relations with Mexico; he's looking for a way to stay in touch with [Mexican President] Lopez-Portillo and he thought this would be a useful thing. He needed it at that particular moment in history; if it had happened at a different time it probably would not have been supported in this way and once that moment passed, the future of it is very much in doubt. So it was important for our purposes as a matter of historical confluence of currents, and that needs to be acknowledged. We have had a problem of strategy, how to keep it going now that the critical moment has passed.

3. Involvement of the Analyst

The personal immersion that is often vital to the O and P perspectives can lead to personal involvement. For example, in an interview by two team members with two key movers from different areas (federal and state) it became clear that both interviewees were interested in getting a small-scale processing plant going to stimulate guayule planting in earnest. An interviewer's constructive suggestion apparently triggered a responsive chord, to judge from subsequent comments we heard.

Such involvement can be helpful and may be difficult to avoid in the personal immersion process, but it also can be dangerous. The assessment can inadvertently turn into a partisan advocate document. This dilemma is faced by an investigative reporter: His role may change subtly into that of a prosecutor or apologist. And he may be "used" by his contacts to "plant" ideas. We will return to this subject in Section XIII G.

D. ANALYSIS (M. ADELSON, H. LINSTONE, AND A.J. MELTSNER)

The T and O perspectives tend to focus on different aspects of planning. The T perspective stresses the technological state-of-the-art and its potential, the need and shortfall, and the economics and environmental constraints. The treatment is largely quantitative. Thus the economic and employment effects of guayule development on rural communities are "shown" to be small in the sense that agriculture accounts for only small numbers of jobs in almost all counties concerned, and many of those are transient. Moreover, the agricultural payroll in the aggregate is also small in almost all counties concerned. No analysis is made, however, of what those numbers actually mean to the groups concerned, nor to the shape of the communities' futures. Nor is there any analysis of what happens to the money involved, except that transient workers tend to spend some of it in other counties. No insight is given as to whether this outflow is compensated for by the money they bring with them from transient jobs in other counties, nor whether the money spent in a county stays there or flows to some city to the account of a major business. Money earned by laborers is, of course, only part of the economic picture. Money earned by farmers or agribusinesses is another matter. Money earned by local farmers is to some extent circulated locally, becoming available for local purposes. In contrast, money earned by a company located in Akron tends to be spent there instead and does not contribute to nearly the same extent to the health of the rural community.

Both the scenarios in the OALS/UA study would tend to place plantations and processing plants owned by the rubber companies in dominant positions in guayule culture and production. Small and intermediate sized farmers and processors would be more or less permanently relegated to positions of economic dependency on major corporate interests, and the financial flow would be rapidly urbanward. The pattern of economic colonialism developed in areas of hevea culture could not be transferred directly to rural U.S. settings. Nevertheless, similar consequences might inadvertently ensue unless early anticipatory steps are carefully designed and executed. At this time, there is no evidence that any serious consideration has been given to that dimension of guayule commercialization.

Early attention is needed: once momentum gathers to move along either of the paths described in Section A.6 of this chapter, little can be done to change paths, despite any degree of public arousal, locally or nationally. Consequently, those whose official responsibility is to the public should deal with that issue now. They could alert others, who might have an active role under some alternative trajectories, to the opportunity cost of failing to participate early, and to make arrangements for facilitating their anticipation in the dialogue and in publicly supported activities. In foregoing such action, responsible officials, government, labor, agriculture, and other affected groups will have made a clear, irreversible, and partisan choice of trajectories.

The argument developed above applies in a different, but equally important, way to Indians living on reservations in the Southwest. Their modes of governance, economic activity, cultural transmission, and political action, as well as personal life-style create a different framework for evaluating the opportunities and threats potentially created by guayule commercialization along various lines. Aside from the purely ethical obligation to consider their values and strategy options—to think about what guayule could mean to them under various trajectories of development and to provide them the chance to protect and develop their own interests as they see them—there are certain larger issues of the relation of Indian interests to those of the rest of the American community. A generally accommodative relationship between the native American nations and the rest of U.S. society can lead to the mutually productive development of the coal, uranium, and other natural resources to be found on reservation land and to nonconfrontive development strategies for increasingly sophisticated Indian communities. A generally exploitive relationship could lead to difficult times for everyone. Thus guayule commercialization must be seen in relation to broader social issues. The kind of isolation that may make analysis simple, crisp, and methodologically attractive papers over the major meanings of the process. Similar thinking certainly applies to relations with foreign nations.

The issues associated with hevea culture and the interests of Southeast Asian nations appear to be in good order. At the recent Saltillo Conference on Natural Rubber, the Malaysian National Rubber Industry stated that it welcomes guayule because it will further the cause of natural rubber. International concern for Malaysian interests is embodied in the International Natural Rubber Organization created in 1979. To date, 24 nations have confirmed the market authority of this body, which allows for a buffer stock of up to 550,000 metric tons of natural rubber to stabilize prices (*New York Times*, Feb. 6, 1982). So events have overtaken the TA.

Relations with Mexico, however, are far more problematic. Without delving into them, we observe that the T perspective does not set the guayule commercialization issue in the larger frame of U.S.–Mexican relations: for example, oil, natural gas, and immigration. Yet, guayule cannot be realistically treated in isolation from those matters if the study is to provide information adequate from a policy guidance point of view.

Whether realistic trajectories alternative to those described in the TA by OALS/UA are possible is not easy to say. We do argue, however, that other perspectives evoke important matters usually omitted from the T perspective and suggest different kinds of action.

The O perspective sees the guayule world in terms of interest groups, coalitions, and actions. Meltsner's O perspective (Section IX B 1) states:

> An appropriate place to start would be in the federal arena . . . What is needed is a new coalition at the federal level.

In October 1980, four months after our O perspective was prepared, we learned of the new proposed plan for joint action by four executive agencies: Department

TABLE 25. A Comparison of Insights Derived from the Three Perspectives—Guayule

TECHNICAL PERSPECTIVE

1. Tests have shown guayule to be a satisfactory substitute for hevea in automobile and aircraft tires (the primary use of natural rubber).
2. In view of the 300% price increase of natural rubber since 1972, guayule is becoming competitive.
3. Guayule development can meet 100% of the projected natural rubber shortfall by 1991.
4. Yield per acre is expected to double between 1985 and 2000.
5. Research needs to be done on the use of guayule to retard desertification.
6. The established view on economies of scale is open to question.

ORGANIZATIONAL PERSPECTIVE

7. There is a highly motivated and dedicated nucleus of researchers who, with research grant support, have been keeping guayule alive. There is excellent communication among them (for example, meetings and newsletters).
8. Research is not the key issue; rather, production start-up raises the question of assumption of financial risk between the tire and rubber companies and the government (federal and state).
9. The U.S. Department of Agriculture has not been aggressive. If implementation succeeds it may act as an agent of change within the department.
10. Inbreeding appears to be a problem in tire and rubber industry management with regard to guayule decision making. Organizational inertia may offer an opening to industry outsiders to jump at guayule commercialization opportunities. The point where control is likely to be exercised is at the processing stage.
11. A number of groups and value systems are not represented in the dialog and decision process (for example, farmers, Indian tribes, and farm workers).
12. The Guayule Commission could become the lead group but has not led much to date.
13. Mexico has had a long history of interest in guayule (wild natural growth, research institute in Saltillo, pilot processing plant), but motivations not readily grasped by U.S. interests due to cultural differences, organizational structure differences, and supply/demand differences.
14. National security considerations may act as the decisive catalyst; fear of increased Asian turbulence is spurred by events in Iran and Afghanistan. The Department of Defense and Federal Emergency Management Agency would then become key elements.

PERSONAL PERSPECTIVE

15. Ed Flynn ("Mr. Guayule Rubber News") is a determined promoter who can be expected to keep the pressure on key actors to move ahead.
16. Representative George Brown (D., California) has been a most effective advocate in the Congress and has been joined more recently by Senator Peter Domenici (R., New Mexico). Texas is lacking a strong Congressional supporter. This suggests potential foci of leverage.
17. Each actor tends to perceive his own prospective behavior and that of his associates quite differently than the others perceive it. Each sees the others' perceptions as distorted. Each therefore interprets a given act differently. This situation discourages formation of intersectoral coalitions and encourages intrasectoral coalitions where perceptions are more similar and mutually comprehensible.

(continued)

TABLE 25. A Comparison of Insights Derived from the Three Perspectives—Guayule
(*continued*)

18. None of the present actors with sufficient power to move unilaterally yet sees enough in it
for him to have a feasible action strategy. Personnel changes must be watched for
indications.

19. There is a crucial difference in perceptions of prospects between those whose careers and
fortune are tied to guayule development and those who must make the commercialization
decisions (advocates versus judges).

20. The "top-dead-center" state of guayule commercialization creates an opportunity for
entrepreneurial invasion from some adjacent sector. Someone with a unique perspective,
technical and political sophistication, and a heretofore-excluded constituency (for example,
native American tribes) could precipitate motion along an unexpected trajectory.

of Defense, Federal Emergency Management Agency, Department of Commerce, and Department of Agriculture. The aim was to develop the capacity to
produce 25,000 short tons of rubber annually by the end of 1989, and over a
ten-year period 80,000 short tons for testing and strategic uses at a cost of $1.32
per lb (1980 dollars). The DOD would provide the incentive or justification (need
for strategic reserves), FEMA the funding under the Defense Production Act,
and the USDA and USDC implementation of the program.[17]

This approach is not far from that envisioned in the Meltsner O perspective
earlier (Section IX B1). The ability to project actions using the O perspective
is encouraging.

In developing the organizational perspective, it is essential that the analysis
be grounded in a specific empirical context. A trade-off has to be made between
superficially examining all conceivable organizations and their policies and viewpoints, and probing in depth a particular set of organizations. Obviously, judgment is crucial in the choice of organizations to be included; criteria such as
likely access, perceived relevance, and decision site play a role.

The decision site is particularly useful in TA because there is often no clear
link to specific policy makers or decision makers. It is certainly easier to specify
a particular arena or site in which various typical actors are likely to engage
each other than to deal with individuals one at a time. The notion of decision
site allows the investigator to estimate the critical place for action and then to
assess organizational actors and their likely interactions. In the case of guayule,
it seemed that the federal site as distinct from state and possible international
sites was the most appropriate. It was at the federal site that coalition formation
had already started and would have to be modified.

The emphasis on coalition formation follows from our concern with political
and organizational feasibility in introducing the technology. For other technologies, this emphasis may be inappropriate, and a greater concern for changes in

[17]See Footnote 16, p. 250.

organizational procedures might be the central focus. If guayule commercialization had already proceeded beyond its immediate political problems, then a microprocedure-oriented focus might have been appropriate.

Personal contact was of great value, in fact, absolutely essential, to obtain meaningful insights for the O and P perspectives. The excerpts in Section IX C indicate how the P perspective tends to interact with the O perspective in illuminating the political aspects (Figure 9). The OALS/UA TA team provided exceedingly useful information, particularly the names of key actors. The Third International Guayule Conference was an ideal setting to meet and interview members of the guayule community.

The differences in insights obtained by the three perspectives are suggested in Table 25, and the distinctions are apparent.

ON-SITE
SOLID WASTE
TREATMENT

B. CLARY and D. WAGNER

A vapor of vapors! Thinnest of vapors! All is vapor!
Koheleth (Ecclesiastes 1:1)

A technology that has been subjected to considerable assessment is decentralized solid waste treatment. Modern urbanized societies have become completely accustomed to centralized sewer-transported systems. The inadequacy of many of the associated waste treatment facilities, as well as the lavish use of water in this process, have raised serious questions concerning both water pollution and potential water shortages. Alternatives to such centralized systems are available and appear worthy of serious consideration, particularly for smaller communities that have usually simply copied the larger cities with similar, but scaled down, versions of centralized systems.

Alternatives involve schemes such as:

- biological systems that convert toilet waste to compost,

- incinerating systems that burn toilet waste,

- aerobic systems that include the traditional cesspool and septic tank/field.

These systems do not require expensive sewer construction or solid waste treatment plants; in addition, they can produce nutrients for the soil.

The first technology assessment was undertaken by the MITRE Corporation (Wenk, 1971) for the Office of Science and Technology in the Executive Office of the President. A decade later a Stanford University team, headed by Ronald Howard did a TA under a grant from the National Science Foundation (Howard et al., 1981). The former is a most impressive systems analysis with detailed tables, impact trees, flowcharts, and dynamic models. It was conceived as a test bed or pilot study for the MITRE-developed, seven-step TA methodology. The T perspective clearly dominates the study. Part of the Stanford study became available during the final stage of the preparation of this chapter. A postscript (Section E) discusses that TA briefly, placing it in the context of the multiple perspective concept. Our comparatively modest look, using O and P perspectives, has been done independently of the Stanford project.

We did the three TA case studies—electronic funds transfer (Chapter VIII), guayule (Chapter IX), and the current one—in sequence, and we note a progressive increase in the numbers of interviews. The EFT study involved about ten and the waste management case 35 (all taped). The study was geographically restricted to Oregon in view of the limited resource commitment. In moving from one case to the next we also became increasingly concerned with the presentation format for the O and P perspectives. There is *a priori* no reason to assume that the format should be the same as for the conventional T perspective. The discussion of communication in conjunction with the P perspective (Section IV B 3) as well as the Health Care case study (Section VII D) suggest that indeed the most suitable format may differ with perspective. As an experimental step in this direction, the glimpses of the O and P perspectives are presented here largely in quotation form. The reason: the most obvious alternative means of communication is to use the words of the individuals interviewed directly.

A. BACKGROUND—A T PERSPECTIVE

1. The Situation Today

The problem of solid waste disposal has been with us for millennia—and was one of the first beneficiaries of technology. Thousands of years ago, India and Rome constructed extensive sewer systems, usually discharging directly into the ground and sea (sometimes with disastrous pollution results). At least two-thirds of the U.S. population is serviced by sewer systems, but less than half is provided with adequate waste treatment.

Prior to 1977 most of the federal dollars allocated to waste treatment were spent on the design and construction of centralized systems. The Environmental Protection Agency (EPA) provided 75/25% match money to states for centralized systems. The 25% local match came from user fees and service district assessments, and until recently, this arrangement was an economically viable method of funding waste treatment. Local areas of relatively high or medium density could absorb the cost of centralized sewers as long as the federal money was paying 75% of the actual cost. On-site systems have until recently been viewed as interim methods until centralized sewers have reached a given area. These centralized systems have been dominated by sanitary engineers and public health officials. On a national level, the EPA oversees and regulates local policies for waste treatment.

In recent years, inflation and governmental budgetary constraints have necessitated a change in accepted practices in the area of waste treatment. The Federal Water Pollution Control Act was amended in 1977 to reflect new criteria in basic standards and to provide incentives for local areas to utilize alternative methods of waste treatment. Regular waste management plans in areas of less than ten persons per acre population density were required to include experimental on-site or subsurface programs in addition to plans for centralized management of waste.[1] The EPA was authorized to pay up to 80% of the cost of local/state experimental programs. This set of amendments marked a change in incentives and a shift in attitude concerning the need to sewer. New concerns—and with them new professional involvements—have surfaced in the wake of the federal financial restructuring.

The feasibility of financing sewers has long relied on federal subsidies, which have become increasingly difficult to guarantee under recent economic conditions. The EPA has suggested that an average household should pay no more than 2% of its annual income for wastewater management. However, a 1979 estimate of per household costs for conventional sewage treatment in a small community is much higher.

Centralized sewers, besides becoming less cost effective for smaller com-

---

[1]Where the density is less than 1.7 persons per acre, centralized sewer systems are automatically considered non-cost-effective.

munities, have other costs associated with them. Effluents are dumped into rivers or lakes after treatment. With a second-stage treatment plant, up to 90% of the undesirable effluent is removed. Although a third-stage treatment process removes up to 97% of these effluents, there are still nitrates and phosphates being dumped into rivers or lakes. There is a risk of these effluents polluting a neighboring community's water supply. Enteric viruses easily survive treatment methods and can exist several months in water. There is a possibility of raw sewage leaks due to faulty lines, and sludge disposal can be a problem. In some areas, sludge is delivered to surrounding farms for agricultural purposes; however, it is only suitable for use on nonfood crops, such as grasses. Another cost associated with centralized waste treatment is the use of purified drinking water. The flush toilet uses four to five gallons of clean water to dispose of human wastes, and centralized systems require still more to carry the sewage through miles of sewer lines and to purify it prior to discharge.

2. On-Site Alternatives

Technical factors. The three basic types of on-site systems are biological, incinerating, and aerobic/recirculating.

BIOLOGICAL

Biological systems—the best known is the Clivus Multrum—are characterized by their production of compost and by their independence of external systems in their operation. All such disposal methods are split systems: because of their inability to function where there is excessive moisture (hydraulic loading) they deal separately with household waterwaste and excretory matter. The grey water[2] disposal system to handle the household waste requires a similar soil type as aerobic on-site systems, but needs only about one-third the square footage.

As with any compost pile, biological toilets require continuous maintenance by the user. Moisture and material balances are necessary for the complete composting of waste, generating the uniform heat necessary for the breakdown in materials. Composting time varies with temperature and ranges from six months to two years. Incomplete composting can result in a health hazard.

The development of biological toilets has occurred largely in Sweden, which has areas where bedrock precludes traditional on-site methods (septic tanks). In 1972 there were about 1000 Clivus Multrums in use in Sweden and 300 in Norway.

Because of composting time, the Clivus Multrum is particularly well suited to seasonal homes. The disruptive effects of excessive moisture make use of this system in wet climates a problem: the ventilation stack can act as a conduit for moisture, thus upsetting the compost balance.

---

[2]Grey water is water uncontaminated by human waste but unpotable.

Oregon reported 28 composting toilets in use in 1980. Studies conducted by the Department of Environmental Quality (DEQ) revealed that over half (16) of the users had excess water problems.

INCINERATING UNITS

Incinerating units have had little public acceptance; they are energy intensive, using electricity to reduce the matter to sterile ash. One brand is aptly named "Destroilet." Like biological toilets, the system is split—it must handle grey water separately from toilet wastes.

AEROBIC SYSTEMS

The most common on-site waste treatment system is the aerobic system. Septic tanks, cesspools, and derivations of these systems, such as mound systems and sand filtering systems are examples. Toilet wastes and grey water are combined and a standard flushing toilet is used. Cesspools are basically a holding tank with little treatment of waste. In most areas of the country cesspools are considered ineffective and are being phased out.

Septic tanks, however, are considered to be traditional and effective systems. By 1977 the EPA policy reflected this view (previously septic tanks were regarded as suitable only for temporary use). Reasons for septic tank failure include poor soil, hydraulic and organic overloading, underdesign, high groundwater, lack of maintenance, conversion of seasonal to year-round use of a home, and increased population density (Lombardo, 1979). Most problems can be readily overcome by sound design or a rational public policy toward growth.

Septic tanks, like other aerobic units, use a leach field to "purify" waste. Ground conditions must fulfill certain criteria to function properly. Soil has to be tested to determine its appropriateness as a field. The size of the field must be adequate for the number of residents using it. Waste filters through the soil, leaving a certain level of phosphates and nitrates behind to break down naturally.

Modifications of the traditional septic tank are designed to accommodate limitations of lot size or soil filtering capacity (a function of slope and/or soil type). They are, in effect, miniature sewage treatment plants.

Mound systems, currently being evaluated at the University of Wisconsin, are designed to deal with soil filtering limitations. As the name implies, the system provides an appropriate field environment through construction of an aboveground filtering layer. The mound system, however, does not address slope problems. It requires a fairly uniform, flat surface.

Sand filtering systems are being developed to deal with soil type and size and slope limitations of the site. Testing of the sand-filtered effluent indicates that there is only about 1/50th of the biological oxygen demand level found in septic tanks. These systems rely on an artificial field construction, as do mound systems. Material is pumped from the septic tank to the sand drain field where "trickling" purifies it. Sand fields are lined with either cement or, in some cases, the natural dura-pan is lined with plastic. Studies are currently focusing on sand drain fields to determine optimal sand type and field size. (There is some indication that current fields are oversized, but no firm data are yet available on the minimum size necessary.) It has been estimated that septic permit denial rates (for example, 50% in one state county) could drop dramatically through the use of sand filtering systems.

Economic and other cost factors. The costs associated with the on-site treatments vary, both in terms of actual dollar costs and other cost factors.

BIOLOGICAL

The 1980 costs of the biological units range from $50 (drum privy) to $1415 (Clivus Multrum). This figure does not include the expense of grey water disposal systems. If the units are installed during construction, the total system costs are comparable to septic tank/drain field costs.

Although the dollar cost of biological toilets is comparable to that of septic tanks, other costs differ. Composting action is a relatively slow means of disposing of waste, and the toilets require considerable user maintenance. Recycling of the composted material can pose problems as well.

The benign nature of grey water has also been questioned. Although some maintain its appropriateness for watering ornamental plants, others suggest that it will have undesirable effects on the soil and will ultimately pose a health hazard.

INCINERATING UNITS

The costs of incinerating units currently preclude their widespread use. These units are energy intensive and, in times of energy shortage concern, are not considered a viable alternative.

AEROBIC UNITS

Costs of aerobic units vary by type. The traditional septic tank/drain field system averages between $900 and $2500, depending on soil conditions, terrain, and linear footage. Sand filtering and mound systems are much more expensive and can run between $6000 and $10,000. Much of the additional cost of these systems can be attributed to their newness: lack of economies of scale and current needs for site-specific design. Should these systems become standard, the costs could be cut dramatically.

Other costs associated with aerobic units are largely public costs. Once in place, units demand little maintenance. However, the systems are water based, which means that dwindling supplies of potable water are used for sewage. In areas with water shortages, such usage is now a significant cost. Also, in areas of extended density, the use of septic tanks may contaminate the soil or ground water. High nitrate loadings are a fairly common problem in areas of high density. Polluting effluents appear less of a problem in sand filter systems than in septic tanks. However, the impact of the units is contingent on density, climate, and soil conditions. Where design and soil conditions are appropriate, environmental impact is minimal.

An additional cost of all on-site waste treatment is the cost of issuing permits, inspecting sites, and testing soil. These costs are dependent on the aggressiveness of the local jurisdiction. However, regulatory cost savings are probably more than offset by environmental costs associated with faulty systems.

Table 26 reviews the major contrasting elements of on-site systems and summarizes the state-of-the-art.

On site marketplace. On-site systems are being adopted in some areas with sewer moratoriums or where sewer referendums have been defeated. Other areas adopting technologies, such as biological systems, have been motivated by environmentally aware residents, the failure of septic tanks, development for seasonal use, and acute water shortages. In Oregon, approximately one-third of the housing units are currently served by on-site systems (primarily septic tanks). Legislation setting standards for biological units has not resulted in significant use. The reasons for such inertia are largely economic: years of federal incentives for centralized systems have resulted in the development of powerful vested interests. These include suppliers, engineers, sanitarians, and construction companies—all specializing in sewers. Only with the 1977 Amendments to the Clean

TABLE 26. Solid Waste Treatment

				Aerobic	
	Sewer	Biological	Incinerating	Septic tanks	Sand filter
CONTRASTING CHARACTERISTICS					
Public awareness	high	low	low	high	low
Public acceptability	high	low	low	high	low
Governmental control	high	low	low	low	low
Governmental acceptance	high	low	low	mixed	low
Environmental impact	high	low	high	mixed	mixed
Homeowner cost	mixed	low	high	mixed	high
Federal cost	high	-0-	low	low	low
Local governmental costs	high	low	-0-	low	low
STATE OF DEVELOPMENT					
Level of Knowledge					
Known/operational	x	x	x	x	–
In development	–	–	–	–	x
Marketing					
Existing production market	x	x	x	x	–
Existing consumer market	x	x	–	x	–
Secondary service market	x	–	–	x	–

Water Act did the EPA establish incentives for on-site systems. Since then, many states have initiated experimental on-site programs, but local areas desiring to institutionalize on-site systems have to take on much of the responsibility in researching the options. Despite these liabilities, the escalating costs of centralized sewers and the decreasing federal money available for them may in the future force growing communities to investigate alternatives.

B. GOVERNMENT AGENCIES—AN O PERSPECTIVE

1. Prevailing Philosophy and Its Change

Until recently, federal policy encouraged development of centralized sewer systems and, as a by-product, local dependency on governmental funding:

> Sewers had to have a financial base to be developed. They still do. That's why we need the federal grants to build the things. No one can build one. I've never seen one built as a planning unit, and I don't know if we ever will.
>
> [a county environmental service official]

The amounts involved have been large—far too large for the resources of most communities:

> As a matter of fact, timing-wise, we have been extremely fortunate in terms of federal money, grant money. We have been the recipient of the 75% federal grant funds for all of our major facilities. We have probably been the recipient of some $40,000,000.   [a county sewage manager]

The end of such subsidized financing is slowly resulting in an attitudinal change in organizations interacting with waste-disposal systems:

> The engineering theory said for years that [on-site systems] are interim systems.
>   That was a prevailing philosophy for a number of years. I don't think that's the philosophy today.
>   We're designing systems that we feel will last many years. In other words, we're planning, we're trying to design systems in approved sites where we feel this site will be adequate indefinitely. And that people won't have any problems 20 years down the line and have to come back to us. Because of the limits on urban growth and the expansions of sewer service, I think it would be foolish for us not to look at sites with the idea that they will perennially be on-site sewage disposal.
>
> [a county environmental service official]

Local governments are beginning to recognize they can no longer depend on federal sewer funding, but change is uneven.
    Supporting professions, such as sanitary engineering, have built up traditions and are resistant to change:

Where they completely ignore the fact—that's where the big hangup is in making these changes—you'll never get any change until you educate the people that are teaching these engineering courses. It's not that they're incapable, it's just that they don't emphasize it and they overlook it in a lot of cases. They'll spend a half an hour on it in the entire curriculum. When you do that, you can't expect them to be able to adapt to looking at on-site as a more permanent type of system.

[a state experimental program manager]

Resistance to alternative waste disposal also stems from government organizations in which innovation is seen as risky, indeed, considering the price of failure:

Innovation does not occur within a governmental agency unless someone internal is interested in it or unless some fairly steady external pressure is applied with a certain amount of directness. . . . There are two reasons for that: you have a multitude of priorities and the inability to answer them all, and therefore when somebody suggests something new and wonderful, your tendency is to throw it in the wastepaper basket because you don't need one more thing. The second one is a very peculiar thing that applies only to government as far as I know and that is the tremendous price that anyone in government pays for failure.

An example in the private sector: The Edsel was a tremendous failure of the Ford Motor Company. The guy who headed that program later went on to become the President of Ford Motor Company. Because all Ford asked after the catastrophe was, "Did you know what the hell went wrong?" And the project manager said, "Sure we do, we know that our pre–World War II marketing methods are totally unreliable in today's marketing. We've analyzed where we went wrong . . . and so we completely revamped our marketing techniques. . . ." The Ford Motor Company went on with the Falcon and the Mustang and just one success after the other from a marketing standpoint. And that's all that they asked—do you know what you did wrong? The private sector accepts failure and that's part of the price you pay for progress. You've got to try stuff out and if it doesn't work you've got to cut your losses. . . .

Government can't accept failure. If somebody fails in the public sector, the political people are all over him because they've got to protect their ass; the editorial writers are all over him . . . and it's this inability to accept failure that has made governmental officials very rigid about trying something new. Suppose we put in a dry toilet and one blows up, you turn to your insurance company and say take care of it. In the public sector you'd expect the resignation of whoever was connected with it, or the demotion, or certainly the end of their career.

[a city manager]

Another administrator sees government as the purveyor of change:

INTERVIEWER: Do you think that these new ideas or innovations, new technologies, have been primarily begun or thought of or implemented by private entrepreneur types, or do you think that the government is doing it?

SEWAGE AGENCY ADMINISTRATOR: I think it's a result of government programs, where you are required to evaluate alternatives prior to being awarded a grant for any project.

The ambiguity arising from such varied perceptions of the governmental role is reflected in perplexity, frustration, and uncertain local response:

Listen. I think federal distribution and pots [of funds] like that, this weird hybrid of Byzantium and Hee-Haw.[3] You know, you can't figure out how it works. Don't you get that feeling? You don't know what's going on but you do know it's something. It isn't just strictly technical and follow things to the letter.
[a county budget analyst]

In addition to this internally generated "weird hybrid of Byzantium and Hee-Haw," federal policy is not equally applicable to all regions of the United States—a source of considerable discomfort to implementing agencies:

It seemed that they saw the whole country as having to develop certain programs and not taking into account the differences in regions within the country. An example, I was in a meeting in Baltimore and they were talking about putting insulation in the walls. And the requirements for wall insulation—the representative was there from Hawaii. He was really in a quandary because they'd have to reconstruct their houses to put insulation in because they only have single walls. There's no place to put the insulation.   [a utility executive]

The incongruities generated by imposing uniform standards on markedly dissimilar regions are further aggravated by the separation between the EPA, which sets guidelines for water quality, and the DEQ, which is responsible for maintaining them.

2. The Politics of Waste Treatment

In Oregon, as in many other states, the Health Department until recently was responsible for subsurface activity.

The vulnerability of local enforcement officers to political pressure led to a transfer and a strengthening of authority and a redefinition of goals:

California was mad at us because we were selling properties that you couldn't even live on. The Health Division finally adopted a rule that said that you can't sell property unless somebody looks at it. Then the sanitarians who were in charge of the thing at that time started looking at some of these pieces of property and saying they weren't any good. That just made the developers and the county officials mad. They just fired the sanitarians and hired one that would say yes. It was that simple. That was going on in _____ County. That was going on at the coast.

---

[3] A hillbilly humor television program.

The State Health Department did not have the budget to do it themselves, did not have the budget to maintain surveillance of what was going on, so they just *carte blanche* delegated it to the counties. The counties—it was run out of their health departments—the state laws were very weak and vague, and all, or for the most part, the counties were subject to their local politics and pressures.

[a state health department official]

This department fell heir to management of the subsewage program in the State of Oregon in 1974. And one of the things that the legislature admonished us to do when they gave us this responsibility—transferred it from elsewhere in the state—and gave a much stronger role in this state program, one of the things they admonished us to do was to develop alternative systems; in this case, they contemplated alternatives to the standard septic tank and drain field.

[a DEQ administrator]

They got a new program, and they've poked it into the existing structure. The existing structure wasn't established to cope with the kind of problems that this thing has.   [a county administrator with close ties to the DEQ]

The transfer of authority to the DEQ did not result in an immediate improvement in the situation for a variety of reasons. Functional change within a bureaucratic organization is never simple. There were staff problems and policy problems, in some ways parallel to those arising at the federal level:

Their staff weren't adequately trained to do the field work which compounded their problem. The regional offices just refused to be serious about the thing. . . . They have the policy setting agents in Portland, but the people who actually execute the policies work for someone else. The guys who set policy, who actually write and modify the administrative rules, have no direct line of control over the execution of these things at the regional level.   [a county administrator]

The magnitude of political pressures associated with determination of subsurface limitations was felt keenly by the DEQ:

Regularly, as we've gone back to the legislature, there's been concern about just the pure agony that's involved in turning people down for a septic tank and drain field. It's hard as an agency to do it, it's harder yet, perhaps, as a legislator to have a constituent turned down, and so there's always been continuing pressure for finding some things that will work on the sites that won't work for septic.

[a DEQ administrator]

But the DEQ operates under multiple constraints: legislative, federal, regulatory, and statutory:

Our commission adopts all the rules on subsurface; counties may and do regularly come in and recommend changes to us, regional rules where they've got a certain stance in their own area that they believe warrants the commission adopting a particular rule that reflects that kind of soil, that kind of weather, whatever. Our rules require that they either have a substantial level of approval from the National Sanitation Foundation or that there be testing that parallels that, that we can look at and conclude that they're appropriate. Our rules require that those systems be subject to some kind of public jurisdiction for supervision.[a DEQ administrator]

The DEQ in turn imposes constraints on local jurisdictions:

> INTERVIEWER: Are most of your rules just the EPA standards, or do you establish your own?
>
> COUNTY SOIL SCIENTIST: No, our rules for site evaluations for construction are right out of the book . . . right out of the DEQ rules. I don't think we were ever more restrictive than the DEQ. We rarely ever give a guy a break unless it can be rationalized using the rules. We try to stay as close as we can to the intent of the regulations, to do otherwise gets you in a lot of problems, gets you in some compromising situation down the road.

The mutuality of constraints is not universally acknowledged:

> Generally, I think that DEQ is doing a reasonable job. I guess the one problem I have with DEQ is what I consider lack of communication with those organizations that they directly impact. [a county official]

The relationship between land-use potential and subsurface activity exacerbates the difficulties for DEQ:

> We're pragmatic, we're engineers. We have a sign in the other room that says, "God made the soil and the State made the law." And we used to stand here like Pilate, washing our hands every day, saying it's not my fault you've got the water table at 14 inches in a clay pan. If I had made it, you'd have four feet of sand. All we do is look at the numbered standard that the State tells us, and we tell you whether it's good or bad. We're the best in the State. We've got soil scientists and geologists. We know what we're talking about. And so we have really a lot of pressure that way. Anyhow the State took that position that they're running a numbered standard for the protection of health and safety. And all of a sudden, after the fact, _____ is very interested in getting that land-use stigma off his agency. That's what's brought the political pressure. We were looked at as *de facto* land-use planners. And antidevelopment because of these restrictive rules.
>
> [a county soil scientist]

These kinds of concerns resulted in a "softening" of DEQ regulations—a response to public concern, which further complicated the duties of implementing agencies:

> They'd like to be able to say, "If you want to be able to build here, it is not us that's stopping you." They want to get the rock out of their pocket. Before, we had a concise, fairly simple set of rules. And they just cut off and said water closer

than 24 inches to the surface at any time during the year, that's it. You just don't build . . . we've had people faint at the counter. I'm not kidding you. The hard ones were the people, little old ladies whose husband had just died, and they bought this thing when they were young, and it was their investment, and now she needed the money because her husband was dead. And I'm going to have to stand there and talk to people like that. The developers, because they were in the business, thought it was too bad.   [a county official]

The DEQ's sensitivity to public opinion possibly reflects the political nature of the director, a gubernatorial appointee:

> RESPONDENT: There was a lot of legislative suspicion, I suppose one would say, of an agency like ours expressing concern, a level of conservatism. The legislature has continued, I think it would be fair to say, to characterize us as having been less vigorous in trying to find alternatives than we should be, although. . . .
>
> INTERVIEWER: So you think you have the reputation as being too conservative?
>
> RESPONDENT: Yeah, I think if I were going to characterize what that view would be out there, it would be that we are more cautious than we should be and that there really is no great reason to be concerned about ground water as we are, for instance. Of course, we disagree with that.
>   We are always mindful, I think, that there is probably a built-in conservatism and I'm particularly sensitive to it, I suppose. Before I went to work with the state I worked in construction for 20 years. I ran a construction company.

The sensitive position of the DEQ is manifested by its enforcement policies, for example, its reluctance to enforce standards. _____ County is inhabited by more than 100,000 people and is not served by sewers. Excessive nitrate readings have been recorded in the groundwater. The area is acknowledged to be a problem.

> INTERVIEWER: So it could be an extremely dangerous situation if it goes on.
>
> DEQ ADMINISTRATOR: I think the most significant thing about it is that [groundwater] could be a future water supply for the City. And I'm not sure what the figure is now, but it can produce something like 100 million gallons of fresh water a day on a sustained basis. That's a major water source. And if something should happen to the water supply at _____, say if Mt. _____ should act up and we had something there, then that would be the first logical place _____ would go for its water supply. And the millions of gallons of sewage that's going into that ground out there certainly poses a hazard to that water source.

Because of this concern, a few rules pertaining specifically to _____County (a moratorium on the use of cesspools and more stringent requirements on the use of septic tanks) were introduced in a rule revision proposal by the DEQ. County officials responded quickly and negatively to rules whose enforcement would generate sure and organized opposition. Following the county's vigorous response, a DEQ administrator explained the state's intent:

> INTERVIEWER: Now I've heard that recently you've issued a new set of regulations. . . . I haven't read them myself yet. . . .
> But what I've heard is that you've put a moratorium on cesspools after 1981, is that what's in there?
>
> DEQ ADMINISTRATOR: OK, that was just a proposal . . . we looked at proposing a moratorium on cesspools after January of 1981. We *did that primarily to get the attention of* _____*County* where most of these installations are occurring.

This interpretation was skeptically received:

> Well, I don't know. He's saying that now. I don't know if he was saying that three months ago. [a county official]

The fact is that the moratorium regulation is currently (1980) being negotiated in terms of goals for having sewers in _____County. Should such goals not be met, what then?

> I think there are a number of things that the Environmental Quality Commission can do and one would be to put a moratorium on new construction in the area. . . . Just close it off. That would be, I think, the most dramatic step that they could take. And beyond that, I'm really not sure. [a DEQ official]

3. Mutual Mistrust

Public opinion of DEQ is not always favorable:

> We formed the government to solve some of our problems, we should never be whipped by our government. That's like being whipped by your newspaper boy. [a citizen activist]

A certain mistrust of citizens is also expressed by government:

> I understand why the DEQ tends to be suspicious of that kind of operation . . . they have no control over the maintenance. There is within the standard technology something called a package treatment plant. Typically used by resorts, or maybe an isolated subdivision or something, that's kind of a miniature waste treatment plant. The DEQ has a lot of experience with people basically just not maintaining them. If you keep them up they can, in fact, work fine. But their experience is that people don't do that. And they tend to be prejudiced, I don't know if prejudiced is the right word, but from that experience they're skeptical. [a county official]

4. Future Options

Centralized systems are easily controlled by governmental units. The counter argument is the greater cost effectiveness of on-site systems. Most interviewees felt there would be a continued need for government regulation.

> I think there will be areas where it will be necessary to have community sewer systems as we know them. Also there are going to be areas within the same general vicinity where you have the alternative systems that can be maintained by the same governmental unit.   [a sewage agency director]

Within that framework, education of affected professions is necessary.

> I think any time you try and change the direction of something that's going on and you become a threat to somebody's livelihood, they are going to resist it. You see that in this case. There are engineers who for 30 or 40 years have done nothing but design sewer pipe and sewage treatment plants. And you go to them and you say that this is all wrong, we're going to do it this way. They're going to at least be very skeptical because they've been doing this one thing for so long. They perceive it as a threat to everything that they know.   [a landscape artist]

Active dissemination of information to those impacted would also facilitate change:

> There are other ways to do it. The thought occurs to me that what you have to do is get to the building people and inspectors and the people who are doing the day-to-day work in this area. If a builder comes to them and says you don't have any sewer out there, you tell me I can install a septic tank, so what am I going to do? If the inspector of the City or the County says another alternative is composting toilets, take a look at that, that's one way you can handle that situation.
> [a utility energy specialist]

Coalitions that would actively further alternative waste disposal systems and evade blocking actions would expedite implementation:

> Presuming [the Clivus Multrum] has been tested in place by people whose impartiality is trusted, the results have been positive and this looked like an alternative, I would start looking for allies in the places that can make the change. That means . . . allies in the Legislature. . . . I would [also] start looking for the local people that can help with that change. . . . Most people spend a lot of time thinking who their natural allies are. The ones they already know about and think of instantly, those are of no help at all. Those are automatics. What you need is to spend a lot of time thinking about people who might be your allies if you convince them.
> [a city manager]

It is equally important to know who the opponents are likely to be:

Speaking of religious organizations, how are things with the Jesuits? The LCDC,[4] whether it admits it or not, would like to put everyone in the state where they want them in the state. And they're using a variety of real and contrived issues to cause this to come about. The LCDC would really like to see nobody outside of the urban boundary except farmers. . . . Obviously one of the ways you keep people out is you don't let them crap. And so LCDC, I think, would be one of the forces in array against the Clivus Multrum. . . . It would be interesting to see the play-off between LCDC and DEQ on this. . . . Both DEQ and LCDC, unlike most state agencies, are theoretically run by a board or commission. Ordinarily I would tell you just the top guy alone runs it, but in this case I think that both of those top guys have to deal with their boards. And the boards, because of the tremendous importance of LCDC and DEQ, the political appointments to those boards are very carefully considered by governors. Those boards are stronger. . . . they make the regulations, which the director carries out.   [a city manager]

Here we get a glimpse of the thinking of the politically astute administrator.

Despite a growing consensus that economics will inevitably force alternatives to centralized sewage treatment in many areas, the path to such a realization will continue to be obscured by institutional ambiguities, clashes, and underlying conflicts of interest:

The real problem with being everybody's friend is that you don't have anything. So if you're going to be the friend of the majority, you've got the people who live in the city who want the state to be decent and clean, then you've got to maintain some kind of control over the land. That's exactly what they did with that on-site sewage disposal rule. The people in the city mandated that those rules be adopted and enforced. And those rules were enforced by people who live in the country. And the country did not like that at all. They've had real trouble with places like that. What's Lakeview want a comprehensive plan for? Tell the seagulls to fly to the dump? You know that things get a little obscure out there. What's very obvious in _____ doesn't make sense in _____. And we had the same problem here in this county. So what they're trying to do now, I think, is come up with some kind of rule that will meet the intent. And that's public health. Protect the public health and safety of the citizens by whatever cost—and nobody ever said it had to be cost effective—there'll be an alternative if you want to develop it.

[respondent]

Interestingly enough, the interviews never raised the long-term possibility of "reruralization" in this country; it was apparently beyond their planning horizon. Such a trend could have a major impact on, or be impacted by, the evolution of on-site solid waste treatment. Table 27 summarizes the issues and options developed by this perspective through interviews.

---

[4]Land Conservation and Development Commission.

TABLE 27. On-Site Waste Treatment

Subject	Interested parties	Policy issue
Land use Development of new housing tracts; rural dispersed housing development	Developers, farmers, municipal governments	Land use policy
Maintenance	Homeowners, state and county health departments	State inspection Stringent rules on types permitted (for example, septic tanks but Clivus Multrum in higher density)
Water use Water shortage potential	Local population and business	Priority setting
Temporary versus permanent use	Sanitary engineers, sewer system suppliers, federal government (funding of sewer systems) municipal governments, state health departments	Reduction of federal funding of sewers, state laws requiring central sewers when density exceeds certain levels

C. FOUR INTEREST GROUPS—O AND P PERSPECTIVES

We now focus on the attitudes and beliefs of four types of people: environmentalists, technologists, home builders, and homeowners.

In the main, the interviewees echo the views common to their interest groups and give us O perspectives. To the extent that they present unique personal arguments, they offer P perspectives. It is not a trivial problem to identify and separate the O and P perspectives without in-depth probing. Here the O perspectives appear to dominate the responses.

The support of environmentalists for on-site solid waste systems stems from their commitment to the concept of "appropriate technology" (AT). Several of the systems fall into this category, and the perceptions of AT advocates are presented.

Second, the perspective exemplified by sanitary engineers and plumbers will be discussed. Values and traditions among these groups have produced a perception of problem solving that can best be described as the "technical fix." They opt for wastewater solutions that follow the capital intensive, high technology, centralized mode. On-site systems represent a different philosophy of waste disposal, so that these attitudes represent a significant roadblock to the implementation of on-site technologies.

If on-site systems are going to be implemented on a wide scale, it will be necessary to convince the homebuilding industry of their cost savings and reliability. Even given the skyrocketing cost of sewage collection and treatment facilities, developers will be unlikely to adopt alternative wastewater technologies if they view them as a risk.

Finally, like the developers, the homeowner is concerned about economics: he or she wants to pay as little as possible for waste disposal. Further, convenience must be considered; this is especially relevant to the biological toilet alternative. Both factors militate against the adoption of alternative systems, although there are scenarios where homeowners may move toward acceptance of on-site technologies.

1. Environmentalists

The support among many environmentalists for alternative on-site sewage facilities stems not only from an analysis of the wastewater problem, but a commitment to a broader concept of technology. The notion, popularized in the 1970s by E.F. Schumacher's book *Small is Beautiful,* is based on a perception of technology that is decentralized, labor intensive, low in capitalization, and achievable with natural or recycled materials.

Underlying the concept of appropriate technology is a strong ideological commitment to an alternative life style. Self-sufficiency is a major theme, along with an idea of how technology should serve society. As one environmentalist said, "Appropriate technology reminds us that before we choose our tools and techniques, we must choose our dreams and values."

Many persons consider AT advocates to be no more than ideologues or persons who are on the fringe of society. Several descriptions of the AT movement provide a good illustration of this perception:

> So from what I see, people who are interested in implementing AT are mostly those people who are in rural areas and want to create their own community, and don't feel that they can make AT work in a large city. They look at it as a full-scale integrated program where they can be entirely self-sufficient, or as self-sufficient as possible. That seems to demand a rural setting. They can have enough acreage to grow their own food and perhaps a little timber on the side.
>
> I personally do not have very frequent contact with AT people other than going to a couple of conferences. But I have detected a fair amount of hostility from those people to the idea that there might be some validity in the centralized sewage concept. Not all the AT people I have run into have expressed that, but there is a certain element that is definitely hostile to the centralized concept.
>
> There's a feeling that environmentalists don't examine too closely, don't care to test scientifically whether or not these things really work. They are so enamoured with the idea of the individual system. . . . If you want a prime example, look at the horrendous problem DEQ is now facing with the wood stove . . . [it] has become almost a religion. . . . It's been a shuddering fact that the majority of wood stoves are horribly inefficient and are tremendous polluters.

However, within the AT community, changes are occurring that may have significant consequences for the development and marketing of alternative on-site wastewater systems. There is a movement away from ideology and toward implementation. Many AT advocates realize that society is not going to switch to a new form of technological development overnight and that ATs are bounded by the same constraints as any technology. To a large extent, this perception has resulted from the attempts to either implement or market appropriate technologies. The consequence has been a shift within the AT movement from an ideological to an entrepreneurial stage. As described by a consultant in the recycling field:

> One of the major problems with innovation, using my example of source separation, is that some people who have attained some position and became source separation advocates in the 1970s, behaved in an irresponsible and provocative position. They overstated the issue, used bad data, developed facilities that failed, and this sort of thing. I think we're starting to see appropriate technologists who can balance a budget, who can do engineering, and write grants.

Solar energy and recycling are examples of AT that have reached this stage of development. However, among environmentalists involved in the AT process, alternative wastewater facilities are seen as being at a very different stage of development. Few of the persons we interviewed saw wastewater as a high priority, although they felt changes in the magnitude of the problem could result in a change in its priority. They expressed considerable dissatisfaction with existing wastewater systems, but also realized the technical limitations inherent in alternative facilities and the problem of getting society to change overnight. What emerges from the interviews is a perspective on change that is oriented toward the long term and further development of the technology. Alternative wastewater systems, as examples of ATs, receive support in the environmental community, but there exists a rather sophisticated perception about the limits of their political and social feasibility, at least in the short run. Consequently, in the near future, alternative wastewater systems are unlikely to receive the same push from AT advocates that solar energy has in recent years. More likely will be the following attitude:

> What is appropriate is going to change by situation, is going to change over time, is going to become more knowledgeable, more creative. You know, using something that I might consider really appropriate might be more so tomorrow. It's tempting to talk in terms of absolutes, to say that composting toilets are always more appropriate than outhouses or central sewage systems. There are some things I'd be tempted to say are never appropriate. For instance, I would be tempted to say that the household garbage disposal is never appropriate, that this method is the worst way to dispose of your garbage, but there may be somebody who has an incredibly good reason for using a garbage disposal, and it might be really an appropriate use.

Finally, the entrepreneurial push within the AT community has fostered an awareness of technical feasibility and the demands of the marketplace. This is evident for both appropriate technologies in general and, more specifically, alternative on-site waste technologies:

> Most people who are working with appropriate technologies are trying to focus on developing systems that require as little maintenance as possible, recognizing that people generally have only so much time and energy that they are willing to put into it.

Although further technical developments may only have limited impact on the adoption of on-site waste systems, given the priority accorded to this technology by AT people, a crisis or some other precipitating event may mobilize AT types into an active push for it. If so, we may see a transfer of many entrepreneurial and technical skills developed by these people while working in other areas of appropriate technology.

2. Technologists

To technologists, problems are perceived in terms of solutions, and solutions in terms of techniques and the individual's experience with them. Garrett Hardin, in a seminal article, "The Tragedy of the Commons" (1968), defines this orientation to problem solving as the "technical fix." It is grounded in a faith that problems can be solved and that science will provide the key. The notion that the problem may be us, or that we will have to change our values, is not part of this view.

Technologists are central actors in the wastewater disposal arena. Engineers design the collection and treatment process and play a role in setting the standards for the industry. Plumbers represent another set of actors. Their role is generally perceived to be simply technical—placing the fixtures and pipe or repairing a home waste system. But their activity goes beyond this. As plumbing inspectors, they have the power to permit or prohibit an individual home's water system and they have substantial influence on the Oregon State Department of Commerce—one of the permitting bodies for alternative wastewater facilities.

A key to acceptance of on-site waste facilities is the attitude of sanitary engineers and plumbers. The extent to which the systems are judged feasible will depend heavily on their opinion. To a significant degree, our interviews indicate a perception among these persons that fits the model of the "technical fix." Wedded to high technology, they tend to favor centralized over other types of solutions and view change with considerable skepticism. As one sanitary engineer described his profession and its response to alternatives:

> The real problem is a tunnel vision that the engineering industry has and agencies typically have on sewers. Traditionally, people have said that they have got to have a sewer as an end product. . . .

The same theme was evident in an assessment of the profession by an architect, who has worked with sanitary engineers. He felt they would be among the last to accept change, if for no other reason than their livelihood is dependent on the status quo.

By viewing problems largely in technical terms, engineers and plumbers quite readily dismiss advocates of alternative systems as largely uninformed idealists. There seems to be the implicit assumption that if these people "knew the truth" they would act otherwise. A plumbing inspector argued:

> Frankly, I think there are many people who are dreamers; they look at things in an abstract manner and don't really look at the pros and cons of something. They just say this is a good idea: We aren't going to use water, we aren't going to pollute the atmosphere, we're not going to do this or that. And they go for the compost toilet.

Another plumber looked negatively on the compost toilet alternative because it didn't fit his perception of what should constitute a toilet and how it should be used. The criticism has merit on technical grounds, but doesn't indicate an awareness that people could be educated to use a toilet in the same way that children have been taught to brush their teeth:

> I argued very strongly at the time they came out with these things; frankly I don't like them. I've been a plumber for some 40-odd years and you get used to a fixture that washes or cleans itself. Generally, with a regular toilet, you've got a flusher on them. It's china, a very clean material, and you've got the flush rim. You've got a full flow of water just below the top of the bowl and it keeps everything pretty well washed out. On a compost toilet, you don't have that, and in the normal course of events, when you sit down on the toilet stool, particularly men, I don't know about women, and especially boys, and urinate, you're going to urinate forward. Well, there's nothing there to wash that away. Urine scum does build up very readily, as you've probably seen in some urinals where they don't maintain the restrooms. Also, if a person has diarrhea or something, which happens fairly regularly, you kind of squirt all over the place and there is nothing there to wash it down other than the person who owns the unit. And whether they will get in there and thoroughly clean those things a couple of times a day, we have no way of knowing.

Over the long term, an important precondition for acceptance of alternative on-site waste facilities will be changes in the attitudes of engineers and plumbers toward what constitutes appropriate wastewater technology. They reject alternative systems on grounds that closely fit Hardin's description of the "technical fix." Further, in response to a question about sand filters, a sanitary engineer stated, "I don't know if the sand filter has been built." This is surprising, because the Oregon Department of Environmental Quality has been involved in a testing program for several years, and the sand filter has been one of the major technologies under investigation.

However, changes are evident in the profession. A consultant in resource recovery, who has one of the few firms specializing in this area, indicated that he receives about one resume a day from graduate engineers who want to enter the field. He said this represents a marked change from the early and mid –1970s when there was little interest in appropriate technologies by engineering professionals. He felt this development was even more significant because most universities had yet to offer a course in AT engineering.[5] Changing attitudes can also be seen in government. As most of the recent funding for centralized systems has come from this source, a shift in governmental attitudes may produce a change in attitude among engineers and professionals in related fields. A statement by an official with the Oregon State Department of Environmental Quality provides an illustration of the tension that is developing within the profession and how on-site technologies may be making inroads:

> On-site. I think that it is superior myself. Engineering theory has said for years that these things are not there to last for more than about 10 to 15 years. That's crazy technological thinking. If you look at nature, and leaf decomposition on the forest floor, there's an equilibrium that takes place. You'd have a mass of leaves taller than this building, or wooden debris and vegetative matter if that didn't take place in nature. Septic systems are designed to be a natural biological environment in somewhat the same sense. If you undersize them or you make some mistake in your technology when you apply it, you're obviously going to have problems. I guess what I am saying is that it is not that tough to counter these problems and expect something to last at least the life of the structure if it is properly installed. There's a few little maintenance precautions, of course, that a guy has to consider, but in the long run it will be one heck of a lot less expensive than sewers. It wouldn't tie up all the resources necessary to operate sewers, plant them in the first place, and this sort of thing.

3. Home Builders

Although home builders are not in the forefront as actors in the sewage disposal arena, they nonetheless play a significant role. It is developers who make decisions about what goes into a home, including the plumbing fixtures. Given the huge capitalization required for sewage projects today, home builders in the urban fringe, rural areas, and small communities are facing major economic problems. As one person we interviewed expressed it, developers work on the margin and any major increase in the cost of a project can stop it. Consequently, if developers can be persuaded that there are cost savings with alternative sewage disposal systems or that they can build in places where they were not previously able to, then these systems will probably be implemented.

A home builder will not be persuaded to adopt on-site technologies on the

---

[5]Universities characteristically tend to lag. In the 1960s universities started space engineering programs so late that the industry demand was already met by the time the first graduates appeared.

basis of any social good it might produce. Developers are prime examples of "economic man," acting in a way to maximize self-interest. Interviews with developers and other persons associated with the industry clearly indicate the importance of the economic issue to developers. For instance:

> Developers will do anything that will save them a buck.
>
> One of the ways alternative systems could be attractive, particularly to groups like the Homebuilders Association and Metropolitan Homebuilders, is if they can decrease the cost of housing. If you don't have to hook up to a sewer, if the developer doesn't have to build a mile of sewer line to get his development hooked up to the major trunk, and if the Clivus Multrum is a less costly alternative, it could promote less costly housing.

Home builders, while profit-oriented, are not risk takers. They must be shown that an on-site system will work. As an urban planner expressed it:

> There's an article on innovative building here and there in the *National Home-builders Journal* on occasion, but not usually. The ordinary developer is someone who uses off-the-shelf technology. By technology, I mean house and home plans. That's where he gets his technology. The average developer is not innovative. He's a guy trying to put his house up as quickly as he can for as low a cost as possible.

In a similar vein, a city manager describes homebuilders in these terms:

> Developers are really hard to sell, that's why I keep going back to this success thing. Developers have been screwed over very badly by untested whims and fancies. The vapor barrier is a tremendous example of this. Lots of people who should have known better got sold on the vapor barrier as an absolute cure-all, as an energy saver, in spite of the fact that the vapor barrier had not been properly tested under Oregon conditions.

To sell on-site technology to developers, an effort similar to the push for wood stoves would seem to be necessary. Home builders are not going to use products unless they produce cost savings and have been proven technically effective. This statement by a public utility executive illustrates the problems faced by on-site advocates in selling their product on the market, especially to developers and others involved in the home-building business:

> I'll tell you of an example that may be related to the waste disposal area. This is wood stoves. When this product first came out, there were a lot of flaky designs. These guys claimed enormous benefits, when, in fact, they were really terrible products. Now they have associations, they police themselves and there are some really good products out. But that doesn't exist now for the compost toilet thing. I think you've just mostly got a very few suppliers of that sort of technology. Most

of them are totally unknown to most people. Until you start seeing these technologies in Fred Meyer,[6] they're not going to make it on the market.

4. Homeowners

In the final analysis, the success or failure of on-site wastewater systems will depend on the marketplace, that is, whether consumers will accept it or not. The problem will be much less with those alternative systems that use standard plumbing fixtures and disposal units, like the septic tank or sand filter, which are sited outside the dwelling. For biological units, like Clivus Multrum and Toa-Throne, that are located inside the home, consumer acceptance is a crucial factor in their implementation.

When queried about composting toilets, our interviewees were nearly unanimous. All said that given the contemporary perception of household sanitation, there are severe limitations to the feasibility of compost toilets. For example:

> You've got to really babysit the toilets. You've got to be able to tolerate flies. They're indigenous. You've got problems if you haven't got spiders and flies in the toilet. Some people don't like that. But if they're there, that means that your composting environment is pretty healthy. You've got odors in a lot of them.

A city manager told us:

> The sand filter is a big hole in the ground filled with a mixed medium. And that can be stuck back in the corner of the lot, but I can see some real eyebrows raised. . . . I can see the neighbors coming unglued. Neighbors have trouble enough with things like refuse heaps and the like.

Another factor is convenience. In more than one interview the "out of sight, out of mind" feature of the flush toilet was emphasized:

> There is no personal responsibility at all. You put a Tidy Bowl Man[7] in your toilet, and that's it. Remember to pull the handle when you're done. What could be better?
>
> What percentage of people would be interested in bothering with a Clivus Multrum system? You know we are creatures of convenience, and I can't think of anything more convenient than flushing the toilet, because it goes away and it never comes back.

Maintenance was another theme that was emphasized. Despite the claims of the advocates for compost toilets, maintenance was perceived as unavoidable,

---

[6] A Northwest hardware and general merchandise chain.
[7] Trade name for a toilet bowl cleaning product.

and the responsibility for this was seen as falling on the shoulders of a reluctant householder:

> And then the compost pile itself, too much urine or not enough urine or not enough heat or too much heat may cause a problem. It has to be totally controlled by the person using it. I think that's the fallacy of the whole thing. They have some of those units that might work pretty well if they're properly cared for all the time, but you just can't control people.
>
> Well, I think the greatest fear, whether you're talking about officials, individuals, or neighbors is that the toilet will be messy and odorous.

But many of the persons interviewed felt a change in householder perception could occur. Another factor leading to attitude change, probably more likely to have an impact in the short run, is economics. Like the developer, the homeowner is an economic animal and responds to the marketplace. One homeowner who had purchased a Clivus Multrum said:

> I wouldn't have pursued the Clivus just for the sake of the environment. At that point, because I didn't have sewers, it was more from an economic standpoint, being able to get the house going faster. Plus, it made sense to have the ability to eliminate a lot of the garbage and to be able to re-use it to fertilize. I guess I've never considered myself a hardcore environmentalist.

He further stated:

> What most people are looking for is some type of financial benefit. I mean, it's going to be rough to find somebody that's just a hardcore environmentalist that's going to go around and preach the gospel on Clivus Multrums when the people you're talking to don't really care. They're surely not going to put one in their house and incur the expense to do it.

D. ANALYSIS

1. The Use of Interview Quotations—Pro and Con

As noted at the outset, we decided to use interviews as the basis for our O and P perspectives on the on-site solid waste management TA. Excerpts from these interviews constitute the framework of the preceding sections.

The T perspective analyst would argue that the excessive use of quotes from interviews is reminiscent of some of the more trite types of television news reportage, where "the man in the street" is asked his opinion on the eruption of Mt. St. Helens. It lends itself to an unreflective presentation of a disjointed hodgepodge of shallow opinions. Quotes should be used only when one wants to catch the special flavor of a significant statement made by an individual, or when it is important to show that a statement made by an individual has not been edited in its representation.

Let us recall some specific examples of quotes.

The homeowner described the convenience of the flush toilet in these words:

> There is no personal responsibility at all. You put a Tidy Bowl Man in your toilet and that's it. Remember to pull the handle when you're done. What could be better.

No diagram, flow chart, or decision tree can hope to make the point so directly and vividly.

The local development commission member characterized the trend-setting user thus:

> Same people that jog. You know, the upper middle class liberal professionals who are into whatever is *now*—Perrier water, Nike brand shoes, and dry toilets.

Similarly, direct quotes dramatically illuminate an organizational view of tactics:

> We looked at proposing a moratorium on cesspools . . . We did that primarily to get the attention of _____ County. . . .

Or the lack of trust in citizens on the part of bureaucrats:

> The DEQ tends to be suspicious of that kind of operation [where] they have no control over the maintenance. . . . The DEQ has a lot of experience with people basically just not maintaining them.

Or the lack of trust in federal bureaucrats on the part of local bureaucrats:

> Federal distribution and pots like that, this weird hybrid of Byzantium and Hee-Haw.

It is our conviction that the use of quotations can increase the effectiveness of O and P perspectives because *the form of expression reflects the perspective as much as does the substance of the statement*. Data- and model-based modes of inquiry are independent of quotations. But a dialectic inquiring system, such as a trial in a court of law or a Congressional debate, places great weight on testimony or speeches. The jury's prime source of information is the word-by-word transcript of oral statements. This does not mean that the O and P perspectives are to be presented entirely, or even principally, in quotation form.

The use of quotes should be guided by:

1. filtering out extraneous material;
2. keeping quotes that provide insights not obtainable with the T perspective, or otherwise obtainable with the O and P perspectives only in a less efficient or less transparent way.

2. Implications

In the brief four-person-month effort, two team members interviewed 35 people, producing 450 pages of typed transcripts. We have only dipped into this material rather than analyzed it exhaustively. In a full-scale TA different regions of the country would have to be considered rather than only the Pacific Northwest. The O and P perspectives do not provide the logical, data-based, and tightly organized analysis we expect from the T perspective, but neither does the T perspective yield the three-dimensional world that surrounds and informs human decision making. Even so, these O and P perspectives have enriched our understanding of the issues raised by this technology:

- the deeply ingrained "flush and that's the end of it" attitude (note: even in Western Europe, which has more areas of water shortage than the United States, there is no rush to on-site solid waste systems);

- the current absence of strong vested interest support for on-site systems— even environmentalists have higher priorities (for example, solar energy);

- the potential impact of federal sewer funding cutoff;

- the reluctance of bureaucrats to innovate; and

- the dependence of a "take off" on real estate developers and home builders (who have enough problems without saddling themselves with new risks).

The added perspectives make it clear why the 1970 anticipation of "a very slow rate of utilization of [individual on-site] systems" (Wenk, 1971:xxiii) continues to be a reasonable forecast despite technological advances. Finally, the possible mutually reinforcing effect between rerualization and on-site waste treatment systems is a potentially significant possibility that should be examined from both T and O perspectives.

E. A POSTSCRIPT—THE STANFORD UNIVERSITY TA

During the final stages of this work a report (Howard et al., 1981) of the Stanford University TA referred to at the opening of this chapter became available.[8] It is interesting to place it, as well as the MITRE Corporation TA (Wenk, 1971), in

---

[8] A second volume, "Case Studies of Household Waste Management" was not in hand at this writing. Hence, all comments in this section refer only to the first volume, "An Application of Decision Analysis to Technology Assessment of Decentralized Waste Treatment Methods."

the context of multiple perspectives. As noted earlier, the MITRE TA is an impressive T-oriented analysis and this is suggested schematically in Figure 20a. The title of the Stanford TA itself is significant: "An Application of Decision Analysis to Technology Assessment: An Assessment of Decentralized Waste Treatment Methods." It hints that the primary interest is methodological rather than substantive.[9] The question here is: how would one describe this volume in terms of our perspectives? In Howard et al. we read:

> Each decisionmaker "sees" the problem differently.   [Howard et al., 1981:29]

> This hierarchy does not describe the formal organization of agencies, but rather it describes our perception of the one in which decisions are actually made.
> [Howard et al., 1981:23]

We note the strong emphasis on decisions rather than technology throughout the document. There is a discussion of individuals: the "economan," "nominal (average) man," "environman," and "analyticman."

All of this suggests that the coverage involves multiple perspectives, as shown by our schematic format in Figure 20b. Three of the types would appear to be P perspectives; the analyticman, the T perspective.

A closer look gives a different picture, however. The economan, nominalman, environman, and analyticman are all idealized and described by the same few variables. For example, the discount rate for one equals the interest rate, for another exceeds that rate, and for a third is less than that rate. These variables all relate to costs. Thus the statement that each decision maker "sees" the problem differently means that he weights, or assigns different values to, the variables— but he "sees" the same few variables as all the individuals. Similarly, the individual types all perceive a logical, manageable sequence of events: condition–problem–solution–consequence–condition. They work in a sophisticated T perspective manner. People's actual perception of decisions does not coincide with this sequence. They may not perceive the problem at all. They may be in a different sequence stage: the EPA may already be up to the problem–resolution decision while individual citizens are still back in the condition-problem stage. A decision may be contingent on the power distribution among participants. This is particularly true in the case of waste treatment as there is a high level of indifference on the part of the man in the street.

The stress on the economics is indicated by the fact that 25 of the 36 figures in the report (excluding appendices) deal with dollar costs.[10] Whereas the individual is viewed in a highly idealized and simplified form, organizations are seen in terms of decisions based on analyticman's cost–benefit calculations modified by a "responsiveness parameter."

---

[9]The Principal Investigator, Ronald Howard, is a widely recognized authority on decision analysis.
[10]The remainder are hierarchies, flow charts, demographic, and technical curves.

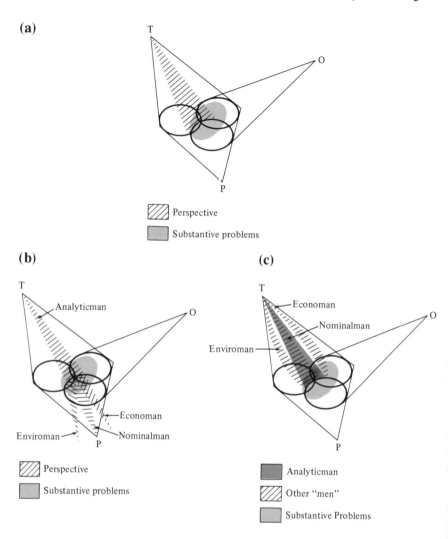

Stanford University TA

FIGURE 20. Schematic of perspectives: Solid Waste Management TA: **(a)** MITRE Corporation TA; **(b)** Stanford University TA, first impression; **(c)** Stanford University TA, second impression.

A cost model has been developed involving physical flows, capital costs, operating and maintenance costs, collection costs, and effluent costs. The decision model provides an elegant way to sweep in not only such quantitative information, but to make use of qualitative information once it is transformed into quantitative terms:

Decision analysis . . . is the latest step in a sequence of *quantitative advances* in the operations research/management science field. [It] is the result of combining the fields of systems analysis and statistical decision theory. . . . A good decision is a logical decision. . . . Decision analysis permits a rational treatment of problems (italics ours) [Howard et al., 1981:123–124].

There is a deterministic phase where the importance of the variables is measured by a sensitivity analysis, a probabilistic phase to represent the effect of uncertainties, and an "additional information" phase in which the previous uncertainties are eliminated.

This is clearly a valuable rational actor approach (that is, T perspective). There are models and data, idealization of individuals and of the decision-making process, that is, reductionism. There is little evidence of organizational drag, mutual mistrust of bureaucrats and citizens, or centralized sewer-focused engineering school curriculum, and little concern with developers and builders. There is no tie-in of organizations that are not in the hierarchy of waste treatment decisions but do have an important impact (for example, the Land Conservation and Development Commission). It is assumed that decisions on this subject can be isolated from other decisions. In sum, organizations and individuals involved in policy formulation and nontrivial decision making rarely, if ever, "see" the decision process the idealized way decision analysis does, that is, entirely from the T perspective.

We conclude that Figure 20c is a far closer representation of the first volume of the Stanford report than is Figure 20b. It is expected that the second volume, the case studies, will draw in different perspectives to provide a good overall balance.

XI

ANALYSIS
AND IMPLICATIONS

M. ADELSON, H. LINSTONE,
A. J. MELTSNER, and L. UMBDENSTOCK

Our increase in knowledge is comparable to that which a man,
interested in learning more about the moon, gets when he climbs
upon the roof of his house to catch a closer look at that luminary.
　　Albert Einstein

There are more things in heaven and earth, Horatio,
Than are dreamt of in your philosophy.

　　Hamlet (Shakespeare)

We have now savored enough sociotechnical systems to develop an appreciation of the role of multiple perspectives. In this chapter, we ponder the experience gained in Chapters V through X and prepare the ground for guidelines to assist the user.

The first point to note is that our illustrations encompass a decision range from global to local, from billion dollar programs to small household systems. We considered the decision to drop the atomic bomb and county watershed management, the wide-body trijet aircraft, and the Clivus Multrum toilet.

Table 28 presents a sampling of significant insights.[1] In the first two sections of this chapter, we examine the insights substantively: in Section A, a qualitative evaluation of one case—the Perinatal Regionalization System Study from Chapter VII, and in Section B, a collective look at the three technology assessments of Chapters VIII, IX, and X.

Following these discussions are three sections concerned with methodological matters. In Section C an approach to a more systematic comparative evaluation of the perspectives is developed. Section D reconsiders the fuzzy aspects of O and P perspectives, while E addresses the important problems of cross-cuing and integration of perspectives.

A. THE PERINATAL REGIONALIZATION SYSTEM CASE—AN EVALUATION (L. UMBDENSTOCK)

The following comments are based on the application presented in Chapter VII.

The perspectives yield quite distinct pictures of an emerging social technology. The T perspective in its well-ordered approach systematically sets out to present its case, implement a plan of action, and evaluate the results. Project staff contribute by establishing system linkages and procedures. In and of itself, however, the perspective misses many role aspects of the staff, and critical elements in gaining entry to organizations as well as inducing change. Nor is it attuned to such factors as "climate," "image," and fundamentals of interpretation found in professional and cultural settings.

The O perspective, meanwhile, emphasizes the intricacies of breaking through the traditional roles and established procedures. Drives are devoted to other priorities at every level of staff, across professions and institutions, and involve the interrelation of personal, economic, and positional factors. Project staff are sensitive to their roles in "others' territory." They look for entrances in relation to all these factors and seek to use existing directions of momentum but find it easy to get caught in their entangling web.

---

[1] We again must point out that the balance of effort or significance among perspectives varies with the object of study. In general, all perspectives are relevant. The omission in Table 28 of the T perspective in the case of the federal bureaucracy and the O perspective in the case of inflation is entirely due to the interest of the sources in the O and P perspectives in one case and the P perspective in the other.

TABLE 28. Examples of Insights Derived from T, O, and P Perspectives

	T	O	P
MILITARY TECHNOLOGY			
USS Wampanoag (Chapter VA1)	New ship superior to ships in other navies. Sea trials very successful, performance exceeded specs.	Ship is a destructive energy in navy society; adverse effect on morale; not a school of seamanship.	Isherwood is a brilliant designer.
M-16 rifle (Chapter VA2)	AR-15 (later M-16) superior in tests and Vietnam; more lethal (faster, smaller bullet); lighter weight permits carrying more ammo.	Marksmanship tradition (accuracy and long range) strong in Ordnance Corps. Ordnance developed M-14.	Stoner develops and pushes AR-15; Col. Neilsen, Gen. LeMay, Sec. of Defense McNamara want it.
Atom Bomb Use (Chapter VA3)	Dropping bomb on Japan without warning most cost-effective alternative; ends war with fewest U.S., Japanese casualties.	Anticipates threat of Soviet expansion; fear of impression of Manhattan Project as boondoggle if bomb not used.	Truman as new president cannot challenge policies, must appear decisive and bold.
OTHER FEDERAL ILLUSTRATIONS			
Federal bureaucracy (Chapter VA4)		Survival network; Congressional staffs No. 1 lobby target; turf protection.	Sec. of Defense Laird has ability to circumvent White House orders.
Inflation (Chapter VA4)	Economists' explanations		"Inflation is fun" or collective vice; excuses spending, evokes self-deception.
LOCAL CRISIS			
Mt St Helens (Chapter VB)	Watershed management an important long-term problem. Traditional flood control: Corps of Engineers builds levees, dredges channels.	Predictions ignored. Resistance to change even after eruption; exception: Cowlitz County control of land use. Multiple flood control measures raise interorganizational problems.	Individual only perceives immediate flood risk.

CORPORATE DECISIONS

Hydroelectric facility (Chapter VIA)	Building 60 MW facility most cost-effective alternative.	Changes in internal structure reduce planning role of Engineering and Rate Depts.	New president brings in outsiders and changes corporate decision process.
Acquisition of electronics company by Acousticon (Chapter VIB)	Venture analysis showed candidate to be an excellent choice for purchase.	Acousticon "culture" favors inhouse, develops rather than buys, is very conservative.	The conservative corporate secretary exercised great power.
Commercial aircraft (Chapter VIC)	Risk analysis shows disastrous outcome if Big 4 airlines split orders between DC-10, L-1011.	Logical analysis may easily succumb to other corporate needs. Bribery is an SOP in foreign sales. "Don't rock the boat" attitude can have deadly long-term impact (for example, DC-10 cargo door problem).	Haughton's leadership, charisma, and negotiating skills saved Lockheed at time of Rolls Royce/C5A crisis. Matching a leader to a situation can be crucial: Mr. Mac's lack of experience with airlines hurt DC-10 marketing.

HEALTH CARE

Nursing education (Chapter VC)	Goals: recognition of nursing school as academically credible higher education center; program efficiency and effectiveness.	Change of organizational vision to "community of scholars"; promotion depends on research, PhD credentials.	Struggle of old-timers to survive; political game of department chairpersons; elitism; morale problems for losers.
Perinatal regionalization (Chapter VII)	Plan to decrease mortality and morbidity based on levels of risk and care; upgrading of level of practice in hospital; evaluation of each stage. Plan also reduces need for costly duplication of services.	Recognition of opportunities inherent in overlapping interests; maintain relationships with hospital chiefs and administrators; assist public hospital in compensating for decreased resources and negative image.	Development of image of regionalization as personally useful; simultaneously noble and pragmatic; sensitive to Black professionals and their unique, controversial role in community.

(continued)

TABLE 28. Examples of Insights Derived from T, O, and P Perspectives (*continued*)

	T	O	P
TECHNOLOGY ASSESSMENT			
Electronic funds transfer (EFT), (Chapter VIII)	Impacts on organizations extensively analyzed (ADL TA). Uncertainties indicated (ADL TA). Impacts of other technologies (telecommunications and computers) on EFT underestimated.	Legislative and administrative recommendations (Commission). Report bought time and public discussion (Commission). New turf arrangements likely; cartels may form around EFT.	McCoy and Fisher have been the driving force in making Banc One a leader in financial services industry (credit card processing, automated tellers, in-home banking). "(TA's) don't have much value to us."
Guayule (Chapter IX)	Guayule a satisfactory substitute for hevea rubber. With surprise-free scenario, 100% of hevea shortfall made up by guayule in 1991; rapid commercialization scenarios also developed.	Research community has provided continuity but lacks leverage for commercialization. Production start-up rather than R&D is the key issue; coalition needed to get guayule off the ground; Dept. of Defense may be most effective catalyst (rubber is strategic material). Tire and rubber companies are risk averse.	Each actor sees his own prospective behavior differently than others perceive it; there is a crucial difference between those who are emotionally tied to guayule and those who must make commercialization decisions; external entrepreneurial invasion possible.
On-site solid waste treatment (Chapter X)	Possible mutual reinforcing effect between reruralization and solid waste treatment systems. Most common on-site systems: aerobic (e.g., septic tanks). With biological systems (e.g., Clivus Multrum) continuous maintenance and separation of grey water and toilet wastes required.	Engineering schools and federal policies favor centralized systems; absence of strong vested interest support (even environmentalists have higher priorities); potential impact of federal sewer funding cut-off; dependence of take-off on real estate developers and home builders.	Deeply ingrained "flush and that's the end of it" attitude; homeowners dislike maintenance; options such as Clivus Multrum attract con men.

The P perspective provides the most immediate grasp of the essential and unique world of the participants, but is the most elusive to deal with. In this situation the role of staff as conveyers and developers of an image and their development of others in this context is quite different than their role seen in the other two perspectives. The subtleties are such that without the measures of progress of the T perspective or the organizational inroads of the O perspective, a project is unlikely to get off the ground.

The openly interpretive role of the analyst appears to generate a number of concerns. One is subjectivity. Each analyst inevitably brings to the problem certain sensitivities and blind spots, the ability to empathize in one situation and total noncomprehension in another. Let us remember, however, that blind spots and filtering occur in the T perspective also. Thus the choice of quantifiable variables and drastic simplifications constitutes filtering. The hope is that each of the multiple perspectives applies different filters so that insights absorbed by the filters in one perspective are transmitted by those in another.

A second concern is replicability. Many insights are replicable in that others can check them, for example, the doctor–administrator relationship. The information is there and can be uncovered by other observers. Their resulting image may differ in some respects, but variations are usually minor. If significantly disparate images are obtained, further probing is called for. To the decision maker, cognition of wide disagreement may be more important than a forced consensus.

1. The P Perspective

The P perspective presents a unique contextual point of view on the topic, formulated experientially and communicated graphically by the analyst.

As each artist presents a unique, personal vision, so, too, the analyst admittedly enters an immersion process. Struggling through enormous amounts of contradictory information, impressions, and mixed emotions, he emerges with an integrated view of the situation or slices of the key tones and shades of the reality at play. This interpretation is offered for consideration or tested by recognition or expanded understanding within the group. If one accepts this possibility, the role of the "analyst" is then opened to a radically different kind of person—the dramatist, storyteller, comedian, poet, and artist.

Each is used to letting go of preestablished frames of interpretation to catch the moment and try alternate frames, to crystallize an image, convey a tone, involve an audience emotionally. Playing a more "straight" role, the columnist, ethnologist, and applied anthropologist may also be appropriate types of investigators. All can deal with insights into conditions of fundamental uncertainty by presenting a coherent and involving view of all the information at hand. Section VII D tried to convey a tone, an insight that could not be obtained by citing objective facts. Yet the heart of understanding this particular region is contained in this section. The linked socioeconomic-political issues described in

Section VII C arise out of the personal and individual/professional/cultural context elucidated in Section VII D; and interplay in very specific ways with policy goals, implementation strategies, and planning facts given in Section VII B. While it should be noted that the data gathered in this perspective are objective (available to anyone who enters the situation without prejudgment, to the extent any researcher does), a filtering process, of course, takes place. It is very consciously employed in the analysis phase—seeking alternate filters of interpretation but ultimately presenting a highly personal one.

2. The O Perspective

The organizational perspective, too, presents a dilemma for researchers. Section VII C tried to demonstrate that the organizational perspective is precisely the way events, decisions, and processes are viewed *by* organizations and organizational units, which are unique, to some extent monolithic entities, with distinct points of view. Thus an attempt to change the practices of a hospital unit may be challenged by the unit not just because its head is paranoid, incompetent, or resistant to change. It may happen because the prerogative of change belongs to someone who, if bypassed, can destabilize the multilayer network of authority, status, working relationships, job satisfaction, retention of employees, and even the definition of situations that make the work setting reasonable. On the other hand, these very linkages make possible radical change that, while ostensibly contributing to one function, greatly enhance linked ones across various groups. The data collection methods of the perspective, then, provide information, but the framework of interpretation falls together at the point where one reaches a closure stage. Again, it can be seen that the organizational perspective depends on more than the traditional research mode involving a preset framework of interpretation. The best investigators for the perspective advocated here would probably be a combination of those sensitive to organizational functioning, such as managers and union representatives, applied anthropologists, group process psychologists, human ecologists, and alternative organization advocates.

Thus the way each perspective collects and analyzes data (the type and organization of information) and the type and role of the researchers should vary greatly depending on the perspective used.

3. Integration

In Section IV C 5 (p. 82), we suggested that the multiple perspectives cross-cue each other, that is, the dominant role (or view or context), of each perspective is monitored and reshaped by the dominant role of the others as shown in Figure 21. Taking each in turn as a basic approach and organizing principle in the development of a plan, we can examine T, O, and P as contexts for the integration of information.

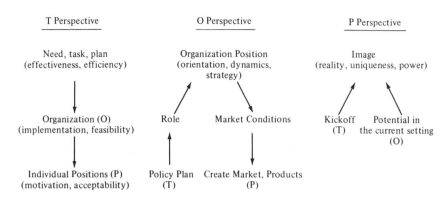

FIGURE 21. Cross-cuing of perspectives.

Use of the T perspective as a context. The basic plan arranges the information hierarchically from the objective abstractions of the need, task, and plan analysis (T) to the implementation constraints of the real world (O) and the motivating components at the individual level (P).

Use of the O perspective as a context. It demonstrates a strategic consciousness: orientation, position, and dynamics. The T perspective provides a policy or plan to consider and adapt vis-à-vis the roles and structure of the institution. It lobbies against whatever is not profitable or enhancing (for example, economically or technologically) and creates markets and products or services for whatever is. The P perspective concretizes an understanding of the "market conditions."

Use of the P perspective as a context. A plan is not merely applied with certain adaptations (trivial details), but is shaped both in its process and its end results by a unique image, forming pervasive power forces. In this context, the T perspective serves as a kickoff, a statement of need and/or formation of possible configurations. The O perspective presents the real-life lay of the land, the current order containing the potential of transformation.

The value of cross-cuing is the resulting depth and richness that such processes evoke. The perspectives are integrated by forming what Hofstadter (1980) calls "strange loops" where there is not figure–ground, but only figure–figure or mutual contexts as in Escher's drawings, Bach's fugues, Gödel's Undecidability Proof, or the mutually encompassing frames in the play *Marat/Sade*. While one can intellectually analyze the lines of the fugue (a stimulating and rewarding exercise) the musical ear registers satisfaction with the whole, pleasingly dynamic and balanced (artistic criteria), a process quite natural and effortless.

4. Communicating Multiple Perspectives

Of key importance to understanding and using multiple perspectives is the fact that not only do the perspectives present a different picture of the matter under consideration, but people who need that information themselves fall into different types—sometimes to the extent that the other perspectives are virtually useless to them.

Whereas Andersen points out that a "common language" can be developed from the perspectives with which to raise issues of concern and make plans, the communication process does not appear so simple. In fact Figure 7 suggested a very realistic basis for miscommunications.

The importance of the perspectives, then, is that they can reach more than one group of people because they provide pertinent information (content focus) *for each type* from its accustomed point of view (style of seeing or hearing). An area that needs consideration is how to present the various types of information in accessible formats. This is not too difficult to conceive. Numbers—whether counts of interrelationships in organizations or scores yielding predictive profiles of key actors—appeal to a rational actor (T type). On the other hand, numbers can be transformed into experiences. The number of standard nursing hours required to fulfill X functions at a specified rate for a certain number of women in labor and delivery means that three times the number of nurses should be on duty. The transformed experience shows that instead of a nurse dashing from one fetal monitoring device to another, the same nurse could comfort an anxious, first-time mother by telling her what to expect and by helping her with breathing exercises to alleviate pain. Numbers can also be dramatized by an example, as columnist Jimmy Breslin does in his picture of the low-income, pregnant mother sitting on the stoop and speaking of kids, poverty, and abortion.[2]

The more important issue, however, *is the enlarging of the capacity of people to see any situation from alternate points of view.* This has not been accomplished unless the perspectives have been developed by the appropriate types who also truly understand another type and are capable of clicking in on an area that can be used as a transition to understanding. The P perspective in this study is conveyed as a distillation of meaning in fictional form to suggest nuances and pervasive "forces." Another means of communicating could have given episodes of interactions from each of the participants' points of view when everyone agrees on some important aspect but the disagreement is very rational.

An important caution is that not all the information gathered should be communicated, even though one necessarily accumulates a vast amount through the multiple perspectives. Reams of notes were not used directly. The striving for

---

[2]We have observed a similar phenomenon in the corporate boardroom. The T perspective analyst is at home with cumulative probability curves and may wish to present his stochastic project analysis to the Chief Executive Officer. To do so effectively, however, he should transform his curves into equivalent statements about odds, for example, the likelihood that the project will net at least $100 million after taxes is one in three.

fuller comprehension rather than integration of detailed information is obvious. The T perspective calls for a choice of critical parameters to consider, the O perspective for portrayal of key interconnections, the P perspective for a basic feel for the whole. What do people need to know to do what they need to do? The perspectives contribute some interesting considerations to the imposition of limits.

B. INSIGHTS FROM THE O AND P PERSPECTIVES IN THE TA APPLICATIONS (A. MELTSNER, M. ADELSON, AND H. LINSTONE)

We now take a different cut at evaluation, focusing on the technology assessments (Chapters VIII, IX, and X). We first observe that the formal TA's (Arthur D. Little, 1975; Foster et al., 1980; Howard et al., 1981; Wenk, 1971) have similarities and differences. In our language, the emphasis may be described as follows:

- electronic funds transfer (EFT) (Arthur D. Little): T perspective on organization (Elements 3 and 5 in Figure 4; also Figure 18a);

- guayule (OALS/UA): T perspective on technology and economics (Elements 1, 2, and 3 in Figure 4; also Figure 19);

- solid waste (MITRE): T perspective on technology and economics (Elements 1, 2, and 3 in Figure 4; also Figure 20a);

- solid waste (Stanford)[3]: T perspective on decision process (Elements 3 and 8 in Figure 4; also Figure 20c).

The implications derived from the O and P perspectives taken in this report are now examined at a more general level.[4]

It may appear that we are rediscovering the wheel, that is, stating commonplace observations about social and individual behavior. It is certainly not our intention to develop a new, or verify an old, theory of organization or individual behavior, but it would be foolish not to expect a certain amount of consistency with previous concepts and empirical evidence. Common points of intersection are bound to occur because they are inherent in the O and P perspectives.

We will commence our discussion with some of the important insights that are a function of individuals, such as the distortion, which comes from partial views; and those organizational factors that slow down acceptance of a new technology, here termed organizational drag. Then we will address some of the interdependencies between a technology and its social contexts.

---

[3]Volume I of the final report.
[4]Some of the lessons learned in doing these three cases are included in Chapter XIII, where they are transformed into guidelines.

1. Participants Have Partial Views

The individual participants involved with a technology have somewhat limited, circumscribed views. The P perspective should uncover the total individual, but frequently we found that the individual wore blinders. Sometimes the partial view would be a function of professional training. In the solid waste treatment area, for example, engineers seemed to see on-site systems as temporary expedients, and their own training predisposed them to favor centralized systems (Chapter X). At other times, the partial view would be a function of professional interests or values. Many of the guayule scientists are more concerned with research on yield than in developing commercial markets (Chapter IX). Then again, partial views can develop from acceptance of certain ideologies or belief systems; thus some environmentalists do not place a high priority on on-site solid waste treatment systems because these systems can encourage development and affect the quality of the groundwater. Finally, selective perception in the form of discounting operates to encourage partial views, for example, bankers seeking short-run governmental regulations and guidelines to cope with some of the long-run technological implications of EFT systems (Chapter VIII).

Individuals are more likely to pay attention to immediate consequences, immediate in the sense of time or causation, than they are to future, distantly occurring consequences. Scientists, too, are not immune to this limitation.

The existence of individual, partial views is not just a restatement of the proposition: where you stand depends on where you sit. For one thing, that proposition assumes an organizational locus for the sitting. Location in some piece of the social structure does inadvertently result in a partial and selective access to information. This partial view can also be reinforced by the organizational actor's having a stake in the outcome and consequently persuading others of the validity of his partial view. Both the inadvertent and deliberate use of a partial view, however, need not stem solely from an organizational location or role; evidently individuals operating outside an institutional home have the same propensities because of value differences, self-interest, prior socialization, ideology, and incomplete information.

Organizations tend to generate their own versions of groupthink, in which the things that "we all know" come to be accepted as true[5] to the point where those contravening them are subject to suspicion or, in the extreme, ostracism. Members therefore take great pains not to be seen as willing to sacrifice their standing for their ideas. Only when an idea has the sanction of belief by those with unquestioned standing (for example, the board and top management, or the successful competition) is it safely espoused by those without such standing.

There are two consequences:

---

[5]The Merleau–Ponty inquiring system, in which the group creates its own reality (see Section II D and Figure 5).

1. When strong individuals come to believe in an innovative idea that has not been sanctified, it may be easier for them to split off and create a new enterprise or join another organization which is in a ready phase.
2. Every effort will be made by individuals interested in a new idea to make it look like one that is already accepted, and to show that it can be integrated without organizational stress or disruption. New wine will be poured into old jugs; in the end it will taste like old wine.

In some cases (perhaps in most of them) the analyst and his readers will be required to impute to the various actors characteristics and/or motivations for which confirming evidence is inadequate. Without such imputation the situation cannot be understood, but that is no excuse for irresponsible attributions. The network of conditions or circumstances in which the imputation occurs should create enough support to justify its consideration by others, whose task is then to inquire as to the portent of the interpretations. For example, in the guayule case, the *fact* that a rubber company executive made a presentation in which he seriously underestimated the prospective cost of land does not readily lead to an interpretation of incompetence or computational error, because such figures are carefully reviewed prior to presentation in any mature organization. At least a suspicion is raised that the underestimate may have been deliberate, just as contractors competing for a job sometimes underestimate costs in order to capture the work. Further work is certainly required to explore this matter, work that could be done only with a more or less continuing approach to TA, rather than a one-shot, episodic one.

2. Partial Views Encourage Distortion

Distortion inevitably accompanies the exercise of partial views. Each participant constructs his own world view, and thus, sees his behavior quite differently from the way the other participants perceive it. Each sees the other's perceptions as distorted. Each, therefore, interprets a given act differently. Thus the leaders of the federal effort to commercialize guayule perceive themselves as proceeding sensibly within their notion of the constraints. Other participants see only ineffective leaders who are more concerned with their own careers than with the development of guayule. Advocates of a technology, whose career and fortune are tied to its development, are likely to be critical of other participants, particularly those who may be playing a decision-making or judgmental role. Some of these advocates are able to operate outside institutional constraints, so they are not likely to appreciate those who operate within them.

Partial views and distortion, of course, make communication difficult. The participants can never be sure they are talking about the same thing, as when the blind men describe an elephant—each of them feels a separate part and on that basis envisions a different whole elephant. Commercialization of guayule does not mean the same thing to both rubber company employees and small farmers from Indian reservations; these participants have very different conceptions of scale and control of production.

It is important to determine whose perspective, and whose language system, is dominating the field at the moment; for that determines in what kind of language any argument will have to be couched, and whose approval will be required for next steps to be designed or taken. It is also important to examine what will be required to substitute a new language system or concept structure, or to augment the existing one with others that may be equally viable and have different implications. In the guayule case, for example, the language of national security, or that of preservation of rural America, may have to join that of rubber company planning or state economic development before forward motion occurs, and the implications that need to be considered may have to be political, labor, community development, or military ones in "assessing" the technology. *Each* of these may benefit from application of *all* of the perspectives.

The existence of distortion can also affect the probability of social acceptance and change. A fragile coalition that supports acceptance of the technology could be formed with the potential distortions obscured or hidden. Each participant joins with the overall objective in mind, not necessarily knowing that there are important differences that can divide them. Then, as the technology moves closer to implementation, experts start working out consequences, differences emerge, and the coalition falls apart.

3. Organizational Drag

In using multiple perspectives, there is a natural inclination to look for factors which may contribute to social change. Some of the factors that resist change or inhibit the acceptance of a new technology can be placed under the rubric of organizational drag.

Other things being equal, decisions leading to gradual onset are easier for people to make than those leading to sudden onset. Organizational costs are higher for sharp changes in direction. If the situation is framed so as to seem to require major commitment and rapid adoption, the fact in itself would tend to delay implementation. It is precisely this framing that seems to characterize those presently active on the guayule scene, and it may be commitment to this way of representing things that accounts for the inability of the technology to get off top dead center. (Exceptions include conditions of high perceived threat, as in the case of U.S. response to Sputnik, or manipulation of oil prices by OPEC.)

Bureaucratic routines, for example, budgeting, can retard acceptance or be used as an excuse not to implement a technology. It is no secret that federal funding for the development of guayule has been slow in coming. A small part of the explanation for this slowness can be found in the organizational drag created by the mechanics, procedures, and timing of budgetary requests.

Another typical way of postponing action is to raise questions and suggest the need for more study, including the formation of commissions and sponsorship of assessments. Generally, uncertainty of knowledge creates a demand for study and for more experts to work on the problem. The assumption behind this behavior is that more information will contribute to decision making, yet it is equally plausible that the intended function of the research is simply to gain time. The EFT Commission is a case in point. Sometimes the organization may require its own study because the study can be used to build internal consensus or has a greater legitimacy than the information that may be available elsewhere. Thus, while the additional research slows down action in the short term, it may actually facilitate social change in the long run. Events, in the form of a receptive climate, catch up and correct, or alternatively support the bureaucrat's inclination to delay in the hope the issue will go away. The practice of defensive research is a well-known industry phenomenon, often designed to stop or slow technical change. In oligopolistic situations, hedging tends to act as a brake on introduction of new technology, because each firm defers to the interests of the others, without necessarily forming an active coalition.

Unfortunately our scope did not allow the opportunity to dig deeply into the complex motivations and incentives of bureaucrats and other organizational participants. Obviously, the organizational context of any new technology is bound to be one of mixed motives where there are some participants who are motivated to take risks and others who avoid them. It is our impression, however, that organizations encourage their members to avoid risk by administering punishments promptly but delaying rewards. As a consequence, the individual in an organization is likely to become progressively more conservative and to discount a future reward in favor of not being punished in the present. The on-site waste treatment case is particularly illustrative of this concern.

The tendency of individual members to avoid risk is also extended to the organization's dealings with its environment. The essence of the notion of organizations is predictability, and it follows that they will try to enact environments that are stable, predictable, and subject to control. In the case of guayule, the rubber companies want large sources of natural rubber under their control; they do not want to face the instability that can come from dealing with a large number of small suppliers. Similarly, central sanitation districts want to reserve some measure of inspection and control over on-site sanitation systems. They would probably prefer a centralized treatment system because, in their view, such a system facilitates monitoring for health hazards. But if on-site systems are going to be used, then they also want to be involved.

Like a parent who does not want to let go of his or her children, complex organizations do not want to let go of any piece of their environment that might affect them. It is quite possible that a decentralized, small-scale approach to the commercialization of guayule would satisfy a large range of needs and also avoid the social costs of a large-scale, capital-intensive system. But the actual choice between small- and large-scale systems is likely to be guided by organizational dynamics rather than cost–benefit calculations.

Too much control, of course, can be counterproductive. In the case of electronic funds transfer, legislation and regulation have been used to attempt to maintain or gain control. It is not clear from our review, however, that the requisite control has been achieved. The use of laws to create a predictable environment has resulted in a patchwork of inconsistencies and short-term accommodations. The controls get more complex and, with some irony, the organization seems to have less control. Laws and regulations seem to create a demand for more laws and rules—thus adding to complexity.

Most organizations adopt standard operating procedures, rules, and regulations to deal with routine decisions and situations. With the objective of protecting one part of the public from another, regulatory agencies try to enforce their rules by issuing permits and judging appeals to depart from building codes and other explicit regulations. One problem with a new technology is that this mass of legal and paper protection is designed to cope with likely adverse effects of the old, rather than the current, technology. The old rules may become a standard for judging the safety of the new technology, despite the agency's interest in promoting the new technology. At a minimum, the old rules will have to be rewritten and go through an extensive approval process. This time delay to make the rules fit the technology is another example of organizational drag.

Finally, we should recall our earlier discussion of the business cycles and phases of companies, which periodically accentuate organizational drag (Section IX B 2).

4. System Boundaries Are Open

In our work, we have placed a technology into its social context, comprising a number of loosely coupled organizations and individuals. This context can be considered a system whose boundary is quite open, accessible, and permeable. Obviously, much that is transpiring within the system determines the reception of the technology, and so it would not be unusual for purposes of investigation to consider the system as closed. But it is particularly interesting to see how external elements can influence internal behavior.

In the case of guayule, one of the potential levers for change is a concern for national security. A major change or the threat of a change in our international sources of natural rubber would trigger a shift in priorities over the urgency for guayule commercialization. We observed the effect of another existing external influence in the case of on-site waste treatment technology. In that situation the federal government, through its grant mechanisms, has encouraged centralized sewer construction and has undercut its own efforts to encourage state and local actors to consider on-site technologies. If the state/local system, as we observed it in Oregon, had a closed boundary, its allocation process would not have been distorted by outside incentives.

When an organizational or system boundary is open, the actors in the environment will influence the behavior of the organization or system. The organization in many different ways comes to terms with its perceptions of its environment. Sometimes it responds simply to an external incentive, but other times it may sacrifice its central objectives. The latter situation is frequently found in the field of regulation, where an enforcement agency is captured by the regulated industry or groups. In our waste treatment case study, we found a state environmental control agency that was coping with the organizations and citizens it was supposed to regulate by trying to be their friend. The agency was perceived to be a weak enforcer. The work *weak,* besides being pejorative, also obscures what is going on. Is the agency weak because it lacks the financial, legal, and other resources to be strong? Are persuasion and friendliness the only strategies available to the agency? We do not know, but it is clear that the agency had open boundaries and was anticipating and reacting to its environment and that the acceptance or rejection of new waste treatment technologies was related to what was going through the holes in its boundaries.

5. Differential Influence of Citizens and Elites

In technical policy areas, where public involvement is minimal, individual actors, such as scientists and other technical elites, are likely to affect policy outcomes. Certainly, in the early days of the development of atomic energy, the views of scientists such as Edward Teller or Herbert York were significant, and ordinary citizens had very little to say. Even in our three subjects of assessment, where the technologies themselves are not particularly advanced or complex, citizen involvement is minimal. In the case of EFT, it is mainly in the hands of computer and banking experts. Guayule, at the moment, is dominated by scientists and production specialists. On-site waste treatment is in the hands of engineers, public health experts, and a few advocates (for example, entrepreneurs and environmentalists). Nuclear power plants that raise Hiroshima-like images of potential destruction in the public mind are something else again.

The more typical lack of citizen involvement is probably due to a variety of factors, only one of which is the sophistication of the technology. Lack of knowledge, itself, can operate as a barrier to activity. In the EFT situation, for example, many people fail to realize that transfers are not made by sending checks or pieces of paper. They assume that the new system more or less works like the old and do not perceive any reason to act or be concerned. The public in general worries about immediate things, so that all an on-site waste treatment system has to do is work "out of sight, out of mind," require no maintenance or plumbing, and not be unduly expensive. There is not much incentive to worry about long-term effects, such as changes in the quality of the groundwater. And the citizen as consumer is indifferent to the source of the rubber in a tire, as long as it lasts and costs about the same as his previous tires.

At this stage of our work, the consequences of citizen indifference are not entirely clear. Some observers of the EFT situation feel, for example, that the passiveness of large numbers of consumers simply slowed down the acceptance of the technology. It might be argued, however, that the elites in that situation were simply not as aggressive as they might have been. One consideration to keep in mind is the extent of the decentralization of the particular technology. The more decentralized the technology, the more individuals have discretion. For technologies such as personal computers and on-site waste treatment, individual preferences can determine the rate and degree of acceptance. How citizens react in their individual decision-making situations also provides clues for likely organizational activity (a function of the P perspective noted in Section IV B 3).

One consequence of minimal citizen involvement is obvious: elites will have more to say. The extent of elite influence, however, depends on other considerations. For example, the influence of a scientific elite will probably be much greater at an initiation or incubation stage of a technology. Guayule is a good case in point, because the network of scientists and researchers has been effective in keeping interest in guayule alive. There has been funding from the National Academy of Sciences and the National Science Foundation; at least two societies have been formed and three international conferences have been held. But all this scientific support in itself has not been sufficient to implement the technology. We are at a later stage of technological change where, to proceed, the support of policy-making elites and organizations from both the public and private sectors is necessary.

6. Coalition Formation and the Political Arena

In discussing the acceptance of a new technology we are concerned not only with the inertia or action of a single organization. The social system, which is our primary concern, represents a loose coupling of a number of organizations and individuals, in other words a coalition. Generally, a technology that is going to affect a large number of people and interests in our society is bound to involve coalition formation. With the exception of small or obscure social change, no single individual or organization has sufficient resources to bring about the conditions for change. American politics is coalition politics, and this rule applies to the acceptance of technology as well.

Once the necessary coalition has been built to sponsor a technology, it is hard to stop. In the case of EFT, it seems that the sponsoring coalition has done its job: the technology is on the track and rolling. This does not mean that everyone who will be affected by the move from paper to machines is aware that they have something at stake; but only that, by the time they find out, it may be too late to do anything about it.

The situation is different with respect to guayule and on-site solid waste treatment. The sponsoring coalitions that can lead to acceptance have yet to be formed. In the case of guayule, the existing coalition does not have adequate political and economic resources to accomplish commercialization. In the case of on-site solid waste treatment, the participants appear to be too atomized to even speak of a coalition. When assessment concerns such new or incipient technologies, the assessor must conjecture about who may be or become stakeholders, create scenarios accordingly, establish structured dialogue, if possible, and produce hypotheses about "event strings" that appear, *a priori,* improbable. This may be unpopular because it may fly in the face of prominent stakeholder interests (including some of the assessor's own) or because it looks like a diversion from the apparently high-probability options. Nevertheless, it serves to raise potentially important issues and "ways of seeing" that are the proper business of TA.

In building a coalition, there is often a leader or power broker. His first questions usually are: Who wil be in the political arena? Who has something to lose or gain? One of the leader's jobs, like the assessor's, is to identify the actors who are involved, who may potentially become involved, and who are not likely to become involved. But not all coalitions are formed by leaders. Some just form naturally, as may be the case with guayule. The guayule coalition started out with a group of scientists and researchers who were in some ways a social club, then was joined by passive federal government agencies and defensive tire and rubber companies. In addition, there were several individuals, not organizationally based, who tried to exert influence through other organizational actors, "powers behind the throne." Farmers, farm workers, and Indian tribes, as potential producers, have not been involved in any serious way in the present discussion and discussion process, although they are likely to have a stake in the outcome.

The lack of producer participation brings up another generalization about coalition formation: the size of the coalition, in terms of diverse interested parties, should be big enough to win, but not so big as to be unstable. The present guayule coalition seems ineffective, and some alteration in its membership, incentives, and level of operation may be required.

From our work, it was apparent that the participation of national security agencies would help the guayule coalition at the federal level. At state and local levels, it may be useful to involve farmers and other producer interests. In short, coalition formation for implementing a technology can occur at various levels of our political system, or in different sectors of our economic system.

Regardless of level, not all affected parties and interests will always be aware that they have something at stake, and so they may not be in the political arena. We would expect that the likelihood of some parties being outside the political arena is higher for a newer technology. In the early stages of the acceptance of a new technology, its proponents and those who have something to gain from its implementation are likely to enter the political arena. The proponents and the gainers make up the sponsoring or supportive coalition. There is some delay before the "losers" enter the political arena and form an opposing coalition. Part of the delay is due simply to the time it takes for the opposition to become aware that it has something at stake, that it is going to lose something from the technology. The complexity is compounded by those who are not "losers" but "choosers." They can influence the form that a technology can take (for example, environmental groups regarding energy).

Another source of delay is related to the mode of implementation, rather than the technology itself. A group may not perceive that it has anything to lose from a particular technology, and be neutral or indifferent to it. At that point, the supportive coalition chooses a certain path for implementation that excludes the group or may be costly to it, and then the loss becomes apparent. For example, small-scale producers are probably not aware that the present coalition in favor of the commercialization of guayule might proceed down a large-scale production path. In some ways the opposing coalition is at a disadvantage, because it needs the supporting coalition and its plans as a frame of reference to recognize that it has something at stake.

7. Characteristics of the Technology

Sometimes in the pursuit of the O and P perspectives we tend to forget that the T perspective will contribute to our understanding of them. The characteristics of a technology influence individual and social behavior, and it is essential to understand the influence. For example, the inadequacy of an existing technology to perform certain organizational and social tasks often creates a demand for a new technology. Surely the manual tabulation of interbank payments and the sheer volume of transactions encouraged financial institutions to look for new technologies, such as those encompassed by electronic funds transfer. And it is no accident that in Oregon about 37% of solid waste management systems are on site; centralized systems would just not fit the less dense and rural areas of the state.

Usually we talk about the applications of a technology, that is, a set of technical conditions that augment the technology and the process of choice. In the case of on- and off-site solid waste management systems, none of the technological choices are particularly novel. We have a variety of means to meet diverse technical conditions: the kind of soil, the drainage, the density of population, and the use. From the interaction between the characteristics of the technology and the technical conditions will come a choice of septic tanks, sand filter systems, dry-composting toilets, or centralized systems. But, as we have seen, this is not the whole story, because technical characteristics and conditions have to be put into a social and individual context. Decisions seem dependent on local, physical, and organizational conditions. Using the P perspective we found that many homeowners perceive on-site systems as a step backward in the direction of outhouses. Moreover, one technical characteristic of a dry-composting toilet is that it requires maintenance. For example, the homeowner has to make sure it is working at appropriate temperatures, or as one informant put it, "You've got to babysit the toilets." With the present system, one just pushes the handle and there is not much personal responsibility. Not only is an on-site system a decentralized technology, but its social context is equally decentralized.

This interaction between the technology and its organizational context or social system is, of course, what assessment is about. It is a subtle and complex business. Sometimes we try to simplify the complexity by adopting technical decision rules; for example, we have been told that the cost effectiveness of sewers becomes marginal with less than ten persons per acre and unacceptable with less than 1.7 per acre (Section X A 1). Yet these technical heuristics may prove to be oversimplified. In cost–benefit calculations, we usually consider the concept of economies of scale as a neutral, technical one. All we have to do is go out and estimate the effects of size or scale on costs. But as experienced practitioners of cost–benefit analysis know, much depends on who is doing the estimating of costs and benefits. In the case of guayule, the tire and rubber companies have their own notions of appropriate scale, and from these notions will come the selection of benefits and the magnitudes of costs. Usually we expect that political actors will discount technical information while pursuing their political interests. What we do not appreciate is how the technical information itself is altered by the same pursuit. Significantly, this applies even to a technological forecast and to risk analysis.

In the latter case, is it not an oversimplification to assume a direct linkage between the technology and an assessment of risk for most situations? Individuals and organizations operate as intervening variables, and their risk-taking propensity is dictated in part by their familiarity with the technology and in part by their own nature, age, and economic standing.

8. Interdependence

Many of the insights we have discussed in the previous pages stress interdependence: between the technology and the social context, between organizations and individuals, and between individuals and their perspectives. Institutions are not isolated in their behavior resulting from technology. They are not closed systems, but are open to influences from their environment. What one organization does affects the behavior of another.

The various organizations and individuals that make up the social context are bound together by a process of social exchange: states accept federal money for decisions in favor of centralized waste management systems; banking interests decide on the location of a financial center in return for a change in interest rates; and individual entrepreneurs promote the commercialization of guayule in exchange for the possibilities of future economic and other gains.

The organizations can also be considered as forming a network with commonly understood expectations and procedures. Recall that one of the reasons given at the outset (Section IV B 3) for the inclusion of the P perspective was that it may shed light on the O perspective. For example, the individual's search and need for personal security is reflected in the organization's resistance to change. An organization may, in fact, be organized to maximize the exercise of P perspectives in formulating an O perspective. Corporations that emphasize decentralization and decision making by consensus, for example, autonomy of product teams and participative management, consciously strive to create an O perspective that is in harmony with the P perspectives of the employees. The assumption is that such an approach is more attuned to the role of the corporation in the coming decades and, specifically, to deal with complex sociotechnical systems problems.[6]

There are other facets as well. Under normal conditions, an organizational network has a high degree of stability. However, the network may be confronted with severe external pressures which endanger that stability. Individuals and their P perspectives may assume a critical role when the network breaks down. Max Weber pointed out long ago that charismatic leaders emerge at a time when social organization is undergoing basic change. This is not to say that P perspectives are only important at such junctures—but they may have a profound impact under such conditions. The Great Depression endangered the United States and Germany—one produced Franklin Roosevelt and the other Adolf Hitler. Their P perspectives were exceedingly influential in generating the New Deal and the Third Reich, respectively. Each drastically altered not only the nature of the countries as organizations, but completely changed their O perspectives.

Let us for the moment consider the case of the wide-body trijets (L-1011 and DC-10) discussed in Section VI C. The organizational network included the airlines, aircraft manufacturers, subcontractors, the Federal Aviation Administration, etc. Dan Haughton maneuvered his corporation through a crisis only by restabilizing a network of organizations (that is, Rolls–Royce, the airline customers, and the British and U.S. governments) that were ready to break an established set of relations.

In the case of Acousticon (Section VI B), the founders' P perspective had permeated the organization for a long period, shaping an O perspective that made other perspectives favoring an acquisition appear alien or intrusive to the corporate culture.

Moving from the retrospective to the prospective, the strong stability of the guayule organizational network—the tire and rubber companies, U.S. Department of Agriculture, Department of Defense, Federal Emergency Management Agency, the southwestern states, etc.—makes it exceedingly difficult for an individual to create a coalition of organizations to undertake the commercialization.

One of the key tasks in a TA is to identify the combination of external circumstances and internal vulnerabilities that would make a P perspective prevail over an established O perspective, for example, to facilitate implementation of

---

[6]Kiefer and Senge (1982) use as specific examples the Kollmorgen Corporation (electrooptics), Cray Research (large computers), Analog Devices, Inc. (analog digital converters), and Dayton–Hudson Corp. (retail chain).

a change and to predict the characteristics of the individual(s) who could effect such reconfiguration of the natural rubber market.

Interdependence also has a time dimension to it. In the case of guayule, there were a number of individuals who were the keepers of the institutional and technical memory of what, in the aftermath of World War II, was considered a discarded and unnecessary technology. It is that memory which is facilitating the commercialization of guayule today. If commercialization succeeds, it may act in the future as an agent of change for the U.S. Department of Agriculture in encouraging a shift in orientation from food to fiber production. Such a shift would also change the incentives of agency officials, who at present are not particularly active in promoting the production of guayule.

Finally, there is a critical interdependence between a technology and its acceptance. Surely a technology that is seen as contributing to a current social good, for the most part, will find easier public acceptance than one that is seen as adding to our list of current social problems. Our nation's unrestrained approval of progress no doubt contributed to the public acceptance of nuclear energy in its early years of development. Moreover, technologies can be promoted in terms of the public interest or in the name of progress, and at the same time serve private and individual purposes. Thus, the EFT technology can be subverted for criminal purposes, and the development of guayule can contribute to the self-advancement of a few individuals. Sometimes these interdependencies can be positive, and other times less so. One thing seems clear: the use of multiple perspectives makes it easier to identify them.

9. Technology Assessment and the P Perspective

The common justifications for expenditure of public funds for TA are:

1. to indicate the need for legislation or to establish that no special need for legislation exists;
2. to support administrative policy, program, strategy, planning, or other action, or to establish that no special need for administrative action exists;
3. to inform a diverse public of prospective consequences and contingencies, so that parties at interest may take appropriate action in a timely fashion.

Translated into operational terms these justifications become as follows:

1. to enable individual legislators and/or their staff workers to combine the results of the TA with other information they have access to, and with the pressures exerted by other parties, interest groups, and individual constituents, to determine if they should (and how they should) introduce, support, amend, or oppose legislation relating to the technology or its consequences;
2. to guide administrators in adjusting policies, programs, strategies, plans or planning processes, personnel assignments, budget allocations, organizational arrangements, leadership style, etc., or in taking other actions

such as forming coalitions, initiating research, modifying criteria for evaluation, or requesting authorization;
3. to provide early warning to investors, consumer groups, corporate managers, community officials, and other decision makers and "actors" of
   prospective opportunities, consequences, and contingencies so they may
   take timely action.

The translation makes it clear that TAs are done so that individuals in various
settings can progress better with their purposeful activities. Technology assessors'
understanding of those purposes, and the means that each actor may use in
fulfilling them, can clearly make TAs more useful. Furthermore, decisions that
each actor makes about a technology, or the conditions of its development or
application, influence the field of "forces" within which all subsequent decisions
are made. Thus, decisions are factors that must be used as input data to TA,
not just as outputs that use TAs. In this sense, *the P perspective,* the perspective
of the individual person, is not just a way to make TAs more useful, it *is
indispensable to TAs because it refers to a major class of essential inputs.*
  If TA is to be useful at all, it will influence the decisions people make about
the technology. To the extent that it is a factor in the decision processes, it is
more manifestly political[7] than knowledge-oriented, "conventional" scientific
research. This is not to say that technology assessors intend to be political. On
the contrary, they typically strive to be dispassionate, to the point where they
conscientiously omit information about people and organizations that may greatly
affect a technology's future. That is just the information that our approach is
striving to reinsert. The methods that have been developed in TA generally
attempt to make results as source independent as possible, that is, to objectify
them. Yet the very attempt to be apolitical is a political choice, based on the
belief that the results are more likely to be accepted and acted on if personalities
and organizational styles are kept out of consideration. In this approach we face
the need to bring what is clearly *subjective* information into the assessment
process without altogether impairing the acceptability of the results.[8] Such information is essential because technology advances along a path steered by human
decisions, which are taken by individuals with particular characters in specific
organizational settings; these decisions and ensuing actions influence subsequent
ones, including who is to make further decisions. This class of information may
sometimes be properly treated via economic models, system dynamics models,

---

[7] The word *political* here indicates only that interests of different individuals and groups are affected differentially,
in terms of wealth, power, status, or other ways. Technology assessment is useful precisely because it can exhibit
such differences. The ethical problem is therefore fundamental, not incidental. Nor is it avoided by choice of
methods, although it may be camouflaged.

[8] Technology assessors frequently collect interview data and may be quite sensitive to value, strategy, and
perceptual issues; but this material seldom finds its way into final reports, and little attention is given to how to
use it.

or statistics. But there are times when specific people and groups make a unique difference, and those must be considered also.

A P perspective implies the possibility of identifying in advance who the key actors in the development of the technology in question are going to be, are likely to be, or may possibly be. To avoid "exponential explosion" of the search process, the technology assessors must have some hypothesis about the trajectories of implementation.

C. POSSIBILITIES OF SYSTEMATIC COMPARATIVE EVALUATION (H. LINSTONE)

Each user brings to the table a unique prior knowledge and mind set—a distinctive perspective or amalgam of perspectives. One hopes that the use of multiple perspectives is beneficial. How can we determine or measure the benefit? Clearly the answer depends on the evaluator's perspective: a resulting decision by the user which looks great to one appears poor to another. And the impression may change over time. To many in the Kennedy Administration, the U.S. intervention in Vietnam was a good decision in 1962 and a poor one three years later.

Despite these difficulties some kind of evaluative effort is desirable. Following is one suggested approach. It is not designed to answer the question posed in the preceding paragraph, but rather to provide the T-oriented analyst a means to measure the impact of the multiple perspectives.

As a first step, a list of insights gained from each perspective is compiled. Tables 20 and 25 serve as examples for electronic funds transfer and guayule commercialization, respectively. Each user is given the list and asked to 1) add any other items that, in his or her opinion, appear to be missing and 2) rank the statements according to measures such as *importance* or *newness*. Table 29 shows the rankings of the ten statements considered most important by each of five persons concerned with guayule commercialization. We note:

- each perspective contributes insights to each user;
- the T perspective makes the strongest showing, followed by the O perspective, then the P perspective;
- as could be predicted, the scientist places the heaviest reliance on the T perspective;
- the USDA official is most O oriented, the entrepreneur most P oriented;
- while the T perspective is significant for all users, interest in the P perspective is the most dichotomized;
- there is considerable similarity in perspective balance 1) between the scientist and the military and 2) between the entrepreneur and the commission member.

We have not examined the newness measure (Nutt, 1977). In general, one

TABLE 29. Example of Importance Rankings for Guayule Commercialization

	Scientist[a]		USDA official[a]		Entrepreneur[a]		Military[a]		Commission member[a]	
Ranking[b]										
10 (highest)	1	T	1	T	1	T	1	T	1	T
9	3	T	14	O	2	T	14	O	3	T
8	4	T	12	O	20	P	3	T	18	P
7	2	T	9	O	18	P	8	O	19	P
6	7	O	2	T	19	P	2	T	20	P
5	12	O	3	T	14	O	18	P	8	O
4	14	O	11	O	12	O	16	P	16	P
3	9	O	8	O	8	O	4	T	17	P
2	15	P	16	P	10	O	7	O	9	O
1 (lowest)	6	T	19	P	16	P	13	O	10	O

WEIGHTED TOTALS OF EACH PERSPECTIVE

Perspective					
T	35	21	19	27	19
O[c]	14	23	11	14	6
P	2	3	22	9	28

MOST IMPORTANT STATEMENTS AS RANKED ABOVE

Integrated rank order	1st	2nd	3rd	4th	5th	6th	7th
Statement No.	1/T	3/T	2/T	14/O	18/P	8/O	12/O

[a]Numbers refer to statements in Table 25.
[b]Of ten statements considered most important by respondent.
[c]Adjusted to account for larger number of statements of O type in Table 25.

would expect some complementary relationship: the T-oriented user would tend to see the T perspective output as most "important" and, being familiar with it, might rate it as the least "new." Correspondingly, this individual would be most surprised by some O and P perspective statements. The reverse would be the case for the other perspectives.

An alternative to rankings is the use of anchored rating scales (Nutt, 1980). Descriptors are selected that incorporate a salient attribute as seen by the user. For example, an evaluation of statements drawn from the perspectives could have one or both of the scale formats in Table 30.

The continuous linear scale is placed next to each statement, and the respondent marks the appropriate point on it. The analyst needs to exercise some caution in view of the likelihood of rating dependencies. A statement may be rated as important because it tells something new, for example. The order of statements in a list may influence the rating also, that is, the initial statements may seem more important or newer than the last statements. Randomization of the order

TABLE 30. Scale Formats

Importance scale	Newness scale
1.00 Crucial, essential	1.00 Complete surprise, no previous inkling
0.75 Quite important	0.75 Mostly new
0.50 Valuable, of significance	0.50 Partly new, partly known
0.25 Of peripheral interest, marginal, low priority	0.25 Only fills in a few gaps
-0- Irrelevant	-0- Nothing new

and use of several evaluators with presumably similar perspectives is feasible with T and O perspectives (but not P perspectives).

It goes without saying that the kind of evaluation considered here is more satisfactory to a T-oriented analyst than to O- or P-focused users. The organizational perspective is likely to bring forth considerations such as ease of routinization of the multiple perspective concept and implications of diffusion of politically sensitive items. The personal perspective may well judge the value of the different perspectives by criteria such as their ability to place the user in an advantageous position vis-à-vis his associates, to provide new leverage in political maneuvering, to avoid surprises. Furthermore, a dominantly O or P perspective person might not be eager to respond to requests which would bare closely held concerns and tactics. At the very least he sees systematic evaluation as an academic exercise.

D. THE FUZZINESS OF THE O AND P PERSPECTIVES (H. LINSTONE AND M. ADELSON)

There are three potential traps in managing the O and P perspectives:

- confusing the *how* with the what, that is, *how* we are looking and *what* we are looking at;
- misidentifying or misreading a perspective;
- confusing O with P.

We discussed the *how* and the *what* in Chapter IV. The Arthur D. Little and EFT Commission reports demonstrate the distinctions. Both looked at organizations—ADL primarily from a T perspective, the Commission primarily from an O perspective (see Figure 18). The makeup of each group provides the clue—largely analysts in one case, senior bureaucrats in the other. Table 31 shows how the guayule case may be represented in terms of the *how* and the *what* according to T, O, and P under each heading. At times we can also interpret the *how* and *what* as *strategy* and *concern* or as *means* and *ends*.

The O and P perspectives are neither unique nor necessarily clearly bounded.

TABLE 31. Distinguishing "What" and "How"

How it is being viewed	What is being viewed		
	Technological elements	Organizational elements	Individuals
T perspective	Federal program officer offers to consider research proposals not covered by commission mandate G requests U.S. information to help him use guayule to slow down desertification in Africa	Rubber companies do defensive research	Private citizen F provides good seeds to stimulate research
O perspective	"State, feds" consider sharing cost of pilot plant NAS reports on promise of guayule	Guayule Commission formed; includes USDA, USDC, BIA, NSF State agency head is directed to procure federal funding rather than being given state funding Congress relates Guayule Commission to Mexico Q discusses employment for his research team with rubber companies if commercialization proceeds.	D sets up network via newsletter E negotiates with industries to sell ERP seed E sets up organization at ___ University to pursue Indian interests in guayule
P perspective	Federal official sees rubber company official as misrepresenting costs of land for guayule culture	Federal official cultivates good relations with Mexicans, alienates rubber companies Private citizen F joins A in hope of promoting decentralized development Congressman promotes interest in guayule	X tries to get R replaced Z tries to get credit for U's idea Entrepreneur issues press release on guayule related matter, commending self

Unlike with the T perspective, a certain fuzziness is unavoidable. An individual may claim his view represents that of an organization, say, the company or agency which employs him. He may believe this is the case or he may wish to hide his personal view—we cannot be sure. He may give two different perspectives at two points in time or to two interviewers. Two individuals in the same organization may give different versions of that organization's perspective on an issue. Both may be valid—one the party line presented in the Annual Report and the other the internal perspective. Or the two may be giving the perspectives of two different divisions in the organization.

Only a handful of the tens of thousands of Lockheed employees had any inkling of the millions dispersed in payoffs, a standard operating procedure in marketing aircraft overseas (see Section VI C 3). The pivotal roles of the Seven Sisters in oil on the international scene only became partially understood with Blair's research (1977). The five grain multinationals constituted a complete enigma to the public until *Merchants of Grain* was published (Morgan, 1979). As Senator Frank Church confessed:

> No one knows how they operate, what their profits are, what they pay in taxes and what effect they have on our foreign policy—or much of anything else about them. [Morgan, 1979:ix].

This came from a member of a legislative body that has authorized billions of dollars in U.S. government subsidies to such companies.

In an information society, the generation of disinformation constitutes a further challenge. The computer provides marvelous opportunities to create such output at unprecedented levels of sophistication.

Another source of fuzziness: If one person is considered to have a P perspective, do two people constitute a group and, as such, have an O perspective? As indicated in Figure 6b, there is a quasi-continuous range from individual to large formal organization. There is little value in pursuing a Talmudic debate about whether a perspective is P or O. However, there is value in determining misrepresentations. We seek perspectives (whether O or P) that are likely to be 1) significant in terms of the policy formulation and decision process and 2) honest representations. At times cross-checks are possible for O perspectives, for example, by interviewing a number of individuals in the same organization. An experienced psychologist, interrogator, or attorney can also make checks on a P perspective.

As we move from T to O to P we follow a path not dissimilar to that of Freud—penetrating from the "professional" to the deeper "political" to the still deeper "persona" layer (Section IV B 3). A P perspective is the most difficult to do well and the easiest to do poorly. It is the most sensitive, the least replicable.

Yet the situation closely resembles that faced by the executive, the jury, or the legislative committee. All seek a variety of perspectives (rather than solely

General Motors' Decision on Downsizing
as reported by William Halal

An awareness of the energy crisis . . . during the early 1970's increased the emphasis on strategic planning at GM. The "down-sizing" decision . . . was formulated in a process of "logical incrementalism" that includes successive steps searching for marginal improvements that comprise the formulation of a new strategic posture. Some major advances in this direction included: the formation of an ad hoc task force on energy in 1972, the approval of the Seville [K] and Chevette [T] car programs which proposed 800–1000 pound weight reductions across the entire product line. . . . [These steps were followed by] formation of a strategic planning department in 1977 at the corporate level (Halal 1980:109).

as reported by Joseph Kraft

I asked Murphy [Chairman of the Board] when that decision had been made . . . Pointing to the sheets he held in his hand, he said, "This is an official schedule of major actions by G.M. It says here that the executive committee approved the K-Car decision on Jan. 23, 1974, and the T-Car on the same day. But I know it's wrong. We didn't make the decision in the executive committee. We made it in the engineering-policy group. It was on December 23."

There had, in fact, been no high level meetings at G.M. on the date described by the Chairman of the Board as D-Day.

[The interviewer then talked to Gerstenberg, Chairman of the Board 1972–74].

Gerstenberg's account . . . was just as flawed as that given by Murphy. For one thing Gerstenberg was wrong about the committee that made things happen.

[It was not all forgetfulness. Tactics were also involved.]

An official of the Department of Transportation said, "Nobody at G.M. could tell you exactly how the downsizing decision was made because nobody knows. Without the [government's] miles-per-gallon standards, G.M. would never have downsized the way it did." That view was endorsed by a Washington lawyer who works for the auto industry . . . He wrote me: "Only when the fuel economy standards were enacted in 1975 did a comprehensive approach to downsizing begin" (Kraft, 1980).

the T perspective) and all must contend with the fuzziness we are discussing here.

It is important to keep in mind at all times that the paradigms basic to the T perspective are not suitable to O and P. The replicability we take for granted with T is a case in point. A jury trial is not replicable—even if there is a retrial. Nor are significant, nonroutine executive decisions replicable. Similarly, with our O and P perspectives, we rarely have the luxury of adequate replicability. Cross-checks should be used where possible, but it must always be remembered that different perspectives may legitimately yield contradictory images.

E. MORE ON CROSS-CUING AND INTEGRATION
(H. LINSTONE AND L. UMBDENSTOCK)

1. The Use of Digraphs[9]

In Section XI A 3 we brought out the cross-cuing among the perspectives for the case of Perinatal Regionalization. We pointed out that this was a vital step in synthesizing the insights obtained into a coherent image.

This aspect of multiple perspectives may also be studied using a technique familiar to T perspective analysis: structural modeling (Linstone et al., 1978).

Consider the Perinatal Regionalization case evaluated in Section XI A. In Figure 21 we presented the cross-cuing schematically. The same basic relations are depicted in standard directed graph (or digraph) form in Figure 22a. This digraph is unsigned and the perspectives form the "elements." If the relations can be represented simply as positive or negative, we may use a signed digraph. Here "reinforcing the attitude toward, or feasibility of, a policy" is shown by a plus sign (+); "counteracting the attitude toward, or feasibility of, a policy" is denoted by a minus sign (−). Thus an arrow marked " + " from T to O might mean that the T perspective analysis presented to the organization favors implementation of the technology (for example, the analysis has demonstrated the benefit–cost ratio of the preferred choice to be the most advantageous of the alternatives considered). An arrow marked " − " from O to T might indicate that the organization resists the same technology decision (for example, its implementation may lessen the leverage of the present power centers in the organization). It should be emphasized that the complexity of the cross-cuing will not always permit representation by a simple " + " or " − " sign.

Figure 22b shows the USS *Wampanoag* example (Section V A 1) as a signed cross-cuing digraph. The advantage of such a digraph is that we can interpret any resulting feedback cycles or loops.[10] Reconstruction of arguments and reasoning presented in decision-making groups points up a striking paucity of such cycles. Axelrod (1976) was puzzled by the lack of cycles in three policy deliberation cases he studied, and Linstone et al. (1978) observed a similar phenomenon in the Carter Energy Plan. The explanation is, we believe, related to the commonly observed lack of follow-through in causal thinking beyond the immediate cause–effect link.

The focus of digraphs on cycles may prove to be one of their most significant advantages because it consciously encourages the search for higher order consequences of decisions or actions—and these may cancel or greatly magnify the expected effects. Thus, the military planner may find that his new weapon, developed to counter an enemy threat, is in turn made ineffective by a change in enemy tactics. And the farmer, spraying his field with insecticide to reduce

---

[9]This section is primarily for readers who are at ease with the T perspective techniques.

[10]The terms *cycle* and *loop* are used interchangeably here to denote directed closed paths, which end at the starting point, such as Figure 22b (but not 22a).

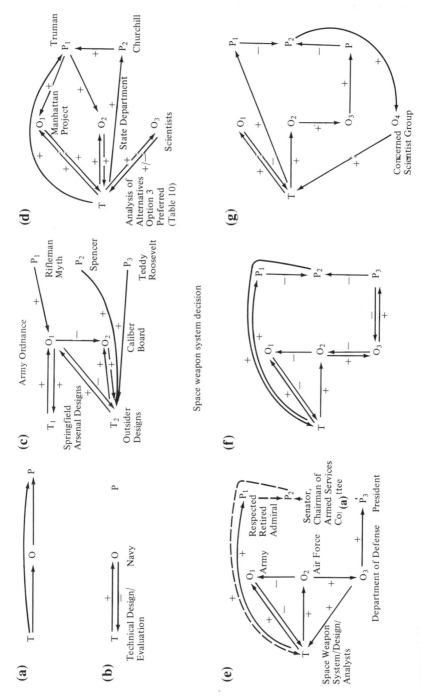

FIGURE 22. Digraphs of the cross-cuing process: **(a)** Perinatal Regionalization, cf. Figure 21; **(b)** USS *Wampanoag*; **(c)** M-16 rifle— history of Army rifle prior to World War II, cf. Figure 10; **(d)** atomic bomb use decision; **(e)** base case; **(f)** a "stop-action" strategy?; **(g)** another "stop-action" strategy.

crop losses, has initial success only to see his losses mounting again as resistant strains emerge.

A loop is positive or impact amplifying if it has zero or an even number of minus signs, negative or impact counteracting if it contains an odd number of minus signs. This corresponds to Axelrod's Rule 1 for paths in cognitive maps. We shall also follow his Rule 2:

> The total effect of point A on point B is the sum of the indirect effects of all the paths and cycles from A to B. If all such indirect effects are positive, the sum is positive; if all are negative, the sum is negative; if some indirect effects are positive and some are negative, then the sum is indeterminate. ["Indirect" here refers to a multisegment path, for example, A to C to B.] [Axelrod, 1976:63–64, 72–73].

The possibility of indeterminacy distinguishes (and constrains) the application of digraphs in policy and decision analysis.

In Figure 22b we clearly have a negative loop (one plus, one minus sign). The T perspective on the ship was a positive one, but the O perspective had a negative impact: the Navy wanted no part of this advanced vessel. We could add arrows to and from the P perspective if we had more information. With more than one O and P perspective (as is normal) each perspective becomes a separate element in the digraph (for example, O_1, O_2, P_1, P_2, P_3). We then also expect arrows connecting, say O_1 and O_2 or P_2 and P_3.

Figure 22c shows seven perspectives interacting in the case of the Army rifle (Section V A 2) prior to World War II. It corresponds to the first part of Figure 10. Army Ordnance (O_1) created Springfield Arsenal (T_1), and the mutual support relationship is shown by the two arrows connecting O_1 and T_1. The Western rifleman myth (P_1) strongly influenced O_1 as shown by the " + " arrow P_1 to O_1. Outsider Spencer (P_2) evolved a different technical perspective (T_2). However, the T_2O_1 relationship is nonsupporting (that is, loop with one minus sign). Teddy Roosevelt also supported an outside design, as did the Caliber Board (O_2), subsequently. The relation O_1O_2 signifies the Chief of Staff's disapproval of the Caliber Board recommendation. We note four loops in this figure:

- $T_1O_1T_1$ positive
- $T_2O_1T_2$ negative
- $T_2O_2T_2$ positive
- $T_2O_1O_2T_2$ negative

Because O_1 was more powerful than O_2, the reinforcing loop T_1O_1 was the dominant positive effect; and T_1 (part of one strong positive loop) triumphed over T_2 (part of two negative and one weak positive loops). We could go one step further in digraph techniques and assign weights to arrows, that is, develop a signed, weighted digraph. We do not recommend such extension—it too easily leads to self-delusion in overinterpreting quantified output.

As another example, consider the decision to use the atomic bomb (Section V A 3). The analysis indicated that all arrows were of positive sign, except for a portion of the scientists, that is, part of O_3T. Thus we have seven loops and all but one is positive (Figure 22d):

- TO_1T positive
- TO_2T positive
- TO_3T positive and negative
- TP_1O_1T positive

- TP_1O_2T positive
- $TP_2P_1O_1T$ positive
- $TP_2P_1O_2T$ positive

It is quite apparent that in these examples the use of digraphs is not essential to an understanding of the cross-cuing. But it is also clear that with little effort one can develop situations where reliance on intuition may be less desirable. Consider the following hypothetical case.

A NATO partner's research and development organization has achieved a technological breakthrough that makes a revolutionary military space weapon system feasible. American analysts at the RAND Corporation and elsewhere have confirmed the technical analysis (T perspective). The U.S. Air Force is enthusiastic because U.S. implementation would be their responsibility and give them a major new project. The U.S. Army is opposed because the funding of a major new Air Force system would drastically reduce chances of a go-ahead for a new Army helicopter system. The Army perspective is denoted O_1, the Air Force perspective O_2. The Department of Defense perspective, O_3, mirrors a general hawkish administration attitude. Key individuals are a retired maverick admiral who is opposed to "wasting" money on space weapons (P_1) and is a close personal friend of the Senator who now heads the Senate Armed Services Committee (P_2), and the President (P_3). The Navy is not represented because it is split on the issue, and its internally conflicting perspectives cancel out. The effect of the interaction of perspectives is as follows:

- $T \rightarrow O_1$, $T \rightarrow O_2$, $T \rightarrow P_1$ positive—the analysis clearly favors the space weapon system; it is transmitted to the Army and Air Force; the influential admiral is slipped a copy by the Army.

- $O_1 \rightarrow T$ negative—the Army orders a study to show that the RAND analysis is faulty (for example, misleading threat assumptions). The resulting loop TO_1T is negative, neutralizing the original analysis.

- $O_2 \rightarrow O_3$ positive—the Air Force formally endorses the RAND analysis and appends it to a go-ahead authorization request to the Secretary of Defense.

- $O_2 \rightarrow O_1$ negative—the Air Force argues against the Army position in the Joint Chiefs of Staff meetings, focusing on allegedly erroneous data in the Army report on this system. In digraph terms this closes the loop TO_2O_1T, which becomes positive and counters the Army's negative TO_1T loop.

- $O_3 \rightarrow T$ positive—the Secretary of Defense likes the RAND analysis and orders it augmented (presumably strengthened). This step also creates a loop, TO_2O_3T, which is positive and reinforces the system support.

- $O_3 \rightarrow P_3$ positive—the hawkish Secretary of Defense pushes the space system with the President.

- $P_1 \rightarrow P_2$ negative—the retired Admiral expresses his strong opposition to such an "utter waste" to his close friend, the Chairman of the Senate Armed Services Committee. Will this negative view create a negative loop, TP_1P_2T?

- $P_3 \rightarrow P_2$ positive—the President listens sympathetically to his Secretary of Defense. He sees that his acquiescence to the space weapon system will help to maintain his own desired image of strength and toughness. He is informed that there is concern over the possible agreement of the key Senator with his Admiral friend. The President counters this by pressuring the Senator to accept his perspective.

- $P_2 \rightarrow T$—the Senator may agree with P_1 or P_3; he does not have a strong independent position on this question. The resulting relation will create either the negative loop TP_1P_2T or the positive loop $TO_2O_3P_3P_2T$.

Thus, the cross-cuing may be represented as shown in Figure 22e. If the $P_3 \rightarrow P_2$ relation prevails, there will be three positive and one negative loops; if the $P_1 \rightarrow P_2$ relation holds instead, there will be two positive and two negative loops. Both relations cannot hold simultaneously without resulting in indeterminacy by Axelrod's Rule 2 (hence the dashed arrows).

One advantage of this mode of representation is that it can serve as the focal point for a group discussion to elicit missing perspectives and cross-cuing relationships. New strategies may be revealed and can be walked through the digraph. For example, a discussion of Figure 22e is likely to raise the following questions:

- Can the Navy (O_5) and the House Armed Services Committee Chairman (O_7) really be omitted?

- Would NASA (O_6) support or oppose T?

- Does the Air Force not have influence on the Senate Armed Services Committee through another Senator (formerly an Air Force Reserve General)? If so, we can connect O_2 to P_2 through the Senator (P_4): $O_2 \xrightarrow{+} P_4 \xrightarrow{+} P_2$. This would create another positive loop: $TO_2P_4P_2T$.

With the aid of graph theory we can probe still further and test the digraph for stability.[11] In the case of typical physical systems, we usually seek stability

---

[11]The following theorems and their proofs have been developed by Roberts (1976). He distinguishes two types of stability. Value stability means that the value of a vertex does not get too large in magnitude. Pulse stability means that the change in value, that is, the pulse, does not get too large in magnitude.

- *Theorem 1:* If a weighted digraph D is pulse stable under all simple pulse processes, then every eigenvalue $\lambda = a + bi$ of D has magnitude $|\sqrt{a^2 + b^2}|$ at most unity.

- *Theorem 2:* Suppose D is a weighted digraph with all nonzero eigenvalues distinct. If every eigenvalue of D has magnitude at most unity, then D is *pulse* stable under all simple pulse processes.

and fear instability. For example, Meadows et al's *Limits to Growth* sees catastrophe in unbounded resource use and population growth. In the case of policy decision analysis, the interpretation is quite different: digraph "instability" means unanimity or strong support for an action or change and "stability" a serious split or suppression of a decision and inaction. In Figure 22d we saw that nearly all loops were positive or reinforcing. This signifies "instability" of the digraph but unanimity or strong reinforcement for the decision to use the bomb.[12] This basic difference in interpretation can also be placed on a more philosophical level: it reflects the contrast between closed physical systems seeking stability and open human/societal systems at the leading edge of evolution, restless and seeking change.

In the hypothetical example of the space weapon system decision, the original digraph (Figure 22e) with either $P_1 \xrightarrow{-} P_2$ or $P_3 \xrightarrow{+} P_2$ included is not pulse stable.[13] If we want to stop any go-ahead, we can test strategies on the basis of changes in the digraph. Consider the following (Figure 22f):

- the President gives a negative signal to the Senator: $P_3 \to P_2$ sign change;

- the Admiral gives a negative signal to the Senator: $P_1 \to P_2$ negative;

- the President gives a negative signal to his Secretary of Defense: $P_3 \to O_3$ negative;

- the Secretary of Defense gives a negative signal to the Air Force: $O_3 \to O_2$ negative;

- the Secretary of Defense does not strengthen the technical analysis: $O_3 \to T$ eliminated.

We now have six loops: five negative and one positive.[14] According to Theorem 1, this digraph is not pulse or value stable, however. An example of a modification which does result in value stability (via Theorems 1 to 5) is shown in Figure 22g. Here the Air Force does not counter the Army nor does the President pressure the Secretary of Defense and he, in turn, the Air Force. The Senator draws in a new group (O_4), concerned scientists who have raised the specter of

---

- *Theorem 3:* Suppose D is a weighted digraph. Then D is *value* stable under all simple pulse processes if and only if it is pulse stable under all simple pulse processes and unity is not an eigenvalue of D.

- *Theorem 4:* Let D be a strongly connected signed digraph with a central vertex which is on all cycles of D. Let a_i denote the sum of the signs of the cycles of length i, where a $(+)$ cycle is counted as $+1$, a $(-)$ cycle as -1. Let s be the largest integer such that $a_s \neq 0$ and $s > 0$. If D is pulse stable under all simple pulse processes, then $a_s = \pm 1$ and $a_i = (-a_s) a_{s-i}$ for $i = 1, 2, \ldots, s - 1$.

- *Theorem 5:* Let D be a strongly connected signed digraph with a central vertex which is on all cycles of D and let $s > 0$. If D is pulse stable under all simple pulse processes, then it is value stable under all simple pulse processes if and only if $\sum\limits_{i=1}^{s} a_i \neq 1$.

[12]While a predominance of positive or deviation amplifying loops suggests instability of the digraph, a predominance of negative or deviation counteracting loops does not necessarily imply stability—it could lead to increasing oscillations; hence the importance of the theorems (Roberts, 1976:188).

[13]Not all eigenvalues have $|\lambda| \leq 1$.

[14]Negative: TO_1T, $O_2O_3O_2$, $O_3P_3O_3$, $TO_2O_3P_3P_2T$, TP_1P_2T; Positive: TO_2O_1T.

a weapon system effect which would be most undesirable for the United States. This had, of course, been ignored in the technical analysis (T).[15]

Examples of representations of real life policy decision cases, yielding more complex digraphs, may be studied in Axelrod (1976). Multiple perspective cross-cuing analysis is also likely to lead to fairly complex digraphs.

Fortunately, the computer can assist in this structural modeling, for example, by displaying the entire set of loops rapidly (SPIN program, cf Linstone et al., 1978).[16] A disadvantage is that, as pointed out earlier, the use of such graphical analysis of cross-cuing is likely to be confined to T-trained analysts.

2. The Use of Delphi

Whereas use of digraphs was labeled a T-oriented technique, Delphi may be viewed as an O/P-oriented approach.[17] It is defined by Linstone and Turoff (1975) as "a method for structuring a group communication process." Elsewhere, it is described as a remote structured conferencing procedure. The key features are use of a panel of participants, iteration, feedback, and anonymity. The panelists' responses are not constrained to the T perspective. In fact, Delphi can serve as the means to construct a shared reality and thus help to develop a group (O) perspective (Scheele, 1975).

Delphi also proves useful in cross-cuing and integrating multiple perspectives. In this role it complements the digraph approach described above.

In the form of a *policy* Delphi (Turoff, 1975), this technique can bring to the fore the various perspectives and facilitate their circulation among the participants, provided they are selected to sweep in the appropriate T, O, and P perspectives. The Delphi exercise should

- clarify the perspectives themselves;
- indicate the most significant conflicts or differences;
- minimize discrimination in favor of any one view;
- suggest the rigidity or flexibility of each perspective (by the change or lack of change in later rounds).

In the form of a *decision* Delphi (Rauch, 1979), this procedure can assist in integrating the diverse perspectives into a decision. It is more action oriented than the policy Delphi and may serve as:

- a prototype integration (see Section IV C 5);
- a means to examine the dynamics of the integration process.

---

[15]Note that there are three negative loops: TO_1T, $TP_1P_2O_4T$, and $TO_2O_3P_3P_2O_4T$.

[16]Interested readers are referred to Linstone et al. (1978) for a survey of structural modeling tools, Roberts (1976) for the mathematics of such graphs, and Axelrod (1976) for "cognitive maps" of political/military decisions.

[17]This accounts for the strident opposition to it by Sackman and some other T-trained analysts. See Sackman (1975), Coates (1975), and Goldschmidt (1975).

It has been used effectively in the first mode for the Perinatal Regionalization case by Umbdenstock (1981).

Her Delphi was initiated following the development of the T, O, and P perspectives as described in Chapter VII. The aim was to design a regional network organization based on the different perspectives through participative action. Following are the steps in this process:

1. *Selection of the Delphi participants.* The choices were based on a) criticality of individuals as determined by the O and P perspective analysis and b) need for representation from the principal organizational and professional decision-making components. There were doctors, nurses, administrators, and nurse educators; these represented private doctors, public hospitals, private nonprofit hospitals, private proprietary hospitals, and Regionalization Project staff. Of 57 invited, 44 actually participated.

2. *Introduction to decision Delphi.* A letter from the Regionalization Project Director and personal discussions with the prospective participants introduced the Delphi to them and put everyone "in the same game."

3. *The first round.* Four 1985 scenarios were provided to the participants; each described a form of organization for attaining regional perinatal goals. The four: regional consortium model, Board of Directors model, pyramid model, and free enterprise at work model. A series of questions on specific mechanisms accompanied each scenario. Each participant was asked to choose the one scenario which would suit him most and would constitute a good system. The questions corresponding to that scenario were then to be answered. (Sample: Each hospital or doctor sets its [his] own protocols. Would this mechanism contribute greatly to a good regional organization? [yes, no]; Would this mechanism work very well for you? [yes, no]). Telephone calls reminded the participants to mail back their responses.

4. *The second round.* Summaries of the first round responses were presented. An opportunity for reaffirmation of the participant's round one choice or a change of mind was provided in the second round. Next, positive and negative factors were to be listed for the preferred scenarios, together with tasks for implementation. The results were picked up in person to speed the process.

5. *The third round.* Each packet was delivered personally and a pick-up time arranged. Controversial issues drawn from the responses were listed. (Samples: Smaller hospitals have little expertise to offer; a loss of doctor-patient relationship would result from the Board of Directors model.) In each case, the participant checked one of the following: I support greatly, I support some, I don't care, I oppose some, I oppose strongly.

The result of the Delphi: a strong preference for the Board of Directors model. All respondents were willing to participate in some future organization. The process itself confirmed the importance of participatory decision making (even if system resources are hierarchical). However, the transition of an organization to a new form requires leadership for takeoff. The lack of this element meant that more interest than energy was generated. Thus a conclusion focused on the importance of timing of the Delphi. The need to enlarge the imaging power of Delphi as a design process was also recognized.

With regard to anonymity, Rauch's comments are interesting. He finds that it is not desirable in a decision Delphi. A participant is only motivated to take the task seriously if he knows who the other participants are. However, Rauch recommends "quasi-anonymity": the names are known but the statements or responses are still anonymous, that is, not attributable to an individual.

3. A Note on Other Analytic Tools

In Section XI E 1, we introduced graph theory as a T-oriented tool to assist in cross-cuing. Let us briefly examine some other analytic tools.

The *theory of games* was the brilliant brainchild of John von Neumann and Oskar Morgenstern (1944). In its simplest form there are two players and each has several options. The payoffs associated with every pair of choices are known to them, as are their objectives, that is, maximizing or minimizing the payoff. The calculus then determines the best strategy for each player. Like probability theory, game theory originated in conjunction with social games.[18] After World War II it was applied to military decision analysis as the following sanitized RAND "problem" suggests:

> Suppose that a pair of Blue bombers is on a mission; one carries the bomb and the other carries equipment for radar jamming, bomb-damage assessment, or what-have-you. These bombers fly in such a way that Bomber 1 derives considerably more protection from the guns of Bomber 2 than Bomber 2 derives from those of Bomber 1. There is some concern lest isolated attacks by one-pass Red fighters shoot down the bomb carrier and the survival of the bomb carrier transcends in importance all other considerations. The problem is: Should Bomber 1 or Bomber 2 be the bomb carrier, and which bomber should a Red fighter attack?" [Williams, 1954:47].

As Schelling observed, the idealization of a conflict required by the theory drastically alters the character of the game. "There is a danger in too much abstractness" (1960:162). It might be said that Schelling anticipated Allison's models. He recognized the unrealistic restrictiveness of the "rationality" assumption and saw the need for a theory of strategy which encompassed what appears to the analyst as "irrationality." Multiple perspectives certainly help to avoid the game theory trap. Consider the following recommendation:

> We may wish to solicit advice from the underworld, or from ancient despotisms, on how to make agreements work when trust and good faith are lacking and there

---

[18]Von Neumann's original 1928 paper was titled *"Zur Theorie der Gesellschaftsspiele."*

is no legal recourse for breach of contract. The ancients exchanged hostages, drank wine from the same glass to demonstrate the absence of poison, met in public places to inhibit the massacre of one by the other, and even deliberately exchanged spies to facilitate transmittal of authentic information [Schelling, 1960:20].

In our framework game theory is inexorably tied to the T perspective and Schelling's discussion leads us to the O and/or P perspectives.

Utility theory transforms a general measure, such as dollars, into a personal preference scale (also known as a utility scale or utiles). This step would seem to take into account the P perspective (for example, predilection of an individual for risk taking). However, the concept, dubious at best, is often doomed to failure by the attempt to calibrate the scale in a pseudoanalytic manner (that is, via the T perspective). Typically, the subject individual is asked a series of standard questions about his risk propensities using a highly idealized, hypothetical situation.[19] The resulting scale is then used to predict his preferred decision (highest expected utility) in a complex real life problem. Further, individuals are compared on the basis of such utility profiles. The resulting "realism" offers as much illusion as instant antiquing applied to new furniture. The complexity of human decision making simply cannot be captured by such superficial number crunching. Our approach would argue that in-depth interviews and other personal contacts are vital in understanding personal preferences, that is, the P perspective.

It is interesting to speculate what the impact of the ubiquitous computer will be on the use of multiple perspectives. Its inherent preference for T perspective tools may either exacerbate the imbalance in favor of the use of the T perspective or encourage the misuse of T tools to derive false O and P perspectives.

It should be noted, for example, that the T perspective comes closer to a "universal language" than the Tower of Babel suggested by the pluralism of O and P perspectives. A multiplicity of perspectives is conducive to heterogeneity, but not to homogeneity. This connection is echoed in Maruyama's comparison (Linstone and Simmonds, 1977:260) of traditional and emerging society characteristics:

Traditional	Emerging
uniformistic	heterogenistic
quantitative	qualitative
classificational	relational
atomistic	contextual
hierarchical	interactionist
unidirectional	mutualistic

---

[19]Example: On a new project described in two sentences which alternative do you prefer—1) the certainty of making a $100,000 profit or 2) an 80% chance of making a $200,000 profit and 20% chance of losing $50,000?

LOOKING AHEAD:
RISK, FORECASTING,
AND PLANNING

H. LINSTONE

The body travels more easily than the mind. . . .We have not really budged a step until we take up residence in someone else's point of view.

John Erskine, *The Complete Life*

Through reason and the methods of science alone we are inadequately equipped to deal with the present problems of metabiological evolution.

Jonas Salk, *Anatomy of Reality*

In Table 28 we had a clear intimation of the broad spectrum of multiple perspective applications. In this chapter we address three areas expected to reap unique benefits from this concept in the next few years. We then call attention to several directions of potentially fruitful research.

A. MULTIPLE PERSPECTIVES IN RISK ANALYSIS

The Three Mile Island nuclear accident investigation recognized the inadequacy of the T perspective in risk analysis:

> A truly unexpected result came out of the Kemeny Commission's study of Three Mile Island. A group that set out to investigate a technology ended up talking about people. In the Commission's own words, "It became clear that the fundamental problems were people-related problems" [*Washington Post,* October 31, 1979].

Table 32 shows how the three perspectives illuminate different views of risk. The T perspective undertakes probabilistic calculations and draws up fault trees, the O perspective deals with standard operating procedures and threats to organizational integrity, the P perspective perceives personal fears and images of horror. Not surprisingly, there is a dramatic difference between actuarial, societal, and personally perceived risk rankings.[1] According to a recent survey, the typical individual views the risk of auto accidents as equal to those of nuclear power, while the actual annual mortality rate of the first is over 500 times that of the second.

The T perspective analysis explains the "distortions" suffered by the P perspective, that is, reasons for disagreement with the statistical probabilities,[2] as follows:

1. Causes of overestimation of risk:
   the layman sees little difference between, say, 1% and 0.001%; thus, very low frequency events (for example, tornado, homicide) are overstressed;
   the media extensively cover dramatic events, even if their likelihood is minute; the image remaining in the mind and in the memory magnify the probability estimate;
   technological steps taken to reduce a recently publicized risk are ignored;
   events having some similarity are equated in terms of risk even if the risks are very different (for example, nuclear weapons and nuclear power stations are assumed to be equally dangerous).

---

[1]See particularly the work of Fischhoff et al. (1981) and Slovic et al. (1981); the recent literature review of Covello (1983) is also helpful.

[2]Our wording here is meant to reflect the typical T perspective view of the individual's "ignorance" of the "true," that is, probabilistically derived, risk.

TABLE 32. Physical Risk as Seen from the T, O, and P Perspectives

T	O	P
Probabilistic	Threat to perpetuation (e.g., of nation, family line)	Type of danger (cancer as the "plague" of this century)
Actuarial		
Expected value calculations	Threat to product line, company image	Time for consequences to materialize (discounting remote effects)
Fault trees	Ability to avoid publicity	
Statistical inference	Political sensitivity (voter anger)	Popular image of horror (nuclear accident)
Fail-safe concept	Definition of acceptable risk varies with organization	Personal experience (e.g., survival of a hotel fire)
Margin of safety design		Age of individual a factor
Applicability of precedent designs	Ease of shifting or diffusing blame and liability	Peer esteem (e.g., teenagers and drugs, smoking)
	No single decision maker	
One definition of risk for all	Ex ante compensation to disarm opposition	Popularization of risk (e.g., nuclear plants and *The China Syndrome*)
Quantification of risk essential	Socioeconomic status as determinant of risk acceptance (life "guaranteed safe" in U.S.)	Ethical overlaps (e.g., religion and gene splicing)
	Cost of product recall, ease of litigation	Archetypal values (e.g., virility and guns, fertility and water)
	Standard Operating Procedure	Risk is danger to some, opportunity to others
	Access to expertise on specific risk	

2. Causes of underestimation of risk:

high frequency events may not be given much media coverage (for example, strokes, asthma);[3]

low frequency is interpreted as low danger and ignored even when consequences are catastrophic (for example, reluctance to buy flood or earthquake insurance for residents of floodplain or earthquake regions);

misunderstanding of probability, that is, if a low likelihood event has just occurred, it cannot occur again for a very long time;[4]

---

[3]Strokes kill 85% more people than do accidents; yet people estimate that accidents take 25 times as many lives as strokes. Asthma kills 20 times as many people as do tornadoes; yet people estimate that tornadoes kill about three times as many people as does asthma (Slovic et al., 1981).

[4]Another example of the fallacy: in tossing coins, a string of five heads in a row means that the chance of a tail on the sixth throw must be greater than 0.5.

the individual has personal immunity to risks perceived to be under personal control, that is, voluntary;

long time lag between the event occurrence and the impact (for example, smoking and lung cancer).

In connection with the last statement we recall our discussion of the different time horizons associated with each perspective (Section II H). Obviously, risks with distant (long-term) effects are discounted by many people in comparison with risks that have immediate impact.

The concept of probability, long imbedded in the T perspective, is that of frequency of occurrence of a repeatable event, that is, the limit of the ratio of actual to total possible occurrences as the latter tends to infinity.

For a nonrepeatable or one-time-only event, such as a courtroom trial, football game, or contract bidding competition, the P-based "degree of confidence" of the individual has been grudgingly accepted as a "subjective probability" by the T-oriented fraternity (see statements 13 and 14, Appendix B II). For example, the statement "I think chances are 2 to 1 that A will win" (the case, the game, or the contract, respectively) reflects a personal judgment and perspective.

In risk analysis we often deal with *very* low probabilities. They signal rare events which normally are, and should be, ignored. However, when the consequences of their occurrence spell disaster, for example, a nuclear strike annihilating Washington, D.C., the event cannot be ignored. A frequency of 0.0001 per year, or one attack expected every 10,000 years, is equivalent to less than 70 deaths per year for Washington. A frequency of 0.00001 per year, or one attack every 100,000 years, implies an expected value of less than 7 fatalities annually. As pointed out in the above listing, the layman (and nearly all of us) cannot differentiate meaningfully among such small probabilities. Even if we could, the associated fatality figures would be misleading anyway and the order of magnitude difference, a factor of ten, inconsequential. The event must be related to the O perspective, specifically to a societal life scale. Once we are in the domain of very low probability *cum* very high magnitude effect, both frequency and subjective probabilities, as well as expected values and probability differences, become practically useless. What does matter is 1) the magnitude of the catastrophic event and 2) the *possibility* that this rare occurrence may take place in our, or our offsprings', lifetime. If an entire community can be annihilated in this time frame, our concern is eminently warranted from the O perspective.[5] The possibility that a society can suddenly break its evolutionary continuity is a calamity, whereas the same number of deaths distributed over time and space is far more bearable. The degree of concentration of the effect

---

[5]The discussion here is equally applicable to other societal entities. A corporation may face a risk of small likelihood and great severity. Example: A metals company has large mines in a Third World country that has had a stable military government for 30 years. Although not currently anticipated, a revolution would nationalize the mines and this loss could force the company into bankruptcy.

in time and space may well be a decisive factor in the O perspective. The possibility, rather than the probability, of communal apocalypse and disappearance of the societal entity weighs heavily on its members; it is analogous to the "endangered species" issue.

Herman Kahn's (1960:20–21) risk analysis *On Thermonuclear War* exhibited a clear T perspective in its extensive use of probabilistic calculations. Expected values led to the conclusion that, with 40 million dead, economic recuperation would take 20 years, and the greatly increased amount of human tragedy "would not preclude normal and happy lives for the majority of survivors and their descendants." The percent increase in genetic damage was expected to be tolerable. But we recall Fallows' concern (Chapter I) that these theoretical scenarios have little foundation in fact. The question is: How much worse is the possible, rather than the probable, outcome for the affected society's future? Not surprisingly reactions to Kahn's T-oriented risk analysis were strident. James R. Newman (1961:197), editor of *Scientific American,* called Kahn's work

> . . . a moral tract on mass murder. . . . This evil and tenebrous book is permeated with a bloodthirsty irrationality such as I have not seen in my years of reading.

And fellow RANDite Richard Bellman was impelled to write to the *Washington Post* (March 5, 1961) that a number of RAND experts do not share Kahn's "troglodytic, apocalyptic visions."

IIASA's extensive risk research project on liquified energy gas (LEG) facilities in four countries (Kunreuther et al., 1982) clearly focuses attention on the O perspective as well as T in reviewing the roles of the various organizational actors addressing risks in siting decisions. Consider, for example, the recognition of the importance of the *process* in reaching the decision. The authors note the sequential nature of such decision making and conclude that the final outcome, that is, the siting of an LEG facility, is a strong function of the way the agenda is set. This stress on the process is characteristic of the O perspective (see Table 8). Another indication is the concern with the differing perspectives on risk by the government agencies at various levels, public interest groups, local residents, and the applicant for the site. In a postscript to the work by Michael Thompson, there is even a hint of the P perspective.

> An adequate theory of risk-handling style will have to go below the institutional level and take account of socially induced variations in individual perceptions of risk and in individual strategies towards risk [Kunreuther et al., 1982:370].

In another place Thompson expands on the contribution of the P perspective. On viewing the poor in the framework of risk analysis he writes:

> Oscar Wilde once said: "If only the poor had profiles, there would be no difficulty in solving the problem of poverty." (He meant that) the trouble was that 'the poor'

could only be perceived by the problem-solvers as an anonymous mass. If only they could discern the features of the poor—perceive them in all their individual diversity—the problem would be solved. The irritating thing about Wilde is not that he is so facetious and so witty . . . but that he is usually right as well [Thompson, 1982:28].

Thompson not only recognizes the relationship between the social context and risk selection, that is, the O perspective, but stresses that risk acceptance, risk aversion, and risk absorption are responses to different risk environments, which an individual constructs for himself, that is, a P perspective (Thompson, 1982:44).

Drim et al. (1962) show that risk perception is at least partially dependent on over 40 personality factors, including sex, economic class, need for achievement, prior experience, obedience, and anxiety. Other studies have indicated highly individualistic responses to semantics and setting, to the information giver, and even the time of day.

Tversky and Kahneman (1974) cite many of the biases that inexorably dominate individual perceptions of risk and completely ignore the scientist's model of risk = (probability) × (consequence). As Slovic has pointed out, the public understands consequences, but does not understand probabilities the way a scientist does. And this problem in turn affects the O perspective. Meltsner (1977) in his study of California earthquake risk asks: "If the earthquake hazard is not to be believed on an individual basis, why should the hazard become any more credible on a community basis?" Following are further examples from studies in physical risk acceptance:

- Otway et al. (1975:16) observe that risk perception is important because the response to risk depends on how situations are perceived.

- Velimirovic (1975) discusses risk perception in traditional societies and compares risk behavior with modern societies, that is, an anthropological view.

- Fischhoff (1980) concludes that people's risk perceptions are colored by their own prejudices and even the way the risks are presented.

- Fischhoff et al. (1981:135–137) state "there are no value-free methods for choosing the most acceptable (risk) option . . . the expertise needed for (such) decisions is dispersed throughout society. . . . If each new perspective has some unique contribution, we may want to lend an ear to parties not often heard in policy-making circles—the poor, the philosophers, the artists—in hopes that their life experiences have something illuminating to offer."[6]

---

[6] Of the seven criteria these authors present for evaluating the suitability of approaches to acceptable risk (53–59), six are T or O focused: T—*comprehensive, logically sound,* and *open to evaluation;* O—*practical, politically acceptable,* and *compatible with institutions.* The seventh criterion, *conducive to learning,* may be appropriate for T, O, and P.

- Turner (1982:79) states "While we cannot throw away our reliance upon systematic, rational thought . . . we need to recognize that many human responses cannot be solely considered in terms of an applied rationality, and that matters of organizational responses to hazard cannot be treated solely as isolated technical problems. . . . Organizational responses . . . are interpenetrated by the interorganizational political economy of our society, and by our own cultural assumptions and attitudes towards risk and hazard."

Finally, we turn to country-by-country political risk analysis, an increasingly popular consulting service provided to international business. Clients are corporations such as Arco, Merck, Bechtel, Goldman Sachs, and Chase Manhattan Bank. Consultants include Henry Kissinger, former National Security Advisor Brent Scowcroft, and CIA alumni William Colby, Richard Helms, Ray S. Cline, and others. The Association of Political Risk Consultants claims to have 375 members in 1983. The comment of an executive of Arco, a client of Kissinger Associates, implies that the inadequacy of the T perspective is appreciated: "You can't quantify political risk. It's judgmental" (*New York Times,* Aug. 7, 1983). Economic and other quantitative aggregations of data, for example social indicators, are not enough. Dror's *Crazy States* (1980) also gives a sterling demonstration of the failure of the rational actor perspective. Going beyond the T perspective calls for insider understanding of local political and social entities' views, as well as native individuals' perspectives. The O perspectives should encompass government and opposition groups; the P perspective must include the elite and the poor, the idiosyncracies of the leaders and their opponents.

It is apparent that risk analysis has plunged successfully into multiple perspectives in recent years. This discussion suffices to establish the link and suggest that it merits much deeper exploration in both directions. Thus the insights already gained in the personal perception of risk should prove useful in applying the P perspective elsewhere, while the experience with the O perspective in business applications may benefit risk analysis.

B. MULTIPLE PERSPECTIVES IN TECHNOLOGICAL FORECASTING

It is a common practice to divide technological forecasting into two complementary types: 1) exploratory or capability forecasts and 2) normative or needs forecasts (Martino, 1972:287). The former focus on what *can* be done in the future, based on the past and present technological capability; the latter focus on what *ought* to be done in the future. Not surprisingly, exploratory forecasts almost always have a dominant T orientation. They involve extrapolations of technology trends as well as analytic models of growth and substitution. In theory, the long planning horizon or low discount rate associated with the T perspective should be of direct benefit to such forecasts. While analysts do use a low discount rate for the future, we observe that they are sometimes inclined to apply a considerably higher discount rate to the past. For example, they may pay excessive attention to short-term trends, extrapolating on the basis of recent historical data only and thus missing the more meaningful, less distorted longer term trend, that is, the "envelope curve" (cf Marchetti, 1977 ff).

The O and P perspectives may insinuate themselves quite subtly into exploratory forecasts. The analyst's tool kit does not force his attention on assumptions and professional biases. These may be based on years of personal involvement in a narrow aspect of technology and communication with peers who think of the future in terms of the same descriptors of capability (see Martino, 1972:566–571).

On the other hand, dominance of the T perspective on the part of the technological forecaster also has an important consequence: It tends to drive him inexorably toward greater technological sophistication in addressing future needs. It is rare to find other options of satisfying needs given equal consideration. We see the result in the imbalance in the intelligence field (Toth, 1980), in the unending efforts to advance technological solutions in the Vietnam conflict, and in the reliance on technical analyses in strategic military planning (Fallows, 1981).

Needs analyses usually reflect the O perspective of the client organization or the P perspective of the forecaster far more strongly than do capability forecasts (Linstone, 1969). A case in point is the defense establishment. We already observed the importance of the O perspective in the case of the Navy's *USS Wampanoag* and the Army's M-16 rifle (Section VA). In both cases, the contemporary analyst would have done poorly if he had ignored the O perspective and based his technological forecast strictly on a future capability estimate using the T perspective.

From 1959 to 1970, Linstone directed four corporate planning "needs analyses" in the area of national defense and space programs. By the time of the fourth of these privately funded projects, our T perspective analysts had made an important discovery: "The gap between what is needed and what is marketable means that a 'needs analysis' is, in fact, a mirage" (Project MIRAGE 85, 1970:116). Our "need" is determined as much by what we like and are comfortable with as by the purely technical requirements. Pilots want aircraft to fly, so that an all-missile force would be organizationally unpalatable, even if technically feasible. It would be a "destructive energy" in the Air Force society just as the *USS Wampanoag* was for the post-Civil War Navy (Section VA1).

Advancement in the Navy traditionally requires experience in commanding ships. Thus the availability of an adequate number of ships must be given consideration in developing normative forecasts.

The familiar adage "the military are always planning to fight the last war over again with better weapons" underscores the centrality of the O perspective. The construction of the Maginot Line in France in the early 1930s assumed that a future war with Germany would be a war of firepower, like World War I, rather than a war of mobility. Yet the technology of tanks and aircraft was clearly advancing at the time. Nor were the slowly changing concepts and standard operating procedures confined to the French military planners. The German High

Command also had little faith in highly mobile warfare and tended to see the future through a rear-view mirror. The *Blitzkrieg* of 1940 was the product of the planning of Hitler and three generals who were outsiders to the vaunted General Staff: von Manstein, von Rundstedt, and Guderian (Rowe, 1959:62,127). Hitler's charisma and personal power meant that a maverick P perspective overcame an entrenched O perspective.

A priority needs list based solely on a T perspective looks very different from one based on, say, T *and* O perspectives. The T perspective takes account of King Richard III's lament, "For the want of a nail the shoe was lost. . . ." so that the list would include unglamorous items such as changes in training and maintenance procedures or in communications equipment. However, a list based on both T and O features the more prestigious items in the firepower and vehicle areas—glamorous aircraft, ships, and weaponry.[7] As Representative J. P. Addabbo (D., N.Y.) recently observed, "the Pentagon doesn't like anything that's small" (*Sunday Oregonian*, April 10, 1983:A14).

In the nonmilitary area, an example of the O perspective determining "needs" is found in the electric utility industry, the largest single sector of the U.S. economy with net assets of about $250 billion. Their claim that healthy industry growth requires an increase of at least 3% annually in electrical demand implies a total capital investment of about $1 trillion by the year 2000 (Lovins and Lovins, 1982:156). In the eyes of Wall Street, there is increasing danger that utilities are overspending themselves into insolvency. Their ingrained O perspective prevents many of them from recognizing that they should view themselves as purveyors, not of electricity, but of energy services (or the financial means of acquiring them). Such a shift could brighten their futures dramatically.

The dialectic approach often seen in the O perspective is beautifully illustrated by the history of energy resource forecasts in the United States. As Wildavsky and Tenenbaum (1981) have shown, the deep division between industrial interests and conservationists on oil and gas resources was already apparent in the early 1900s. Each side seized on the 1908 U.S. Geological Survey (USGS) estimates to confirm its policy stand.[8] Many forecasts have been made since then. Except for the World War I and II periods, each faction habitually accuses the other of manipulating these forecasts for its own selfish purposes. Table 33 suggests the different views on resource forecasts. It becomes clear that the forecasts are the servants of policies already determined or preferred rather than being prerequisites for policy formulation. The T perspective quests for more accurate forecasts in this area are thus rather irrelevant.

---

[7]Examples: Although close air support of ground forces is an extremely important air mission of maneuver warfare, the Air Force prefers strategic bombing, and is traditionally unenthusiastic about the subservient and unglamorous mission to assist tactical Army operations. It prefers the faster F-16 fighter to the slower A-10 even though slow speed may be vital in this task. Similarly, the glamorous new Bradley infantry fighting vehicle (nearly $2 million each) is preferred by the Army to its 1960 M-113 armored personnel carrier ($80,000 each) despite the former's severe operational handicaps (*Time*, March 7, 1983:14).

[8]At that time, USGS forecasted total U.S. oil resources between 10 and 24.5 billion barrels and indicated that we would run out of oil between 1935 and 1943. In 1974, USGS (Vincent McKelvey) estimated a range between 200 and 400 billion barrels.

**Another Organizational Perspective
on the Navy's Career Officers**

Defense lawyer Barney Greenwald after a few drinks at a party celebrating the
court martial acquittal of Lt Steve Maryk, executive officer of the mine sweeper
USS *Caine* (the proceeding effectively destroyed the Navy career of its commanding
officer, Capt. Queeg, nicknamed "Old Yellowstain"):

> I'm coming to Old Yellowstain. Coming to him. See, while I was studying
> law 'n' old Keefer here was writing his play for the Theater Guild, and Willie
> here was on the playing fields of Prinshton, all that time these birds we call
> regulars—these stuffy, stupid Prussians, in the Navy and the Army—were
> manning guns. Course they weren't doing it to save my mom from Hitler,
> they were doing it for dough, like everybody else does what they do. Question
> is, in the last analysis—last analysis—*what* do you do for dough? Old Yel-
> lowstain, for dough, was standing guard on this fat dumb and happy country
> of ours. Meantime me, I was advancing my little free non-Prussian life for
> dough. Of course, we figured in those days, only fools go into armed service.
> Bad pay, no millionaire future, and you can't call your mind or body your
> own. Not for sensitive intellectuals. So when all hell broke loose and the
> Germans started running out of soap and figured, well it's time to come over
> and melt down old Mrs Greenwald—who's gonna stop them? Not her boy
> Barney. Can't stop a Nazi with a lawbook. So I dropped the lawbooks and
> ran to learn how to fly. Stout fellow. Meantime, and it took a year and a half
> before I was any good, who was keeping Mama out of the soap dish? Captain
> Queeg.
>
> Yes, even Queeg, poor sad guy, yes, and most of them not sad at all,
> fellows, a lot of them sharper boys than any of us, don't kid yourself, best
> men I've ever seen, you can't be good in the Army or Navy unless you're
> goddamn good. Though maybe not up on Proust 'n' *Finnegan's Wake* and
> all.

(H Wouk, *The Caine Mutiny*, pp 446–447)*

*For a discussion of the question of denial of individual responsibility vs loyalty to the system raised by
The Caine Mutiny, see Whyte, 1956: 269–275.

In cases where a forecast is done by organization A for client B and few
constraints are imposed by B, the biases of A may be decisive for the forecast.
If A is experienced in a certain forecasting technique, it is likely to prefer its
use in responding to B—whether or not it is most suitable. A may also be
subconsciously influenced by the possibility of future grants or contracts from
B—and avoid forecasts that may alarm B.

Thus the organizational perspective explains constraints and core assumptions
which strongly affect the forecasts (Ascher, 1978:199). Standard operating pro-

TABLE 33. An O Perspective on Oil Reserve Forecasts

	When prices are high	When prices are low
Industrialists favor	High forecasts	Low forecasts
	"Major new supplies can be found if prices are high."	"Higher prices are needed to bring on more supplies."
Consumers favor	Low forecasts	High forecasts
	"Oil is no longer the solution."	"No need to raise prices."
Conservationists favor	Low forecasts	Low forecasts
	"High prices encourage overproduction."	"Low prices encourage overconsumption."

Source: Wildavsky and Tenenbaum, 1981:300.

cedures, morale needs, as well as incrementalism and tradition determine the forecasts in important ways. And the personal perspective also merits recognition. In a thoughtful essay on "Why Forecasters Flubbed the '70's," *Time* (Jan. 21, 1980) recognized a paradox:

1. forecasters remain human beings and, as such, have optimistic or pessimistic biases;
2. forecasters are "triumphantly rationalistic," and exaggerate this aspect in human behavior.

One often wishes the forecasting community would exhibit such awareness of the "self."

As noted in Section XI E 2, one technique which openly admits O and P perspectives is Delphi (Linstone and Turoff, 1975). It can preserve P-focused individuality, that is, it will not suppress the maverick, because no consensus is forced. In its early stages of development, it was viewed primarily as a forecasting technique, and this remains a major area of application.

In sum, the conscious use of multiple perspectives in technological forecasting should prove quite valuable—at the very least they bring to the surface vital core assumptions and minimize self-delusion.

C. MULTIPLE PERSPECTIVES IN CORPORATE PLANNING

This is another important area where the potential of the multiple perspective concept is apparent.[9] Most major corporations today have planning units, variously termed "corporate development," "strategic planning," "business planning," etc. (Halal, 1980). There are many models of the planning cycle (for

---

[9]In this connection, also recall the illustrations in Chapter VI.

example, 4, 7, 9, or 12 steps), and much has been written about various analytical aspects, such as forecasting techniques, top down and retrogressive planning, cybernetic modeling of the corporation, and environmental scanning. These reflect the T perspective of the analyst.

Figure 8 has already alerted us to the fundamental dilemma encountered if we move beyond near-term planning: the O and P perspectives tend to have a much shorter planning horizon than the T perspective (Section IV C 2). Yet the executive rightly feels that he needs the multiple perspectives. It appears, therefore, that he must either forego strategic planning or rely on his own resources to augment the T perspective. Halal (1980:57–58), in his survey of strategic management in 25 major U.S. corporations, found that:

> skillful executives do not rely primarily upon the outcome of formal planning. . . . They base their decisions on heuristically derived knowledge that is internally tested and found to be intuitively true and senseful, rather than upon a literal interpretation of complex data and analyses that often seem esoteric and doubtful. . . . The decision maker continually gathers opinions, pieces of data, new ideas, etc., through exchanges with persons that are trusted and respected. . . . The essence of strategic decision making, therefore, is remarkably similar to the process that has been described by artists, writers, scientists, and others who are involved in producing creative works.

Increasingly, corporations are becoming convinced that "an operating manager is his own best strategist" and are cutting back their T-focused planning staffs. We already noted the importance of intuition to executives in the quotations in Section IV B 3. There are some leaders who have an unusually long planning horizon; their P perspective reaches out beyond that of their associates and leads them to effective strategic planning. The alternative is to replace such planning by experimentation.

Recently, Peters and Waterman (1982) studied 43 particularly well-run U.S. companies. They also concluded that success is correlated to the ability to go beyond the "rational model," that is, beyond the T perspective. The most effective managers are biased toward action rather than analyzing a problem to death. They are people oriented, and they encourage individuals to innovate—to a degree that may seem to verge on irrationality. And they don't penalize experiments that fail, but use them as important learning experiences (see the City Manager's comment in Section X B 1, p. 270).

Not surprisingly, strategic planning consulting firms are broadening their thinking beyond strategy to include staff, style, skills, systems (of communication), structure, and shared values—the inevitable acronym: "The Seven Ss." The interaction among these is seen as the basis for incremental forward movement of the company (Kiechel, 1982b:39). It should be obvious that this shift signifies a *de facto* change to multiple perspectives.

The CEO may indeed see the role of strategic planning as one of raising the awareness of his people in the future, extending their usual horizon, and reducing their parochialism. This role may be far more valuable than the generation of formal plans. Too often a division adopts a defensive attitude due to fear of the future (for example, new business line development seen by a department as a threat to its own integrity) or inbreeding leads to fatal misjudgment of the environment (for example, ritualistic trend extrapolation using obsolete core assumptions).

Attention to the complacency-inducing effect of shared values two decades ago might have shocked our automobile industry into vigorous action. Yates (1983) addresses himself to this situation in his study of *The Decline and Fall of the American Automobile Industry*. In the words of a former General Motors executive, Detroit's auto executives "live together, they work together, they drink together, they play golf together, they think together." The result is executive myopia in planning.[10] The top executives are yearly given cream-of-the-crop cars that are maintained free of charge for them, washed daily, and filled with gas in the company garage. Thus they do not sense the aggravations of the common, garden variety car owner. The executives are concerned that their cars ride comfortably on Michigan's flat highways, start and stay warm in the cold winters, keep cool in the hot summers, and carry a family and its gear to and from Upper Peninsula summer homes. This they accomplish beautifully. In all fairness, it should be pointed out that the Mercedes and BMW, built within 100 miles of the Alps, analogously reflect their executives' concern with mountain driving, for example, precise steering.

It is increasingly evident that many other American corporations have suffered severely from this handicap—one only needs to point to the shipbuilding and steel sectors (see also Hayes and Abernathy, 1980). In a society that is undergoing a rapid and profound shift—from industrial to information society—even an individual corporation's far-sighted manager/strategist or its extensive in-house experimentation may not suffice.

Let us use an analogy. Driving a car in the darkness of night on an unfamiliar highway requires either high-beam headlights or a reduction in speed. If another car does have high-beam headlights and we do not, it will soon overtake us.

In Japan, the government long ago recognized the limitations of industrial long-range planning. It created the Ministry of International Trade and Industry (MITI), before World War II, to formulate and facilitate implementation of "industrial policy." Thus a focal point for long-range planning is provided, and it becomes action-directed. The dominant perspectives are two: 1) the technical and 2) the national as O perspective. Such planning subordinates any individual corporation's O perspective to that of the country, a situation often characterized as "Japan, Inc."[11]

---

[10]Akron's tire and rubber industry has suffered similarly from shared values, as was noted in Section IXB2 and Table 25.

[11]This does not mean that intraindustry competition is stifled. Examples: Japan has nine automakers, the U.S. five; Japan has five mainframe computer manufacturers, the U.S. ten, Europe three (Sawada, 1983). Neither does it imply that the corporate leadership is forced to accept MITI's recommendations. Soichiro Honda, for example, did not follow MITI's advice concerning the U.S. market, preferring to rely on his own advisers and experience (Honda, 1983).

In a flexible and pragmatic manner, MITI has served as a catalyst to assist Japanese industry to:

- reconstruct key sectors after the almost total destruction of World War II, for example, electric power, coal, iron, steel, and fertilizer companies in the 1945–1952 period;
- pursue a "dynamic comparative advantage strategy" in capital-intensive sectors with high growth potential and higher added value, for example, synthetic textiles, petrochemicals, machinery in the 1952–1960 period;
- follow a "trade liberalization strategy" in the 1960–1973 period;
- initialize a "positive or active industrial policy" to support promising sectors for the 1980s and an "adjustive industrial policy" to deal with declining sectors (both policies since 1973) [Sawada, 1983].

Knowledge-intensive, high-technology industries are being nurtured through subsidies (for example, for super large-scale integration research involving five firms), and alternative energy sources are given strong R&D assistance.[12] On the other hand, the high-cost coal mining, textile, and basic material industries have been declining. Long-range planning in such cases focuses on adjustment (for example, disposing of obsolete excess capacity, joint ventures in developing countries) or phase-out, while protectionism is eschewed. MITI helped the shipbuilding industry to scrap over 40% of its capacity when it became less competitive in the 1970s.[13]

There is an unexpected and thought-provoking implication that evolves from MITI's effective long-range planning ability. Recent work by Mensch (1979) and Graham and Senge (1980) on technological innovation strongly indicates that there is a connection between Kondratieff (approximately) 50-year economic cycles and technological innovations. A Kondratieff cycle comprises the sequence prosperity-recession-depression-recovery. Technological advances are classified as follows:

- basic invention: discovery of a new idea or technical process;
- basic innovation: the first practical application of the invention on a significant scale, creating a new type of human activity;
- improvement innovation: incremental advances of an existing technology that do not alter its fundamental nature.

The interest here is in basic inventions and basic innovations. The most interesting findings are that 1) basic inventions and basic innovations cluster, the latter

---

[12]MITI is providing $400 to $500 million to the Fifth Generation Computer Project for hardware R&D (*Business Week*, Dec. 14, 1981). A few years ago, it helped to put Mitsubishi, Kawasaki, and Fuji into the commercial airframe business.

[13]By contrast, the United States continues to spend $500 million per year and provides $6.3 billion in loans and loan guarantees to prop up its ailing shipbuilding industry (Magaziner and Reich, 1982:250–252). Until recently, Great Britain followed a similar policy.

distribution showing much less dispersion than the former, and 2) the clustering correlates well with the Kondratieff cycles.

Specifically, basic innovations come in spurts at the end of the depression phase of the cycle. When the economy is moving through recovery and prosperity, the emphasis is on "safe" improvement innovations rather than the more risky basic innovations. At the end of a depression, there appears to be greater willingness to move into more radical innovations. As an example of this correlation, the end of the Great Depression saw a bunching of major basic innovations. The period from 1930 to 1945 introduced atomic energy, jet engines, computers, nylon, and radar—each creating new industries.

The implication of the Kondratieff cycle is that the next bunching of basic innovations will occur prior to the year 2000. Obvious candidates include bioengineered drugs, home information systems, robotic systems, and electric cars.

Basic innovations cannot be judged using conventional payback periods and discount rates. Their returns are slow at first and huge later (Graham and Senge, 1980:306). The MITI's focus on long-range planning is thus particularly compatible with the pursuit of basic innovations and may place Japan in a uniquely favorable position to exploit the next cluster period.

Not surprisingly, MITI resonates with the private sector in its attitude toward technology assessment. Like nearly all of U.S. industry, Japanese companies and much of MITI's staff view TA, like environmental impact studies, as a hindrance to the desired pace of technological development (Randolph and Koppel, 1982:366–367; see also Footnote 5 of Chapter II).

The Japanese approach is interesting because it shows how a change in O perspective—from single corporation to ministry—can overcome the inadequacies in planning horizon. At first glance, it would appear that there is a U.S. counterpart in at least one area: the U.S. Department of Defense. It takes responsibility for long-range planning, for example, in strategic weapon systems. But the analogy is superficial: it is itself the client (or customer), and we have seen (Sections V A and X II B) that its O perspective may make it at times more past than future oriented.

France also has a tradition of national strategic planning in support of the private sector. Its administrative elite developed a sophisticated planning process under General de Gaulle. Corporations are encouraged to participate by means of government subsidies, orders, and favors. The 1967 Plan Calcul in the information technology area, for example, provided 1906 million French francs in assistance to French computer manufacturers (Botkin et al., 1982).

Indeed, the O perspective contributes in several ways to an understanding of U.S. difficulties in retaining its leadership in the shift of the advanced countries from an industrial, capital-based society to an information, knowledge-based one. Two more examples:

- The Japanese concept of management melds the people in the organization in the sense that a) each person is exposed to the others' P perspectives (for example, through discussions, job rotation) and b) the resulting poly-

ocular vision of each person facilitates mutual accommodation and formation of an O perspective. Superficially it would appear that the organization and its people are "synonymous" (Peters and Waterman, 1982:39).
It is more accurate to say that this flexible process reinforces societal
cohesion—and this, in turn, makes a major shift in the society easier to
accomplish. Americans tend to prize individualism and self-interest over
national interest except in time of all-out war. Thus the planning horizon
tends to be restricted and national strategic planning weak, specifically in
comparison to that of Japan and France in the high-technology sector.

* Older organizations have more political power than budding ones, hence
more influence in governmental decisions. Labor unions are strong in
obsolete industries, and large old enterprises have had a long time to
develop political ties. By contrast, young companies are naive politically
and ineffective. Hence, the obsolescent companies obtain government assistance much more readily. The one major exception in the United States
is the military/industrial complex. Its success may be in no small part due
to the unique and fortuitous bond between politically potent old components, the Army and Navy, and young high-tech components, the Air
Force and aerospace/electronics companies.[14]

As the O perspective points to the U.S. disadvantages, the P perspective helps
to focus on this country's advantages. There are unmatched opportunities to
transform individualism into leadership. Botkin et al. (1982) suggest the following recent examples collectively as one American response to MITI's activities
in advanced information technology:

1. A governor's initiative:
   James B. Hunt, Jr, Governor of North Carolina, was instrumental in obtaining a $24.4 million grant from his state legislature for construction,
   equipment, and initial operating costs of the Microelectronics Center of
   North Carolina. Hunt is unfazed by state bureaucracy and feels that:

   only the governor can bring it all together. I doubt you'll ever get maximum effort
   without a strong governor. You need the leader who will go out and take the initiative
   to get more resources [Botkin et al., 1982:106].

---

[14]A concrete result: the growing dependence on extremely sophisticated and expensive weapon systems with
relatively low combat readiness. As a 1980 Pentagon systems analysis warned: "Our strategy of pursuing ever
increasing technical complexity and sophistication has made high technology solutions and combat readiness
mutually exclusive." (*Time*, March 7, 1983:16) Note that the effect is a striking reversal of the situation prior to
World War II and the formation of the military-industrial complex, for example, the Navy's resistance to the
advanced *USS Wampanoag* a century earlier (Section VA1). In both cases, it would be impossible to explain the
defense procurement program without resorting to the O perspective, that is, by a T perspective alone. (See also
Section B of this chapter).

2. A corporate vice-president's initiative:

   Erich Bloch, an IBM executive, was the mover in creating a consortium of some 20 corporations to eventually channel $50 million annually into pure research in semiconductors and computers. This Semiconductor Research Cooperative will direct its commitment to a handful of universities for work in selected generic areas. This approach will simultaneously enhance the supply and quality of degreed professionals.

3. A corporate president's initiative:

   John Young, the Chief Executive of Hewlett–Packard, has taken the lead in inducing 17 companies to contribute $13 million for the creation of a Center for Integrated Systems at Stanford University. The Center is expected to do research in computer science and electrical engineering as well as provide 100 master's degrees and 30 doctorates annually. The U.S. Department of Defense is contributing another $8 million.

4. A university professor's initiative:

   Robert M. Hexter, Professor of Chemistry at the University of Minnesota, developed another university/industry partnership to upgrade electrical engineering/computer science education and research. The Microelectronics and Information Systems Center at the University of Minnesota was initially capitalized with $6 million to be applied toward matching grants from other sources.

5. A former Defense Department executive's initiative:

   William Perry, a recent Under Secretary of Defense for Research and Engineering, recognized the need for an Electronics Education Foundation and helped the American Electronics Association set it up. High-technology industry members are expected to contribute 2% of their current research and development budgets to a pool for use primarily in grants to raise faculty salaries ($10,000 each) and support students through fellowships ($15,000 each).

6. A computer entrepreneur's initiative:

   Dr. An Wang, founder of Wang Laboratories, has created the Wang Institute of Graduate Studies. It is neither a trade school nor a feeder for his company; rather, it is attempting to provide top quality master's level education in software engineering. High salaries are attracting a first-rate faculty, and the stifling constraints of traditional academic settings are avoided.

A schematic representation of the corporate planning perspectives based on Figure 5 is shown in Figure 23. Issues may arise from the interplay of any of the elements shown (see also Figure 4b). Examples are the company's products with the physical or technological environment, the business units with competitors and governmental agencies, key individuals with each other, and the products with their external societal environment. The recognition of the exis-

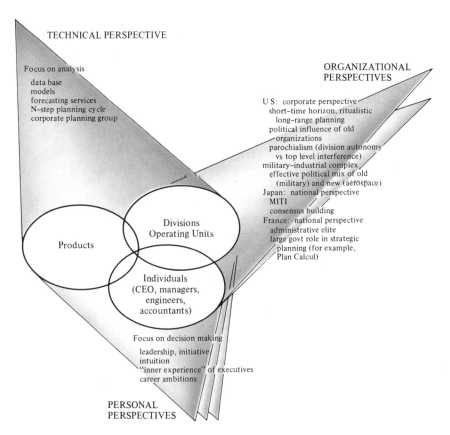

FIGURE 23. Multiple perspectives in corporate planning.

tence of issues and their definition depend strongly on the perspective; as values vary, so will the ranking of issues. The significance of sports fishing (Section VI A) and values of Indian tribes (Linstone, 1981c) to hydropower development cannot be captured by the T perspective, but becomes apparent with the O and P perspectives. Similarly, the different issue emphases faced by a utility in developing liquified energy gas facilities in different countries become evident only through the use of multiple perspectives (Kunreuther et al., 1982). Thus issues management is strengthened.

One practical advantage of the multiple perspective concept not previously stressed is its potential to compress the time for the decision-making process. The simultaneous attention to several perspectives not only facilitates cross-cuing, but shortens the need for serial consideration of different perspectives. The executive saves considerable time if he can short-circuit the more conventional procedure, that is, ordering a lengthy T perspective analysis, recognizing its limitations, then seeking organizational perspective input, and finally soliciting various individual perspectives. Furthermore, he can thereby reduce the total *cost* because the T analyst knows that he may concentrate on those aspects that lend themselves to a T perspective and need not worry about the others being pursued in parallel. Thus none of the perspectives waste time searching for the Holy Grail of comprehensiveness.

Finally, even the stock market can readily be seen in terms of our perspectives. In *The Mind of the Market* (1981:20–21), Charles Smith observes:

> Why is the [stock] market so contradictory? The most important roots of these contradictions are the conflicting perspectives different persons have of the market and the different interpretations of market events which these varying perspectives generate. . . .Different assumptions regarding the underlying structure generate very different accounts of 'what' is happening.

He identifies four professional perspectives:

1. *The Fundamentalist.* Market values reflect local, national, and global *economic* conditions. The *New York Times, Wall Street Journal,* and *Barron's* are avidly read. The general attitude is that of a conservative financial advisor.
2. *The Cyclist/Chartist.* There are underlying patterns and rhythms to be grasped, a transcendent *order* to be discovered.
3. *The Insider.* Institutional influences and social relationships are the key. Contacts are nourished and "the boys with the money" are watched to draw forth inside information. People are more important than reports as sources.
4. *The Trader.* The market is a sporting game in which intuition and chance are important. There must be a "feel for the market." Psychology is appreciated: some companies catch the imagination of the street while others do not. We also have the spectacle of the brokerage house "groupies" trailing with pencil and paper the current in-house guru who has a hot streak picking stocks to buy and sell.

In our terms of reference (1) and (2) are T perspectives (the former quasi-Lockean, the latter quasi-Leibnizian), (3) is an O perspective, and (4) is P. Smith notes, however, that few professionals are pure, that is, true believers who rely solely on one perspective. Usually their perspective is more fuzzy; the balance or mix is apt to be influenced by the immediate objective, for example, selling stocks or newsletters. Not surprisingly the result for the consumer is often confusion. Smith (1981:153) concludes:

> What our analysis of the market indicates is that it is useless to attempt to select one orientation, one logic or one purpose and ignore the others; it indicates that [the] mind is inherently multi-facet and any attempt to deny this will only lead to an incomplete picture of whatever subject is being studied.

D. AREAS FOR RESEARCH

The reader who has arrived at this point will have noted diverse fertile areas for further (interparadigmatic) research. We simply list some of the most interesting ones here.[15]

1. Differential Discounting (Sections II H and IV C 2)

The T, O, and P perspectives tend to have different discount rates, hence different planning horizons (Figure 8). This mismatch inhibits important tasks, such as strategic planning. We do not know enough about the variations among organizations and individuals. Is there much variation among Third World nations in discount rate? What is the significance of socioeconomic status in determining rates for individuals?

Means to reduce the gap in time horizons also deserve attention. Linstone (1973; 1975) has suggested two ways (Figure 24): 1) moving the distant crisis or opportunity well within the organization's or individual's current planning horizon or 2) extending the present planning horizon farther out. As noted earlier, we discount in physical space as well as time (Figure 24a). Telecommunications have been successful in drastically foreshortening the space dimension, for example, bringing the distant Apollo landing and Kennedy assassination events vividly into our living room. Technology has been far less effective in foreshortening the time dimension. Orson Welles' broadcast of H.G. Wells' *War of the Worlds* is a rare example. In some instances it may be possible to substitute space for time and then compress the space dimension by telecommunications (arrow S in Figure 24a). Distant space/near time is used as a surrogate for distant

FIGURE 24. Space time perception: (a) moving crisis or opportunity closer; (b) extending perception out. *Source: Linstone, 1973:337.*

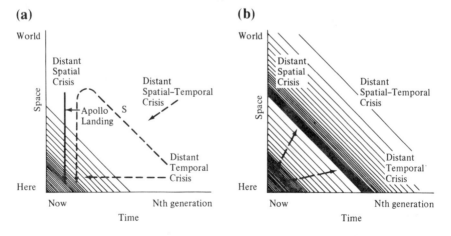

---

[15]We have not forgotten our "nagging worry" of Section IV C 6. Possibly the concept of "interparadigmatic research" itself should head the list of areas to be examined.

time/near space. A future situation of concern to us will be more readily comprehensible if we can find a current analog somewhere else in the world. Option 2 may be achievable by the slower process of education, particularly at the elementary and high school levels. Japan's MITI can be seen as an organizational approach to extending the planning horizon (Section XII C). Its longer range view permits it to serve as *de facto* strategic planner for Japanese corporations where desired.

2. Improvement in Forecasting (Section XII B)

The significance of the O and P perspectives for normative forecasting has been described. They are unavoidably entwined in the core assumptions that constitute "the major determinants of forecast accuracy" (Ascher, 1978:199). Work is now in progress on analyzing the forecasting process of the Bonneville Power Administration in terms of multiple perspectives (Sapp, 1983). Detailed examination of the impact of O and P perspectives on selected governmental agency and corporate forecasts would provide a basis for developing guidelines to improve the process.

Duncan's (1969:112–114) review of the state-of-the-art of social forecasting proposes the idea of cohort analysis as a means to improve our understanding of social change. The concept has, of course, been exploited in demographic forecasts for several decades. Its wider use is based on the reasonable assumption that each cohort develops its own perspective on issues. This perspective is developed during the formative years (in home and school) and strengthened by constant contact with peers. Thus each cohort has its own biography and will respond differently to external stimuli. The potential of developing "cohort perspectives" in some depth (O_1, O_2, O_3, . . .) as a tool in social forecasting deserves study.

3. Risk Analysis (Section XII A)

The centrality of individual and group perceptions of physical risk, as contrasted to actuarial or statistically calculated risk, is now recognized even by strongly T-oriented analysts (Starr and Whipple, 1980). The importance of the subject today suggests the desirability of research to shed light on the question: Does the conscious use of multiple perspectives signficantly increase the insights in risk analysis?

Case studies are needed on both voluntary, individually controlled risks (for example, smoking or drug use) and involuntary risks not individually controlled (for example, nuclear radiation, carbon dioxide air pollution, chemical waste management).

4. Identification of T-O-P Balance in Individuals (Section IV C)

It is important in any application of the multiple perspective concept to draw in diverse perspectives and simultaneously to avoid mistaking one perspective for another. Does a specific O perspective put forward in an interview really represent the designated organization, or is it actually a personal perspective? It would be desirable to develop means to facilitate the identification of a perspective type or dominance of one perspective in a mix. The problem is related to that of determining psychological profiles. Appendix C suggests a start in this direction, but much deeper examination of this subject is in order. Another facet of considerable interest is the stability or instability of perspectives and mixes held by individuals.

5. Cross-Cuing and Integration of Perspectives (Sections IV C 5 and XI E)

A decision maker frequently is presented with a series of perspectives that are then "processed" in his mind and lead to a decision. Similarly, a jury hears witnesses and summations by the attorneys, "processes" such input, and reaches a decision. In each case, the "process" may well be a mysterious one, difficult to predict or even to analyze *a posteriori*. How does one perspective support or neutralize another? Why is one perspective weighted heavily and another ignored? There exists no neat formula for integrating perspectives. (If there were, the analyst could do the integration for the decision maker—and possibly even replace him altogether!)

The subtleties and complexities of this "process" are such that we do not anticipate a "solution."[16] However, research may begin to illuminate some aspects of the process and inform the analyst about the number and variety of perspectives to use.

6. Communication Techniques for O and P Perspectives (Section IV C 3)

Means to obtain input and transmit output for the O and P perspectives certainly differ significantly from those familiar to T perspective analysts. Interviews clearly play an important role but other methods, such as participant observation and guided group dialogue, require closer examination in connection with the multiple perspective concept. Lendaris' survey (1979) offers a suitable starting point.

This brief list gives ample evidence that, with this book, we have only taken a few steps on a very challenging and fascinating path.

---

[16]Indeed, a "solution" would have awesome implications. Computers might then be programmed to perform high level decision making and initiate the replacement of top level executives!

XIII

GUIDELINES FOR USERS
OF MULTIPLE PERSPECTIVES

H. LINSTONE and A. J. MELTSNER

ALICE B. TOKLAS (AT HER DYING FRIEND'S BEDSIDE): "Gertrude,
  Gertrude, what is the answer?"
GERTRUDE STEIN: "What is the question?"

For us there is only the trying, the rest is not our business.

    T. S. Eliot

In this final chapter, we translate the lessons learned into 16 guidelines that, we hope, will be useful to those who wish to apply multiple perspectives. *The discussion is relevant to a broad spectrum of sociotechnical systems in contexts of governmental policy making, corporate strategic planning, issues management, regional development, or systems implementation.*

A. EXPERIENCES TO DATE

The first classroom exercises using multiple perspectives were carried out by Linstone in January–March 1977 in the University of Washington's Program for the Social Management of Technology. Students individually developed term papers on subjects of their own choosing. The subject had to have both social and technological content and permit personal information gathering by the student. Excellent term papers using the three perspectives were developed on subjects such as the West Seattle freeway extension, the cruise missile, and a local methadone project.

The multiple perspective concept has now become the heart of the last quarter of the basic three-quarter graduate course "The Systems Approach" in the Systems Science Doctoral Program at Portland State University. Three of the illustrations in Chapters V and VI—the Atomic Bomb Use Decision (Section V A 3), the Willamette Falls Hydroelectric Project (Section VI A), and the Electronic System Market (Section VI B)—were originally prepared as student term papers.

The concept was used in the doctoral dissertation on Perinatal Regionalization, which is condensed into the case study in Chapter VII, Sections XI A and XI E 2. It was also introduced into a technology assessment recently carried out for the Institute for Water Resources of the U.S. Army Corps of Engineers by a team including several contributors to this volume (Linstone et al., 1981c). The subject of the six-month effort was National Hydropower Development over the next 20 years. Another doctoral dissertation now in progress is examining the influence of the different perspectives on the Bonneville Power Administration's forecasting process (Sapp, 1983).

We have found that multiple perspectives are easily taught and grasped, not only by graduate students in U.S. universities, but by practitioners in other countries. In March 1981, it was included in a workshop presented at the Applied Chemistry Research Institute (CIQA) in Saltillo, Mexico. The exercise there was based on the guayule case examined in Chapter IX.

In April 1981, an exercise on multiple perspectives was conducted in the context of the Policy Analysis and Planning Workshop sponsored by the United Nations Development Program in Vina del Mar, Chile. A sketch of the exercise follows. The group consisted of 20 students (male and female, aged 25 to 35) and all were previously unfamiliar with the concept. Many did not have a working command of English, and simultaneous translation was used. One morning (about four hours) was devoted to an explanation of multiple perspectives for the entire group, using material from this work. Slides and a blackboard were available for this purpose.

One afternoon was given to an exercise applying the concept. The problem: a hypothetical regional economic development plan formulated by GEICOS.[1] This plan involves four countries—Argentina, Bolivia, Chile, and Paraguay— in the creation of a port outlet for their imports and exports in northern Chile. The students were familiar with the general outlines of the GEICOS concept. They were divided into four groups of five students each. Their task was to consider the port development from the following perspectives (each group one perspective):

a. technical,
b. organizational—GEICOS executive staff,
c. organizational—an agency in a participating government,
d. individual—a stevedore at the port of Antofagasta before and after announcement of the port outlet development by GEICOS.

Each group was asked to summarize its perspective in written form. Excerpts from these summaries follow:

Group (a): The market study shows that increased commercial activity and transport generate capital and resource needs in several areas: energy, port infrastructure, telecommunications, and roads. Three sites are considered: Iquique, Tocopilla, and Antofagasta. Of these, the last named appears best, using cost–benefit as the criterion; the second is a possible additional facility. Antofagasta has considerable installed capacity; the largest additional investment will be for storage silos and containers. In the area of telecommunications, also, the available equipment in Chuquicamata should suffice.

Group (b): The executive staff of GEICOS is composed of five private businessmen representing the five member nations with a rotating president and meeting place. The primary task is to create the operating structure. The locations are assumed to be Antofagasta and Arica.[2] GEICOS grants to Chile administration of the ports in its territory and the use of Chilean labor in construction and operation of port facilities. GEICOS arranges unrestricted transport for Argentina from the Atlantic to the Pacific within a specified corridor. The hope is to increase Argentine exports to the Far East. Businessmen of member nations are encouraged to bid on highway and railway expansion to the ports. Thus, governmental opposition in these countries to the project is reduced. Japan's aid is sought to initiate negotiations with Brazil to include that country in the project. The project is viewed to be of such

---

[1]Grupo Empresorial Integracion Centro Oeste Sudamericano, an international organization of forward-looking South American businessmen, whose main goal is the economic, social, and cultural integration of the west central area of South America.

[2]Given more time and intergroup discussions, the port location(s) would be the subject of an agreement between the first and second group work periods.

magnitude and benefit to the participants that it will significantly influence the relaxation of tensions in the entire region.

Group (d): Before Project Announcement. Juan Verdejo found out from another stevedore they planned to develop commercial routes from Salta, Tucuman, and San Salvador de Jujuy, as well as Bolivia and Paraguay to permit shipping out of Antofagasta. This news made him very happy because it meant hiring of stevedores by the port. The news went around among groups of people at the soda fountain where they usually met. When he arrived at his house in La Estrella, he told his wife so that she could let her brother know as he was without work. It turned out that he had gone to San Fernando for a temporary job harvesting beets. Thus, the timing was good; he would be ready if the project should become a reality. . . . Two days later the news seemed to be confirmed. The shopkeeper on the square was talking about it with the wife of Pancho Perez, who worked in the customs bureau. He saw grave problems as the present traffic created various difficulties. Juan Verdejo got into the discussion claiming it was certain they would install more cranes in the port. . . .

After Project Announcement. [After the signing] everything was activity. They began to raise piles for a new dock, they brought more cranes. . . . When we got together for lunch, there was a Bolivian immigrant and an Argentinian strumming his guitar. But trouble started when the water supply ran short. Mercedes (the wife) had to get in line at the water trough on the corner. Also prices began to rise. The government had to put up temporary structures for the new laborers. Juan could not make extra money in renting out rooms since his children occupied all available space. . . . Things got ugly when the Argentinians started arguments about our stealing three islands in the south from them and more than one man fell in a dark corner of the pier facing a Chilean. The Peruvian workers talked among themselves in low voices. . . .

It is evident that the general idea was captured by the students despite the foreign language, different culture, and short explanation time.

In 1982, Bowonder proposed application of the multiple perspective concept to environmental and energy policy decision making in India. One of the problems he considered was the Silent Valley Hydroelectric Project in the state of Kerala. Controversy erupted when the State Electricity Board decided to authorize construction of a dam and reservoir for the generation of electric power, and the Indian Planning Commission approved the project. The public outcry focused on the assertion that implementation would destroy a tropical rain forest unique in the country. Although less than ten percent of the forest would be used, it was claimed that rare flora and fauna would be endangered. The Indian Government appointed a committee which recommended that the Silent Valley area should be preserved as a National Biosphere Reserve, at least until the year 2000. Consequently, the Indian Government requested the State to stop work on the project while the Electricity Board hotly contested the committee's report. The State now passed the Silent Valley Protection Bill, which created an environmental monitoring committee and underscored several key points: 1) the claims of uniqueness are not supported by known facts, 2) the socioeconomic considerations compel the State to press the government of India to reverse its position, and 3) the State will do everything possible to protect the fauna and flora of the area. This Bill, in turn, led to formation of a new Government of India–Kerala State Committee to resolve the conflict.

Bowonder draws on the T, O, and P perspectives to show that they are useful in facilitating the decision process. Examples of his perspective statements follow:

T: The creation of a large body of water, the opening up of the tree canopy, and the inevitable introduction of exotic plants will cause major ecological changes, and highly specialized local species will succumb.

T: Of the various hydroelectric projects in the country and also the state, the Silent Valley project will submerge the minimum area per unit of stored energy due to the high natural head and depth of the reservoir.

O: The Kerala State Electricity Board has already spent over $2.5 million and it is not fair to ask them to give up the project [Chairman of the Board].

O/P: It is an injustice to the people of this region to keep postponing action by raising more objections and appointing more study groups, after already having given clearance to the project and accepting 17 conditions for conservation [a resident of Silent Valley].

Examination of the perspectives points in each case to a tendency toward polarization (for or against), self-serving selection of information, and oversimplification. But it also suggests paths out of the impasse, such as reduction of the dam height or creation of an autonomous Silent Valley protection agency to monitor the local environment. Bowonder points out that the perspectives can provide the key to the identification and formulation of acceptable compromises (Bowonder, 1982).

The use of multiple perspectives must take into consideration unique local cultural aspects. Kerala is not typical of Indian states. Its historical ties to other countries and openness to outside influence are reflected today in a higher literacy rate, superior social services, and less elitism than the rest of India. Thus representative perspectives are likely to be more accessible in this region than elsewhere in the country. The elitist character of Indian society in general may create unique barriers to the proper development of some perspectives[3] (Sen, 1982).

B. PLANNING THE MULTIPLE PERSPECTIVE EFFORT

The first question: Is the problem to be addressed likely to benefit from the application of multiple perspectives? Our attention has been focused on sociotechnical systems, and the answer is clearly affirmative. However, there are

---

[3]One example of elitism is a well-developed system of higher education but a grossly inadequate system of elementary education (only 36% of adult Indians are literate).

many problems of such a nature that the T, O, and P perspectives can be decoupled, for example, purely technological problems in research and development of physical systems. Low level decision problems can often be decoupled in terms of our perspectives; high level problems rarely can. Assuming that the initial evaluation suggests the use of multiple perspectives, we next face the question of personnel selection: who should do the work?

In Section IV C 1, we exposed the common misconception that an interdisciplinary mix of professionals (say, an engineer, an economist, a sociologist, and a systems analyst) is most suitable.[4] For multiple perspectives, we need an *interparadigmatic* mix, that is, individuals who have been nurtured on different inquiring systems.[5] Thus, one of the most important members of the National Hydropower TA team (Linstone et al., 1981c) was a lawyer; he has a very different sense of regulatory issues than does an engineer. We are not assuming either party has an *a priori* familiarity with the regulations; rather, they tend to emphasize different perspectives (O and T, respectively). The T-O-P profile test in Appendix C may prove helpful in identifying individuals with different strengths.

Guideline #1—Plan the effort to assure an interparadigmatic mix rather than merely an interdisciplinary mix. (Example: engineer plus lawyer plus writer plus businessman if you are using a team).

The team members complement each other, and their interaction generates insights that would not have emerged otherwise. Consequently, the team *process* design, which anticipates the conflicts and facilitates their interplay, is an important aspect.

Our experience has been that the depth of a team's immersion in the subject matter is often a good criterion for gauging the results. One has to "live" with the issues for some time and get a true "feel" for them. For this reason, a six-person effort over four months is far less likely to be successful than a three-person effort over eight months.

Guideline #2—Aim for deep transdisciplinary immersion in the subject matter. This takes time. The perspectives cannot be meaningfully developed by throwing together a crew of technologists, economists, and systems analysts for a fast-paced, data-gorged, and model-driven analysis done in a pressure cooker.

---

[4]By extension, a team composed only of academics is likely to be a disaster.

[5]A pure T, O, or P type is as uncommon as a well-balanced individual. Most people appear to exhibit an unbalanced amalgam (for example, stronger T and weaker O and P) reflecting their particular personality and background (see Section IVC).

An important advantage of a team effort is the ability to pursue the multiple perspectives simultaneously rather than serially, at least until the integration stage. This saves considerable time, a point much appreciated in the world of business.

> Guideline #3—Keep the time within reasonable bounds by having the team do the T, O, and P perspectives in parallel.

We do not want to leave the impression that a team is a necessity. There are individuals who have an appreciation and good balance of T, O, and P perspectives, but they are *rarae aves*. Da Vinci was a technologist and artist, H. G. Wells a mix of scientist and writer. Many of the most successful modern executives are well-balanced mixes of perspectives. If such a person can be found, he or she may be as valuable as, or more valuable than, a team in creating a useful multiple perspective product. We note that several of our case studies are one-person products: Mt. St. Helens (Section V B), the nursing school (Section V C), the Willamette Falls Hydroelectric Project (Section VI A), the electronics company acquisition (Section VI B), and the health care system (Chapter VII). The insider, observing activities from day to day, identifying the key actors, and isolating false issues, has unique advantages in doing the O and P perspectives. Linda Umbdenstock exemplifies this situation in the health care case. In the area of hydropower, Hussein Fahim's one-man TA of the Aswan Dam is a recent example (1981). With this advantage comes the disadvantage of greater political sensitivity. Another concern is the longer time needed for such effort.[6]

> Guideline #4—Keep in mind that there do exist individuals who have a good balance of T, O, and P perspectives. If you can find such a person, he or she may do as well as a team if the time constraint is not severe.

C. AN APPROPRIATE BALANCE

It is not possible to give an *a priori* prescription for the relative effort to be allocated to T, O, and P perspectives. In the absence of any other information, we would recommend a partition into equal parts, that is, one-third the total number of person-months on each perspective. It may be a crude rule, but it is

---

[6]It does not follow that one person doing three perspectives takes three times as long as three persons doing the perspectives in parallel. A cost savings can be expected.

almost certainly better than the 90% T perspective approach so frequently seen (see Section XI B). With experience the practitioner will develop a sense for the appropriate balance in any given case. A newly emerging technology (for example, recombinant DNA) may call for more emphasis on the T and O perspectives, while a current technology or organizational transformation is likely to produce richer O and P perspectives (as, for example, guayule).

Guideline #5   Strive for an appropriate balance among the T, O, and P perspectives.

D. FOCUS ON ISSUES

Issues vary with perspective. Since they are the focus of decision making, it is important to identify the key actors and perspectives (organizations, individuals) early. A quick minianalysis at the outset may be helpful in drawing forth a first cut list of critical issues. In this way, we avoid movement along a path which later proves to be tangential, with an absence of significant perspectives and an imbalance of issues (Linstone et al., 1981c; Coates, 1981).

Guideline #6—Consider as an initial step the development of an "issue paper," giving a first approximation to the major issues and identifying key actors and perspectives.

E. SELECTION AND USE OF O AND P PERSPECTIVES

Section XI D discussed the fuzziness of the O and P perspectives. The cautionary remarks there can be readily translated into two guidelines:

Guideline #7—Don't confuse *what* you are looking at with *how* you are looking at it, that is, the object examined and the means or perspective used to examine it.

> Guideline #8—Once the issues indicate the key technological, social, and individual elements, select the perspectives. There will probably be several O and P perspectives significant for policy formulation and the decision process. Recognize that you will not capture all of them and that fuzziness cannot be completely eliminated. Remember that cross-cuing among perspectives can prove very valuable.

The choice of O perspective(s) depends on the context of policy making that frames the decisions about the technology. For example, if the decisions about it are likely to be a function of one particular organization, then an O perspective should reflect that organization's myths and modus operandi. The practitioner will find that the P perspective lies deepest and presents him with the most difficult challenge.

There are many gradations betweeen a clearly labeled individual and a well-defined formal entity (county, company, agency, etc.). Also, the perspectives themselves are inherently dynamic and will change over time. Furthermore, different perspectives may well yield contradictory images. Comparisons are always recommended. A useful example of the synergistic interaction of perspectives, that is, cross-cuing, is provided in Section XI A 3 (recall Figure 21).

In dealing with an emerging technology, one should recognize the empirical difficulty of using multiple perspectives when the technology is mainly in the hands of a coterie of scientists and engineers, and the rest of the potentially interested participants have only latent and inchoate opinions about it. Such situations call for an aggregative effort to determine the locus of decision and assess the possibilities of coalition formation. In addition, for these technically dominated situations, it is also important to use the P perspective to bring out differences and similarities with respect to *beliefs* and orientations about the physical reality and the consequences of the technology. Such an approach will complement the technical aspects of the analysis by indicating potential conflicts and possible lines of technical development. Of course, as the technology matures, in the sense of developing a more textured political and social environment, the emphasis on the P perspective would probably shift to understanding the *values* of a wider circle of potential participants. No longer would it make sense to apply the P perspective just to technical participants when nontechnical ones would be equally or more relevant.

In using the P perspective, the *number* of individuals to which the perspective is applied has to be severely limited. One should particularly look for individuals who are likely to act outside of an organizational or institutional role and who would affect outcomes (because they will not be included in O perspectives).

F. THE PERSISTENT PROBLEM OF LONG-RANGE ANALYSES

In Section IV C 2, we agonized over the difficulty in dealing with long-range impacts and policy questions. The different horizons associated with the three perspectives (Figure 8) laid bare the dilemma. We cannot escape the fact that future-oriented studies are difficult to perform well, to the degree that they must evaluate impacts and policies at distant target dates. The T perspective, then, has troubles with core assumptions, the O perspective is accustomed to disregard long-range planning (Table 8, Figure 8), and the P perspective has difficulty envisioning a future that involves changes in many variables at the same time.[7] The result in a TA is usually either a brave, quixotic effort to rely on a long-range T perspective that falls very wide of the mark, or a shift of attention from distant impacts to closer-in aspects such as implementation strategies and paths. It is here that analysis and assessment have the strongest links to policy making and that the O and P perspectives provide the most potent support. Similarly, corporate planning must normally bring its time horizon closer in than desired by the T perspective analysts, so that the O and P perspectives can fill their vital roles in the decision-making process (Figure 23).

How do we, then, best try to fulfill the spirit of the "what-if" policy analysis? Keeping in mind the advice given in Chapter XI, we have three guidelines:

Guideline #9—Use all three perspectives (T, O, and P) as far out in time as they jointly reach.

Guideline #10—Keep revisiting the analysis and never consider it complete. Revise and refocus all perspectives at intervals.

Guideline #11—Keep eye and ear open to locate individuals with strong O and P perspective orientations and longer-than-average time horizons.

In seeking individuals compatible with Guideline 11, one should not confuse them with faddists: today's upper middle class "cause" may have little to do with tomorrow's key issues.

---

[7]Most individuals readily picture one or two changes *ceteris paribus*.

G. ON INTERVIEWS

Guideline #12—Use skilled interviewers to develop the O and P perspectives. You cannot rely on conventional documentation.

We would like the interview subject to speak for himself or herself without our providing some clue as to what we want to hear. We want to understand and see things from the other person's point of view. Ethnographers and other skilled field investigators are quite sensitive to this problem and have taken steps to reduce, control, or at least identify the sources of bias. Regardless of whether we conduct several independent analyses, corroborate our findings with participant observation, do repetitive intensive interviewing with the same informant, or extensive interviewing with a variety of participants, there is bound to be some mixing of the observer and the observed. The interviewer at least has to be clear about which perspective he or she is using in the field, in the subsequent analysis, and in the write-up.

In any event, we will be dealing with individuals to obtain the necessary information. In employing the T perspective, for example, we may be interested only in rational cause-and-effect linkages or the relation between physical components, but have to elicit the information from an individual who reflects both organizational and technical concerns. Trying to use the O perspective we may see that a particular organization will be central to the outcome. We would then take that organization as an empirical referent and proceed to work on describing roles. But in interviewing a number of individuals, we would soon discover that these individuals are not necessarily confined by their organizational roles in their responses. Indeed, the same informant may provide information for understanding several perspectives. An actor could also behave in idiosyncratic ways which may be outside his institutional role. The consequences of the idiosyncratic behavior are essential for specifying the P perspective; the institutional role is essential for specifying the O perspective. Consider Admiral Rickover's pursuit of nuclear submarines. Some of what he did reflected the U.S. Department of the Navy, while the maverick in him reflected his own propensities, independent of the organizational context.

At some point in the analysis, we have to make simplifying and perhaps distorting assumptions about what we are learning from the multiple perspectives. As noted, what we think we have learned about an individual's behavior via the P perspective may not be what that individual feels or thinks at all. Yet, what we observe or infer may be quite acceptable and important. Suppose that the *total thrust* of what we have learned from a variety of sources indicates that an organization is dragging its feet in implementing a decision about a new technology. Then it will be of only slight significance that a civil service informant feels that he is protecting some interest instead of creating red tape. True, one person's regulation is another's red tape, but this is a difference of perception that can usually be assumed away. Similarly, in the analysis using the O perspective, we are likely to assume that certain organizations will operate, for our purposes, as monoliths. Obviously, organizations are composed of many individuals with differing values, goals, and beliefs, but this fact should not prevent us from assuming the organization, as a coalition, can act in concert. Distortions that do not affect major findings should be ignored.

In some ways—but only some—a model interviewer is the Italian journalist, Oriana Fallaci. Here are two views:

> Hers is a mind of intuitions, of instincts. It is a very bright mind, as one quickly finds on reading her interviews [Howard, 1981].

> Fallaci caught that mood . . . She wrote history in the Roman style; she sought psychological, not factual, truth. [Kissinger (an interviewee), 1979][8]

Our experience since 1977 has developed from interviews conducted by students in conjunction with graduate class term papers, to the more than 100 sessions carried out as part of a 1981 TA (Linstone et al., 1981c). There have been numerous one-to-one interviews (for example, Chapter X), but two interviewers operating as a team have also been used (for example, Chapter VII). Recording has usually been done in one of two ways: summarization immediately after the interview or taping of the interview. The latter is superior to the extent that it constitutes a more accurate memory and minimizes distortion or bias by the interviewer.

The interviewer must be a good listener and sensitive to nonverbal communications. We found male academics often rigid in their questions and poor listeners, trying to implant ideas rather than receive them.

Care must be taken to preserve anonymity (that is, no attribution), or other constraints imposed by the interviewee and ethical questions may arise to confound the interviewer. He or she may be subject to manipulation, being "used" to plant ideas, or becoming brainwashed, slowly turning into an advocate or apologist.

Finally, Hannah Arendt reminds us that "truthfulness has never been counted among the political virtues, and lies have always been regarded as justifiable tools in political dealings" (Arendt, quoted in Meltsner, 1976:284).

To design a field strategy for using multiple perspectives, the first question to ask is: Who cares about this system or problem? Individuals and organizations who care and are concerned about it are more likely to come into the political arena than those who are indifferent. In the early stages of the investigation, we

---

[8]Studs Terkel's oral histories offer another useful model.

do not have to worry about whether that concern is supportive or hostile, only that it is a likely indicator of future activity and behavior.

We do not start trying to create a scientific random sample but more of a snowball sample, going from one key informant to another on the basis of leads.[9] For future technology, we are likely to go to the scientists or the designers or the technology and then proceed from producers to likely policy makers, consumers, and other groups who may act on, or be affected by, the technology. With an existing or near-term technology, it is possible to start with any concerned informant; and the more knowledgeable, the better. Within the resource constraints of the effort, it is preferable to be expansive in choosing people to interview or otherwise observe. Some people from analogous fields may have useful perspectives, and others may represent views which will become relevant in the future.

We should have an interview schedule to start with, but as the investigation proceeds, we should be prepared to be opportunistic and adapt it to emerging issues. The initial schedule can be based on a literature review. Generally, we should not expect policy makers and individuals who are distant in time and concerns from the technology to have specific knowledge and preferences; the aim of such interviews is to get at underlying predispositions that later on in the analysis phase of the investigation we can use to make appropriate inferences. For a future emerging technology, it may be desirable to use short scenarios or hypothetical questions to get at these predispositions, but we should be very careful not to put words in the mouth of the informant.

In view of the central place of such personal contacts in the pursuit of the O and P perspectives, more detailed guidelines are provided in Appendix A (see also Bogdan and Taylor, 1975; Dexter, 1970; Murphy, 1980; Spadley, 1979).

H. POLITICAL SENSITIVITY

It has been said earlier that only the T perspective has the luxury of being neutral and politically harmless—but the price is high; it may, by itself, also prove rather useless. The O and P perspectives reflect the realities of human beings, encompassing both the "original sins" of greed, crime, and war, and the "divine touch" of creativity, leadership, and concerted action *pro bono publico*. Political sensitivity may not arise as a problem in purely technological activities such as systems design. But it is inescapable in strategic planning, decision analysis, issues management, risk analysis, and technology assessment. There are no simple answers; each case has unique aspects. Following are some alternatives which a multiple perspective effort should consider:

---

[9]One must be alert that successive recommendations do not simply reinforce one point of view.

1. provide the final output in two (or even three) parts, reflecting different levels or areas of sensitivity (for example, one part the client can distribute widely, another to be held in house);
2. present each part of the output in two forms: one written, the other oral;
3. use sensitive material implicitly rather than explicitly;
4. substitute quotable references, statements, and examples that communicate the same idea as unquotable ones;
5. transform unquotable material into fictional format.

Options such as these may be anathema to the T perspective purist, but they are recognized by every executive and bureaucrat.[10]

Guideline #13—Recognize the political sensitivity of the O and P perspectives. Carefully evaluate how to communicate insights in an inevitably political setting.

I. COMMUNICATION

Guideline #14—Adapt the medium to the message, that is, fit the mode of communication to the perspective.

Different perspectives invite different modes of communication. For communicating the O perspective, consider the use of excerpts or summaries of interviews, oral briefings, scenarios, and vignettes together with the conventional type of report. For the P perspective, all of the above, with the exception of the conventional report, merit consideration (see Table 9).

A talented communicator can also use the P perspective to get all of the perspectives (T, O, and P) across to a wide audience. However, only rarely is this a practical option; outstanding writers are rarely available, and use of media is constrained by the project budget.

---

[10]A naive or careless American analyst could conceivably find himself in a position less favorable legally than that of the investigative newspaper reporter: his writings on the O and P perspectives are not covered by the First Amendment ("freedom of the press") in the Constitution. In dictatorships, any departure from the T perspective and the "official" O perspective may prove unhealthy.

J. INTEGRATION

> Guideline #15—If at all possible, leave integration of the perspectives to the user or decision maker. At the very least, cross-cuing links should be pointed out, however. Prototypes of the full integration process may also prove helpful to the client.

Since a client or decision maker may integrate the T, O, and P perspectives in a unique way based on personal values or insights, it is usually preferable for the analyst to maintain the integrity of these perspectives as separate or distinct, without trying to prejudge his integration process. It will then be apparent to the client which insights emerge from each perspective.

However, the option of developing the cross-cuing interactions among the perspectives into one or more prototype or sample integrations for the client should also be considered. A good analogy is the courtroom trial. The jury has heard many witnesses (that is, perspectives). The prosecuting and defense attorneys develop linkages and weave them into integrated accounts for the jury. This decision-making group may accept such prototypes or ignore them and create its own integrated picture from the various perspectives as a basis for its decision. At a minimum, the analyst should examine and exhibit possible interactions and relationships among the several perspectives. The cross-cuing process may be facilitated by the use of digraphs (see Figure 22).

Finally, the use of multiple perspectives makes communication with policy makers easier because the analyst soon appreciates the orientation and language of various policy makers. In a sense, multiple perspectives enhance our knowledge of the audience and the kinds of communication means which are appropriate to the specific situation.

K. OTHER USES OF MULTIPLE PERSPECTIVES

> Guideline #16—Remember that multiple perspectives can add insights to facilitate decision and action for a wide spectrum of sociotechnical systems problems and issues.

The illustrations in Chapters V through X and XII cover not only technology assessments, but also military and corporate planning as well as education and health care delivery. They encompass large and small systems, national and local in scope. The reader should not hesitate to explore other uses of interest.

L. LAST WORDS

"The only principle that does not inhibit progress is: anything goes" [Feyerabend 1978:23]. Thus, Feyerabend echoes Singer's pragmatism in the use of inquiring systems [Churchman, 1971]. He adds that only by going outside the circle of an accepted corpus of theory will its limitations become clear. Hence, a pluralistic approach is seen as essential for the expansion of knowledge.

This line of argument suggests that the O and P perspectives make us see the limitations of the T perspective, just as three-dimensional space helps us understand the limitations of one-dimensional space.

The ultimate value of the multiple perspective concept may be to spur the redefinition of "systems analysis" in the realm of human–social–technological systems.

Finally, the reader might recall the "Catch 22" noted in the introduction (Chapter I): one cannot deal with an *inter*paradigmatic concept using intraparadigmatic procedures. In concrete terms, we cannot hope to "validate hypotheses" such as the correctness of a set of perspectives. After presenting the multiple perspectives, we cautioned ourselves and subsequent researchers not to build a "theory" of multiple perspectives or attempt a "rigorous formalization" of the concept (Section IVC6). It is an appropriate note on which to end. When we see the first set of equations involving perspectives $x_1, \ldots, x_n$ and the first computerized model for weighting or integrating perspectives, we will have come paradoxically full circle—right back to the T perspective.

REFERENCES

Adams, J. G. U. (1972), You're Never Alone with Schizophrenia, *Industrial Marketing Management* 4, 441–447.

Akutagawa, R. (1952), *Rashomon and Other Stories,* translated by Takashi Kojima, Liveright Publishing Co., New York.

Allison, G. (Sept. 1969), Conceptual Models and the Cuban Missile Crisis, *The American Political Science Review* 63 (3), 689–718.

Allison, G. (1971), *Essence of Decision: Explaining the Cuban Missile Crisis,* Little, Brown and Co., Boston, Mass.

Amara, R. (Sept. 1980), *The Futures Field,* Institute of the Future, No. P-95.

Amrine, M. (1959), *The Great Decision,* G. P. Putnam's, New York.

Andersen, D. F. (Aug. 1977), *Mathematical Models and Decision Making in Bureaucracies: A Case Story Told from Three Points of View.* MIT: Ph.D. Dissertation.

Archer, D. (1980), *How to Expand Your SIQ (Social Intelligence Quotient).* M. Evans Co., New York.

Art, R. J. (1968), *The TFX Decision: McNamara and the Military,* Little, Brown and Co., Boston, Mass.

Art, R. J. (1973), Bureaucratic Politics and American Foreign Policy: A Critique, *Policy Science* 4 (4), 467–490.

Arthur D. Little, Inc. (1975), *The Consequences of Electronic Funds Transfer: A Technology Assessment of Movement Toward a Less Cash/Less Check Society.* Prepared for the National Science Foundation, GPO, Washington, D.C.

Ascher, W. (1978), *Forecasting: An Appraisal for Policy-Makers and Planners,* The Johns Hopkins University Press, Baltimore, Md.

Ashby, W. R. (1956), *An Introduction to Cybernetics,* Chapman and Hall, Ltd., London.

Axelrod, R. (ed.) (1976), *Structure of Decision: The Cognitive Maps of Political Elites,* Princeton University Press, Princeton, N.J.

Banc One Corporation (1981), *Annual Report,* Columbus, Ohio.

Banc One Corporation (1982), *Quarterly Report 1* Columbus, Ohio.

Berlin, I. (1967), *The Hedgehog and the Fox,* Weidenfeld and Nicholson, London.

Berlinski, D. (1976), *On Systems Analysis: An Essay Concerning the Limitations of Some Mathematical Methods in the Social, Political, and Biological Sciences.* The MIT Press, Cambridge, Mass.

Blackburn, T. R. (1971), Sensuous-Intellectual Complementarity in Science, *Science* 172, 1003.

Blackman, A. W., Jr., Seligman, E. J., and Sogliero, G. C. (1973), An Innovation Index Based on Factor Analysis, *Technological Forecasting and Social Change* 4 (4), 301–316; reprinted in Linstone, H. A., and Sahal, D., (eds.), *Technological Substitution*, Elsevier, New York, 1976: 69–84.

Blair, J. M. (1977), *The Control of Oil,* Pantheon Books, New York.

Board of County Commissioners of Cowlitz County (1980), *Cowlitz County Request for Special Legislation* (Report to Federal and State Legislative Delegations).

Bogdan, R. and Taylor, S. J. (1975), *Introduction to Qualitative Research Methods,* John Wiley and Sons, New York.

Bolkosky, S. M. (1975), *The Distorted Image: German Jewish Perceptions of Germans and Germany, 1918 1935,* Elsevier, New York

Borsting, J. R. (1982), Decision-Making at the Top, *Management Science* 28 (4), 341–351.

Botez, M. C. and Celac, H. (1981), *Global Modelling . . . Without Models?,* HSDPGPID-51/UNUP-258, United Nations University Department, New York.

Botkin, J., Dimancescu, D., and Stata, R. (1982), *Global Stakes: The Future of High Technology in America,* Ballinger Publishing Co., Cambridge, Mass.

Boucher, W. (Dec. 18, 1979), oral communication.

Boulton, D. (1978), *The Grease Machine,* Harper and Row, New York.

Bowonder, B. (1982), Multiple Perspective Concept for Content and Policy Analyses: Energy and Environmental Examples, Administrative Staff College of India, Bella Vista, Hyderabad, India.

Braudel, F. (1972), *The Mediterranean and the Mediterranean World in the Age of Philip II* (vol. 1), translated from the French, Harper and Row, New York.

Brim, O., Jr., Glass, D. C., Lavin, D. E., and Goodman, N. (1962), *Personality and Decision Processes: Studies in the Social Psychology of Thinking,* Stanford University Press, Stanford, Calif.

Brodheim, E. and Prastacos, G. P. (1979), The Long Island Blood Distribution System as a Prototype for Regional Blood Management, *Interfaces* 9 (5), 3–20.

Buskirk, R. H. (1974), *Modern Management and Machiavelli,* Cahners Books, Boston, Mass.

California Dept of Food and Agriculture (1982), *On the Feasibility of Commercial Development of Guayule in California,* Sacramento, Calif.

Canetti, E. (1962), *Crowds and Power,* The Viking Press, New York.

Cannon, L. (1982), *Reagan.* Putnam, New York.

Churchman, C. W. (1968), *Challenge to Reason,* McGraw Hill, New York.

Churchman, C. W. (1971), *The Design of Inquiring Systems,* Basic Books, New York.

Churchman, C. W. (1977), A Philosophy for Planning, in *Futures Research: New Directions,* H. A. Linstone and W. H. C. Simmonds, eds., Addison-Wesley Publishing Co., Reading, Mass.

Churchman, C. W. (1979), *The Systems Approach and Its Enemies,* Basic Books, New York.

Churchman, C. W. (1982), *Thought and Wisdom,* Intersystems Publications, Seaside, Calif.

Cicco, J. A., Jr. (Jan. 5, 1982), Wanna Fix Your Firm? *New York Times* 25.

Coates, J. F. (1975), In Defense of Delphi, *Technological Forecasting and Social Change* 7 (2), 193–194.

Coates, J. F. (June 1976), Technology Assessment—A Tool Kit, *Chemtech* 372–383.

Coates, J. F. (June 2–3, 1977), The Need to Study the Social Impacts of EFT, Boston: Presentation to Conference on EFT Research and Public Policy.

Coates, V. T. (1981), *Policy Issues in Hydropower Development*. Institute for Water Resources, Ft. Belvoir, Va. U. S. Army Corps of Engineers.

Coates, V. T. and Fabian, T. (Jan. 30, 1981), *Technology Assessment in Europe and Japan*. Washington, D.C.: Dames and Moore, Policy Analysis and Technology Assessment Group.

Colton, K. W. and Kraemer, K. L. (1980), *Computers and Banking*, Plenum Press, New York.

Cook, G. (June 1979), R_x for the Maladies of Health Care: A Medical Revolution in the Making, *The Futurist* 179–189.

Cook, G. (Oct. 5, 1982), Comment CC49 on Electronic Information Exchange System (EIES), Conference on Computers and Society.

Cortner, H. J. and Richards, M. T. (March–April 1983), The Political Component of National Forest Planning, *Journal of Soil and Water Conservation* 79–81.

Covello, V. (1983), The Perception of Technological Risks: An Overview, *Technological Forecasting and Social Change* 23, 285–297.

Crandall, D. R., Mullineaux, D. D. R., and Rubin, D. R. (1975), Mt. St. Helens Volcano: Recent and Future Behavior, *Science* 187 (4175), 438–441.

Crowell, F. A. (1980), Evaluating Programs for Educating Mentally Retarded Persons, in *Educating Minimally Retarded Persons in the Mainstream*, J. Gottlieb, ed. University Park Press, Baltimore, Md.

Culbert, S. A. and McDonough, J. J. (1980), *The Invisible War: Pursuing Self-Interests at Work*, Wiley and Sons, New York.

Cyert, R. N. and March, J. G. (1963), *A Behavioral Theory of the Firm*, Prentice-Hall, Englewood Cliffs, N.J.

Davidson, J. W. and Lytle, M. H. (1982), *After the Fact: The Art of Historical Detection*, A. A. Knopf, New York.

DeJouvenel, B. (1967), *The Art of Conjecture*, Basic Books, New York.

DeParle, J. (May 1983), Advise and Forget, *The Washington Monthly* 15 (3), 40–46.

DeTocqueville, A. (1966), *Democracy in America* II, Knopf, New York.

Dexter, L. A. (1970), *Elite and Specialized Interviewing*, Northwestern University Press, Evanston, Ill.

Dror, Y. (1968), *Public Policy Making Re-examined*, Chandler, San Francisco.

Dror, Y. (1980), *Crazy States*, Kraus reprint, Millwood, N.Y.

Dror, Y. (1982), *Policy Analysis for Rulers*, unpublished.

Drucker, P. (April 8, 1973), New Technology: Predicting Its Impact is Perilous and Futile, *New York Times* Section 3, 1.

Dugger, R. (1982), *The Politician: The Life and Times of Lyndon Johnson*, W. W. Norton & Co., New York.

Duncan, O. D. (Fall 1969), Social Forecasting—The State of the Art, *The Public Interest* (17) 88–118.

Dunlap, R. E. (Sept.–Oct. 1980), Paradigmatic Change in Social Science, *Amer. Behavioral Science* 24 (1), 5–14.

Ehrlichman, J. (1982), *Witness to Power: The Nixon Years,* Simon and Schuster, New York.

Elboim-Dror, R. (1982), Israel: Sisyphean Reform Cycles, in G. E. Caiden and H. Siedentopf, eds., *Strategies for Administrative Reform,* D. C. Heath and Co., Lexington, Mass.

Etzioni, A. (Dec. 1967), Mixed Scanning: 'Third' Approach to Decision Making, *Public Administration Review* 27, 385–392.

Fahim, H. M. (1981), *Dams, People, and Development: The Aswan High Dam Case,* Pergamon Press, New York.

Fallows, J. (1981), *National Defense,* Random House, New York.

Fallows, J. (Dec. 16, 1982), Review of Carter's *Keeping Faith: Memoirs of a President, N. Y. Review of Books,* 3–11.

Federal Water Pollution Control Act (1977).

Feyerabend, P. (1978), *Against Method,* Verso Editions, London.

Fischhoff, B. (1979), Consent in Risk-Benefit Decisions, *Technological Forecasting and Social Change* 13 (4), 347–357.

Fischhoff, B. (Oct. 20, 1980), quoted in Risk Assessment's Role in Regulation Debated, *Chemical Engineering News,* p. 30.

Fischhoff, B., et al. (1981), *Acceptable Risk,* Cambridge University Press, Cambridge, Eng.

Florman, S. C. (1976), *The Existential Pleasures of Engineering,* St. Martins Press, New York.

Forrester, J. W. (1968), *Principles of Systems,* Wright-Allen Press, Cambridge, Mass.

Forrester, J. W. (1971), *World Dynamics,* Wright-Allen Press, Cambridge, Mass.

Foster, K. et al. (April 1980), *A Sociotechnical Survey of Guayule Rubber Commercialization* University of Arizona, Office of Arid Lands Studies, Tucson, Midwest Research Institute, Kansas City, Mo.

Freud, S. (1937), Analysis Terminable and Interminable, in *Collected Papers* (vol. 5) (J. Strachey, ed.), 316–357.

Fried, J. and Molnar, P. (1978), *Technological and Social Change: A Transdisciplinary Model,* Petrocelli Books, New York.

Fuglesang, A. (1977), *Doing Things . . . Together: Report of an Experience in Communication Appropriate Technology,* Dag Hammarskjold Foundation, Uppsala, Sweden.

Gardner, M. (Dec. 1981), Mathematical Games, *Scientific American* 18–31c.

Georgescu-Roegen, N. (1972), *The Entropy Law and the Economic Process,* Harvard University Press, Cambridge, Mass.

Glansdorff, P. and Prigogine, I. (1971), *Structure, Stability and Fluctuations.* Wiley Interscience, London.

Godson, J. (1975), *The Rise and Fall of the DC-10,* D. McKay Co., New York.

Goldschmidt, P. (1975), Scientific Inquiry or Political Critique? *Technological Forecasting and Social Change* 7 (2), 195–213.

Gore, J. (Nov. 1979), Case Study: Perinatal Regionalization, Presentation to the Annual Meeting of the American Health Assoc.

Graham, A. K. and Senge, P. M. (1980), A Long-Wave Hypothesis of Innovation, *Technological Forecasting and Social Change* 17 (4), 283–312.

Hadamard, J. (1945), *The Psychology of Invention in the Mathematical Field,* Princeton University Press, Princeton, N.J.

Halal, W. E. (1980), *Strategic Planning in Major U.S. Corporations.* Study prepared for General Motors Corporation at George Washington University, Washington, D.C.; see also *Technological Forecasting and Social Change* 25 (3), 239–261 (1984).

Hardin, G. (Dec. 1968), The Tragedy of the Commons, *Science* 162 (3859), 1243–1248.

Harrison, E. F. (1975), *The Managerial Decision-Making Process.* Houghton-Mifflin Co., Boston, Mass.

Harvard Business School (1982), *Banc One Corporation and the Home Information Revolution,* prepared by K. J. Freeze, HBS Case Services, Boston, Mass.

Hayes, R. H. and Abernathy, W. J. (July–Aug., 1980), Managing Our Way to Economic Decline, *Harvard Business Review* 58 (4), 67–77.

Hegel, G. W. F. (1860), Philosophy of History, in *The Age of Despots,* J Addington Symonds, ed., Putnam Press, New York.

Heilbroner, R. L. (1974), *An Inquiry into the Human Prospect,* W. W. Norton & Co, Inc., New York.

Hetman, F. (1973), *Society and the Assessment of Technology.* Paris: Organization for Economic Cooperation and Development.

Hill, P. H. et al. (1979), *Making Decisions,* Addison-Wesley Publishing Co., Reading, Mass.

Hiltz, L. and Turoff, M. (1978), *The Network Nation,* Addison-Wesley Publishing Co., Reading, Mass.

Hofstadter, P. (1980), *Gödel, Escher, Bach: The Eternal Golden Braid,* Vintage Books, New York.

Holling, C. S. (1977), The Curious Behavior of Complex Systems: Lessons from Ecology, in *Futures Research: New Directions,* H. A. Linstone and W. H. C. Simmonds, eds. Addison-Wesley Publishing Co., Reading, Mass.

Holsti, O. (1976), Foreign Policy Formation Viewed Cognitively, in *Structure of Decision: Cognitive Maps of Political Elites,* R. Axelrod, ed. Princeton University Press, Princeton, N.J.

Honda, S. (1983), personal communication.

Hoos, I. R. (1972), *Systems Analysis in Public Policy: A Critique,* Univ. of California Press, Berkeley, Calif.

Hoos, I. R. (1979), Societal Aspects of Technology Assessment, *Technological Forecasting and Social Change* 13 (3), 191–202.

House, E. (1977), *The Logic of Evaluative Argument* (CSE Monogr. 7), Center for the Study of Evaluation, University of California, Los Angeles.

Houston, J. (1976), Prometheus Rebound: An Inquiry into Technological Growth and Psychological Change, *Technological Forecasting and Social Change* 9 (3), 241–258.

Howard, J. (April 1981), A Woman, *Quest/81,* 14–18, 86–87.

Howard, R. et al. (April 1981), *An Application of Decision Analysis to the Technology Assessment of Decentralized Waste Treatment Methods.* Stanford University Engineering-Economic Systems Dept., Stanford, Calif.

International Communication Agency (Oct. 25, 1981), Soviet Elites: World View and Perceptions of the U.S., Office of Research Study. Quoted by M. Marder, LA Times-Washington Post Service, *Sunday Oregonian,* A-14.

Jantsch. E. (1972), *Technological Planning and Social Futures*. Cassell/Associated Business Programmes, London.

Jay, A. (1968), *Management and Machiavelli*, Holt, Rinehart, and Winston, New York.

Kahn, H. (1960), *On Thermonuclear War*, Princeton University Press, Princeton, N.J.

Kahn, H. (1982), *The Coming Boom*, Simon and Schuster, New York.

Kaje, R. (1977), Bringing the Feminine Into Forecasting, *Futures Research: New Directions* H. A. Linstone and W. H. C. Simmonds, eds., Addison-Wesley, Reading, Mass.

Kellen, K. (1968), On Problems in Perceiving Other Nations and Systems, *Security Studies Paper No. 15*, University of California, Los Angeles, Calif.

Kellen, K. (1980), Is Inflation Fun? *Technological Forecasting and Social Change* 17 (1), 1–5.

Kellerman, B. L. et al. (1979), *Making Decisions: A Multidisciplinary Introduction*. Addison-Wesley, Reading, Mass.

Kennedy, J. F. (1963), Preface to *Decision in the White House*, by T. Sorensen (quoted in *Essence of Decision*, by G. Allison, p. vi), Columbia University Press, New York.

Kiechel, W. III (1981), New Management Strategies, *Fortune* 104(7) 111–126; (8), 139–146; (9), 181–188; (10), 148–154.

Kiechel, W. III (June 1982a), Executives Without Degrees, *Fortune* 105 (13), 119–120.

Kiechel, W. III (Dec. 1982b), Corporate Strategists Under Fire, *Fortune* 106 (13), 34–39.

Kiefer, C. F. and Senge, P. M. (1982), Metanoic Organizations in the Transition to a Sustainable Society, *Technological Forecasting and Social Change* 22 (2), 109–122.

Kissinger, H. (Dec. 7, 1968), quoted in *New York Times*.

Kissinger, H. (1979), *The White House Years*, Little Brown and Co., Waltham, Mass.

Kissinger, H. (1982), *Years of Upheaval*, Little, Brown, and Company, Waltham, Mass.

Kluckhorn, C. and Mowrer, O. H. (1944), Culture and Personality: A Conceptual Framework, *American Anthropologist* 46 (1), 1–29.

Kraft, J. (May 5, 1980), Annals of Industry: The Downsizing Decision, *The New Yorker* LVI (ii), 134–162.

Kunreuther, H., Linnerooth, J. et al. (1982), *Risk Analysis and Decision Processes: The Siting of LEG Facilities in Four Countries*, Preliminary Draft, International Institute for Applied Systems Analysis, Laxenburg, Austria (to be published by Springer Verlag).

Langer, W. C. (1972), *The Mind of Adolf Hitler*, Basic Books, New York.

Larkin, J., et al. (June 20, 1980), Expert and Novice Performance in Solving Physics Problems, *Science* 208 (4450), 1335–1342.

Lawless, E. W. (1977), *Technology and Social Shock*, Rutgers University Press, New Brunswick, N.J.

Lee, D. B., Jr. (May 1973), Requiem for Large-Scale Models, *AIP J.* 163–178.

Lendaris, G. G. (1979), On the Human Aspects in Structural Modeling, *Technological Forecasting and Social Change* 14 (4), 329–351.

Lewin, K. (1948), *Resolving Social Conflicts: Selected Papers on Group Dynamics*, Harper and Row, New York.

Lewin, L. C. (1969), *Report from Iron Mountain*, Dell Publishers, New York.

Lewin, T. (March 9, 1969), Business and the Law, *New York Times* 28.

Linstone, H. A. (March 1968), *Corporate Risk Analysis for Commercial Aircraft Programs,* Corporate Development Planning Dept., Lockheed Aircraft Corp., Burbank, Calif.

Linstone, H. A. (1969), When Is a Need a Need?, *Technological Forecasting and Social Change* 1 (1), 55–71.

Linstone, H. A. (1973), On Discounting the Future, *Technological Forecasting and Social Change* 4 (4), 335–338.

Linstone, H. A. (1975), Book review of M. Mesarovic and E. Pestel's *Mankind at the Turning Point: The Second Report to the Club of Rome, Technological Forecasting and Social Change* 7 (3), 331–334.

Linstone, H. A. (1980), On the Management of Technology: Old and New Perspectives, in *Decision Models for Industrial Systems Engineers and Managers,* P. Adulbhan and M. T. Tabucanon, eds., Bangkok, Thailand: Asian Institute of Technology.

Linstone, H. A. and Simmonds, W. H. C. (1977), eds., *Futures Research: New Directions.* Addison-Wesley Publishing Co., Reading, Mass.

Linstone, H. A. and Turoff, M. (1975), *The Delphi Method: Techniques and Applications.* Addison-Wesley Publishing Co., Reading, Mass.

Linstone, H. A. et al. (1978), *The Use of Structural Modeling for Technology Assessment* (Rept. 78-1), Futures Research Institute, Portland State University, Portland, Ore.

Linstone, H. A. et al. (1981a), The Multiple Perspective Concept, *Technological Forecasting and Social Change* 20 (4), 275–325.

Linstone, H. A. et al. (1981b), *The Multiple Perspective Concept,* (Report 81-1), Futures Research Institute, Portland State University, Portland, Ore.

Linstone, H. A. et al. (1981c), *Technology Assessment of National Hydropower Development* (vol. 1), Institute for Water Resources, U. S. Army Corps of Engineers, Ft. Belvoir, Va.

Lombardo, P. (Nov.–Dec. 1979), Alternative Waste Water Planning for Small Communities, *Compost Science/Land Utilization* 20, 16–29.

Lotka, A. J. (1956), *Elements of Mathematical Biology,* Dover Books, New York.

Lovins, A. B. and Lovins, L. H. (1982), Electric Utilities: Key to Capitalizing the Energy Transition, *Technological Forecasting and Social Change* 22 (2), 153–166.

Lowenthal, A. F. (1972), *The Dominican Intervention,* Harvard University Press, Cambridge, Mass.

Loye, D. (1978), *The Knowable Future,* J. Wiley and Sons (Wiley-Interscience Publication), New York.

Machiavelli, N. (1851), *The History of Florence* 2.

Magaziner, I. C. and Reich, R. B. (1982), *Minding America's Business: The Decline and Rise of the American Economy,* Harcourt Brace Jovanovich, New York.

Malcolm, J. (Dec. 1, 1980), The Impossible Profession, *The New Yorker,* 150–151.

March, J. G. and Simon, H. (1958), *Organizations,* Wiley, New York.

Marchetti, C. (1977ff), articles in *Technological Forecasting and Social Change,* beginning with 10 (4), 345–356.

Marchetti, C. (1983), On the Role of Science in the Post-Industrial Society: 'Logos'— the Empire Builder, Keynote address, St. Paul de Vence Conference, 19–21 May 1981. Reprinted in *Technological Forecasting and Social Change* 24 (3), 197–206.

Martino, J. P. (1972), *Technological Forecasting for Decisionmaking.* American Elsevier Publishing Co., New York.

Maruyama, M. (1984), New Developments in Asian Theories of Management, *Technological Forecasting and Social Change* (to be published).

McNaugher, T. L. (Winter 1980), Marksmanship, McNamara, and the M-16 Rifle: Innovation in Military Organizations, *Public Policy* 28, 1.

McPhee, J. (1981), Minihydro, *The New Yorker* LVII (1), 44–87.

Meadows, D. et al. (1972), *The Limits to Growth*, Universe Books, New York.

Meltsner, A. J. (1976), *Policy Analysts in the Bureaucracy*, University of California Press, Berkeley, Calif.

Meltsner, A. J. (Dec. 1977), *Seismic Safety of Existing Buildings and Incentives for Hazard Mitigation in San Francisco: An Exploratory Study* (Report to NSF), UCB/FFRC-77/28, Berkeley, Ca; Earthquake Engineering Research Center, College of Engineering, University of California.

Meltsner, A. J. (Summer 1979), Don't Slight Communication: Some Problems of Analytical Practice, *Policy Analysis* 5 (3), 367–392.

Meltsner, A. J. and Bellavita, C. (1983), *The Policy Organization*, Sage Publications, Inc., Beverly Hills, Calif.

Mensch, G. (1979), *Stalemate in Technology: Innovations Overcome the Depression*, Ballinger, Cambridge, Mass.

Meyers, H. B. For Lockheed (Aug. 1, 1969), Everything's Coming Up Unk-Unks, *Fortune* 80 (2), 76–81, 131–134.

Michael, D. N. (1973), *On Learning to Plan—and Planning to Learn*. Jossey-Bass Publications, San Francisco, Calif.

Miller, J. G. (1978), *Living Systems*, McGraw-Hill, New York.

Miller, R., Enhancing Impact Assessment Through A Synthesis of Two Divergent Approaches, Doctoral dissertation, Systems Science Doctoral Program, Portland State University, Portland, Ore., in progress.

Miser, H. J. (1980), Operations Research and Systems Analysis, *Science* 209, 4452, 139–146.

Mitroff, I. I. (1974), *The Subjective Side of Science*, Elsevier-North Holland, New York.

Mitroff, I. I. and Blankenship, L. V. (1973), On the Methodology of the Holistic Experiment: An Approach to the Conceptualization of Large-Scale Social Experiments, *Technological Forecasting and Social Change* 4 (4), 339–353.

Mitroff, I. I. and Kilmann, R. H. (1975), On Evaluating Scientific Research: The Contribution of the Psychology of Science, *Technological Forecasting and Social Change* 8 (2), 163–174.

Mitroff, I. I. and Turoff, M. (1973), Technological Forecasting and Assessment: Science and/or Mythology? *Technological Forecasting and Social Change* 5 (2), 113–134.

Morgan, D. (1979), *Merchants of Grain*, Viking Press, New York.

Morison, E. E. (1966), *Men, Machines, and Modern Times*, The MIT Press, Cambridge, Mass.

Morton, L. (Jan. 1957), The Decision to Use the Atomic Bomb, *Foreign Affairs* 35 (2), 334–353.

Mowery, D. C. and Rosenberg, N. (1981), Technical Change in the Commercial Aircraft Industry, 1925–1975, *Technological Forecasting and Social Change* 20 (4), 347–358.

Murphy, J. T. (1980), *Getting the Facts*, Goodyear Publishing Co., Santa Monica, Calif.

National Academy of Sciences (1977), *Guayule: An Alternative Source of Rubber*, National Academy of Sciences, Washington, D.C.

National Commission on Electronic Funds Transfer (1975), *EFT and the Public Interest,* National Commission on Electronic Funds Transfer, Washington, D.C.

Nehnevajsa, S. and Menkes, J. (1981), Technology Assessment and Risk Analysis, *Technological Forecasting and Social Change* 19 (3), 245–256.

Newhouse, J. (1982), *The Sporty Game,* A. A. Knopf, New York.

Newman, J. R. (March 1961), Two Discussions on Thermonuclear War, *Scientific American* 204 (3).

Nutt, P. C. (1977), An Experimental Comparison of the Effectiveness of Three Planning Methods, *Management Science* 23 (5) 499–511.

Nutt, P. C. (1979), Influence of Decision Styles on Use of Decision Models, *Technological Forecasting and Social Change* 14 (1), 77–93.

Nutt, P. C. (1980), Comparing Methods for Weighting Decision Criteria, *Omega,* 8 (2), 163–172.

Otway, H. J., Pahner, P. D., and Linnerooth, J. (Sept. 1975), Societal Values in Risk Acceptance, Paper presented at the Annual Meeting of the American Institute of Chemical Engineers, Boston (also IIASA Rept. RM-75-54).

Perlmutter, A. (May 3, 1980), The Courtship of Iraq, *The New Republic,* 182 (18) 19–24.

Peters, C. (1981), *How Washington Really Works.* Addison Wesley Publishing Co., Reading, Mass., for interesting reviews, see *Technological Forecasting and Social Change* 19 (2), 197–202.

Peters, T. J. and Waterman, R. H., Jr. (1982), *In Search of Excellence,* Harper and Row, New York.

Pfaff, W. (May 1980), Think Tanks: Think Again, *Quest/81,* 79–80.

Plamenatz, J. (1972), ed., *Machiavelli,* Fontana/Collins, London, Eng.

Polmar, N. and Allen, T. B. (1982), *Rickover,* Simon and Schuster, New York.

Porter, A. L. et al. (1980), *A Guidebook for Technology Assessment and Impact Analysis.* Elsevier North Holland, New York.

Prigogine, I., Allen, P. M., and Herman, R. (1977), Long Term Trends and the Evolution of Complexity, in *Goals in a Global Community* (vol. 1) E. Laszlo and J. Bierman, eds., Pergamon Press, New York.

Project MIRAGE 85 vol. III, (DPR-87) (April 1970), Corporate Development Planning Dept., Lockheed Aircraft Corp.

Quade, E. S. and Boucher, W. I. (1967), *Systems Analysis and Policy Planning,* Elsevier, New York.

Quade, E. S. and Miser, H. J., *Handbook of Systems Analysis,* to be published.

Randolph, R. H. and Koppel, B. (1982), Technology Assessment in Asia: Status and Prospects, *Technological Forecasting and Social Change* 22 (3/4), 363–384.

Rauch, W. (1979), The Decision Delphi, *Technological Forecasting and Social Change* 15 (3), 159–169.

Riedl, J. J. (June 19, 1978), Statement before U. S. Congress, House Committee on Agriculture, Subcommittee on Department Investigation, Oversight, and Research; and Committee on Science and Technology, Subcommittee on Science Research and Technology: The Goodyear Tire and Rubber Company.

Rittel, H. W. J. and Webber, M. W. (1973), Dilemmas in a General Theory of Planning, *Policy Science* 4 155–169.

Roberts, F. S. (1976), *Discrete Mathematical Models,* Prentice-Hall, Inc., Englewood Cliffs, N.J.

Rowan, R. (April 23, 1979), Those Business Hunches are More Than Blind Faith, *Fortune* 99 (8), 110–114.

Rowe, V. (1959), *The Great Wall of France,* Putnam Press, London.

Sackman, H. (1975), *Delphi Critique: Expert Opinions, Forecasting, and Group Process,* D. C. Heath, Lexington, Mass.

Salisbury, H. E. (Nov. 17, 1980), De-professoring Foreign Policy, *New York Times* A23.

Salk, J. (1983), *Anatomy of Reality: Merging of Intuition and Reason,* Columbia University Press, New York.

Sampson, A. (1981), *The Money Lenders: Bankers in a Dangerous World,* Hodder and Stoughton Ltd. (Coronet edition), Kent, England.

Sapp, J. (1983), *Electricity Demand Forecasting in a Changing Regional Context: The Application of the Multiple Perspective Concept to the Prediction Process.* Ph.D. Dissertation (in progress). Portland State University, Portland, Oregon, Systems Science Ph.D. Program.

Sawada, J. (1983), Government Industrial Policy for a Healthy World Economy, talk presented November 10, 1982, at the Woodlands Conference on Sustainable Societies, Woodlands, Texas, *Technological Forecasting and Social Change* 24 (2) 95–105.

Scheele, D. S. (1975), Reality Construction as a Product of Delphi Iteration, in *The Delphi Method: Techniques and Applications,* H. A. Linstone and M. Turoff, eds., Addison-Wesley Publishing Co., Reading, Mass.

Schelling, T. C. (1960), *The Strategy of Conflict,* Harvard University Press, Cambridge, Mass.

Schneider, H. W. (1948), ed., *Adam Smith's Moral and Political Philosophy,* Hafner Publishing Co., New York.

Schoenberger, W. S. (1970), *Decision of Destiny,* Ohio University Press, Athens, Ohio.

Schorske, C. E. (1981), *Fin-de-Siecle Vienna: Politics and Culture,* Vintage Books, New York.

Schwebs, D. (1981), Book Review of *How Washington Really Works,* in *Technological Forecasting and Social Change* 19 (2) 199–202.

Schwebs, D. and Sprey, P. (1981) (Formerly OASD/Systems Analysis), oral communication.

Searle, J. R. (1982), Minds, Brains, and Programs, in *The Mind's I: Fantasies and Reflections on Self and Soul,* D. R. Hofstadter and D. C. Dennett, eds., Basic Books, New York.

Sen, A. (Dec. 16, 1982), How Is India Doing? *New York Review of Books,* 41–45.

Simon, H. (1958), *Administrative Behavior,* MacMillan, New York.

Simon, J. L. (June 27, 1980), Resources, Population, Environment: An Over-Supply of False Bad News, *Science* 208 (4451), 1431–1437.

Simon, J. L. (1981), *The Ultimate Resource,* Princeton University Press, Princeton, N.J.

Siu, R. G. H. (Spring 1978), Management and the Art of Chinese Baseball, *Sloan Management Review* (MIT) 19 (3), 83–89.

Slovic, P. et al. (1981), *Facts and Fears: Understanding Perceived Risk,* (manuscript), Decision Research, Inc., Eugene, Oreg.

Smith, A. (pseudonym) (1972), *Supermoney,* Random House, New York.

Smith, C. W. (1981), *The Mind of the Market,* Rowman and Littlefield, Totowa, N.J.

Spadley, J. P. (1979), *The Ethnographic Interview,* Holt, Rinehart, and Winston, New York.

Starr, C. and Whipple, C. (1980), Risks of Risk Decisions, *Science* 208, 1114–1119.

Steinbruner, J. D. (1968), *The Mind and the Milieu of Policy-Makers: A Case History of the MLF*, Ph.D. dissertation, MIT.

Steinbruner, J. D. (1974), *The Cybernetic Theory of Decision*, Princeton University Press, Princeton, N.J.

Steiner, G. A. (1981), The New Class of Chief Executive Officer, *Long Range Planning* 14 (4), 10–20.

Stimson, H. S. (Feb. 1947), The Decision to Use the Atomic Bomb, *Harper's* 194 (1161), 97–107.

Sullivan, J. B. (1976), A Public Interest Laundry List for Technology Assessment: Two Dozen Eternal Truths About People and Technology, *Technological Forecasting and Social Change* 8, 439–440.

Svedin, U. (Oct. 8, 1980), Scenarios, Technology and Development, Paper presented at the Conference on Natural Resources and Regional Development, the Semi-Arid Regions Case, Cocoyoc, Mexico.

Thom, R. (1975), *Structural Stability and Morphogenesis*, W. A. Benjamin, Inc., Reading, Mass.

Thompson, M. (Dec. 1980), Political Culture: An Introduction, (working paper WP-80-175), International Institute for Applied Systems Analysis, Laxenburg, Austria, also published as Fission and Fusion in Nuclear Society, *Newsletter of the Royal Anthropological Institute* 41.

Thompson, M. (1982), The Cultural Approach to Risk: The Case of Poverty, in H. Kunreuther ed., *Risk: A Seminar Series*, International Institute for Applied Systems Analysis, Laxenburg, Austria.

Thompson, W. I. (1971), *At The Edge of History*, Harper and Row, New York.

Thompson, W. I. (1976), *Evil and World Order*, Harper and Row, New York.

Thompson, W. I. (1978), *Darkness and Scattered Light*, Anchor Books, Garden City, N.Y.

Tolstoy, L. (1869), *War and Peace*, Epilogue II, translated by L. and A. Maude, Simon and Schuster, New York, 1958.

Toth, R. (Dec. 30, 1980), *Los Angeles Times*, 1.

Toynbee, A. (1972), *A Study of History* (revised and abridged by A. Toynbee and J. Caplan), Oxford University Press, Fairlawn, N.J.

Trotter, R. G. (1971), The Cuban Missile Crisis: An Analysis of Policy Formulation in Terms of Current Decision-Making Theory, Doctoral dissertation, University of Pennsylvania, Philadelphia.

Turner, B. A. (1982), Organizational Responses to Hazard, in H. Kunreuther, ed., *Risk: A Seminar Series* (Rept. CP-82-S2), IIASA Collaborative Proceedings.

Turoff, M. (1975), The Policy Delphi, in *The Delphi Method: Techniques and Applications*, H. A. Linstone and M. Turoff, eds., Addison-Wesley, Reading, Mass.

Tversky, A. and Kahneman, D. (Sept. 27, 1974), Judgement Under Uncertainty: Heuristics and Biases, *Science* 185, 1124–1131.

Umbdenstock, L. (1981), The Perinatal Regionalization Project: A Study in Form and Development, Doctoral dissertation, Systems Science Doctoral Program, Portland State University, Portland, Ore.

Velimirovic, H. (Nov. 1975), *An Anthropological View of Risk Phenomena* (Rept. RM-75-55) International Institute for Applied Systems Analysis, Laxenburg, Austria.

Vietmeyer, N. D. (June, 19, 1978), Statement before U. S. Congress, House Committee on Agriculture, Subcommittee on Department Investigation, Oversight and Research; and Committee on Science and Technology, Subcommittee on Science Research and Technology.

von Foerster, H. (1972), Responsibilities of Competence, *J. Cybernet.* 2 (2), 1–6.

von Foerster, H. (1977), The Curious Behavior of Complex Systems, in *Futures Research: New Directions,* H. A. Linstone and W. H. C. Simmonds, eds., Addison-Wesley Publishing Co., Reading, Mass.

von Neumann, J. and Morgenstern, O. (1944), *Theory of Games and Economic Behavior,* Princeton University Press, Princeton, N.J.

Ways, M. (1967), The Road to 1977, *Fortune* 75 (1), 93–95, 194–195.

Weinberg, G. M. (1975), *An Introduction to General Systems Thinking,* Wiley-Interscience, New York.

Wenk, V. D. (June 1971), Water Pollution: Domestic Wastes, in *A Technology Assessment Method* (vol. 6), MITRE Corp., Washington, D.C.

White, G. (1969), *Strategies of American Water Management,* University of Michigan Press, Ann Arbor, Mich.

White, L., Jr. (1974), Technology Assessment from the Stance of A Medieval Historian, *Technological Forecasting and Social Change* 6 (4), 359–369.

Whyte, W. H., Jr. (1957), *The Organization Man,* Doubleday Anchor Books, Garden City, N.Y.

Wildavsky, A. and Tenenbaum E. (1981), *The Politics of Mistrust,* Sage Publications, Beverly Hills, Calif.

Williams, J. D. (1954), *The Compleat Strategyst,* RAND Corp., Santa Monica, Calif.

Wouk, H. (1951), *The Caine Mutiny,* Doubleday, Garden City, N.Y.

Yates, B. (1983), *The Decline and Fall of the American Automobile Industry,* Harper and Row, New York.

Zadeh, L. A. (1965), Fuzzy Sets, *Information Control* 8 (3), 338–353.

APPENDIX A

SOME GUIDELINES FOR IMPLEMENTATION OF THE O AND P PERSPECTIVES IN A TECHNOLOGY ASSESSMENT

A. J. MELTSNER

A. BASIC PROCEDURE

The following guidelines are intended to provide a schematic outline of the activities that are necessary to implement organizational and personal perspectives for the analysis of sociotechnical systems. They are not intended to take the place of the numerous books on qualitative research and elite interviewing.

1. Prefieldwork

1. Read relevant material on the proposed technology, on past but similar technologies,and on the policy processes associated with these past and present technologies.
2. Develop a preliminary list or map of the key actors (both individuals and collective or organizational) who have been or might be involved with the proposed technology. One basis for selection is who cares or who has something to gain or lose by the introduction of the technology, and one clue to possible involvement is past involvement.
3. Delimit the site or area or scope of investigation on the basis of an issue paper. The point is to have a representative sample of informants but also to recognize the limits of research resources. If need be, delimit the subject technology.

2. Fieldwork

The interview process will be discussed in Part B of this Appendix.

3. Analysis

From the typed interviews and other written material analyze the feasibility of the proposed technology. From the organizational perspective determine whether the technology is congruent with the way the present organization functions. Does the technology have to change or does the organization have to alter its tasks and structure? Similarly, for the personal perspective, look to see whether the technology is likely to be adopted by private and public policy makers. If so, which *type* of individual will push for such adoption and which *type* of individual will oppose it. Who are enthusiasts? Who has leverage and exercises it? Can alternative implementation paths be defined? Suppose each path is followed to fruition, what then? A check list of questions is presented in B5. Such questions are generic to technology assessment (TA) and the material from each perspective should be examined to elicit insights.

B. ON INTERVIEWING

The actual interview can be characterized by the personality and motivation of both the interviewer and the respondent, the physical setting of the interview, and the topic being discussed. Some people are pleasant and helpful as a matter of course; others are just as naturally grumpy and obstructive. One setting can be quiet and conducive to an engaging dialogue, while another is like being on a rush hour bus. Some topics are controversial, others barely able to generate a yawn. The analyst must be able to determine quickly the kind of interview it will be and adopt an appropriate strategy. Here is a brief description of some of the types of people you can run into in an interview and some suggestions about how to get the most out of them.

1. Interviewee Types[1]

The "technician". This is the man or woman concerned with details, precision, and accuracy to the point that it borders on being anal compulsive. The stereotype of an engineer is an example of this role. If you are interviewing this person, your major problem is that he spends so much time talking about irrelevant (to you) details that you have a difficult time getting to the larger issues. This is the person who not only cannot see the forest for the trees, he can't see the trees because he's too busy looking at an insect crawling around the bark of one of the trees. If you find yourself, as an interviewer, stuck with this kind of person, you can either cut the interview off as soon as possible, or, more usefully, take advantage of the situation to ask him about some issue about which you really do need details—such as the inner workings of a processing plant or the methodology a laboratory assistant follows when he gets a sample of water he has to analyze.

The pretender. This is the person who does not belong where he is. He is pretending to be competent, but it soon becomes obvious to you that he does not know the first thing about the topics you're studying, even though he should know. You have made a mistake interviewing this person. If there's no way to use this person, the best thing to do is have a pleasant conversation for a

---

[1]Appreciation is expressed to C. Bellavita who suggested some of these types and developed the images.

reasonable amount of time and then leave. Don't forget to review the process you used to reach the conclusion that this was a person you ought to interview; you might be able to learn from that.

The busy executive. This person makes it very clear through his behavior that he has a great deal of work to do, most of it is important, and you're lucky you got an appointment at all. The telephone rings and people walk in and out asking for decisions or audiences. The best thing here is to know what you want to talk about in specifics; don't go on fishing expeditions. Work in between the spaces or interruptions. Be prepared to summarize the last answer he gave you, or the last partial answer, when he asks, "Now, where was I?"

The teacher or helper. This kind of person realizes that you are a "student" in the general sense of the word and enjoys being in the position of someone with superior knowledge. He honestly goes out of his way to be helpful to you by rephrasing your questions or guiding you in certain directions. It is easy to get seduced by this kind of person. He is so helpful and informative that you sometimes leave the interview knowing a lot that you did not know before, but knowing little about what you came to get. Because he considered himself a "teacher," he gave you what he thought was "best" for you instead of listening to what it was that you really wanted.

The protector. This person is interested in protecting what he has. You have come with a request for information, and he is not sure why you want it. He can be afraid of what you will do with the information, of what your hidden agendas are, or of who put you up to this. He can resent the fact that you are butting your nose into his affairs, that you are questioning his ability to do his job—in a word, he is afraid of you for one or several of many reasons. This is a tendency. You can see the signs of it when you arrive at his office; he may be nervous, brusque, quiet, or recalcitrant. He views you as a potential threat. If you do nothing to put him at ease, you are not likely to get much out of the interview. If you can overcome that initial fear, you may end up with some useful information. Most of the time there is little that you can do to overcome the fear that is inside him—whatever manifestation it takes. You need to be extremely tactful.

The boaster. This person's world revolves around himself. He sees all things in terms of a stage on which he is the true center. He is good for getting negative information about others. It is usually heavily biased, but once you make the proper allowances, he may provide some inside information you are not likely to get elsewhere. Frequently this person will also be dissatisfied with the organization, and he is a good source for gossip about other organizations.

The weathervane. This individual's stories change each time you see him. You will get a feeling for today's climate of opinion. The information reflects the individual's high discount rate. The current information may be useful, but interpretation is not.

The counterpuncher. This individual tries to turn the relationship interviewer-interviewee around, that is, he would like to ask, rather than answer, questions. Possible reasons are a wish to cover up, an interest in the interviewer's project, or the desire to find out what others have told the interviewer. Try to determine quickly whether you can get the interview back on track.

The patient on the couch. This interviewee uses the opportunity to unburden himself. You are the psychiatrist/priest and he is the patient/confessor. His own problems may indeed reflect organizational problems; at the other extreme you may only become enlightened about his unhappy family life.

The angel. This person is not common to this planet—at least not that we have discovered. Essentially, this person knows just what you want to find out, gives you the information in such a way that you cannot help but understand it, and can also use it to make pithy and profound empirical generalizations. He also tells you what you did not ask but should have. He is a pleasant conversationalist and devotes the time you ask for directly to you.

2. Preparation for the Interview

1. Read exhaustively but critically whatever field you are exploring. Immerse yourself in the subject matter so that in an interview you can isolate a statement that does not fit and begin to wonder why it does not fit. This is where the payoffs come, that is, comparing the mismatches and then trying to discover why they exist.
2. Get to know roughly as much about the important facts as the people you're talking to and be able to turn those facts this way and that way without the constraints of people who are actually in the institution. By reading and interviewing eventually you should be able to think like someone actually dealing with the technology and make little fantasy decisions to see how those decisions might change outcomes. It is not only useful but fun to get to that stage.
3. Avoid being sponsored by an organizational "has-been" or known troublemaker. However, the has-been himself may be a valuable subject. Often a vice-president is "kicked upstairs" into, say, corporate planning, as a decompression chamber before retirement. Such a person may be relaxed and provide a highly perceptive long-range view of the organization. He can be objective since he is out of the rat race.
4. When someone refuses, have a sponsor or friend of interviewee help set up the meeting.

5. Avoid complex, detailed explanations about the project; say just enough to get the interview.
6. Try to schedule an interview so as to avoid interruption and distraction.
7. When asked, state that the length of the interview depends on the interviewee. If pushed, understate the time requirements slightly. Do not give the feeling that the interview will take a great deal of time.
8. Do not schedule interviews too closely to try to save time. You need to think and have some unscheduled time as well as travel time.

3. The Interview—General

1. Be punctual.
2. Consider using two people to interview a person, either together or separately. This may be important where questions of race, insider–outsider positions, style and personality differences, complementarity, or orientation for the study might prove significant.
3. Consider the advantages and limitations of tape recorders carefully. What is very effective with one person can turn another person off. An alternative is to use a tape recorder immediately after the interview while your impressions are fresh.
4. Interview all actors in an unstructured manner. Try to get an understanding of what is being said from the actor's own frame of reference. Under no circumstances use the proposed technology as a directing device or as a way of focusing the responses. In the case of the O perspective try to find out what the particular person does and how that affects the functioning of the organization. In the case of the P perspective, try to elicit the propensity of the actor to support or oppose the proposed technology by ascertaining basic beliefs, values, world-views, and motivations.
5. Follow up clashes of information for interpretation and refinement. Use questions like "On whom do you rely to get _____done? To get word through?" "Someone mentioned _____: do you agree?"
6. Look for phrases like "off the record" or "what you don't understand is _____."
7. Play "what if?" This can make the interview particularly useful. The worst that can happen is that the person interviewed will not know how to play this game. He may be so rigid that nothing beyond standard operating procedure (SOP) or business-as-usual has ever come to mind. The best that can happen is that the interviewee will know how to play and will turn up all sorts of impact and policy-related points.
8. Always ask a few more questions than you have on the list when an interview starts. During World War II, a CBS correspondent talked with an injured Marine pilot in a hospital for an hour about the details of the pilot's being shot down and parachuting into the water, and as he was leaving he remarked that the pilot seemed rather badly hurt for having

been dropped gently into the water by the parachute. It was only then that the pilot thought to mention that his parachute had not opened.[2]

9. Do not assume anything and particularly do not worry about asking silly questions. Stop the interview if the person you're talking to says something you do not understand. Most people really enjoy talking about things they do and think and, while you will run into someone occasionally who will claim that he thinks the question is foolish or ignorant, most of the time people really want to make things clear and will be patient until they are.

10. Do not hesitate to interview someone from whom you anticipate little additional information, because an atmosphere of trust can boomerang if certain people feel left out. If someone recommends a number of sources he is sure will be of use, at least one should be contacted to show you do take the whole interview seriously. If a group perceives certain people as key or "important," the credibility of your approach is at stake.

11. Be observant to "test" situations. Sensitivity to information that must not be traced may be tried before other information is given to the interviewer. You can get better information only to the extent you have already gotten some good information. Catching on to inside humor is a good test also; it shows what one knows.

12. Circulate bits of information that are interesting but will not betray confidences in order to trace communication patterns.

13. Select your "targets of interest" carefully. Start with someone you have an "in" with or feel comfortable with. Add to or drop from the list as you go along, being sure to maintain a cross section.

14. To the degree that interviewing is investigative reporting it is nothing more than old-fashioned detective work. Put together little scraps of information one piece at a time until things fit together. If one scrap is wrong, nothing will fit. Investigative reporting is commonly seen these days to involve efforts to discover what's wrong, as in "Watergate," but it is as easily applied to discovering what went right or simply what went on.

4. The O Perspective Interview

1. When you're exploring an institution always start at the bottom, but keep going until you get to the top. Any situation looks very different to people at all levels of an organization. If you settle for the view from middle management you will miss even more. Often it is very useful to talk first to someone who has a good overview of the area—a terrain specialist who likes to talk and knows everybody. From this interview refine a list of actors.

---

[2]Personal communication, Jack Burby.

2. Be sure to get to "front line people" (that is, the workers doing the task) as well as top and middle management in an organization. The comparison allows tracing lags, SOPs, and relationships.
3. Be able to recognize "middle level *information*" and distinguish it from vague generalities, trivia, and petty office intrigues without particular value.
4. Try to allow sufficient time for a second pass through the organization and with the informants. One purpose of the second pass is to fill in gaps in understanding, but it is also possible at that time to ask more directed questions dealing with the proposed technology.
5. Try to find out what the particular person does and how that affects the functioning of the organization.
6. Find the "doorkeepers"—to get in, to know how to get in, and to learn the view of the world from that office. Often those easiest to talk to are now power holders so the entrance must be achieved step by step.

5. Starter Question List for a Technology Assessment using T, O, and P Perspectives (Arranged by Elements of Figure 4b)

Element	Question
1. Technology	a. Do YOU really understand the subject technology well?
	b. How do the technologists see its advantages and disadvantages?
	c. Read relevant material on the proposed technology, on past but similar technologies, and on the policy process associated with these past and present technologies.
	d. From typed interviews and other written material analyze the *feasibility* of the proposed technology.
	e. Would problems with the subject technology implicate a group or class of technologies?
	f. What might happen if the technology became very widespread or was vastly scaled up?
	g. Which seemingly unrelated technologies could have a major impact on the one under assessment?
2. Physical and environmental setting	a. What are the anticipated beneficial and adverse effects on the physical environment?
	b. Are there low probability impacts that would be of large magnitude?
	c. Are there high-likelihood impacts that are currently assumed to have low magnitude?

d. Are there impacts that are difficult or impossible to detect with current sensing or monitoring systems?

e. What impacts might be caused by synergism with other technologies?

3. Sociotechnical setting

a. Who are the likely beneficiaries and victims?

b. Develop a preliminary list or map of the key actors (both individuals and collective or organizational) who have been or might be involved with the proposed technology. One basis for selection is who cares or who has something to gain or lose by the introduction of the technology and one clue to possible involvement is past involvement.

c. What organizations are "responsible" for monitoring and for regulating the technology?

d. What are the appropriate SOPs for each organization?

e. How does information flow through each organization?

f. How centralized or decentralized is each organization?

g. What organizations might become involved if serious problems or alarm developed?

h. What are appropriate policies to deal with the technology from a cost-benefit point of view?

4. Technopersonal setting

a. What individuals have a strong personal stake in the technology and possess power?

b. Are there impacts that may galvanize specific individuals to action and, if so, what kind of action?

c. How will this technology help or hurt progress toward the career objectives of the key actors?

d. Does organization X have to hire or fire people (as a result of the new technology)?

e. Whose task is made more difficult or easier by the technology? How?

f. Which *type* of individual is likely to push for adoption and which type of individual will be opposed to it?

g. How does the technology change the way you make decisions?

h. Which individuals have taken strong public stands regarding the technology?

5. Organization
   actors

    a. What are the official aims of the organization/group?

    b. What are the unstated aims of the organization/group?

    c. Is there a difference in perception between the technologists and organization X regarding the meaning and significance of the technology (for example, due to the technologists confusing peers with clients).

    d. How does the technology impact the official aims and the unstated aims?

    e. Which organizations/groups compete most directly for financial resources with organization/group X?

    f. What is the most effective way to change SOPs in organization X?

    g. What does the organization chart look like? How does it differ from the real power structure? Who controls policy?

    h. What does organization X consider to be the most serious misconception on the part of the technologists?

    i. What are the organization's vulnerabilities to influence?

    j. Will or should the SOPs of the organization/group change as a consequence of the new technology?

    k. Who are this organization's strongest friends and strongest enemies?

    l. Are there conflicting jurisdictions among regulatory/control agencies?

    m. What plans do regulatory/control agencies have for monitoring the new technology—continuous, one-shot, periodic?

    n. When and how are SOPs circumvented in organizations?

    o. What links exist among research organizations and commercial interests?

    p. What kind of legal actions have been taken involving the technology?

6. Individual actors

    a. What does the psychological profile of each key actor look like?

    b. What are the career objectives of each key actor?

    c. What links exist between "experts" in the field

and manufacturers/promoters of new technology—research funding, consulting, prior jobs, etc?

d. What links are there between regulatory actors and manufacturers/promoters?

e. What *type* of individual is likely to support/oppose the technology?

f. Who are the "strong" individuals?

g. Who is a risk taker? Who is a risk avoider?

h. Who is a maverick? How is he faring?

i. Who is a long-range thinker (or low discounter)?

j. Who is vulnerable to influence?

7. Political action

a. What strategies and tactics are likely to be tried?

b. What coalitions are feasible?

c. How do the styles of play of the key actors compare?

d. Are issues regarding this technology linked to other political/technological issues?

e. How can money be used most effectively to influence policy relating to this technology?

f. What trade-offs are possible to help achieve agreements?

8. Decisions

a. What are likely/desirable/unlikely/undesirable decisions? Why?

b. Are decisions part of organizational politics or ad hoc?

c. What decisions have been avoided or neglected and by whom?

APPENDIX B

ADDITIONAL BACKGROUND FROM THE LITERATURE

B. CLARY, H. LINSTONE, and A. J. MELTSNER

In this Appendix we provide additional supporting material from the literature. Section A deals with the analysis of formal organizations and is based largely on Meltsner's published checklist (1972) and *Organizational Elements of Analysis*. Section B draws in propositions suitable to the T, O, and P perspectives.

A. ORGANIZATIONAL ELEMENTS OF ANALYSIS[1]

Before proceeding to analyze a formal organization, the policy analyst should take into account his objective in performing the analysis. If the objective is to do a technology assessment, for example, then it is important to pay attention to the relationship between aspects of the technology and the possible organizational consequences in terms of altered design and operational procedures. If the objective is to evaluate a program, it will be important to examine those aspects of the organization that are directly related to program output.

This checklist identifies some of the design elements of a formal organization that you will want to examine in an analysis. A design element is simply some aspect of the organization that can be manipulated or changed to alter its structure and processes.

1. Preliminary Boundary Design Elements

The first step in analyzing a formal organization is to identify it. Such an identification is entirely arbitrary and is related to the nature and purpose of the analysis. The analyst is expected to make some sort of a boundary around the organization that may be more or less coterminous with the way the organization is perceived by others. At a minimum, a boundary must be drawn around the organization that separates it from its environment.

---

[1]We recall from Sections IVB2 and IVC (Figure 6b in particular) that the term *organization* has been used very broadly to include informal groupings and societal entities. Here the term will be used in its narrower connotation.

Members. Once the line or boundary around the organization has been drawn, it will then be possible to identify the *members* of the organization, those people who work in it or in some way perform tasks that are associated with the organization. This is not always an easy element to identify, because members may be augmented in a variety of ways; for example, one could identify the over 3000 staff members as part of the U.S. Congress rather than limiting the definition simply to the elected officials. In addition to knowing who are members, it may also be important to understand how these members are recruited and replaced over a long period of time, what type of training is necessary for past performance, and what are their orientations toward the organization.

Environment. The environment of an organization is not simply a residual. The organization is connected to its environment by important linkages with individuals and other organizations which impart limitations, supply resources, or place demands on output. It is essential to identify these linkages and to understand what kinds of exchanges take place. This is often done by interviewing members of the organization itself *to see how they perceive their environment.* For example, are the necessary inputs always available? Can the outputs always be distributed? Are there competitors for both resources and markets? What is the role of regulators and unions? Do the people in the organization perceive the environment to be routine or stable, changeful, predictable, or unpredictable? Moreover, the environment also has a physical dimension. Consider the physical characteristics of the facility or the plant as well as the location of the organization and their effects on behavior.

Task, goals, and technology. The organization must be able to carry out various types of activities: identify a desired outcome, develop a belief about how to achieve that outcome, maintain and adapt to changing circumstances, and be able to control the necessary resources to do all these things. As a preliminary element of analysis, it is important to determine the nature of organizational work, identify the tasks performed, and ascertain how, if at all, these relate to the technology used by the organization and to the diverse goals of its members.

What kind of technology does the organization use to achieve its objective? Is it like a production line where each task must be done in sequence, like an employment agency or bank that links people who want to be interdependent, or is it composed of a variety of techniques used in combination to achieve some goal such as a hospital, or a research institute? Do people know with certainty how to accomplish their objective? Do the methods they use produce the desired outcome? A grammar school or a community mental hospital would be an example of an organization where the members do not have a clear idea how to accomplish their objective. We really don't know how to teach children to read or to produce mental health; alternatively, it is very clear how to produce shoes and pocket calculators.

In theory there is an interaction between the nature of the tasks an organization performs and the organization's environment that is reflected in the structure which the organization takes on. Organizations with similar tasks facing the same kind of environment should look alike. At one extreme is the organization in which the members know how to achieve their goals but they face an unstable environment—oil companies or microprocessor companies. At the other extreme is the organization in which the members do not know clearly how to achieve their objective but the environment is stable—primary schools and mental hospitals. There can be four possible combinations: the organization has a clear idea how to achieve its objectives and faces a stable environment or an unstable environment; the organization does not have a clear notion how to achieve its objective and faces a stable environment or an unstable environment. In theory each of these four types will develop different sorts of *allocation design elements* and *control design elements*.

2. Allocation Design Elements

Under this heading, the analyst will examine those elements that are generally static and are usually allocated during initial formation of an organization or during a process of reorganization. The notion of allocation design elements has to do with the division of tasks, allocation of responsibility for completion of those tasks to members of the organization, and possible linkages to the environment.

Structure. The structure of an organization is the vehicle by which the organization tries to achieve the desired outcome with the least expenditure of resources. The structure of an organization is a way of dividing up tasks, specifying particular roles and positions in the organization, and allocating responsibility. When analyzing the structure of an organization, which we usually think of as a "hierarchy," the analyst must identify *the network of roles* that is intended to accomplish the various tasks. Sometimes a network can result in a very tall hierarchy or a pyramidal shape. Other times it can be quite flat or more collegial in the way it operates.[2] It is possible to look at any organizational chart and see what is considered to be the formal structure, but many important relationships do not appear on the formal chart, and it is the analyst's task to identify those informal aspects of organizational life that might affect structure. Some examples are status, cliques, and social controls via informal norms. In some production settings informal social controls cause employees to curtail output, which affects the organization's production. The status of employees can often influence the distribution of tasks in ways not specified in formal job descriptions.

---

[2]See also Section IV B 2, particularly Table 7.

Power and resources. A supplementary aspect of the allocation of roles and tasks is the allocation of power and political resources. In each particular role, whether formal or informal, there will also be a set of resources, so that the occupant of that role can accomplish the particular task that is assigned to it. Such resources involve economic and noneconomic aspects. A holder of a particular position can have resources that deal with the control of information, the distribution of material rewards such as pay raises, the monopoly over computer time, and so on. It is important for the analyst to identify not just those occupants who appear to be powerful and have considerable resources, but those who actually exercise their power by using their resources to accomplish the assigned task or some other objective. Thus sometimes it is a mistake to see the person at the top of the organization as the one who is in control and has many resources while, in fact, to accomplish organizational tasks, it is essential that persons at the top gain the cooperation of those that are supposedly "below" on the hierarchy. The analyst should not mistake reputation for power with the actual exercise of it. A way to identify power is to see where dependence exists. *Power is the inverse of dependence.* To the extent that you are dependent on someone else for information, cooperation, resources, etc., then that person has power over you. Since the exercise of power is a relationship, the analyst has first to sort out the resources which individuals at various levels in the organization have and then proceed to describe typical power relationships.

3. Control Design Elements

Once the first cut has been made at examining the allocation design elements, which for our purposes can be considered to be more or less *static,* it is important to examine the more *dynamic* aspects of organizational life which alter these allocation design elements. Most of these processes are aimed at the basic organizational problem of control—how to accomplish certain tasks which the leaders and resource holders of an organization want to see accomplished. It is usually understood that an organization will use up most of its energy and resources to accomplish the primary work. However, a great deal of this energy is also devoted to trying to control what is being done and to insure compliance.

In a general sense, this has to do with coping with *unpredictable occurrences* originating both from within the organization and from the environment. Some examples of unpredictable occurrences or sources of uncertainty are employee discretion and variable skill levels, changing factor and labor markets, changing technology, shifting consumer tastes, changing regulations, etc. Unpredictable occurrences are generally seen as undesirable because they mean that the organization's resources are unused or diverted from the primary tasks of the organization and performance is reduced. Organizations carry out several types of behavior that have to do with coping with uncertainty: communicating information, coordinating tasks, making both routine and nonroutine decisions, and developing routines, rules, and incentive systems.

Again, in theory, the nature of these coping behaviors probably depends on the type of task and the source and extent of uncertainty. For example, when people do not know clearly how to do what they are trying to do and the source of uncertainty is external, such as in storing nuclear wastes or curing cancer, then the organization will develop a different set of methods for communicating information, coordinating tasks, and motivating employees than will a bakery or a MacDonald's, where it is clear how to make eclairs or wrap Big Macs, and the source of uncertainty is primarily internal in terms of variability in human skill.

Communication. The communication process is a good first place to look at how the various design elements interact. Here the analyst will try to examine the information and formal information systems. These systems include how the organization gathers intelligence from the environment so that it may react to changing circumstances, processes information internally within the organization, and how it transmits information to the environment. For example, how does the organization receive information from the outside—journals, verbal communication, clients, customers, professional meetings, etc.? When a person in the hierarchy knows something, whom does he tell it to? How does he pass on this information? And what happens to it in the process of passing it on? How does the organization transmit information to the environment—memos, advertising, public relations, press releases, etc.?

It is important to understand that communication as a process should not be restricted to formal management information systems, but should be extended to the general processing of information via grapevines, coffee breaks, lunch with colleagues, social occasions, etc.

Decision making, routines, and rules. Once a general understanding of the flow of information is gained, it will then be possible to concentrate the analytical effort on identifying the standard operating procedures (SOPs), or the routes and rules, by which decisions have been made and continue to be made. The members of every organization have a set of *programmed responses* to stimuli which they regularly face in the performance of tasks and accomplishing work. That is to say, not every situation requires a new decision, because rules and routines have been established for handling those aspects that have previously been decided in the history of the organization. Sometimes these SOPs will be written down in manuals. Other times they will be unwritten rules that people absorb, know, and apply. It will be important for the analyst to identify the central nonwritten as well as the written rules that are related to the particular purpose or objective of the analysis. For example, if the analyst were looking at the effectiveness of a new high school program that made extensive use of individually directed study periods, an unwritten rule that dictated that teachers send troublesome students to the library rather than to the principal's office would be central. In general, the analyst should identify those rules that organizational members apply to the performance of tasks, to the maintenance of the organization (such as personnel replacement), and to adaptation activities (such as planning schedules).

Decision making, nonroutine coordination of tasks. Not all decisions can be made according to SOPs. New situations arise that may not have been anticipated in the past, yet it is important for decisions to be made to coordinate the various tasks of the organization and to plan future activities. Therefore, it is important for analysts to identify a sample of central key, nonroutine, "nonprogrammed" decisions. The question here is to find out how the members of the organization make decisions on nonroutine matters. Now, while it is not possible within the limits of the available time in analyzing an organization to examine all central nonroutine decisions, it will be important to have what may best be considered a representative sample of such decisions. The organization essentially is an open entity receiving a variety of stimuli from its environment that affect the nature of organizational tasks. It is important to examine those aspects of decision making that show how the organization deals with changes in its environment, such as changes in the demand for the organization's output, in the supply of resources, in the available technology, new federal regulations and court rulings, etc.—those aspects of change which can have considerable impact on the organization over time. Generally, it is possible to trace decisions that the members of the organization believe have been important or will be important in the future. Try to identify who makes the decisions and where they are made.

Incentive reward system. A central method of control over the performance of tasks in an organization is accomplished through the use of explicit and implicit incentive or reward systems. Each organization will have several different ways of rewarding its members, and the analyst should not look only for monetary or financial rewards. The organization may offer several nonmonetary incentives such as prestige, visibility, social connections, and the like. Often an organization will be able to control its members by appealing to intrinsic or altruistic motivations or by relying on professional norms. Other organizations may resort to more physical or coercive measures. The nature of reward systems is probably as varied as the motivations of the members of the organization. One way to determine the structure and use of the reward system is to ask members why they work at the particular organization.

B. A SAMPLING OF STATEMENTS ILLUMINATING THE PERSPECTIVES

Using Table B-1 (drawn from Table 8 of the main text) as a starting point, we bring together 101 statements descriptive or characteristic of perspective traits. They serve us as assertions, maxims, or postulates in place of formal propositions. Their sources comprise a spectrum ranging from Machiavelli to as yet unpublished material, and they are illustrative rather than comprehensive. We have

TABLE B1. Multiple Perspectives (Drawn from Table 8)

	Technical (T)	Organizational (O)	Personal (P)
1. Goal	Problem solving Product (study, design, explanation)	Stability and continuity Process Action and implementation	Power, influence, prestige Status maintenance or improvement
2. Modes of inquiry	Abstraction and modeling Data and analysis	Dialectic/adversary Negotiated reality/consensual	Intuition, persona, individual reality Experience, learning
3. Constraints	Problem simplification by limiting variables, relations Cause and effect Need for validation and replicability	Fractionating/factoring problems Problem delegation or avoidance Agenda ("problem of the moment") Bureaucracy often pervasive Political sensitivity and expediency Loyalty, credentials Restricted access by outsiders	Hierarchy of individual needs Each construes attributes of others Inner world (subjectivity)
4. Characteristics	Prediction Optimization (best solution) Quantification Use of averages, probabilities Trade-offs Uncertainties noted many caveats ("on one hand . . .")	Recognition of partial unpredictability Long-range planning often ritualized Satisficing (first acceptable, rather than best, solution) Incremental change, slow adaptation Parochial priorities Standard operating procedures Compromise and bargaining Uncertainties avoided Fear of error	Need for certainty, beliefs Creativity and vision of the few Cope with few alternatives or variables only Filter out images inconsistent with past experience Focus on simplistic hypotheses rather than scanning many Leaders and followers, mystique Fear of change and unknown
5. Communication	Technical report, briefing	Directive, conference Hortatory language with public Private language with insiders	Narrative (story), discussion, speech Importance of personality

used an artifice to underline the differences of perspectives, that is, in the mode
of expressing the statements. Hence most are paraphrases rather than direct
quotations.

Some statements can be associated with more than one perspective, and these
will be identified by Greek letters as follows:

$$\phi\text{—O and P}$$
$$\rho\text{—T and P}$$

1. T Perspective

GOALS

1. The prevailing objective is maximization of expected utility (EU), for example,
   the highest benefit/cost ratio.[3] The objective constitutes the decision rule or criterion
   which guides the decision maker in his choice for a course of action. Economic
   choice is "a way of looking at problems" [Rubinstein, 1976:315, Hitch, 1965:53].
2. The most important task of management . . . is to be able to assess the values of
   lost opportunities. The determination of opportunity costs is essential in the application of all operations research models. [In measuring these costs] one must
   try to estimate the optimal use of the released funds [Churchman, 1982:13, 98].

MODES OF INQUIRY

3. Science and its knowledge and approach are the cornerstone of systems analysis,
   although it more nearly resembles engineering in its focus on choice and action.
   It deals with systems combining people, the natural environment, and various
   artifacts of man and his technology.
   Systems analysis uses the methods of science insofar as possible.

   • Results can be duplicated by others.

   • Calculations, assumptions, data, and judgments are reported explicitly and
     thus are subject to checking, criticism, and disagreement.

   • Conclusions are not influenced by personalities, reputations, or vested interests
     [Quade and Miser, to be published 1, 23, 25, 26].

4. The essence of systems analysis is to construct and operate within a "model," an
   idealization of the situation appropriate to the problem. Only in rare cases is it
   possible to make a convincing comparison of alternatives without a quantitative
   analysis [Quade and Boucher, 1967:11, 48].
5. [Operations research] is based on the conviction that the factors affecting . . . operations can be measured quantitatively and that there exist common
   laws obeyed by the basic variables. . . . The main problems concerning operations

---

[3]If the cost is fixed, the alternative with the highest effectiveness or benefit is selected; if the effectiveness level
is fixed, the alternative with the lowest cost is chosen.

research today are the discovery of such laws and the development of techniques . . . for rapid, simple application [Kimball, 1953:145].

6. General systems theory is a set of related definitions, assumptions, and propositions which deal with reality as an integrated hierarchy of organizations of matter and energy. General living systems theory is concerned with a special subset of all systems, the living ones [Miller, 1978:9].

7. Control systems are of two types: cause-controlled systems and error-controlled systems. In the former, the control measure is defined directly by the disturbance (e.g., an electric toaster is a cause-controlled system). In the latter, there is a comparison between desired and actual output, with a corrective feedback being a function of the measured deviation (e.g., an autopilot in an aircraft) [Kramer and de Smit, 1977:110–125].

8. Living systems can be structured in seven hierarchical levels: cell, organ, organism, group, organization, society, and supranational systems. Systems at all these levels are open systems composed of subsystems which process inputs, throughputs, and outputs of various forms of matter, energy, and information. Systems at each of the seven levels have the same 19 critical subsystems [Miller, 1978:1].[4]

9. Steady states in all living systems are controlled by negative feedbacks. A living system is self-regulating because in it input not only affects output, but output often adjusts input [Miller, 1978:36].

10. All systems that change through time can be represented by using only levels and rates. The two kinds of variables are necessary but at the same time sufficient for representing any system [Forrester, 1971:18].

CONSTRAINTS AND CHARACTERISTICS

11. Decision analysis imposes a logical structure on the reasoning that underlies any specific decision. It quantifies the considerations, however subjective, which enter into any decision. A complex decision is decomposed into separable components, often in the form of a decision tree, on which any given decision maker's perceptions can be explicitly represented and quantified. Their logical implications are deduced according to established mathematical procedures [Brown et al., 1974:5].

12. A decision-making model contains five main elements:

- An objective which is a statement of what the decision-maker wants.

- States of nature that constitute the environment of the decision model and are not controlled by the decision maker.

- Alternative actions which the decision maker controls because he can select whichever action he wishes.

- Outcomes that are the results of a combination of an action and a state of nature.

- Utilities that are measures of satisfaction or value which the decision maker associates with each outcome; measures often involve cost and effectiveness [Rubinstein, 1976:315].

---

[4]Note that these are prime numbers, following a curious pattern in systems analysis.

13. Decision making can be classified according to four states of knowledge:
    (a) under certainty—each action always results in one known outcome;
    (b) under risk—a known objective (frequency type) probability is associated
        with each outcome;
    (c) under uncertainty—each action can result in two or more outcomes, but the
        associated objective probabilities are not known;
    (d) under conflict—the states of nature are replaced by courses of action available
        to an opponent who is trying to maximize his objective function.
    The mathematical tools corresponding to these types are:
    (a) optimization theory;
    (b) objective probability theory;
    (c) subjective probability theory, other decision rules (e.g., maximin, maximax,
        Hurwicz, and regret); and
    (d) game theory [Rubinstein, 1976:311].

φ14. A Bayesian regards it as meaningful to talk about the probability of a hypothesis
    A given evidence B. He is ready to incorporate intuitive probability into statistical
    theory and practice, and into the behavior of humans, animals, and automata
    [Good, 1965:8].

15. Rational analysis may be divided into two phases: problem formulation and
    solution. The first phase may be the more critical of the two, but receives the
    least attention in the literature [Anderson, 1971:112].

16. When the process of selecting an alternative is simplified by fixing certain char-
    acteristics that may, in fact, vary, the resulting selection is called a suboptimum.
    Such simplification is both necessary and permissible [Quade and Boucher,
    1967:63].

17. For an analyst to gain control over a system, he must be able to take at least as
    many distinct actions, i.e., as great a variety of countermeasures, as the observed
    system can exhibit. Variety is a measure of complexity (Ashby's Law of Requisite
    Variety) [Hare, 1967:136–138].

18. The solution is only as good as the data we are using. The model may be great,
    but our information about the problem may be poor ("garbage in, garbage out")
    [Lucas, 1976:2–4].

2. O Perspective

GOALS

19. Our organization has a sense of its own identity [Ingalls, 1976:50].

20. There is nothing more difficult for us to carry out, nor more doubtful of success,
    nor more dangerous to handle, than to initiate a new order of things [Machiavelli,
    The Prince, quoted in Buskirk, 1974:15].

21. This rule should be observed by all who wish to abolish an existing system . . . and
    introduce a new one. . . . It is important to retain in such innovations as much as
    possible existing forms [Machiavelli, *The Discourses,* quoted in Buskirk, 1974:132].

22. Good models are crisply focused on a few problems. Our operating units split
    their attention between a host of imprecisely defined goals. Formal models have
    little to say explicitly about how to allocate attention among multiple, imprecisely
    defined goals [Andersen, 1977:226].

23. A study group considers a broader range of alternatives than we do in our organization. It is apt to recommend actions beyond our ability to implement; for example, policies requiring interagency or interdepartmental coordination. Formal models with a focus on strategic problems and abstract representations of our organizational capabilities exacerbate this tendency to infeasible policies [Andersen, 1977:233–234].

24. Given a problem, we examine alternative courses in an incremental fashion, based on our routines. Policy results from the routine execution of our organizational capabilities [Allison, 1971:84–85, 209].

25. Before our organization can begin to change how it views a problem, it is necessary that several key managers first change their thinking, thereby breaking the self-reinforcing nature of cognitive realities. Hence, analysts who desire to change shared problem definitions must at least implicitly assume the role of a teacher [Andersen, 1971:379].

26. We avoid difficult decisions about alternative goals by avoiding tradeoffs. We attend to incompatible goals one at a time. For example, the US Navy in Hawaii in 1941 had two goals: (a) to train pilots for attacks, and (b) to carry out reconnaissance. There were not enough aircraft to do both, so the Navy concentrated on (a) [Allison, 1971:92].

27. In our American power structure, the dominant factor is economic interests [Hunter, 1953:102].

28. We are very likely to select and implement alternatives which reflect our existing organizational goals [Allison, 1971:90–91].

29. Our organization is never satisfied with the gains we have achieved, e.g., our budget, our profits, our number of employees. [Edelman, 1967:154]. Example: no defense budget is ever adequate to the military, no wage level to the union.

MODES OF INQUIRY

30. Policy recommendations result only partially from model-based analysis. To a large degree, our final recommendations will be influenced by our organizational capabilities and the nature of the linkages established with other units [Anderson, 1977:221].

CONSTRAINTS AND CHARACTERISTICS

φ31. In our decision making, complete rationality is never possible [Edelman, 1967:68].

32. Hierarchy is basic in Japan's culture from the family to industrial enterprises to international politics. Caste has been a rule of life through all of Japan's recorded history [Benedict, 1946:43–75].

φ33. The self-disciplines of another culture are always likely to seem irrelevancies to observers from our culture. Example: In Japan, the phraseology and practice of self-discipline have a recognized place in life. It is a principle of Japanese psychic economy that the will should be supreme over the almost infinitely teachable body. It is their conviction that the body itself has no laws of well-being so dominating that they must be obeyed at all costs. In other words, when it is a matter of serious affairs of life, the demands of the body, no matter how essential to health, should be drastically subordinated [Benedict, 1946:228–230].

34. Our internal operating setting is our bureaucratic environment [Andersen, 1977:210].
35. Our "reality" is often socially constructed within our organization. It is contextually created from prevailing shared assumptions about a specific situation or problem. Agreement permits action (Merleau-Ponty Inquiring System) [Scheele, 1975:42–44].
36. We perform functions in routine and standardized ways, even in novel situations where innovative responses are demanded [Allison, 1971:83].
37. We must distinguish between nonimplementing staff and implementing operating units in our organization [Andersen, 1977:211].
38. One of our operating units may take action which constrains the options open to another unit. The activities of the unit are, over time, closely circumscribed by the actions of other units [Andersen, 1977:214].
φ39. The leadership echelon in our organization has an esprit de corps which makes it easy to decide who "will carry the ball" on a problem. The others subordinate themselves readily on a temporary basis [Hunter, 1953:66].
40. We focus on our organization's interests; we look at the individual's interests only as our organization interprets them [Whyte, 1957:440].
φ41. A problem for our organization is that the professional man tends to be career-oriented rather than company-oriented. (Not surprisingly, the most effective R&D laboratories are also the most tolerant of individualism [Whyte, 1957:446].
42. We tend to extend our control over those activities which strongly support the achievement of our main goals, even if these activities do not themselves constitute our major missions [Thompson, 1967:39–40].
43. We subdivide problems and delegate the pieces to different units in our organization [Allison, 1971:80].
44. Our organizational hierarchy fractionates not only problems but also information. Only at the top is there broad information about all the activities as well as the external environment. This provides the basis of power at the top [Ingalls, 1976:112].
45. Our operating units function under pressure to meet constraints. Of necessity, these operations are characterized by expediency. Models create a long-run, somewhat abstracted view of policy questions that is not compatible with the perspective of our operating units [Andersen, 1977:224].
φ46. In organizational decision making, we rarely have the time to consider all the costs and benefits of a given strategy. The necessity for action, not the search for an optimum choice, is the hallmark of our decisions [Allison, 1971:178].
47. Usually a decision depends on agreement among several participants; we bargain and compromise to reach a decision [Allison, 1971:174–175].
48. The potential for conflict in our organization grows as outside forces require compromises among our decision makers [Thompson, 1967:138–139].
49. When we have settled questions, there is constant pressure for conformity [Hunter, 1953:181].
50. In important affairs, it is necessary for success that the principal authority should reside in one man only [Machiavelli, *The Discourses,* quoted in Buskirk, 174:259].
51. Our organization normally dislikes publicity: (1) the media feed much more on bad news (e.g., scandal, financial crisis) than on good news (e.g., steady growth); and (2) power can usually be exercised more effectively behind the scenes than under the glare of publicity [Hunter, 1953:183].

52. The flow of information in our organization is downward in larger volume than it is upward. Policy determination is not made by the professional understructure in any organization—be it corporation, government, or university [Hunter, 1953:248].

53. Our organization must deal with two kinds of changes—operating methods and goals. Both are very difficult to effect, the latter even more so than the former [Michael, 1968:92].

54. The more ambiguity exists about our goals and future, the more inhouse power bases and political players we must contend with [Thompson, 1967:129].

55. Long range planning is usually done at the top and becomes institutionalized; we tend to disregard it in our operations since they are geared to short-term considerations [Allison, 1971:84, 92].

56. Our organization reduces uncertainty through day-to-day negotiations with our operating environment. Policy models are characteristically unconcerned with day-to-day operations in any detailed and explicit way [Andersen, 1977:227].

57. External shocks cause our organization to adapt. Decision rules which lead from one state to a preferred state are likely to be used again in the future [Cyert and March, 1963:100].

58. In dealing with administrative enforcement of rules, we often play a game. Example: most drivers exceed the 55 mph speed limit, and occasionally warnings or tickets are issued. Outrage occurs only when it is no longer played as a game, e.g., when every violator is ticketed, as in a village speed trap [Edelman, 1967:44].

59. Public programs usually benefit small groups. We can use political activity to obtain quite specific, tangible benefits if we are well organized. [Edelman, 1967:4–5]. Example: many regulatory agency decisions only ostensibly benefit the public, but in actuality benefit the regulated industry.

COMMUNICATION

60. As bureaucrats, many of us are convinced that the issues of politics are now so technical and intricate that the individual cannot be expected to understand them or be alert to their consequences [Mills, 1956:347–348].

61. As a political elite, we carefully orchestrate perceptions for the general public, playing on mass needs, hopes, and anxieties. They are usually ignorant of the real issues, i.e., the actual goods, services, and power conveyed by their vote. What they get is *not* what they see [Edelman, 1967:2].

62. A large part of the prestige of dictatorships is based on the fact that they are credited with the concentrated power of secrecy. In our democratic society, a secret is dispersed among many people, and its power is thus weakened [Canetti, 1962:295].

63. In appeals for political support with the mass public, we tend to use hortatory language. Phrases such as "safeguard the public interest," "promote peaceful negotiations," and "redress the imbalance" are nothing more than emotional appeals for political support [Edelman, 1967:134].

64. Administrative language or jargon is imposed on us by minor bureaucrats, not leaders. We resent their authority over us and tend to respond with anger, humor, or ridicule [Edelman, 1967:142].

65. We use bargaining language to gain the support of those with whom we negotiate. We use hortatory language to provide rationalizations appropriate to those who must justify their actions (e.g., a lobbyist uses such approach with a congressman).

But we use bargaining language when logrolling in a legislature or when negotiating a contract [Edelman, 1967:146].

66. We use legal language in our contracts and statutes. Such language consists almost entirely of definitions and commands. This distinctive jargon is the near-exclusive property of lawyers and a concomitant of the "lawyerization" of our society [Edelman, 1967:138].

3. P Perspective

GOALS

67. As an engineer, I have an instinctive flush of pride in the machine . . . every man-made structure has a little bit of cathedral in it, since man cannot help but transcend himself as soon as he begins to design and construct [Florman, 1976, 126, 130].

68. [Those of us who] rise from private citizens to be princes merely by fortune have little trouble in rising but very much in maintaining our position [Machiavelli, *The Prince*, quoted in Buskirk, 1974:19].

φ69. To shape events, my actions must not only take place in an unstable environment, but my position must be strategically appropriate (e.g., not at too low a level in the hierarchy) [Greenstein, 1970:44–45].

70. A novel insight may change my thinking. If I am a manager, I can move this insight from my private domain toward a shared reality by creating new artifacts, coining a new vocabulary, establishing new formal organizational connections, and fostering new informal social contacts [Andersen, 1977:384].

71. My self-interest may lead me to "do unto others before it is done unto me" [Solman and Friedman, 1982].

φ72. The likelihood of my activity having an impact increases to the extent the environment is unstable, i.e., admits of restructuring [Greenstein, 1970:42–43].

73. I react to a political action because I see it as a personal threat or reassurance. Its objective consequences are of much less concern to me [Edelman, 1967:6–7]. Example: Hitler received the support of many a lower middle class German because it was comforting to be able to blame one's economic hardships on a specific, recognizable group, i.e., the Jews.

74. I not only pass information to another person in accordance with the needs of the tasks to be performed, but also to demonstrate my personal superiority or advance my personal status [Burns and Stalker, 1966:152].

CONSTRAINTS AND CHARACTERISTICS

φ75. I am not secure as Prince in my domain while those whom I have deprived of it are still alive [Machiavelli, 1972:250].

76. I am buffeted by contradictory norms evolved in the social institutions I interact with; and as a result, my behavior is often ambivalent [Mitroff, 1974:16].

77. As a ruler I can best describe my decision making process as *fuzzy gambling*. I face vast qualitative as well as quantitative uncertainties and the rules of the gambles change unpredictably. Added handicaps are distortions in the input I receive and undue positive feedback from sycophants [Dror, 1983:4–7].

φ78. My power and role in problem solving is determined by the way the problem or situation is defined [Allison, 1971:174–175].

79. I cannot approach issues objectively; my background, experiences, and roles are bound to influence my perception [Allison, 1971:211].

φ80. My personality structure (e.g., values, style) may be influenced or changed by the group or organization into which I am placed. For example, I may adopt the values and modus operandi of my predecessor, even though I derided and attacked him while I was an outsider [Edelman, 1967:85].

81. The position shapes the personality of the individual; i.e., my ego is to a considerable degree formed by my social setting—and I can be broken by being removed from it. [Edelman, 1967:108]. Example: General MacArthur became a living legend through his situation (e.g., by his prolonged physical absences from the U.S.).

82. The following steps are important means to pursue my own path (or alignment) successfully in an organizational setting:

- I am aware that I cannot understand the rationale behind someone's behavior or "objective" presentation of the facts until I understand the alignment which underlies that person's orientation.

- I must make sure the other person knows that I know.

- I must give others the essence of my own perspective on what I am trying to accomplish, but I need not fill in the obvious.

- After revealing my alignment, I do not grab control by immediately proposing an alternative course of action.

- I try to negotiate so as to add a person to the network of those who respect me for fairness; such person may be on my side in the future.

- If I must take a unilateral, unpopular course of action, I signal the others in advance.

- I do not take an irresolvable conflict personally.

- I recognize that my own alignments will change as I have new experiences and learn of others' realities [Culbert and McDonough, 1980:204–207].

83. I may still voice discontent even if my interests are taken care of. Example: a worker wants higher pay; a conservative complains even when the federal government is run by conservatives [Edelman, 1967:154].

84. As a leader, I prefer to maintain a distance from subordinates. I see my role as one of control rather than responsiveness. Since "familiarity breeds contempt," my power may be diminished by an active give-and-take relationship with subordinates [Hunter, 1953:231].

φ85. As a person able to make independent decisions, I am part of a relatively small group. As an executor of policy, I am part of a very large group [Hunter, 1953:113].

86. As an individual with power, I focus my attention on problems in which I have a definite interest. This leaves some domains in the body politic without strong top level representation [Hunter, 1953:103]. Example: President Lyndon Johnson's overriding personal interest in domestic issues.

87. In the practical world of handling immediate problems, I will lay aside some principles to achieve success [Hunter, 1953:231]. Example: bribegiving is tolerated by chief executives of major corporations to clinch important sales despite the high personal ethics exhibited by them in other matters.

88. A subtle and essential technique I use as an administrator is to blur issues. I find that clarification and sharpening of issues is not always desirable [Levin, 1970:15].

89. I can control a meeting and attain agreement by careful preparation—choosing the presenter of my proposition, selecting discussants, prearranging questions and answers [Hunter, 1953:183].

90. If I exercise power, publicity can drastically magnify or weaken my effectiveness [Hunter, 1953:183]

91. The greater my personal political skill, the less is my need for an initially favorable position or manipulable environment to achieve an impact [Greenstein, 1970:45–46].

92. The more years of experience and exposure I have had in a certain subject, the less variation there is in my current response to an issue or question about it. I will have developed preconceptions and attitudes leading to a highly predictable reaction [Greenstein, 1970:52].

93. I tend to think in terms of stereotypes and oversimplifications since I cannot recognize or tolerate ambiguous and complex situations. When I am insecure, this tendency is exacerbated [Edelman, 1967:31].

94. I resonate strongly with, or respond emotionally to, certain stimuli, and they influence my actions disproportionately [Greenstein, 1970:59]. Example: voting for political candidates on the basis of a single issue such as abortion.

95. As an individual at the middle or lower level of my organization, I have no voice in policy determination [Hunter, 1953:248].

96. As a user of a technology, I have a very different perception of it than does the designer or engineer [Morison, 98–122].

97. The current demographic and technological changes curtail many opportunities that I, as an individualist, have valued. But they also bring many new ones that I value more. They make room for greater variety and require higher intelligence, more capacity for human relations, and greater self-control [Vickers, 1973:83].

98. I tend to gear my ambitions to my age. Example: In the US, congressmen should arrive between ages 35 and 50, governors between 45 and 50, senators between 45 and 60 [Schlesinger, 1966:175–192].

COMMUNICATION

99. When I bargain with others, I play games. Rarely do I have the necessary information to make a rational decision. Since I play a number of such games at the same time, I may easily misperceive situations and develop misexpectations about the behavior of the other players. This leads to miscommunication with them [Allison, 1971:178–179].

100. The major threat at every level of communication is the lack of an "appreciative system" sufficiently widely shared to mediate communication, sufficiently apt to guide action, and sufficiently acceptable to make personal experience bearable. (An appreciative system is an interconnected set of largely tacit standards of judgment by which I both order and value my experience.) [Vickers, 1973:112, 122].

101. As Roosevelt saw it, the first task of an executive is to guarantee himself an effective flow of information and ideas. . . . He persistently sought to check and balance information acquired through a myriad of private, informal, and unorthodox channels and espionage networks. At times, he seemed almost to pit his personal sources against his public sources [Neustadt, 1960:156].

REFERENCES

Allison, G. (1971), *Essence of Decision: Explaining the Cuban Missile Crisis,* Little, Brown and Company, Boston.

Andersen, D. F. (1977), Mathematical Models and Decision Making in Bureaucracies, Doctoral dissertation, MIT.

Benedict, R. (1946), *The Chrysanthemum and the Sword,* World Publishing Co., New York.

Brown, R. V., Kahr, A. S., and Peterson, C. (1974), *Decision Analysis for the Manager,* Holt, Rinehart and Winston, New York.

Burns, T. and Stalker, G. M. (1966), *The Management of Innovation,* Tavistock, London.

Buskirk, R. H. (1974), *Modern Management and Machiavelli,* Cahners, Boston.

Canetti, E. (1962), *Crowds and Power,* Viking Press, New York.

Churchman, C. W. (1982), *Thought and Wisdom,* Intersystems Publications, Seaside, Calif.

Culbert, J. A., and McDonough, J. J. (1980), *The Invisible War: Pursuing Self-Interests at Work,* John Wiley and Sons, New York.

Cyert, R. M., and March, J. G. (1963), *A Behavioral Theory of the Firm,* Prentice-Hall, Englewood Cliffs, N.J.

Dror, Y. (June 7, 1983), *Forecasting for Rulers,* paper presented at *Third International Symposium on Forecasting,* Philadelphia.

Edelman, M. (1967), *The Symbolic Uses of Politics,* University of Illinois Press, Urbana.

Florman, S. C. (1976), *The Existential Pleasures of Engineering,* St. Martin's Press, New York.

Forrester, J. W. (1971), *World Dynamics,* Wright-Allen Press, Cambridge, Mass.

Good, I. J. (1965), *The Estimation of Probabilities: An Essay on Modern Bayesian Methods,* MIT Press, Cambridge, Mass.

Greenstein, F. (1970), *Personality and Politics,* Markham, Chicago.

Hare, Van Court, Jr. (1967), *Systems Analysis: A Diagnostic Approach,* Harcourt, Brace and World, New York.

Hitch, C. J. (1965), *Decision-Making for Defense,* University of California Press, Berkeley.

Hunter, F. (1953), *Community Power Structure,* University of North Carolina Press, Chapel Hill.

Ingalls, J. D. (1976), *Human Energy,* Addison-Wesley, Reading, Mass.

Kimball, G. E. (1953), A Philosophy of Operations Research (abstract), *Operations Research* (vol. 1).

Kramer, N. J. T. A., and de Smit J. (1977), *Systems Thinking,* Leiden: Martinus Nijhoff.

Levin, A. (1970), *The Satisficers,* McCall Publishing Co., New York.

Lucas, H. C., Jr. (1976), *Why Information Systems Fail,* Columbia University Press, New York.

Machiavelli (1972), *The Prince, Selections from The Discourse and Other Writings,* J. Plamenatz, ed., Fontana/Collins, London.

Meltsner, A. J. (1972), Political Feasibility and Policy Analysis, *Public Administration Review* 32, 859–867.

Michael, D. (1968), *The Unprepared Society,* Basic Books, New York.

Miller, J. G. (1978), *Living Systems,* McGraw-Hill, New York.

Mills, C. W. (1956), *White Collar,* Oxford University Press, New York.

Mitroff, I. I. (1974), *The Subjective Side of Science,* Elsevier, New York.

Morison, E. (1966), *Men, Machines, and Modern Times,* MIT Press, Cambridge, Mass.

Neustadt, R. E. (1960), *Presidential Power,* John Wiley and Sons, New York.

Quade, E. S., and Boucher, W. I. (1967), *Systems Analysis and Policy Planning,* Elsevier, New York.

Quade, E. S., and Miser, H. J., eds., (to be published) *Handbook of Systems Analysis* (vol 1).

Rubinstein, M. (1976), *Patterns of Problem Solving.* Prentice-Hall, Englewood Cliffs, N.J.

Scheele, D. S. (1975), Reality Construction as a Product of Delphi Interaction, in *The Delphi Method,* H. A. Linstone and M. Turoff, eds., Reading, Mass.: Addison-Wesley, 1975.

Schlesinger, J. A. (1966), *Ambition and Politics: Political Careers in the United States,* Rand McNally, Chicago.

Solman, P., and Friedman, T. (1982), *Life and Death on the Corporate Battlefield,* Simon and Schuster, New York.

Thompson, J. D. (1967), *Organizations in Action,* McGraw-Hill, New York.

Vickers, G. (1973), *Making Institutions Work,* John Wiley and Sons, New York.

Whyte, W. H., Jr. (1957), *The Organization Man,* Doubleday Anchor Books, Garden City, N.Y.

APPENDIX C

SAMPLE T–O–P PROFILE TEST

Subject: National Hydropower Development 1981–2000

Background: Three levels of added capacity are to be considered and their impacts assessed. Level I—25,000 MW, Level II—45,000 MW, and Level III—75,000 MW. The study is sponsored by a government agency.

Instruction: Select the ten statements below that you consider the most significant and rank them (10 = most significant, 9 = second most significant, etc.)

1. Hydropower presently supplies about 4% of total U.S. energy _____ and 13% of electricity needs. Under low-demand growth rates hydropower development can supply 20 to 60% of the additional electric energy needs by 2000. As demand growth rates increase, the hydropower contribution declines.

2. Level I is achievable with the existing institutional framework _____ and is the only one politically feasible under current conditions. Level II requires a very active strategy with a rather sophisticated balance between federal and state, as well as public and private sector development.

3. Few dams have been built in the past two decades in the United _____ States and the American hydropower equipment industry has aged. There are few training opportunities today.

4. Jurisdictional conflicts and overlapping agency programs impede _____ nonfederal development at federal dams. Negotiation of memoranda of understanding between agencies or enactment of clarifying legislation is needed.

5. "(Colonel X) was really good. He came in the midst of the dam _____ and levee controversy. The first time he attended a meeting he took a lot of abuse. People were really mad. He introduced himself and then stood there for half an hour or so while people

screamed and hissed and yelled. He took it and he listened. I
wrote him suggesting that if something could be done to beautify
the levees it would really reduce opposition to them. He brought
in some really good landscape architects and they came up with
plans. . . . They transferred him before (the implementation
could be) completed. It's a lot better."

6. Three hydropower system characteristics of particular interest   _____
   are 1) its ability to meet peak demands, 2) its ability to store
   energy, and 3) its nonconsumptive use of natural resources.

7. An entrepreneur on a regulatory agency: _____

   [They are trying to] carve out an empire in which some waf-
   flebottom who knows nothing about the situation can obstruct
   the orderly use of power.

   He went to Washington to deliver copies of the dam feasibility   _____
   study. He was appalled to find a building larger than his state
   capitol, was sent to yet another, and still another.

   All three of these things were full of people who spend all their
   time obstructing.

8. The cumulative impact of demand reductions due to energy   _____
   conservation can be as much as 25 to 35% of total U.S. energy
   needs.

9. While agency officials are required to hold public hearings, they _____
   are not required to listen.

10. The major uncertainty affecting the likely power generation mix _____
    stems from the expected contributions of solar and nuclear power.

11. A Congressional aide: _____

    It is not appropriate to reexamine public decisions. It is not a
    worthwhile use of the taxpayer's funds to tell him how much
    you save if you build. It is a public disservice to embarrass the
    elected representatives of the people who have made decisions
    on issues.

12. For Level I two-thirds of the additions are at existing dams,   _____
    equally split between federal and nonfederal projects. For Level
    II half the additions are at existing, half at new sites. Again
    there is an even split between federal and nonfederal. For Level
    III two-thirds of the additions are new construction, mostly
    federal projects.

13. Sport fishermen have organized a powerful lobby whose inter-   _____
ests must be addressed in any hydropower development program.

14. Hydropower is at present a low-priority agenda item. Because   _____
of its potential relative to other energy sources, a significant
upgrading of priority is unlikely unless a national crisis occurs.
In that case Level III may be in order and it requires direct
Presidential involvement.

15. An entrepreneur's view on permits: _____

> Anybody who sits on their rights is left out and that's how it
> should be. You have to exercise your rights in order to claim
> them.

16. "X is the Bonaparte of hydropower."   _____

17. There has never been a dam failure at a U.S. hydropower   _____
facility.

18. Attainment of Levels II and III involves significant material and   _____
personnel shortages; Level I implies no major impacts.

19. Technologies are often assessed by the same agencies that pro-   _____
mote them; hence they become advocacy briefs.

20. Key federal water official Y sees himself as a "businessman"   _____
of hydropower: "I see the government as a broadly based
corporation. I want to stay in business, to show a profit for the
nation."

21. On minihydropower: _____

> Utilities now must purchase any excess electric power you pro-
> duce. It's a guaranteed market. You have no lab. You have no
> inventory. You have no receivables. No payables. You don't
> have to have salesmen running around. The utility is your one
> and only customer. You have a watt-hour meter that tells them
> what you have generated, and there is no question about their
> paying their bills. . . . As the price of oil inflates, the utility
> will be paying us more, but the creek will still be free [McPhee,
> 1981].

22. The dependence of the United States on imported oil is still   _____
significant. Over half the national energy needs are supplied by
the combination of imported oil and electricity.

23. Hydropower is a clean, renewable, tested, and underutilized   _____
source of power. Nuclear power is dirty, expensive, and feared.

The average American believes the risk of nuclear power equal
to that of auto accidents "although statistically the annual
mortality rates favor nuclear power by a ratio of 1:500."

24. "You have to understand what part of our heritage has been _____
stolen from us because of past dam construction. . . . When
man despoils a work of man, we call him a vandal. But when
man despoils a work of nature, we call him a developer. Now
we intend to build more dams" [*The Statesman-Journal*].

25. Indian tribe lawyer.   _____

> For the last 200 years the Indians have played Bank of America
> in terms of resources. They've locked them up in a vault and
> saved them.
>   The Indian people want to be able to drink clean water and
> to breathe fresh air, and they think that that is just as important
> as running hair dryers in the Northwest.

26. The site-specific nature of development problems militates against _____
standardized institutional procedures for authorization and funding of projects.

27. "The Southwest is not running out of water—it's running low _____
on cheap water. The reform of water pricing would not halt the
Southwest's growth, nor would it cause general hardship. Instead, the Southwest would begin to use water more intelli-
gently, as it eventually must" [*Fortune*].

28. A consultant on hydropower: _____

> Federal water policy? There isn't any. None. There's a lot of
> clashing rights, a lot of programs without cohesion, and no
> effective mechanism for coordination.

29. "The federal government can't do small jobs. It can't work with _____
small interest groups. It can't deal with mayors and city fathers.
It is incapable of comprehending what it is they're doing. It is
big, aloof, intimidating. Big federal agencies make bad vibes
in a small town—they are not institutionally geared to that."

30. Of the 106 water resource subregions, 17 have or by 2000 will _____
have a seriously deficient supply of surface water. In almost
every case hydroelectric power competes to some degree with
other water uses.

Of the thirty statements, ten are of each type of perspective. The following table offers a key for determining totals (weighted according to ranking) for each perspective type.

Statement	Perspective Type	Statement	Perspective Type
1	T	16	P
2	O	17	T
3	O	18	T
4	O	19	O
5	P	20	P
6	T	21	P
7	P	22	T
8	T	23	P
9	O	24	P
10	T	25	O
11	P	26	O
12	T	27	T
13	O	28	P
14	O	29	O
15	P	30	T

AVERAGED STUDENT GROUP SAMPLE OF PROFILE TEST:

Weighted Totals	Ranking of Statements	
T: 21.25	1st # 2 type O	6th #13 type O
O: 21.25	2nd #18 type T	7th #26 type O
P: 12.50	3rd # 1 type T	8th # 4 type O
55.00	4th # 6 type T	9th #22 type T
	5th #16 type P	10th #20 type P

Sources: Sullivan, J.B., A Public Interest Laundry List for Technology Assessment, *Technol. Forecast. Soc. Change* 8, 439–440 (1976). Linstone, H. et al., *Technology Assessment of National Hydropower Development*, Nero and Associates, Inc., Portland, Oregon, 1981. McPhee, J., Minihydro, *New Yorker* (Feb. 23, 1981). *The Statesman Journal*, Salem, Oregon (Feb. 22 and 25, 1981). *Fortune* (Feb. 23, 1981).

APPENDIX D

THE PERSPECTIVES AND THE BRAIN: SOME CONJECTURES

H. LINSTONE

Since the 19th century it has been recognized that the brain's left and right neocortex hemispheres specialize in different tasks. People injured by strokes or gunshot wounds to the brain's left side frequently have difficulty with speech or writing. A lesion on the right side can result in the inability of the subject to recognize his or her own face in a mirror or photograph. It has been claimed that the left neocortex excels in calculation, reading, speaking, and similar linear or sequential activities, while the right neocortex is superior in spatial, perceptual, manipulative, artistic, and nonverbal skills.[1] The left side tends toward the rational and analytic, the right toward the intuitive and holistic. Research provides considerable support but also shows that the lateralization is by no means sharp and permanent. As is typical of complex living systems, there are safe–fail characteristics (see Section II B). Cross-cuing links the two hemispheres by many pathways. Furthermore, the brain can regenerate some synaptic fields and compress them into less than normal space. Each hemisphere, independently, has the ability to learn and can thus compensate at least in part for failures in the other.[2] Recent Japanese research suggests that language learning in childhood plays a role in shaping the division of labor in the brain hemispheres, resulting in significant differences between Japanese and Western patterns of sound processing.[3] It becomes clear that the separation of functions does not lend itself to simple, sharp, permanent, or universal boundaries. However, such caveats do not deny the existence of functional asymmetry. And there are impacts relevant to our concerns.

Rowan[4] reports that the testing of chief executive officers of corporations using an electroencephalograph revealed a preponderance of right-hemisphere-dominated types, suggesting the importance of holistic, intuitive thinking in the decision-making arena. It has also been suggested that women often tend to have

---

[1]Sagan, C., *The Dragons of Eden,* Ballantine Books, New York, 1977: Chap. 7. Gazzaniga, M.S., *The Integrated Mind,* Plenum Publications, New York, 1978: 45–59.
[2]See, for example, the work of Roger Sperry, the 1981 Nobel laureate.
[3]Sibatani, A., The Japanese Brain, *Science 80* 1(8), 22–27 (Dec. 1980).
[4]Rowan, Those Business Hunches Are More Than Blind Faith, *Fortune* 99 (8):110–114 (April 23, 1979).

a stronger right-brain orientation than men.[5] This may account for recent research by a Johns Hopkins group claiming that boys do significantly better than girls in Mathematics Scholastic Aptitude tests.[6] Our experience with the Multiple Perspective Concept, while not a scientifically adequate sample, did provide hints that women may be particularly valuable in handling the P perspective and men the T perspective. It is, in fact, tempting to deduce a certain correspondence between the characteristics of the perspectives sketched in Table 8 and the descriptions of left and right neocortex strengths noted above: T—left, O—left and right, and P—right.

Another highly individual characteristic significant for our applications is mentioned by both Gazzaniga and Loye.[7] The ability to plan ahead is apparently related to the integration of left and right neocortex functions in the forebrain. Gazzaniga observes that inability to plan ahead is typically noted in patients with frontal lobe disease. Loye speculates that far-sighted leadership is associated with a particularly effective forebrain capability. Loye's experiments further suggest that personality differences (for example, masculinity–femininity, extroversion–introversion) are reflected in differences in forecasts. For example, a majority of the "tough-minded" types predicted a better future for us by the year 2000, whereas a majority of the "tender minded" predicted our future would be worse.[8] As forecasting is an important facet of planning, one should not be surprised to find that personality makes its imprint on the planning process itself, just as it does on the development of the technology.

Future research must determine the significance of these controversial conjectures.

---

[5]Kaje, Bringing the Feminine into Forecasting, *Futures Research: New Directions* (H.A. Linstone and W.H.C. Simmonds, eds.) Addison-Wesley, Reading, Mass., pp. 65–76, 1977.

[6]*Science* 210:1234–1235 (1980).

[7]Gazzaniga, op cit., Loye, *The Knowable Future*, Wiley Interscience, New York, p. 141, 1978.

[8]Loye, Personality and Prediction, *Technological Forecasting and Social Change* 16:229–242 (1980).

INDEX

Italicized page numbers indicate that the terms are to be found in tables or figures. Page numbers followed by fn indicate that the terms are to be found in footnotes.